Radical Intellect

Radical Intellect

Liberator Magazine and
Black Activism in the 1960s

....

CHRISTOPHER M. TINSON

The University of North Carolina Press   Chapel Hill

© 2017 The University of North Carolina Press
All rights reserved
Set in Charis by Westchester Publishing Services
Manufactured in the United States of America

The University of North Carolina Press has been a member
of the Green Press Initiative since 2003.

Library of Congress Cataloging-in-Publication Data
Names: Tinson, Christopher M., author.
Title: Radical intellect : Liberator magazine and black activism in the 1960s / Christopher M. Tinson.
Description: Chapel Hill : University of North Carolina Press, [2017] | Includes bibliographical references and index.
Identifiers: LCCN 2017009457 | ISBN 9781469634548 (cloth : alk. paper) | ISBN 9781469634555 (pbk : alk. paper) | ISBN 9781469634562 (ebook)
Subjects: LCSH: African Americans—Political activity—History—20th century. | Liberator (New York, N.Y.: 1961) | African American political activists. | African Americans—Periodicals. | African Americans—Civil rights—History—20th century. | Anti-imperialist movements—United States—History—20th century. | Social movements—United States—History—20th century. | Black power—United States—History—20th century. | African Americans—Race identity—History—20th century.
Classification: LCC E185.615 .T59 2017 | DDC 323.1196/073—dc23
LC record available at https://lccn.loc.gov/2017009457

Cover illustration: Front cover photograph, *Liberator*, June 1964 (courtesy of Pete Beveridge).

Portions of this book have been previously published in a different form as "Manning Marable and the Triumph of American Liberalism in *Malcolm X: A Life of Reinvention*," in *A Lie of Reinvention: Correcting Manning Marable's Malcolm X*, ed. Jared A. Ball and Todd Steven Burroughs (Baltimore: Black Classic Press, 2012); "'Harlem, New York! Harlem, Detroit! Harlem, Birmingham!': Liberator Magazine and the Chronicling of Translocal Activism," *The Black Scholar* 41, no. 3 (Fall 2011): 9–16.; and "'The Voice of the Black Protest Movement': Notes on the *Liberator* Magazine and Black Radicalism in the early 1960s," *The Black Scholar* 37, no. 4 (Winter 2008): 3–15. Used here with permission.

Myrtle Hines
Desmond Bevel
Charles Mac Tinson
William "Bill" Little
Al Hines

Contents

Acknowledgments, xi

Prologue, 1
Inscribing Liberation: Contexts and Conditions of Black Radicalism

1   Voices of Black Protest, 13
    Contours of Anticolonialism and Black Liberation

2   Spokespersons and Advocates, 38
    The Contested Intellectual Life of African Independence

3   Radical Commitments, 74
    The Promise of Black Women's Activism

4   Rebellion or Revolution, 120
    The Challenge of Black Radicalism

5   New Breeds, Old Dreams, 185
    Liberator *and Black Radical Aesthetics*

Epilogue, 235
Refusing to Go Quietly

Notes, 243

Bibliography, 281

Index, 299

Illustrations

Daniel Henry Watts, 1969, 21

Lowell "Pete" Beveridge and Hortense "Tee" Beveridge, Fort Dix, New Jersey, 1953, 26

Lorraine Hansberry, 1964, 79

Gloria Richardson, 1963, 82

Rev. Albert Cleage 1963, 126

Adam Clayton Powell, 1964, 150

Carlos Russell interviewing Malcolm X, 1963, 161

Malcolm X holding daughter, 1965, 175

Dan Watts and student Quinton Wilkes, 1971, 238

Acknowledgments

A book project is never the work of a singular individual alone. I have been blessed to know and benefit from the knowledge, expertise, and company of many amazing people.

First and foremost are my partner, Kyngelle, and our son, Caiden: thank you for your love and patience and for immensely supporting my work; my incredible mother, Marie L. Hines Tinson; LaShawnda, Jennifer, Leslye, Ted, Jade, Resean, Hunter, Dominic, Rene Monroe and family; BJ, Terrance, Sly, Bruce, Karl, G, Dre, Steve, Itch, Tina, and Aaron—Tinsons, Hines, Normans, Russells, and Williams wherever we be. I hope you all are proud of this athlete-turned-scholar. Special thanks go to Vilaire Charlot; Kevin, Fabienne, and Ayanna Maxwell; Nitza Martinez and family; and Gil and Kim Traverso. To my first schoolteachers, Mrs. Thompson, Mrs. Lacefield (RIP), and Mrs. Hunter, thank you for planting the seed of love for learning. Your unwavering support has lifted me up for years.

Thanks go to the *Liberator* family whom I met through this work: Carlos E. Russell, Pete Beveridge, C. E. Wilson, Ossie Sykes, Richard Gibson, and the family of Dan Watts; and also Askia Touré, and Calvin Hicks; special appreciation goes to the *Liberator* crew who passed away before the completion of this book: Clayton Riley and Charlie Russell. This would not have become a book without you all and the work you did and continue to do.

Thanks go to my mentors, Ernest Allen, John Bracey, and Bill Strickland, whose names opened many doors with many of the activists I interviewed for this book and who have been a reservoir of knowledge and materials since the beginning; also, huge thanks and praise go to Esther Terry, James Smethurst, Ekwueme Michael Thelwell, Dayo Gore, Steve Tracy, Manisha Sinha, Nancy R. Mirabal, the great Wade W. Nobles, Nelson Stevens, Maddie and Roberto Marquez, Amilcar and Dee Shabazz, Agustín Lao-Montes, Joye Bowman and John Higginson, Charles E. Jones, Akinyele Umoja, Susan Tracy, and Sabine Broeck (University of Bremen, Germany). Thanks also go to the College of Ethnic Studies at San Francisco State University, the Africana Studies department at California State University Dominguez Hills, and the W. E. B. Du Bois Department of Afro-American Studies at University of Massachusetts Amherst.

Many thanks go out to *The Black Scholar*, the *Journal of African American History*, the National Council for Black Studies, the Association for the Study of African American Life and History, and the TRGGR Media Collective.

Many thanks to the staff at UNC Press, especially my editor, Brandon Proia. Thanks also to Jad Adkins, Michelle Witkowski, and Jen Burton. You all have been professional and in my corner throughout the process. Thank you to the anonymous readers of earlier drafts of this book. Your critical feedback made this a much better book.

The staffs at the following libraries and library collections were of great help to this work: the John Henrik Clarke and Larry Neal Papers at the Schomburg Center, and especially archivist Stephen Fullwood; the W. E. B. Du Bois Library at University of Massachusetts Amherst; the Robert W. Woodruff Library at Atlanta University Center; Amherst College Special Collections; Harold Cruse Papers and George Breitman Papers at NYU's Tamiment Library; Joellen El Bashir at the Moorland-Spingarn Research Library at Howard University; Patrice M. Kane at the Fordham University Archives and Special Collections; and Peter Higgins at WGBH Boston archives.

The colleagues and dear friends who have inspired my work and kept the path lit are many: Carlos Rec McBride, Jonathan Fenderson, K. C. Nat Turner, Anthony Ratcliff, Viveca Greene, Wilson Valentín-Escobar, kara lynch, Amy Jordan, Korina Jocson, Sujani Reddy, and Jennifer Guglielmo (who deserves a special shout out for providing incredible advice, energy, and feedback at critical stages of this project), Ousmane Power-Greene, Dana Finkelstein, Omar Dahi, Suheir Hammad, Micaela J. Díaz-Sánchez, Allia Matta, McKinley Melton, Tanisha Ford, Whitney Battle-Baptiste, Trevor Baptiste, Johanna Fernandez (NYC), Noura Erakat, Aracelis Girmay, Djola Branner, Daniel Kojo and Anna Schrade, Branwen Okpako, Sonya Donaldson, Hiba Bou Akar, Rachel Amma Engmann, Jutta Sperling, Roosbelinda Cárdenas, John Murillo, Sara Lennox, Bob Rakoff, Marlene Fried, Frank Holmquist, Eva Rueschmann, Jonathan Lash, Lynn Pasquerella, Hassan Johnson, Thabiti Asukile, Orisanmi Burton, Cedric Gilmore, Morris Jones, Mary Bombardier, Karina Fernandez, Evelin Aquino, Charles Payne, Tricia Loveland, Shelly Perdomo, Carla Wojczuk, Connie Wun, Deroy Gordon and Zahra Caldwell, Davarian Baldwin, Jakobi Williams, Mike Funk, Vanessa Lynch, Jorge "Pop Master" Fabel and UZN, Theresa "Mama Kuji" Cooper Gordon, sister-in-struggle Jacquelyn Smith-Crooks, Ingrid "Mama Ing" Askew, Judyie Al-Bilali, Andrea Battle, Sebastian Weier (Germany), Jamal Watson, David

Goldberg, David Lucander, Shawn Alexander, Russell Rickford, Sam Roberts, Christina Greer, Saulo Colon, Sean Arce, Jelisa Difo, Keita Grace, Revan Schendler, Chyrell George, Jean Sepanski, and Carol Boudreau.

I have also drawn great inspiration from the radical intellectual work of Sonia Sanchez, Robin D. G. Kelley, Mumia Abu-Jamal, Russell "Maroon" Shoatz, Jalil Muntaquim, David Gilbert, Ashanti Omowali Alston, Bobby Dellelo, Don Perry, Lawrence Jackson, Vijay Prashad, J. Kēhaulani Kauanui, Betsy Casañas, Tina Reynolds, Frank Wilderson, Ruthie Gilmore, and Fred Ho (RIP).

My past and current students have been my lifeline in the academy, especially Aurelis Troncoso, Gabby Nzinga Garcia, Langston Sanchez, Sackona Fitts, Dykee Gorrell, Toni Stone, Kwasi Tre Brooks, Kamika Bennett, Lyla Bugara, Andrew Stachiw, Brittany Williams, Elzbieta Putrycz, Brenda Herrero-Moreno, Elydah Joyce, Maddy Miller, the entire Decolonize Media Collective, and Students Against Mass Incarceration (Hampshire College chapter). Last, I cannot forget all my basketball comrades at the Holyoke YMCA, especially Charles Winston—thanks for keeping me fit, competitive, and getting my mind off work!

As Kendrick put it, "We gon' be alright!"

Radical Intellect

Prologue
Inscribing Liberation: Contexts and Conditions of Black Radicalism

....

We build our temples for tomorrow, strong as we know how, and we stand on top of the mountain, free within ourselves.
—Langston Hughes, "The Negro Artist and the Racial Mountain" (1926)

Radical Intellect is a political and cultural history of one of the lesser acknowledged, but widely influential, periodicals of the 1960s and early 1970s, *Liberator* magazine. More than the story of a periodical, however, this history is concerned with the political and cultural work of a loosely assembled collective of activist-intellectuals and artist-intellectuals in the era of mass protest, decolonization, and "militant transnationalism."[1] In recent years there have been a range of works that have mentioned *Liberator*, and a few shorter articles and chapters have discussed its role as a pivotal outlet of the period.[2] Yet, none of these exhaustively cover the spectrum of personalities, shifts, ebbs and flows, and moments of tension and consternation that contributed to the periodical's overall impact, as this book sets out to accomplish. More than simply recording the news events, the magazine's work was that of inscription. By inscribing liberatory politics, *Liberator* stood at the crossroads of knowledge production and insurrection. Placing this periodical's engagement with black radical perspectives at the center of a history of U.S.-based radicalism opens observation to important shifts taking place in black and Third World political struggle up to and after the articulation of Black Power in the middle of the twentieth century. However, with *Liberator*'s emergence at the beginning of the decade, in 1960–61, in many ways it anticipated Black Power, and its origins can and should be traced to earlier forms and ideas of radicalism.

As with nearly all black radical projects in this period, *Liberator* positioned itself in relation to anticolonial movements in Africa and elsewhere around the world where populations of color were attacking and abandoning colonialism. Yet, supporting African liberation, alongside a robust articulation of demands for human recognition in the United States was its central aim throughout its ten-year existence. Ambitiously, it sought to serve as a respectable platform to address conditions facing African descendants in the United States.[3] In this sense, an appraisal of its impact is long overdue. *Radical Intellect* reveals just how serious readers and activists associated with *Liberator* took Langston Hughes's concluding statement from his 1926 essay. *Liberator* might not have been the temple of Hughes's imagination, but it certainly sought to stand atop the racial mountain as an exemplar of a liberation project untethered from the disciplinary forces of racial capitalism and imperialist democracy at home and around the world.

The rise of black radicalism in the 1960s can be found in the successes and failures of the civil rights movement, although black radical perspectives date back at least to the eighteenth century.[4] Indeed, as my use of the quote from Hughes's famous essay intends to highlight, many of the questions activists and artists faced in the latter half of the twentieth century were engaged by African American thinkers decades prior, and indeed long after. The achievements of the civil rights movement, including the *Brown* decision, Montgomery bus boycott, direct-action sit-in protests, and the simultaneous sense of shared commitment and demonstration of courage in the face of racial violence that accompanied civil rights demonstrations, were inspirational to all who were engaged in the black freedom struggle. However, the limitations on its broad-reaching effectiveness proved to be an equally potent catalyst in the emergence of black radicalism. The inability of the civil rights movement strategies based on nonviolent protest and victories in the court system to bring about structural political and economic change to the United States is perhaps the most significant factor contributing to the (re)emergence of black radicalism in the United States in the middle of the twentieth century.[5] As with much of the political left in the history of the United States, the central issue for many was economic justice and political empowerment at the crossroads of race and culture. Achieving autonomy in a context of stagnant wages, shrinking labor opportunities, and protection could not be guaranteed absent aggressive agitation. Added to these issues on macro and micro levels was the issue of police violence and general hostility meted out to black people in general and the black poor most viscerally.

Even as the civil rights movement achieved its greatest legal, and to some degree spatial, victories, many black people in the United States felt that their material reality had not changed. Although Supreme Court victories and the passage of the Civil Rights and Voting Rights Acts heightened expectations and the anticipation of substantial improvements in their lives, black people found themselves still victims of oppression in the form of Ku Klux Klan and White Citizens Council violence, police brutality, and widespread poverty. Fed up with the intransigence of mounting violence directed toward civil rights workers and organizations, the failure of liberalism, and a gradualist pace in securing social, political, and economic enhancement, many black activists and artists tapped into the deep well of black radical thought and espoused a more assertive anticapitalist perspective, which included armed self-defense and the call for a revolutionary alternative to existing political and economic structures in the United States.[6] Indeed, many questioned the validity of the American government and expressed cynicism toward its defense of African American entitlements to citizenship. This radicalism was paralleled by the simultaneous spread of anticolonial and anti-imperialist movements in Africa, Asia, and Latin America. In this sense, I argue that black radicalism is inherently internationalist. As the historian Robin D. G. Kelley posits, some radicals "were internationalist before they were nationalists."[7] Though U.S.-based radicalism responded to the immediacy of domestic conditions, it always carried with it a global vision of struggle.

The perspective that the political and economic structure of the United States had to change to allow African Americans the opportunity to control their own destinies, and for equity and social justice to be achieved was the radical thread of this era. The shift in approach to securing rights accompanied a shift in the identity of many young activists. This newly formed identity emphasized cultural heritage and stressed the need for political autonomy, economic self-sufficiency, and control over the communities in which they lived. Black radical perspectives embraced aspects of cultural nationalism, with an emphasis on identity and heritage and on what they called revolutionary nationalism,[8] which perceived African Americans as an "internal colony," defined as an "oppressed nation" inside the U.S. borders. This theory included an emphasis on self-determination, political autonomy, economic self-sufficiency, the preservation and appreciation of black culture, and the view that "the African American struggle is intimately tied to the struggles of the 'Third World' against imperialism."[9] Though they were part of the long freedom movement, black radicals were distinctively critical of the civil rights establishment's steadfast adherence to nonviolence and moral suasion.

Radical Intellect explores the history of the *Liberator* magazine as a critical political and cultural formation of the 1960s and early 1970s, which grew out of the tradition of labor and left-oriented radicalism as well as earlier forms of Black Nationalism at the turn of the twentieth century. At its height of influence, the *Liberator* provided an indispensable forum where many of the national and international concerns facing black people could be discussed. Moreover, it offered a platform for voices and perspectives opposed to the political mainstream. In its early days as the organ of the short-lived Liberation Committee for Africa, *Liberator* delivered cutting-edge political, social, and cultural aspects of black radicalism that significantly shaped the political debates among black radical artists and activists over the long decade of the 1960s.

Liberator, a New York City-based magazine and ad hoc think tank, stands as a critical example of how the shifts in identity, perspective, and strategy taking place in black radical thought and practice in this period were articulated to a broad public. Initially formed to provide support for and raise consciousness of decolonization in Africa, as well as to generate attention to struggles for radical social change in the United States and abroad, it lay at several interconnected points of black liberation. These include the issues of civil rights and political, economic, and cultural forms of Black Nationalism, as well as the role of black women in black liberation, Black Power, pan-Africanism, and black internationalism, reflecting the diversity of black radical thought and thereby serving as an important case study for analyzing this period. These crosscurrents and parallel movements are central to the history of the magazine and some of its most influential members specifically, as well as helping to describe the general complexity of black liberation politics in this period. It therefore requires rereading this period as being one of considerable ideological diversity within a broadly conceived anticolonial, antiwestern perspective.

The *Liberator* reflects the diverse "ingredients," or core aspects, of black radicalism, illuminating a mixture of ideological strategies available to activists, intellectuals, and artists of the period. Drawing upon nationalist, Pan-Africanist, and black internationalist concepts, among others, it reflected a perspective that was simultaneously antiracist, anticolonialist, anti-imperialist, and anticapitalist. Thus, through its diverse repertoire of oppositionality the *Liberator* became a critical site of black radical thought and politics in the decade between 1960 and the early 1970s. It formed an important nexus of the various strands of black radicalism—Black Nationalist, pan-Africanist, and community feminist,[10] as well as Old and New Left— that converged during the 1960s, and in doing so proved to be a critical voice in the politics of Black Power and Black Arts and a key space of political and cultural criticism.[11]

In the telling of this history I explore the origins, career, and demise of the *Liberator* magazine, as well as some of the major and historically significant issues it covered, including the attention it paid to both domestic and international causes and events. It is important that *Radical Intellect* probes the backgrounds and experiences of key figures, including Daniel H. Watts, Lowell Pete Beveridge, and Richard Gibson, among numerous others, who were pivotal members of the *Liberator* staff at different points throughout the career of the magazine. Analyzing the personal motivations of the core and associated staff members who worked voluntarily for the magazine yields a greater understanding of the varieties of skills, knowledge, and experiences that shaped the *Liberator*'s content and career. In this way, my research is intended as a contribution to a rapidly expanding body of historical monographs, biographies and autobiographies of the black freedom movement of the 1960s and 1970s.

I investigate several questions in the telling of *Liberator*'s history. I am chiefly concerned with the ways in which *Liberator* helped to define the black radicalism of the period. Where did it stand on the principle ideological tensions ("integration versus separatism," "domestic colonialism versus American citizenship," "nonviolence versus armed self-defense," and "capitalism versus socialism") of its day? The gulf between the integrationist rhetoric of the National Association for the Advancement of Colored People (NAACP) and the separatist philosophy of the Nation of Islam (NOI) was one such tension. Though the magazine appeared to appreciate the antagonistic stance toward mainstream black political leadership vocalized by the NOI, it was skeptical of religious remedies to black oppression, which also extended to its criticism of King's efforts. *Liberator*'s writers persistently questioned the relationship of African Americans to the state, and consistently sought alternatives to the existing political institutions, while always pursuing the question of power. Through its stubborn opposition to mainstream black political attitudes, how might the *Liberator* be said to have anticipated the rise of Black Power? In addition to the support for alternative and autonomous black politics, African Americans grappled with self-defense. What was its perspective on the use of violence in self-defense? Though the magazine espoused Black Nationalist perspectives, what were its writers' opinions on strategic alliances with whites? What, if any, economic analysis did *Liberator* offer? Were these ideas markedly different from the analyses of other organizations and publications? Thinking globally, how did the magazine embrace internationalist activities and perspectives? How does the concept of black internationalism, as employed more recently by scholars such as Brent Hayes Edwards, Cynthia Young, and others,[12] extend beyond traditional notions of pan-Africanism, and how might their discussion contribute to our understanding of the internationalism of the *Liberator* and the Liberation Committee for Africa? In thinking about the magazine's radicalism, we might ask, how did *Liberator* engage with socialism as a solution to black peoples' condition?

Radical Intellect is largely concerned with the political outlooks cast in *Liberator* as an activist repository of black radical thought that is also part of a radical black journalistic tradition. Historically, the black press has been critical in meeting the institutional, cultural, entrepreneurial, and often political needs of black communities nationwide. Publications such as *Freedom, Freedomways, Negro Digest/Black World, Soulbook, Black Dialogue,* and the *Black Scholar* provided spaces where the political, economic, and aesthetic questions of black liberation were discussed.[13] Though *Black Scholar* is currently the only publication of the era still circulating that emerged out of the politics of the period, all the aforementioned periodicals shaped how we understand the multiple dimensions of Black Nationalism, black radicalism, and black internationalism. In this way, Lawrence Jackson's exhaustive narrative, *The Indignant Generation: A Narrative History of African American Writers and Critics, 1934–1960,* is an indispensable contribution to this scholarship. His work fills a critical void in the history and understanding of the overlapping collectives of activists and writers who each contribute in their own way to black radical politics in the twentieth century. Writing served as a premier form of activism for many in this era. Often analysis, poetry, short stories, and novels had an even greater impact on people's thinking than taking to the streets in direct-action protest. In writing circles and organizing collectives, activists found the confidence of voice and strategy that helped to shape the direction of movements. These were also spaces where individuals came to understand and navigated their own commitments. Most important, these spaces were also critical for reflection and the reconsideration of beliefs, values, and principles.

James Smethurst's provocative and detailed study, *The Black Arts Movement,* argues that the history of black journals tells us a great deal about the black liberation movement.[14] The writings of these activists are arguably their most indelible form of activism. In addition, his work explores the regional manifestations of the Black Arts Movement and has contributed greatly to the historiography of the period by tracing the flourishing of Black Arts in the South and Midwest regions of the United States, as well as the more widely recognized coastal locations of New York and California. By expanding the geographic focus beyond New York City to include such sites as Chicago, Detroit, and New Orleans, the Black Arts movement is not only more accurately rendered as national, but is also rendered as *translocal* in scope and influence. In other words, such studies help us rethink the connections between individuals, organizations, and communities. Smethurst's study also refocuses our attention on the intricate relationship between the Communist Party and Black Nationalist organizations in the post–World War II era through the 1970s.

In addition to noting the complexity of racial and class oppression against which much of the Black Arts Movement was directed, Smethurst's work also investigates the significance of gender in the politicized aesthetics of Black Arts. Yet, whereas he views gender as a critical component of a broadly defined Black Nationalism, other scholars center their analyses of Black Arts and Black Power on the role women's radicalism has played in critiquing forms of nationalism by direct participation in existing Black Arts and Black Power organizations and in the formation of their own. They have also gone beyond merely documenting women's participation to explore the ways in which aspects of radical politics are gendered as male or female, which deepens our understanding of *intramovement* ideas and practices.

Kimberly Springer, Rhonda Y. Williams, and Benita Roth, among numerous other scholars have investigated the multifaceted role of women, as well as their thought, perspectives, and activism in this period, and have probed the depths of masculinity and gendered definitions of nationalist projects and activity in black liberation politics. Springer's and Williams's work each greatly contributes to efforts to unpack the male-centered discourses and perspectives in the thinking and writing of Black Power and Black Arts figures and organizations. Springer's *Living for the Revolution* adds to the scholarship by probing the complex organizational lives of black women in the Black Power era and beyond. Similarly, Rhonda Y. Williams's work on radical grassroots black women's movements exposes the ways in which such efforts were instrumental in mobilizing campaigns against poverty and deteriorating and unsafe living conditions in urban areas throughout the United States.[15] Sociologist Benita Roth has offered a compelling interpretation of the overlaps, conflicts, and departures that emerged between the organizing efforts of African American, Chicana, and white second-wave feminist movements. As she argues, these efforts represent "a linked set of cases," which reveal both parallels and divergences.[16]

Such studies are rewarding demonstrations that female challenges to masculinist rhetoric were alive and well in the 1960s. The scholarly efforts of Springer, Williams, and Roth, not only point out women's activities alongside those of their male counterparts, they also demonstrate how black and

Inscribing Liberation   7

Third World women rethought and redefined the terms of liberation. In so doing, they carved out space for a particular liberation discourse that made women's and men's liberation politics inseparable while critiquing the discourse of masculinity within Black Power and other expressions of Black Nationalism. These contributions have expanded the analytical terrain on which black liberation politics are worked out and understood.

Collectively, these studies view this period as one of dynamism and complexity, and as one that resists easy categories. In other words, these studies take a broader view of the impulses and stakes of black liberation. As historian Peniel Joseph writes in the introduction to his edited volume, *The Black Power Movement*, this research "builds on this complexity, by outlining a panoramic view of the black freedom struggle, highlighting previously undocumented traces, origins, and evolutions" of the radicalism of the 1960s.[17]

Though *Liberator*'s politics drew from a well of resistance and alternative knowledge produced by African descendants since the eighteenth century, like its peer publications, it can be viewed as a part of what Lauren Kessler calls "the dissident press." Kessler identifies several main functions of dissident publishing outlets. As "external communicators," these outlets were formed to "educate the unconverted," cover ideas not represented in the mainstream, and serve as "internal communicators" to those who shared their perspective, while providing them with a platform for discussion and debate. One other dubious feature bears upon dissident publications: Without adequate organizational and financial support, they were most often "shoestring operations that could not mount the circulation and promotion campaigns necessary" to make a large impact outside a community of the already converted. Still, the existence of these publications and the accompanying activism of writers and editors played a crucial role in the broadening of ideas in the public sphere.[18]

Radical Intellect seeks to expand the discussion of these political journals by exploring the particular history of *Liberator*, a periodical that has long provided ample source material for much of the recent scholarship on the political and cultural activism of the 1960s and 1970s, but whose own origin, development, and contribution have yet to be fully explored until now.[19] As one of the most important sites of black radical political strategy in the heady and tumultuous days of the 1960s, it provided a platform for discussion and debate that assembled a plethora of critical commentators, thus contributing to global expressions of black radical thought and culture of the period and long after.

The Black Radical Tradition

Radical Intellect situates *Liberator* within the Black Radical Tradition. This tradition embraces an understanding of the centrality of the social, historical, political, and global construction of race and the attendant persistence of racism in America's legal system and practice of government; a working-class consciousness, especially among black workers; a commitment to self-defense, including the use of violence; a critique of global racial capitalism; and an international and transnational understanding of black struggle.[20] Black women's experience in the movements of the 1960s added a heightened sense of gender awareness to African American radical politics. The sharp analyses, cultural production, and committed activism of women such as Angela Y. Davis, Ella Baker, Jo Ann Robinson, Sonia Sanchez, Abbey Lincoln, Toni Cade Bambara, and Fran Beal, among a host of others, forever altered the radical landscape. To use one example, Beal's widely anthologized article, "Double Jeopardy," set the standard for analyses of the deep-rooted oppression black women face. It is important that she grounded her analysis in a critique of capitalism's destructive features, concluding, "Black women must take an active part in bringing about the kind of society where our children, our loved ones, and each citizen can grow up and live as decent human beings, free from the pressures of racism and capitalist exploitation."[21] Radical black women forced many organizations to reevaluate their commitments to liberatory politics and the total liberation of African American communities.

Writing in 1968, Robert L. Allen posed an important question to black radicals who found themselves at the crossroads of Black Nationalism, Marxism, and the rhetorical potency of Black Power. Analyzing Stokely Carmichael's radical public pronouncements and those he published with Charles Hamilton in the book *Black Power*, Allen wondered how activists and militants such as Carmichael intended to "restructure the system," or whether he was essentially calling for reforms within the existing system. With Carmichael as a starting point, Allen inquired about the degree to which those who espoused radical ideals effectively analyzed conditions that contributed to black disenfranchisement and poverty, and whether these radicals could develop and propose "programs" as solutions to the multifaceted and numerous obstacles to black liberation. Posed toward the latter end of the 1960s, Allen's questions paralleled those that radical or left-leaning people and organizations had consistently raised generations before.[22]

The impact of radical ideals was not confined to the realms of politics and economics only, but also extended into theories of American education.

In their introduction to *Radical Ideas and the Schools* (1972), editors Nelson, Carlson, and Linton., sought to provide a definition of radicalism, stating: "Although radicalism may be merely a label applied to any idea that differs from one's own, a clearer statement of the dimensions of radicalism would include the idea of basic opposition to the popular mores, opinions, and values of a given society at a particular time. In these terms, a radical idea would be one that proposes a dramatic or extensive change in a major aspect of the life pattern of any culture."[23] For black radicals the "popular mores, opinions, and values" of the United States included racism, colonialism, violence, political disfranchisement and economic exploitation. And the "dramatic or extensive change" radicals called for could be found in the popularization of the term *Black Power*, the ten-point platform of the Black Panther Party, and the Revolutionary Nationalism of the Revolutionary Action Movement (RAM).

Nelson, Carlson, and Linton argue that radicalism can be considered positive or negative depending on the individual or group espousing radical ideals. Negative radicalism is that which condemns what is wrong with society without proposing alternative solutions to the existing problems. Positive radicalism, they posit, is comprised of radical ideals that "propose idyllic situations for the good of all men without necessarily castigating the present condition of man."[24] Yet, they admit that most radical social theories combine both positive and negative radicalism. Other aspects of radicalism, according to the editors, include a commitment to thorough change in a given society and the willingness to use violence if necessary to achieve goals, though there have also been nonviolent radical acts as shown by the passive resistance and civil disobedience of Mahatma Gandhi and Martin Luther King Jr.[25] It is important that scholars are just beginning to appreciate King's radicalism.[26] Furthermore, Nelson, Carlson, and Linton argue that radicalism often forms a "mosaic of dissent" that includes both a critique of existing institutions and proposals for change. Though Nelson, Carlson, and Linton's use of the phrase "mosaic of dissent" may help explain *Liberator*'s role in the public sphere, mere dissent was but one part of its strategy.

In addition to its work promoting dissidence, my view of *Liberator*'s function shares much in common with what the scholar of radical traditions, Anthony Bogues, and others have argued: that black radicals constitute a particular tradition of political thought and action. As Bogues has maintained, black radical intellectuals wrestled with the very concepts and society they sought to transform, instead of merely opposing them. He notes, "Any observation of black radical intellectual production would illustrate that the central figures of this tradition were explicitly political, seeking to organize, having the courage to stand by or break with organizations and programs while developing an intellectual praxis that made politics not a god but a practice for human good. Theirs was not just a practice of social criticism but oftentimes of organized efforts to intervene in social and *political* life."[27]

In this sense, *Liberator*'s writers' ambitious and sometimes unwieldy intervention into the complexities of transformative struggle remains a paramount example of active political engagement. Its radical outlook embraced race, class, an incipient gender critique, and a firm conception of global struggle. Its perspective included Black Nationalism and traditional U.S.-based internationalism, which allowed it to connect national movements to global events. Though I am arguing that black radicalism includes forms of Black Nationalism, not all black nationalisms are radical.[28] For example, groups such as the NOI espoused some of the core aspects of Black Nationalist thought. The NOI philosophy is largely based on a strong sense of racial solidarity and organization along both religious or spiritual and ethnic lines over a consistent critique of capitalism and reordering of gender roles. Nonetheless, a commitment to a sense of racial justice within a global anti-imperialist framework is central to this tradition of thought and activism.

Following this prologue, the first chapter details the origins of the *Liberator* as an outgrowth of an internationalist ad hoc organization called the Liberation Committee for Africa and the creation of their periodical, *Liberator*. In tracing the group's commitment to a pan-African, black internationalist, or militant transnationalist perspective, that chapter reveals the overall approach of the periodical and its chief influences. The second chapter locates African independence and liberation struggles at the heart of *Liberator*'s early work. It looks at the role of African intellectuals in the United States and the contestation over African independence. In the 1960s, as many African students and petitioners came to study at American universities and colleges or represent newly independent nations at the United Nations, many came into contact and built friendships with a range of writers, organizers, policymakers, and activists. This chapter discusses the strategic importance of such engagements and the resulting impact on the periodical.

In the third chapter, *Radical Intellect* traces the impact of women radicals on both the magazine and the community around it. In that chapter, I demonstrate that though *Liberator* was slow in embracing an outright feminist stance, it was a space where some women radicals published their analyses of the impact of social policy on black communities and offered their own critiques of the stakes of liberation throughout the 1960s. Even during its decline in the early 1970s, *Liberator* consistently published articles and book reviews, notably by key female figures such as Toni Cade Bambara and others, whose careers in black women's activist and literary circles would blossom long after the *Liberator* ceased publication. As editor of the groundbreaking anthology, *The Black Woman*, I argue that Bambara's *Liberator* writings, largely in the form of book and film reviews as well as short stories, anticipate her contributions to African American literature and politics from the 1970s until her death in 1995.

In chapter 4, I take a close look into the dynamics and challenges of black radicalism as revealed in *Liberator*'s analyses of global conditions facing African descendants at home in the United States and globally. Here I focus on the challenges that black radicals confronted that allowed *Liberator* to blossom as a "mosaic of dissent," espousing radical critiques about the role of the state and sharply critiquing a global economic order that routinely exploited black bodies that often resulted in what Dan Watts editorialized as "the obsolescence of the Negro." This chapter also documents the impact of and controversy surrounding seminal figures such as James Baldwin, Harold Cruse, and Malcolm X on *Liberator*'s radicalism, influencing the magazine's espousal of the possibilities of alternative politics.

The inseparability of culture and politics in black radicalism is as central to this book as it was to *Liberator* itself. As such, in the fifth chapter, I analyze the role of black radical aesthetics in shaping *Liberator*'s contribution to radicalism, arguably its most significant. *Liberator*'s balance of culture and politics can partially be attributed to the impact of such figures as Larry Neal, Askia Touré, Amiri Baraka, and other influential activist-intellectuals, including visual artists and jazz musicians of the period. Although the final issue of *Liberator* appeared in 1971, the radicalism it proffered extended well into the next decade. And though many organizations came and went over the decade, the politically charged landscape that *Liberator* helped interpret would require a new commitment to struggles against the carceral regimes of police, and the punitive hand of the neoliberal state. A brief epilogue follows the discussion of black radical aesthetics that looks at the *Liberator* legacy through Dan Watts, its longtime editor in chief. Overall, *Radical Intellect* looks back even as it looks forward. As it details *Liberator*'s work inscribing transnational liberation politics of the 1960s, it imagines how such work might be done today. As the late Detroit-based sage-activist Grace Lee Boggs put it, history is as much about the future as it is about the past.[29]

1 Voices of Black Protest

Contours of Anticolonialism and Black Liberation

....

> Africa has become the magic word and the new hope.
> —John Henrik Clarke, "The New Afro-American Nationalism" (1961)

Anticolonialism, decolonialization, independence, anti-imperialism, self-governance, and self-determination were watchwords of a black new world order in the 1960s. John Henrik Clarke's observance bespoke considerable energies devoted to the cause of African liberation given by black bodies scattered around the globe, and most especially those asserting themselves throughout cities large and small in the United States. To embrace, digest, and implement the visions embedded in these concepts would not only require analytical sophistication and political agility. These concepts also necessitated a clear plan for the reordering of massive populations of human activity, modes of resource extraction and exchange, commerce, infrastructure, decision-making authority, and long-range vision. Nearly every black activist or intellectual navigating and making sense of Cold War fractures was required to hold forth on any combination of these issues. If not simply to understand this changing world for themselves, such activists were expected to galvanize an increasingly anxious black public on the verge of long-awaited political and social possibilities. *Liberator* seized the black political imagination as if receiving a call from on high. It would be the space where these issues were argued about and clarified with force. Moreover, it would be "the voice of the black protest movement," as it declared across its masthead by 1962. By the mid-1960s, even mainstream journalists such as Mike Wallace would call it "the sounding board for the angriest black writers in the black community."[1] *Liberator* injected itself into the confluence of several strands of transnational debate and local organizing, seeking to give voice to a range of political demands. From the standpoint of its editors, it would be the periodical that announced the death of colonialism to the world. It would be the magazine that proudly reflected Du Bois's vision of a "rising tide of color," shaking up the world with black and brown bodies poised to rewrite the history of world leadership. While energized to seize the moment, the activist-writers that made *Liberator* a go-to voice in black movement activities in the north were up against a countervision led by a U.S. government hell-bent on keeping Africa free of Soviet influence. More directly, *Liberator* writers and readers alike encountered the chagrin of white liberal American intellectuals and expressly anticommunist commentators, who not only questioned African Americans' allegiance to Africa, but also bristled at the idea that some black people in the United States would prioritize African affiliation over American citizenship.

In 1959, the journalist turned lecturer from the Massachusetts Institute of Technology and American Committee on Africa (ACOA) executive member, Harold R. Isaacs, speaking to an assembly of Africanists at the second annual meeting of the American Society of African Culture (AMSAC), queried: "Can we say that in acquiring a new image of Africa now, the Negro American is really engaged in acquiring nothing less than a new image of himself?"[2] The new image of Africa of which Isaacs spoke was the burgeoning shift in African American consciousness toward Africa as it shed the skin of direct colonial rule. Africans on the continent and black people in the United States were paving a united road toward a new day, the thinking went. As numerous writers have pointed out, the attitude of diasporan Africans toward Africa has undergone a number of historical shifts, ebbs, and flows since the mid-1890s. Consciousness of Africa has been the source of both hope and consternation.[3] These African-centered global imaginings would be given new life in the 1960s. For his part, Isaacs would be part of a swelling American anticommunist, liberal interest in African independence, and African American political identification with Africa. And as the Year of Africa continued to attract the world's attention, AMSAC and ACOA would find an eager adversary in the Liberation Committee for Africa (LCA) and its organ, *Liberator*.

· · · · · ·

Of all the African connections that piqued LCA political curiosity and catapulted it into existence, the independence of Ghana, Kwame Nkrumah's charismatic brand of pan-Africanism and his political fortunes, and the Congo Crisis, resulting in Patrice Lumumba's assassination, loomed largest. All the *Liberator*'s coverage of Africa pivoted from these two pan-African pressure points. James Meriwether effectively demonstrates African Americans' attraction to African independence as he highlights several key moments in African history that galvanized entire hemispheres of black activism in the first half of the twentieth century.[4] The LCA was one of the formations that owed its existence to histories of black struggle, having grown out of earlier traditions of activism. Yet the late 1950s and early 1960s marked a new epoch in African and African American struggles.

The sixteen African nations that gained independence from colonial rule in 1960, in name if not in effect, nonetheless signaled a sea change to African Americans that was nearly as profound as it was to Africans themselves. This explosion of political independence was subsequently dubbed the Year of Africa, oddly enough by Adlai Stevenson himself according to some accounts. By 1961, the total number of nominally independent nations numbered twenty-eight. The expedience of this movement carried with it numerous complicated and contentious issues, which surfaced as a hindrance to national stability. Largely owing to Cold War alignments, newly independent nations required support from international allies to sustain their autonomy and to guarantee that basic goods and services could be distributed to their citizenry. As new nations, they were not self-sufficient enough to determine how such relationships to the outside world would generate a stable degree of economic productivity. As such, these nations were torn between the influence of the United States and that of the Soviet Union. Others, inspired by the 1955 Bandung Conference, were determining whether a course of nonalignment was tenable.

At the local level, African nation-building initiatives confronted the question of what type of political system would be incorporated, what economic system would be put in place, and how regional differences would be resolved to the success of the national unity. Important, too, would be issues concerning the changes in social and cultural customs as a result of national imperatives toward progress, which resulted in clashes between tradition and modernity.[5] So described, Nkrumah's attempts underscore the multitudinous internal and external facets of nation building in this period, which sought to build a broad sense of cohesion in order to advance the cause of continent-wide unity. He, for one, believed that Ghana's independence mattered slightly unless it was connected to the independence of other nations, as only then could continental unity be achieved.[6]

The *Liberator*'s emergence out of the global anticolonial and domestic antidiscrimination politics that flourished in the late 1950s and 1960s meant its task was in many ways already outlined—utilize the skills and tools of activist journalism to push for African liberation.[7] This necessarily included a vibrant and vocal distrust and dissatisfaction with western society, especially its governing institutions. The core staff of the periodical saw themselves as part of the critical vanguard of U.S.-based activists charged with interpreting and analyzing the impact of African liberation on domestic struggles in the United States and vice versa. The *Liberator* staffers, especially its editor in chief, the bombastic and disgruntled Dan Watts, sought to develop close ties with African diplomats, students, artists, and workers and use these connections as leverage for African American representation at the United Nations, among other goals. Watts was a once-promising New York City architect, who had been hired by one of the most prominent architectural firms of the day, Skidmore, Owings and Merrill. After his demand for promotion to partner failed, he found himself increasingly disenchanted with the profession and the racial glass ceiling of corporate America. Prior to leaving, however, Watts formed a group called the Committee for the Advancement of the Negro in Architecture (CANA), where he would meet Pete Beveridge, who also had an interest in architecture, an awareness that would later serve as safety net. It is interesting that another organization carried a similar acronym and is perhaps better known, the Committee for the Negro in the Arts (CNA), which broke down numerous racial and gender barriers in the hiring practices of the entertainment industry. It is uncertain if these groups had any direct relationship, yet it is likely that Watts was inspired or encouraged by the arts committee to form an organizing unit for his profession. Gathering himself after the crashed hopes of a life in architecture, Watts threw himself headlong into local and international struggles for justice.

In June 1960 the newly established LCA issued a press release that announced the basis of its formation and provided its Statement of Aims, effectively announcing its arrival on the scene. Its opening statement connected the struggles of African people to black people in the United States, plainly stating, "Freedom and equality for Americans of African descent is inextricably linked with the freedom of Africans in their home lands."[8] It went on to pinpoint four aims that reflected their belief in the inextricable bond between African and African American struggles. Its stated aims were:

> To work for and support the immediate liberation of all colonial peoples
> To provide a public forum for African freedom fighters
> To provide concrete aid to African freedom fighters
> To re-establish awareness of the common cultural heritage of Afro-Americans with their African brothers[9]

These broadly conceived aims did not provide a blueprint of how these goals would be accomplished, nor did they reveal a particular ideological perspective or leaning. That would have to be worked out through engagement with the issues. One example of how the LCA hoped to support African independence occurred toward the end of 1961, when the organization solicited financial contributions to send to families in war-torn Northern Rhodesia, yet it would be the flashpoints of Congo and Ghanaian independence that LCA allied itself with.[10] The Congo Crisis brought the LCA out of the shadows and well into the center of debates concerning African independence. These aims reflect the LCA's attempt to provide a vital platform where people could exchange ideas, and where the politics of African and African American liberation could be explored and brought into lived reality. Moreover, these points of emphasis express an active pan-African consciousness that highlights the significance of the African liberation and its relevance to black struggle in the United States. Moreover it envisions a diasporic project based on reciprocal political support and a common vision of tangible empowerment.

At its inception, the LCA sought support from both the black community and white activists and writers who viewed themselves as allies. Under the title, "What Africa Means to Americans," the LCA placed a full-page ad in *The Nation*, where it stated that its membership "includes Americans of all races," and expanded on its stated aims. Though it was primarily concerned with the global black community, in its early goings it explicitly welcomed solidarities that cut across racial and class lines. Over the next year, the LCA sought to "make permanent that unity of purpose and effort" displayed at the UN protest supporting slain Congolese leader Patrice Lumumba in February 1961, adding that its intention was to "give Africans a voice here in the United States." Last, recognizing its function as a disseminator of information, it sought "to inform all Americans of Africa's proud heritage, long obscured by racist myths."[11] Indicated in this ad were the political, cultural, and epistemological registers that would occupy this small, fluid grouping throughout its ten-year existence.

In an organized act of defiance, a week following Lumumba's murder, Black Nationalist organizations and individuals based in Harlem, joined with several other New York–based Black Nationalist groups at a meeting of the UN Security Council on February 15, 1961. A riot broke out, according to the *New York Times*, when, during the speech of UN Security Council Ambassador Adlai Stevenson, guards arrested a woman who stood up to protest his speech. According to Dan Watts, as reported in the *Times* article, the demonstration was intended to be a peaceful one. But when Stevenson announced his support for UN secretary general Dag Hammarskjöld, the person many knew to be responsible for the protection of Lumumba, a woman stood up in protest and "guards rushed for her."[12]

According to Richard Gibson, "It was [Robert F.] Williams who inspired that much publicized and highly effective demonstration in the United Nations Assembly after the American-inspired murder of Patrice Lumumba." Mae Mallory, a New York City activist and close associate of Williams, influenced the protest from the beginning. Gibson's neighbors, Max Roach and Abbey Lincoln, also participated. Williams was away on a speaking engagement and Gibson had to report at CBS News, and thereby missed the demonstration.[13] Perhaps, in this instance, playing coy, Watts indicated to the press that the demonstration was not intended to be more than a display of civil disobedience. However, On Guard for Freedom leader Calvin Hicks offered his take on the disruption that offered different details. As he recalled, the demonstration was intended to be disruptive. During Stevenson's speech, a visiting Cuban student in solidarity with the Lumumba protesters stood up and threw an object in Stevenson's direction. As guards hurried toward the student, chaos broke out in the chamber. In Hicks's words, "We tore the place up."[14] As expected, early press accounts reported Washington officials' effort to discredit the action, calling it "Communist inspired."[15]

Adlai Stevenson was one of several high-ranking architects of U.S. relations with newly independent Africa. Stevenson, a typical Cold War liberal, surely expected there to be a vocal and energized opposition to his appointment as U.S. representative to the United Nations in January 1961. But as a friend of civil rights for African Americans, he may not have expected it to come from a collective of black radicals who had made their way into UN chambers to hear him speak on the crisis in the Congo. A May 1960 article he penned for *Harper's Magazine* spoke directly to where he believed Africa was heading in the language customary of lively Cold War concerns. He began by bemoaning the "perpetual tribal turbulence of the pre-colonial past," underscoring what he believed to be the West's achievement—peace. But this could only be maintained with more western influence, not less. Ultimately, it was America's, not Africa's, interests that mattered most: "If non-involvement or neutrality is to be the aim of the New Africa—coupled with a determination to keep itself free from any external domination, whether from the dying colonialism of Europe or the rising imperialism of Russia and China—the aim is certainly compatible with America's hopes and interests." Stevenson proceeded to lay out a plan that, for all the ink spent, amounted to a warning more than a plan.[16] Stevenson had long expressed interest in postcolonial Africa, ever since his years as governor of Illinois from 1948 to 1952. In the 1950s, his opinions and ideas about independent Africa had become more strident,[17] and by the mid-1950s he was holding forth and traveling regularly to Africa. This *Harper's* article had summarized viewpoints that had long been aired in the public. The liberal Democrat, who campaigned for president in 1952 and again in 1956, was known to some as a "champion" of civil rights gradualism.[18] As it turned out, the same liberal concerns expressed toward black demands in the United States would mirror his attitudes toward independent Africa. Regardless, his interests and outspokenness cohered into enough credibility to earn his appointment as U.S. ambassador to the United Nations from 1961 to 1965.

On January 21, 1961, the LCA issued an immediate press release, a copy of a telegram sent to the attention of Mrs. Patrice Lumumba in Leopoldville. Signed by Dan Watts, the letter stated, "Your husband, Premier Patrice Lumumba, remains the legitimate head of the Congo, and the symbol of liberation for all Africans at home and abroad. The arrest and public abuse of Premier Patrice Lumumba has aroused the sympathy of many Americans, black and white." Watts then called for all interested to petition the United Nations and demand the immediate release of Lumumba.[19] Although the news was not released to the world press, Lumumba had been killed four days prior to Watts's press release, on January 17, 1961. The deaths of Lumumba and his associates, Maurice Mpolo and Joseph Okito, were not announced until February 13, 1961.[20] When the news was finally made public, the LCA fired off another press release. This time it denounced the U.S. government, UN secretary general Dag Hammarskjöld, and Hammarskjöld's assistant Ralph Bunche as the individuals responsible for Lumumba's capture and murder.[21]

Upon receiving news of Lumumba's assassination, On Guard for Freedom, Harlem Writer's Guild members, and other Black Nationalist and left-oriented groups felt it was their responsibility to demonstrate their anger and discontent in front of the world leaders assembling at the United Nations. These activists demanded accountability for the untimely and unnecessary death of Lumumba and his close associates. On Guard for Freedom leader Calvin Hicks could not recall exactly the specifics of the plans for follow-up after the protest, but the consensus among all the groups involved was an indictment of the United States for its complicity in Lumumba's unwarranted death.[22] Writing in the *New York Times*, Lorraine Hansberry defended the protest action in a letter to the editor following an earlier one from James Baldwin, saying she too wished she had been there. Eschewing prevailing and accepted notions that Lumumba was assassinated because of "pro-Soviet" influences, Hansberry defended his outspokenness and principled commitment to independence, which had attracted western animosity. Independence, according to U.S. officialdom, "remains an intolerable aspect in colonials in the eyes of imperialists," Hansberry argued. Finally, the acclaimed playwright thought it absurd that UN representative Ralph Bunche saw fit to apologize for the disturbance of his more militant black brothers and sisters. Hansberry scoffed and thought the apologies were misdirected: "I hasten to publicly apologize to Mme. Pauline Lumumba and the Congolese people for our Dr. Bunche."[23]

Dan Watts seized the moment and made sure journalists covering the protest would hear from him if they heard from anyone. Then and there he proudly announced the formation of the Liberation Committee for Africa, which had been officially formed the previous June. From that moment forward the LCA was one among many that saw its charge as exposing the role of the U.S. government in disrupting the political and economic freedom anticipated throughout newly independent Africa, which for them mirrored the limitations on citizenship in the United States. The pages of the *Liberator* would thereafter be dedicated to documenting and disseminating information about the struggles for black liberation in the United States and around the world. Inspired to build on the energy captured at the protest, the LCA, which came to focus on publishing *Liberator* as its main objective, would utilize the passion and talents of a politicized group of cultural workers. Many would become stalwarts in the Black Arts and Black Power movements or produced work that proved deeply influential to this movement.

In March 1961, under a masthead that read "Liberation" (as this first issue was called) in bold lettering, *Liberator* ran a five-page analysis of the Congo Crisis and U.S. complicity in the assassination of Patrice Lumumba, written by Beveridge. This incident, calculated by western forces in concert with local anti-Lumumba factions in the Congo, thousands of miles away, catapulted *Liberator* magazine into a national debate on African liberation. The LCA, during its short existence as an organization before yielding to its central and more influential role publishing *Liberator*, would dedicate itself to domestic lobbying efforts on behalf of African independence. At its start, the newly named *Liberator* was still little more than a five-page newsletter of LCA activities, interests, and opinions, mixed with a few notable community events and briefings on African political leaders. And though Lumumba and the Congo Crisis loomed large in the formation of the LCA, Congo was but one flashpoint in a larger project of transnational

Daniel Henry Watts, 1969. Steve Larson / Denver Post / Getty Images.

advocacy for African liberation. The coverage of independence in Africa is telling of the magazine's scope, which was central to its organizing and political outlook. It saw the domestic struggle for justice in the context of global liberation efforts. When the LCA was formed, it had in its purview the winds of national liberation sweeping across Africa. Almost as soon as it formed, it took serious the responsibility of conducting advocacy, coordinating panels, offering lectures, and taking out ads in mainstream newspapers to dramatize its positions from protesting Lumumba's assassination to standing against nuclear testing.[24]

Their earliest organizational documents show that Dan Watts, Richard Gibson, and Pete Beveridge founded the LCA, though the bulk of the work was primarily Watts and Beveridge's responsibility. Gibson would play a distant role throughout the life of the organization, submitting articles sparingly but not responsible for the day-to-day business of the group. Gibson, a former Fair Play for Cuba Committee (FPCC) organizer who worked for CBS News and was later a correspondent and English-language editor for the radical Algeria-based journal *Revolution Africaine*, was also a longtime friend of Watts since the days when they shared the same New York City apartment building, in the late 1950s and 1960s.[25] At one point he sought to secure a press pass for his friend Watts, but to no avail. Later on Gibson would establish an international news service under the banner "Richard Gibson Reports," which was designed to supplement wire reports about Africa and distributed to editors of periodicals around the globe. Most of his later reports published in *Liberator* appeared through this dispatch.[26]

Gibson had been involved in a number of debates throughout the late 1950s as one of several notable black expatriates in Europe, including Richard Wright, William Gardener Smith, and James Baldwin. Gibson had returned to the United States in 1958. Though bred in the United States, he had traveled widely, which proved impactful on his political evolution. The writing, arguments in print and in person, and most of all, travel pushed him to reconsider the promises of white American liberalism. Gibson was foremost a writer who, like most of his generation, used writing to critically explore the dynamics of race and published a novel in the United Kingdom. Gibson also had his share of feuds, notably one with Harold Cruse, who seemed to never enter a fight he didn't like. In 1959, Gibson was among a coterie of panelists at the "Negro Writers and His Roots" conference held in New York City. The question of roots, source material, and indigenous African American culture lay at the center of the conference theme. To a lesser degree, concerns over the political orientation and ideology of the black writer would also figure prominently. Here, Gibson was among many participants with a growing dissatisfaction toward American notions of assimilation as a salve to the problem of racial and spatial discrimination. As a writer and journalist with a questioning, if not cynical, view toward the possibilities facing black people in the United States and the prospects of future racial reconciliation, Gibson would spend subsequent years organizing in the leadership of the New York chapter of the FPCC, and traveling extensively throughout Africa. As a self-styled documentarian of the uneasiness of African nationalism, he nonetheless devoted much of his time attempting to make sense of the meaning of this new political era for black and white radicals in Africa, Europe, and the United States.[27] Notably as well, Gibson was chiefly responsible for one of the most influential events that fanned the embers of black radicalism, recruiting a who's who of black radical activists and writers to visit Cuba in 1960. Subsequently, Gibson would work on behalf of the Algerian National Liberation Front (FLN) in Algeria while continuing to write.[28]

According to Gibson, in addition to being prompted by his departure from the architecture firm, Watts was also inspired to engage in the international black freedom movement by Gibson's work with the United Nations and his role in FPCC.[29] Around the time Gibson was working for CBS News, he also acquired a position with the FLN Observer Mission to the United Nations while living in New York, though the details of his role there are not clear. He worked at CBS News until the FPCC was engulfed with controversy concerning its origins and membership.[30] According to him, this controversy may have been the reason he was given a fellowship to Columbia University, a credential he used to gain access to the United Nations.[31] Dan Watts' friendship with Gibson provided him with a model for a life of self-styled activism, journalism, debate, and travel that Watts came to desire. Unfulfilled by, and ultimately rejecting, the professional world of architecture, Watts's career may not have taken the course he initially sought, but it would be the one, for better or worse, for which his name would be known. Watts and Gibson would mutually benefit from each other's work throughout the 1960s. Watts's magazine would publish Gibson's reports, and those reports served to keep *Liberator* relevant as a site documenting the struggles of African nationalism throughout the decade.

Early on, the workload of the incipient LCA would have to be divided evenly, though, naturally, the members of such a small collective would each have to do a great deal of work. LCA organization letterhead indicate Watts as chairman, Gibson as executive secretary, and Beveridge as research director and editor. In December 1961, they announced the members of the LCA executive committee, which listed Watts as chairman, Beveridge as secretary, and Evelyn Battle as social director.[32] The community of African and African American activists throughout New York brought together Evelyn Battle and Ernest Kalibala. Battle, who was then a senior at Fordham University, would go on to play a key role in *Liberator*'s day-to-day operations. Kalibala, originally of Uganda, was then pursuing the Ph.D. in Business Administration at New York University as fellow of U.S. Steel. The couple married in 1962.[33]

Though Watts, Beveridge, and John Henrik Clarke were listed as the initial editorial board of the *Liberator*, Watts and Beveridge were primarily responsible for the collection of articles, meeting deadlines, copyediting, printing, and distribution, while Clarke devoted much of his editorial energies to *Freedomways*.[34] Though the *Liberator* would eventually publish the writings of Julian Mayfield, Carlos Russell, Askia Touré (Rolland Snellings), Amiri Baraka (Leroi Jones), Abbey Lincoln, Richard B. Moore, Sonia Sanchez, James Baldwin, Larry Neal, Toni Cade, and others, it initially relied solely on a tiny cadre of three individuals: Watts, Beveridge, and Gibson, or on the occasional letter or article from veteran activists such as Clarke and Richard B. Moore.[35]

Beveridge served as production editor of *Liberator* from 1961 to 1965, when he departed the organization due to the heightened sense of racial autonomy and the growing intolerance toward whites supporting the black liberation movement.[36] Beveridge worked with a number of organizations throughout the 1950s and 1960s. Notably, he served as education director for the Brooklyn chapter of the Association for the Study of Negro Life and History, participated in several events sponsored by AMSAC before their CIA ties were discovered, helped to organize an ad hoc group called Action for South Africa, and was a member of the Brooklyn Reform Democratic Club, which helped elect Shirley Chisholm to local office. From 1959 until 1963 he was also a member of the Communist Party.[37] His work with the LCA, however, would occupy most of his time through 1965. And once he was nudged away from *Liberator*, he "retooled" himself and trained as an interior designer, later turning that training into a profession.

An equally important figure was Pete's wife, Hortense "Tee" Sie Beveridge. Tee was as devoted as Pete to the cause of African liberation and the politics of black liberation in the United States. As an African American, however, the politics of race and liberation struck her in dramatically different ways. The only account of Tee's activist life is a brief biographical sketch written by Pete at the time of her death in 1993. They had been married for forty years. Hortense Sie was born to African American and Liberian parents. Her mother, Rachel Hall Sie, was a domestic worker from Baltimore who relocated to New York as part of the flow of African Americans moving to the urban north in the 1920s. Her father, Thorgues Tor Sie Sr., was a Kru-speaking Liberian student from Grand Cess, on the southwest coast of Liberia. Tee was born in 1923, shortly after her parents' union. Though Tee did not grow up with her father, when he was home their dwelling was a regular meeting place for a community of Liberian seamen docked in New York. Tee succeeded in school and earned entrance to Hunter College, where she majored in social work. In college she was introduced to the Communist Party. She believed this to be one of the only organizations that spoke to the triple oppression of black, working-class women. Joining the party as a student, she would take up an active role in the Labor Youth League. She subsequently left school after her sophomore year and immersed herself in radical politics. It would be well over two decades before she would return to complete her college degree.[38] Following her departure from school, she spent two months traveling throughout Central and Eastern Europe, attending an International Youth Conference while there. As would be expected in this period, such activity quickly drew the attention of the Federal Bureau of Investigation (FBI). It summarily opened a file on Tee dating back to January 1953 and up through September 1962.[39]

A Harlem resident just returning from Europe, Tee extended her activism in the Harlem-based CNA, while taking night classes in film at NYU. CNA helped her gain an apprenticeship as a film editor. It is likely that the experience in Europe—with the emergence of documentary realism as an effective medium to convey political and grassroots struggle—inspired her interest in film. In any case, Tee subsequently decided to make a career in film editing, a challenging prospect considering this area of filmmaking was typically the exclusive reserve of white males and involved a rather secure father-son apprenticeship-turned-inheritance. Tee would become one of the first women and the first black woman allowed membership in the Editors' Local of the International Alliance of Theatrical Stage Employees (IATSE), which protected the path she had set upon.

By the 1950s Tee's activism brought her to the Council on African Affairs (CAA). The CAA frequently recruited a range of activists, students, and professionals. One of these recruits was a graduate student in African History at Columbia University, Pete Beveridge. Tee and Pete would meet while doing work for CAA. Pete's scholarly skillset assisted the composition of

Lowell "Pete" Beveridge and Hortense "Tee" Beveridge, Fort Dix, New Jersey, 1953. Courtesy of Pete Beveridge.

several articles in CAA's *Freedom* newsletter, whereas Tee was more of a strategic organizer. They could not have known at the time that they would spend the next phase of their life together. Yet, as activists who spent time organizing around New York and traveling to Washington, DC, to protest the arrest and death sentence of Julius and Ethel Rosenberg, their commitment to freedom and their affection for one another grew. As Pete recalled, the Mayflower Pancake House was one of the only integrated restaurants in the DC area then. Pancakes would be the main-course meal for many of their dates. Pete was drafted into the army just as the Korean War was coming to a close. Despite opposition from family, some friends, and no less an authority than the U.S. Army, Tee and Pete decided to formalize their union, and they were married at St. Philip's Church in Harlem.[40] Shortly thereafter, Pete received a less than honorable discharge from the army for refusing to sign a loyalty oath, a decision that would be reversed years later, due in part to Tee's organizing of the Servicemen's Defense Committee, a group that performed essential legal and political work to exonerate soldiers discharged for refusing the oath. From that moment, however, both he and Tee would come under the watchful eye of the FBI.

It would be Tee's work hosting African students and activists visiting the United States in the era of decolonization that would demonstrate her commitment to supporting African liberation. Tee sponsored numerous African students studying in the United States. One of these visitors, Christie Doe of Liberia, was actually her cousin. Others included Eddy Gyando of Ghana, Oliver Tambo of the African National Congress in South Africa, Vusumzi Make of the Pan-African Congress (South Africa), Jareretundu Kozenguizi of the South West National Union (SWANU, Namibia), Markus Kooper, the religious leader from Namibia and one of the main petitioners on behalf of his country at the United Nations, and Mbrumba and Jane Kerina. Mbrumba is credited with renaming Namibia from its geocolonial placard, South West Africa.[41] Mbrumba Kerina had established a lobbying group called Action for South Africa, which drew support from the CAA and attracted the interest of the ACOA.[42]

While providing respite to would-be or aspirant leaders of African independence struggles, Tee Beveridge also played a leading role in the Brooklyn chapter of the Association for the Study of Negro Life and History (ASNLH), heading up campaigns to expand the teaching of African American history in all sectors of the education system throughout New York.[43] Pete recalled inheriting a wide circle of comrades upon meeting Tee, including Ernest Chrichlow, Elayne V. Jones, Sidney Poitier, Ruth Jett, Roy De Carava, Rosa Guy, Alice Childress, Leo Hurwitz, Jacob Lawrence, and Ray Lev, among others.[44] Though there are no known mentions of Hortense Beveridge in the historical literature, it is evident that she played a deeply committed role as a long-distance runner[45] and principled participant in several overlapping projects. Her erasure may be attributed to the fact that she did not leave behind any writings or speeches, yet her contribution should not go unnoticed. In addition to these activities, Tee made a fairly successful living as a film editor. She is credited with several documentary shorts, documentaries, and features, the most well-known being the Blaxploitation-era flick *Honeybaby, Honeybaby* (1974), which starred Diana Sands and Calvin Lockhart, and the documentary *Fundi* (1981), which was centered on the life of pioneering activist Ella Baker.[46] Tee Beveridge, though far lesser known, stands alongside Abbey Lincoln, Rosa Guy, Maya Angelou, Lorraine Hansberry, *Liberator* staffer Evelyn Battle-Kalibala, and numerous others who devoted their lives to the work and activism of African independence and black liberation. These and many other lesser-known women would continue this work long after, well into the next decade.

Besides AMSAC, which early on counted numerous left-leaning artists and writers among its rank, the LCA would have to compete with yet another group with an equally broad reach. The ACOA was founded in 1953 by pacifist clergymen George Shepard and George Houser, with the goal of supporting African liberation struggles through a mixture of missionary activity and largely pro-western political engagement. ACOA's contacts were broad owing to its roots in the church, and it subsequently drew the attention of virtually every stripe of African student and potential leader, including African American pacifists Bayard Rustin, Bill Sutherland, William H. Booth, Wendell Foster, columnist Chuck Stone, and civil rights activist Martin Luther King Jr.[47] Two of ACOA's most prominent members, Peter and Cora Weiss, traveled extensively throughout Africa, racking up a Rolodex of numerous African students, activists, and would-be leaders, including Pascoal Mocumbi of the Mozambique Liberation Front (FRELIMO), FRELIMO leader Eduardo Mondlane, and Amilcar Cabral.[48] ACOA's friendly relationships were efforts to court left-leaning and potentially socialist leaders in Africa in the hopes of steering them toward western influence.[49] By any measurement, LCA and ACOA were headed in two radically different directions. ACOA was funded and privileged with certain connections not available to LCA. As a liberal, civil-society, white-led outfit that held fast to its anticommunist and religious origins, ACOA was able to make significant end roads with U.S. policymakers. Often serving as an intermediary between U.S. officials, UN representatives, and African petitioners, it arranged speakers' bureaus and events, such as "Africa Freedom Day," that featured Tom Mboya, Kenneth Kaunda, Oliver Tambo, Mbrumba Kerina, and others, including, on at least one occasion, James Baldwin. None other than President John F. Kennedy was encouraged by their work: "Your meeting today is symbolic of America's dedication to . . . freedom everywhere, and reflects again the welcome which Americans have throughout their history accorded to champions of human liberty."[50] ACOA summed up its activities by reminding potential supporters and board members alike of its intentions: "It is the fervent hope of the ACOA that our Government may more and more reflect, in her actions towards Africa, our own heritage of liberation from colonial rule."[51] In their estimation, independent Africa had more in common with the United States than with African Americans *within* the United States, who viewed these struggles as interdependent. During the Kennedy Airlift, however, other formations, such as the African American Students Foundation (AASF), set up meetings between the eighty-one Kenyan students who had made the first trek to the United States and such notable African American figures as Jackie Robinson, Lorraine Hansberry, and Malcolm X in September 1960.[52] Clearly, LCA viewed itself as the ideological rival to both AMSAC and ACOA. As an ideological heir of the CAA it is evident that LCA sought to form a grassroots counterweight to the explicit anticommunism of the more recognized groups. Although it had been forced to disband by 1955 under McCarthyism, the CAA had a profound influence on the African liberation support and political activism of a host of individuals and groupings in the post–World War II era. As historian Penny Von Eschen has explained, the group, led by Paul Robeson, W. E. B. Du Bois, and Alpheaus Hunton, was becoming a formidable presence in shaping anticolonial ties between African Americans and Africans. Its critique of American empire during the 1940s attracted relentless government scorn, and as a result the group suffered irreparable repression during the Cold War.[53] Throughout its organizing life, LCA come face-to-face with the question of how to win over African students and UN petitioners while lacking the institutional supports many of them needed. While its principles naturally shaped its political work, it was poised to fight on at least two main fronts: on behalf of African independence and against the power brokers of racial capitalism in the United States. While rarely bemoaning these complexities, LCA's work reveals the challenges of actually providing essential support to the African liberation struggle, supporting the proud call of decolonization, and staying firmly anti-imperialist, all while drawing support from black communities in the United States.

Though the LCA's ties to African diplomats were never as secure as was hoped, Watts galvanized what effort he could muster to let the nation know that African independence demanded Afro-diasporic attention. Moreover, he urged that black people should play a critical role in their own sociopolitical destinies as well as that of Africa. Such an approach was designed to create space to participate in globally recognized institutions, to pressure the U.S. government against colluding with western nations in the *recolonization* of Africa, and to rectify what left-wing, anticolonial activists considered colonial relationships on the home front. Collectives such as *Liberator* punctuate the understanding of this era's local organizing as a period of heightened anxieties and consciousness, as well as political and creative activity. Anticolonial projects were as much about shifting the balance of power in the United States as about promoting and building global solidarity against imperialism.

Like most outfits of its day, *Liberator*'s origins intimately connect to the three individuals who inaugurated the pamphlet-cum-magazine. Later, growing in size and reliability, the LCA established a subsidiary unit called the African American Research Institute, which continued to publish *Liberator*, though the group still used LCA as its distribution arm. The galvanizing impact of African independence and attendant anticolonial struggle on black activists, artists and intellectuals in the United States was crucial to *Liberator*'s beginnings. As an organization determined to build grassroots solidarity with African independence movements, it provides the clearest evidence of how they perceived their proximity, even if largely political and regionally remote, to the struggles unfolding on the African continent and their meaning for justice seekers on the U.S. side of the Atlantic.

The early days of the organization and magazine's career reveal its attempt to balance coverage of Africa with coverage of domestic struggles for justice coupled with local acts of self-determination. These impulses reveal much about the range of activist strategies available in the period and demonstrate the ambitious efforts of this small but influential group of committed individuals. These voices—at times harmonious and at others discordant—facilitate greater attention to the scope and dynamism of black activists and their political relationship to Africa in this period. Though Watts seemed to cut his teeth in attempting to organize black architects, the Lumumba protest at the United Nations was his and LCA's coming-out party.

Between AMSAC, ACOA, the United Nations, and U.S. officialdom, grassroots-level agitators such as the LCA were almost certain to be left out of any policy conversation concerning Africa's future direction. Yet it was clear that not only was the United Nations the right stage, but Stevenson, as spokesperson, was perhaps the right target of protest. To the LCA and their comrades, protesting that the United Nations represented a necessary strategy rather than a philosophical commitment or belief in the UN process. Dominated as it was by western interests, LCA associates knew far better than to hitch their hopes and dreams fully to this platform. Instead, LCA and its associates throughout New York and indeed the nation were demonstrating a contemporary form of black universalism that imagined human possibility unhinged from the constraints of western imperialism and the hurried political desires of U.S. patriotism.[54]

Thus, the political climate around the protest that erupted in the wake of Lumumba's assassination spurred black radicals throughout New York City into greater action, even if it meant they would be under the watchful eye of the government, though this would not be a new circumstance for many of them. Although it seemed to have emerged out of purely political concerns, the action also revealed personal ties. Many members of On Guard for Freedom were also members of the Harlem Writers Guild (HWG). Its leader, John O. Killens had traveled extensively throughout Africa.[55] Some HWG members, such as novelist Rosa Guy, spoke and read in French. For

Guy, her work as a writer and activist would allow her to meet and befriend many of the French-speaking Congolese and West African students and government representatives visiting or studying in the United States. These organizations had already been paying close attention to the crisis brewing in the Congo and were closely following events in Africa generally. And many had already spoken publicly or written statements of solidarity or support for Lumumba. Moreover, interest and personal alignment with the destiny of Africa was hardly a new concept in black communities.[56]

The LCA embraced a straightforward pan-Africanist perspective through an internationalism centered on African independence. African independence movements drove the activity of the committee and occupied a significant portion of the *Liberator*'s contents, especially in the early years of the publication. As events unfolded in Africa, *Liberator* frequently offered analyses rarely seen in print. As a periodical, it went where the action was, took bold positions, and made efforts to stay close to issues local people cared about. Far from the think-tank, policy-oriented style of many government-funded organizations or nongovernmental organizations (NGOs), the LCA would be a gathering space of black radical discontent with western influence in Africa. It shared with many a form of pan-Africanism that appreciated some sense of the political and cultural unity of African descendants, while also fully embracing local exigencies of considerable difference. Africa's problems were its own but were inextricably tied to African descendants around the globe.[57] It was a uniquely shared condition of multiple forms of oppression, rooted in history and reflected in contemporary racial and class antagonisms that would offer the committee its most enduring links throughout the black world. Though not all black internationalist perspectives are based on a belief in African and African American political or cultural unity, the LCA was one organization that articulated this unified vision even as it did not adhere to or offer a strict definition. The committee unwaveringly (and often times romantically) supported African independence, and maintained the view that African independence weighed heavily upon the fight for equality and political power in the United States. Moreover, it reflected the view that African and African Americans should have a place at the table of world leadership.

The LCA emerged from one of the translocal hotbeds of Africa-centric activities. John Henrik Clarke's considering Africa both a "magic word" and "new hope" was no understatement. A number of New York–based nationalist groups interested in the liberation of African people and descendants formed organizations in this period. Even educational organizations such as the Association for the Study of Negro Life and History (formed by Carter G. Woodson in 1915) formed part of this milieu, and several key LCA members participated in local chapters of that professional organization. Moreover, Abbey Lincoln and Max Roach (who composed the African liberation themed "WE INSIST! Freedom Now Suite" in 1960) lived in the same apartment building as Dan Watts, his wife Marilyn Lieberman Watts, and Richard Gibson, and were equally concerned about African liberation and the black freedom struggle in the United States.[58] While U.S. officials were recruiting black artists and writers to travel abroad in hopes of demonstrating democracy's success, not all artists were interested if this meant denial of the hard truths of racism and marginalization widespread throughout the United States. Lincoln's Cultural Association for Women of African Heritage (CAWAH) would be one of the few organizations that embraced radicalism led explicitly by black women.

Groups such as On Guard for Freedom, led by Calvin Hicks and Sarah Wright;[59] the United African Nationalist Movement, led by James Lawson; as well as the Universal African Legion, Inc., and the African Nationalist Pioneer Movement, led by Carlos Cooks; among a number of other groups, all viewed the liberation of Africa as part of the struggle for black liberation in the United States.[60] Some of these formations viewed themselves as late expressions of Garveyism and proclaimed black people worldwide as African people, but each, in their own way, helped the New York grassroots radical landscape that challenged U.S. orthodoxy, and informed wide swaths of communities on African affairs. As such, New York City was a cornerstone of Black Nationalist political and literary activity in the 1960s.[61] *Liberator*'s presence on the scene brings into closer focus New York City as a fertile urban landscape for black radical activity. Many of the individuals associated with the periodical had participated in numerous local political struggles throughout the city and were members of political and cultural groupings prior to, during, and long after their work with *Liberator*. Far from appearing out of the clear blue, *Liberator* staffers came to the periodical already deeply invested in the political fate and economic fortunes of black communities around the globe. Such connections reveal *Liberator* as beneficiary and benefactor of black radical thought in this period.

Proclaiming itself "The Voice of the Black Protest Movement" atop its full-length inaugural series, *Liberator* eagerly published articles that demanded the right to self-government, emphasized self-determination, and advocated the struggle for political, economic, and cultural autonomy, hallmark aspects of black radical thought in the twentieth century.[62] Equally central to its outlook was its criticism of racial capitalism's function in the perpetuation of African and African American exploitation. In fact, the Liberation Committee, like many other internationalist-oriented organizations, saw capitalism as the nemesis of all freedom-seeking peoples engaged in the overthrow of colonialism and imperialism. It therefore wrestled with a socialist solution, although owing to its ties to the old black Left, it sought to avoid sectarianism and the dogmatism found in adhering to prescribed party lines. This meant, among other things, that it explicitly demonstrated support for newly independent African, Latin American, and Caribbean countries that were at least open to strategic solidarity against the West.

Liberator relied on a range of personal contacts. Watts obtained a printing deal through family ties. His wife at the time, Marilyn, was the niece of a Brooklyn printer named Maurice Golden. Watts arranged to have the magazine printed through Golden's shop at a lower price than he would normally charge, and Watts and his associates were responsible for the distribution. According to Marilyn, distribution was a problem Watts regularly lamented.[63] About a year later, Rose and James Finkenstaedt joined the *Liberator* collective. Along with Beveridge, these were the only other white associates that gained LCA's trust and held consistent working relationships with the organization.

Rose's involvement emerged alongside her evolving political consciousness and willingness to play a supporting but active role in black liberation efforts while a Ph.D. student at Columbia University. In the early years of the magazine, Rose would contribute a number of penetrating, insightful articles. James Finkenstaedt, who was vice president of William Morrow publishers, got involved through his wife's urging. James (also known as "Fink") and Charlie Russell, another staff writer and brother of basketball star Bill Russell, took over the responsibilities of magazine distribution to local bookstores, newspaper stands and vendors. According to Rose, newsstands in Queens, Brooklyn, Greenwich Village and the Lower East Side often carried the magazine. Though his ball-playing days were long eclipsed by the stardom of his brother (National Basketball Association legend Bill Russell), Charlie put his 6'7" imposing frame to good use in occasionally "convincing" reluctant vendors to sell the magazine. Regarding national distribution, Rose recalled Watts saying that the *Liberator* was being read in San Francisco and Detroit, owing to the militant translocalism of both cities, but "otherwise it was a New York operation."[64] Nonetheless, the letters to the editor reveal that the magazine was attracting the attention of readers as far away as Detroit, Michigan; Silver Springs, Maryland; Lake Charles, Louisiana; Memphis, Tennessee: Berkeley and Downey, California; Laramie, Wyoming; Seattle, Washington: and all over the five boroughs of New York City.

As the magazine was not a moneymaking, advertisement-driven venture, Watts and Beveridge often used their personal finances to cover the costs of publishing, which put strains on their families. For a short while this seemed feasible; politics was the driving force anyway. According to Beveridge, these costs were generally more than they were able to recoup through memberships, subscriptions, and other forms of revenue such as book sales through its book service, which carried signature titles in history, literature, and politics.[65] Though they were able to attract a number of established and up-and-coming writers, Watts was rarely in a position to compensate them for articles. Though there are no indications of exactly how many members the LCA had, a summary of finances published in June 1961 indicated that membership dues, literature sales, magazine subscriptions, and contributions donated to cover costs for ads in the *New York Times* brought in a modest $4,395. Their overall expenses at the time totaled $3,218.[66] Though a good public gesture, this was the last time the LCA published a financial summary of this type. And although many writers and artists published in *Liberator*, very few were actually members of the LCA, and those that were continued to work in multiple capacities.

Richard Gibson's activities in this period ranged from serving as acting executive secretary of FPCC, to participation in the Monroe Defense Committee (MDC), "a broad, non-partisan defense committee" established to support Robert F. Williams. As Calvin Hicks, the committee's executive secretary, stated in a letter soliciting support for the MDC, "The committee was organized and is sponsored by many individuals who may not agree with each other on the way in which full equality for Afro-Americans is to be achieved. However, they do agree that the oppression, brutality and travesty of justice in Monroe, N.C. which forced Robert F. Williams to flee for his life must be rectified."[67] The MDC sponsor list, as identified in Hicks's letter, contained the names of a number of important political and cultural figures—many of whom published in the *Liberator* or were close associates of the LCA—including James Baldwin, John Henrik Clarke, Richard Gibson, Jesse Grey, Leroi Jones, Paule Marshall, Julian and Ana Mayfield, Bayard Rustin, Dan Watts, Max Roach and Abbey Lincoln, Ruby Dee, Ossie Davis, and Maya Angelou, a grouping that in this instance transcended ideological differences to include some civil rights militants as well as committed radicals.[68]

Though many of these connections were political in nature, some were personal. Angelou was at this time married to Vusumzi Make (pronounced ma-key) of the Pan-African Congress of South Africa. According to Gibson, Make, who was "the darling of black militants" in New York City, was also a key influence on the formation of the LCA. "Like Williams," Gibson contends, "[Make] was convinced that an armed struggle would be necessary to end white rule in South Africa." Make's role in supporting the liberation struggle in the United States for black rights was thus an extension of the struggle against South African apartheid.[69] Though Make did not have an extended engagement with LCA, he did participate in a number of LCA events. He was a featured speaker alongside authors John O. Killens, James Baldwin, and journalist William Worthy at a May 1961 public forum entitled, "Nationalism, Colonialism and the United States—One Minute to 12!" that was hosted by the LCA. In April 1962, one of the few articles Make published in the United States was printed in *Liberator*. In the article, Make sought to provide a context for the ongoing struggle against apartheid South Africa, but tellingly demonstrated the complicity of the North Atlantic Treaty Organization (NATO) countries in the apartheid regime's massacring of black South Africans. NATO "aid," Make wrote, assisted the buildup of a military state in South Africa. He emphasized how ammunitions and tanks purchased from Britain were used in the Sharpeville and Langa massacres of March 21, 1960. Since that time, he warned, "The South African regime has been preparing for . . . a civil war."[70] This was additional justification of the LCA's role assisting African liberation. Make's description of liberation efforts would be an early example of *Liberator* efforts at continued coverage of strained, yet potent, political vision and tumult on the continent. Above all, *Liberator* stressed independence, whether that was found in its support of political independence in the United States and abroad, in its support for culturally relevant education, or in challenging the media representation of the black liberation struggle.

If supporting the promise and project of African liberation was a core element of LCA activity, attention to the civil rights movement in the United States occupied the second column of its racial justice work. From its inception, the LCA began to the political left of the civil rights establishment. It opposed a steadfast adherence to nonviolence when black people were confronted with violence in the North or in the South. Distrustful of liberalism and gradualist approaches to social change, *Liberator* was naturally skeptical about the discourse of integration. Watts and his crew tended to disregard any talk of integration that did not include a deep critique of economic segregation. In a sense, activities of dissidents and controversial figures such as Robert F. Williams, Mae Mallory, and William Worthy drew the praise of *Liberator* writers. Virtually any black activist who received the scorn or indifference of the mainstream was welcomed among *Liberator* ranks.

In June 1961, the editors carried an unsigned article on the Freedom Rides, which provides an example of its viewpoint regarding the civil rights struggle occurring throughout the South, albeit from its northern perch. The *Liberator* hailed the importance of the Freedom Rides for "giving new life to the liberation struggle at home." The Freedom Rides had not only demonstrated to the world that race relations in the United States were still marked by acts of white savagery, but the rides had also "quickened the pace and raised the level of struggle." However, they did not support the riders' steadfast adherence to nonviolence. Moreover, the LCA argued, "By announcing ahead of time that they will not fight back, the Freedom Riders have given license to the most degraded and cowardly elements to indulge in mob violence."[71] Though supportive of the Freedom Riders' effort to test the Supreme Court's prohibition of segregation in interstate travel, the LCA, like many others, shared the belief that the riders must have government protection. Recognizing that nonviolence would not prevent violence nor guarantee protection, the LCA expressed support for the African American community's right to self-defense. This perspective made it the natural adversary of the political perspective of the established black leadership, including individuals such as Martin Luther King Jr., Whitney Young, and James Farmer, figures whom it routinely criticized. Instead, the LCA promoted the activism of Robert F. Williams, Mae Mallory, Malcolm X, Gloria Richardson, Adam Clayton Powell, and Albert Cleage, and championed the pan-Africanism and anticolonial concerns of W. E. B. Du Bois and Kwame Nkrumah. And yet, a focus on prominent figures such as these loses sight of just how widespread these activities were. Informal, ad hoc, issue-specific coalitions formed under the broad umbrella of decolonization, self-determination, and liberation and were as instrumental in furthering these politics and key to their dissemination.

John Henrik Clarke's identification of the LCA as one of many groups reflecting a new sense of militancy, what he called "New Afro-American Nationalism," proved prescient.[72] What Clarke could not have known at the time was just how dedicated to the cause Watts and his crew would become. In Clarke's view, considering African and African American struggles as inherently linked in the effort to defeat imperialism also marked a simultaneous shift in identity.[73] For the black activists associated with the LCA, this was a shift they were eager to make. Formed in a political milieu that had been sliced in two by the Cold War, splintered by the emergence of New Left politics, and shaped by the continued struggle for civil and human rights for African Americans in the United States, the LCA was a small, yet pivotal formation that was dedicated to domestic and international black liberation and committed to radical sociopolitical transformation. Chief among the issues it confronted in a vehement campaign were racial torture, political erasure, and spatial segregation. Having announced their arrival and intention to mobilize resources and energy in the service of African independence and civil rights militancy, the *Liberator* would expressly position itself as a mouthpiece of black radical thought throughout the 1960s.

2 Spokespersons and Advocates
The Contested Intellectual Life of African Independence

> The pattern that sets the course for the intellectual as outsider is best exemplified by the condition of exile, the state of never being fully adjusted, always feeling outside the chatty, familiar world inhabited by natives, so to speak, tending to avoid and even dislike the trappings of accommodation and national well-being. Exile for the intellectual in this metaphysical sense is restlessness, movement, constantly being unsettled, and unsettling others. You cannot go back to some earlier and perhaps more stable condition of being at home; and alas, you can never fully arrive, be at one with your new home or situation.
>
> —Edward W. Said, "Intellectuals and Exile," *Representations of the Intellectual*

African American grassroots groups prepared to support African liberation had their work cut out for them. On one hand they were poised to influence U.S. policy in Africa; on the other hand the work of liberation was right outside their New York City door. Desiring to influence the course of African independence and inspired to take their domestic disputes global, African American radicals would have to organize more effectively, be unafraid of the most spontaneous debate, stay prepared for an impromptu protest, and offer fresh but hard-hitting analyses that could rarely be found elsewhere. Independent Africa unleashed a wave of debate on all aspects of African life. Lawrence Jackson captured the expectations facing advocates and spokespersons to great effect when he states, "By the end of the 1950s, to hold the post of representative authority for black America, a writer would have to appeal to the streets, seem capable of commercial success, be independent of orthodox communism, and espouse a radicalism that would make whites as uncomfortable as middle-class blacks."[1] Just who would speak for Africa's future: black Americans, white Americans, Africans themselves, or some combination of these? Said's notion of exile, of being in and out simultaneously, at once at home and away, effectively adds understanding to the quality of engagement expected of *Liberator* writers, an expectation that was in many ways of their own choosing. In Said's view, the intellectual exile prefers "to remain outside the mainstream, unaccommodated, unco-opted, resistant," working through a self-conscious and purposeful "productive anguish." "Exile," he argues, "means that you are always going to be marginal, and that what you do as an intellectual has to be made up because you cannot follow a prescribed path." He contends that such bodily awareness is not experienced as "a deprivation and as something to be bewailed," but rather a "unique pleasure" gained from going after the problems of the world as one sees fit.[2] Said seems to have insightfully captured *Liberator*'s *raison d'être* and that of an entire generation of iconoclasts. Yet Jackson's observation does not rule out mainstream attention. To be sure, *Liberator* oscillated between Said's poignant description of the exiled intellect and Jackson's sense of the high stakes of indignation.

If officially recognized platforms for African American defenders of African liberation were still out of their reach, they would need to establish them. Thus, *Liberator* eagerly joined a vast pool of commentary on Africa and its relationship to the world that had reached a tipping point in the 1950s, as independence seemed just within reach. Debating Africa's future became a cottage industry unto itself. This debate raged in the early part of the 1960s, and *Liberator* intended, with limited resources, to turn the Year of Africa into the Decade of Africa. While *Liberator* set its sights on battling mainstream liberal opinion, its influence is perhaps best understood in the context of a tradition of grassroots black radicalism. These groups can be viewed along an ideological spectrum, from ultra-nationalist groups such as the African Nationalist Pioneer Movement, a late and politically conservative offshoot of the Garvey Movement, to socialist-influenced, Black Nationalist anticolonial groups such as the Liberation Committee for Africa, to groups that were *anti*-nationalist groups domestically but *pro*-nationalist in regard to Africa, such as the NAACP and American Society of African Culture (AMSAC).

John Henrik Clarke had presciently identified several organizations that fall along this spectrum as evidence of a new sense of nationalism spreading throughout black communities in the United States.[3] Clarke focused on the more or less grassroots formations of African-identified liberation support groups such as the Muslim Brotherhood, the Universal African Nationalist Movement (UANM), the Cultural Association of Women for African Heritage (CAWAH), the African Nationalist Pioneer Movement (ANPM), On Guard Committee for Freedom, the Provisional Committee for a Free Africa, and the Liberation Committee for Africa (LCA). For his part, Carlos

Cooks was long known as a staunch defender of African liberation, stretching back into the 1950s. Ever the propagandist, Cooks established several pamphlets, newsletters, and other print materials, such as *The Black Challenge* and *The Street Speaker,* that proselytized for African freedoms.

On the other end of the spectrum of Africa-inspired activity, the venerable scholar St. Clair Drake highlighted some of the more established and better-funded organizations and institutions. As a scholar of the African diaspora, Drake understood, and to some degree, appreciated better than most, African Americans' attraction to Africa. Some of these organizations were nongovernmental organizations (NGOs) financed by the American government, or otherwise private corporations that fostered intellectual and humanitarian or other relationships with Africa from the 1950s to 1960s. Such groups include the African-American Institute, Operation Crossroads Africa, the African Studies Association, the American Committee on Africa (ACOA), AMSAC, the Peace Corps, and the American Negro Leadership Conference on Africa. As Drake observed, ideological positions had to be considered in the relations between African Americans and Africans, and for that matter, American intellectuals in general in this period, as not all groups agreed on the meaning of African independence for American activists and intellectuals.[4] Indeed, as Brenda Gayle Plummer writes, "AMSAC provides an example of how a clandestine government agency played an active role in scattering the seeds of a movement that it was simultaneously trying to contain."[5] AMSAC epitomized western Cold War interests. "A Western victory in the cold war required the recruitment of emerging states and their most important citizens: new classes and politicized youth who would share elite values," Plummer contends. "While the goal of independence for the global South would be upheld, broader critiques of the international behavior of Western powers were disallowed or deemed subversive of world order."[6]

In many ways, AMSAC, ACOA, and the LCA help to characterize the general makeup of the African American and white liberal interest in Africa in this period. They represent a continuum, which was enumerated by Clarke and Drake. More than any other Africa-oriented group in this period, AMSAC attracted the attention (and later the scorn) of *Liberator* writers, especially in the first two years of the publication. AMSAC, whose stated objectives were to further understand and support the cultural achievement and political development of newly independent Africa, was formed in 1957 partially in response to the activity of the Council on African Affairs (CAA), which emerged from left-wing tendencies. As it turned out, AMSAC was financed by the Central Intelligence Agency (CIA) Committee on Race and Class in World Affairs (CORAC), and was led by men such as Horace Mann Bond and John A. Davis, ties that drew considerable controversy. The significance of AMSAC in this period stems from the esteem it received in elite intellectual and government circles, where it was encouraged to track, discuss, and debate the role independent Africa would play in world politics. As an organization with institutional recognition that attracted scholars, artists, entrepreneurs, and ambassadors, it also reflected U.S. governmental and corporate interests in Africa, a dubious aspect of its work to say the least. Through these connections, however, AMSAC also sponsored a number of art exhibitions and writing projects that highlighted the cultural exchanges between Africans and African Americans. Some of these initiatives included the work of Jacob Lawrence, Elton Fax, Saunders Redding, Randy Weston, Chinua Achebe, David Rubadiri, Thomas Melone, Kofi Antubam, and Afewerk Tekle.

AMSAC's publishing projects also included important collections of African American writing on Africa, such as the seminal *Africa Seen by American Negro Scholars* (1958), which included essays from St. Clair Drake, Martin Kilson, William Leo Hansberry, Lorenzo Turner, Pearl Primus, Mercer Cook, Rayford Logan, E. Franklin Frazier, Adelaide Cromwell Hill, and other first-rate African American scholars. AMSAC was also responsible for the publication of *The American Writer and His Roots* (1959), which included writing by Julian Mayfield, John Henrik Clarke, and St. Clair Drake, and finally *Pan-Africanism Reconsidered* (1962), which published the presentations and debates at the Third Annual AMSAC international conference.[7] The fact that the CIA, in whole or in part, funded all of this activity was certain to fan the flames of dissension and distrust. But it is also a consequence of African Americans' and liberal white intellectuals' passionate, if sometimes naïve, identification with Africa.

When the LCA formed it was foremost out of a rejection of the U.S. diplomacy, European western influence, and American liberal anticommunism that ran through the United Nations, the White House, and nongovernmental organizations like ACOA and AMSAC. By contrast, the left-wing political milieu out of which the LCA grew made anti-imperialist struggle in Africa central to its perspective, which distinguished the group from much of the attention paid to African independence. A January 1962 *Liberator* editorial questioned the role of the United States in Nigeria, specifically critiquing the establishment of an economic enterprise named the American-Nigerian Chamber of Commerce, Inc., whose plans were already underway. Though Nigeria could not afford to respond explicitly to the calls for a "United States of Africa," to which Kwame Nkrumah actively subscribed, LCA, owing to its general pan-Africanist proclivities, still held that country in high regard. The editors were swift to point out that "part of the stated purpose of the new organization is to provide intercourse between American and Nigerian businessmen," but went on to reveal that "this part of the program is handicapped from the beginning, since, possibly by oversight, no Nigerians were placed on the board of directors." The list of companies represented in this new economic venture were IBM, Chase Manhattan Bank, A.C. Israel Commodity Corporation, Mobil Oil, Chase International Investment Corporation, Westinghouse, RCA, Bank of America, Pepsi, Texaco, Farrell Lines, and First National City Bank of New York. This heavy corporate interest in Nigeria alarmed LCA writers, as it was evident that U.S. economic interests were equal to its political interests in Africa, moves that erased differences between the U.S. and the European nations who had established political and economic control across Africa decades earlier.[8] Later, *Liberator* republished an editorial from the Nigerian-based *African Pilot*, which questioned the role of Ford Foundation grants to Nigeria when American cities suffered. "We believe that charity begins at home," it read. "It is all well to help build a hostel at Ibadan, but how much better would it have been to rid Detroit, Pittsburgh, and New York of Negro ghettoes?"[9] American corporate interests abroad were part and parcel of the mounting evidence that pointed to U.S. designs toward empire.

As far as NGOs went, the pages of *Liberator* contained open criticism of AMSAC's efforts in Africa. In the February 1962 issue, the editors ran an article entitled, "A Cold Reception for AMSAC in Nigeria," and went on to dramatize the dissatisfaction growing around AMSAC's activities. "The Nigerian press," it reads, "has virtually poured cold water on any future programs of the American Society of African Culture, more popularly called AMSAC here, with their criticism of the first AMSAC tour in Lagos, Nigeria, last December [1961]."[10] The March issue ran an art review entitled, "Why AMSAC Festival Was a Flop" and went on to critique some of the performances as lacking knowledge of Nigerian culture or wasting the talents of otherwise phenomenal artists by scheduling them alongside artists they had never before accompanied. By far the most comical of the critiques of the festival performances was put forth in the question that concluded the review: "But what on Earth has Madame Butterfly got to do with African Culture?"[11] The editors never missed a chance to critique AMSAC's presence in American foreign policy circles, and early on they perceived that

AMSAC's cultural directive was little more than a smokescreen for American political positioning on the continent. For *Liberator* activists, who had earlier been envious of the organization's more structured diplomatic relations with African dignitaries, it was not hard to level critique at an intellectual arm of U.S. imperial policy. It is important that this critique in *Liberator* anticipated revelations that AMSAC was a front for the CIA.

While coming to the realization that pan-African unity was less stable than first imagined, LCA expressly allied itself with the Casablanca faction of African nationalists, who were open to some form of continental unity and Eastern bloc affiliation. It also however continued to support Nigeria's course of nationalism, which pulled it away from continental cohesion in favor of focused attention on exigencies within its own borders. In this way, the LCA embodied what can be called a Casablanca-plus-one political outlook, which saw no contradiction in solidarity with both Nkrumah and Azikiwe, as indicated by the coverage it accorded the leaders of both Ghana and Nigeria in back-to-back issues in July and August 1962. This also suggests that *Liberator* associates were sensitive to the continent-specific exigencies to be resolved, while among U.S.-based black activists, both Nkrumah and Azikiwe enjoyed a nearly equal amount of acclaim.

In the March issue of that year, *Liberator* published a statement from Azikiwe congratulating Nkrumah on the fifth anniversary of Ghana's independence. Azikiwe's statement shows that, unlike in AMSAC, the division between Ghana and Nigeria on the question of continental unity did not adversely affect the LCA vision of a liberated Africa, and perhaps neither were positioned to appeal fully to the political interests of black people scattered throughout the diaspora.

> On behalf of the people of the Federation of Nigeria I send you sincere greetings on the occasion of Ghana's Fifth Anniversary as a free sovereign and independent state. In this respect I congratulate you and the people of Ghana in the spirit of one pioneer nationalist to another pioneer nationalist in the struggle for human freedom in Africa. . . . And may God strengthen you and your people to forge ahead and contribute your fair share to the solution of world problems and the unity of Africa. My dear Kwame, come thunderstorms at home come deliberate fabrications in the foreign press come vagaries of human life all African nationalist[s] are genuinely dedicated to the manumission of Mother Africa from foreign yoke with the positive goal to enable Africans to live like free men and

free women in free African states enjoying fundamental human rights under rule of law. Fighting for such eternal principles you can always count on me and the people of Nigeria as worthy comrades in arms in this common struggle. Once more accept sincere assurances of our high esteem.

                Fraternally yours, Nnamdi Azikiwe, Governor-General[12]

Despite the fraternal respect shown in Azikiwe's message, the disagreement between Ghana and Nigeria on the question of continental unity and pan-Africanism was palpable. One might look to the fact that Nigeria did not make a public effort to attract and enlist assistance from the African diasporic community in the same way Nkrumah did, as evidence of its attitude on black global unity. Considering this, it might seem that there was no sense of global solidarity emergent from Nigeria. Upon closer look, however, local activists, and not necessarily those with ties to government leaders, shared in a vision of Africa's global redemption. The reality was that these countries were very different and faced different sets of political challenges as they moved toward decolonization. The challenges of pan-African unity had more to do with exigencies on the ground, which pivoted on the ownership and distribution of extractable resources, than hard-line ideological positioning.

The World and Africa: *Liberator* and African Independence

If W. E. B. Du Bois's classic post–World War II polemic, *The World and Africa,* proved Africa's importance to the world,[13] for *Liberator* it might have read in reverse: "Africa and the world," as the periodical centered its global coverage on African independence. Like Du Bois, *Liberator* reflected the growing sense of urgency to rid the world of colonialism with a critical eye on who it perceived to be the world's largest perpetuator and beneficiary, the U.S. government. Its guiding perspective viewed the victory over imperialism squarely in the fight against racist capitalist oppression in the United States. *Liberator*'s coverage of the independence movement in Africa was passionate and determined, if at times eager and disjointed, as it drew on extant resources to impact American foreign policy toward Africa. *Liberator*'s continental coverage was independent, interpretive, and galvanizing. It was equally chaotic, shifting, and at times difficult to grasp as its writers made efforts to track closely the sudden changes of the immediate postcolonial period.

Yet, in its role as watchdog of U.S. foreign policy toward Africa, *Liberator* also highlighted efforts to uproot colonialism on the continent accurately. In an editorial discussing the importance of the All-African Peoples Conference, its global perspective of domestic struggle is evident: "This Conference, attended by over 200 delegates representing 69 parties, organizations and unions from 36 African countries was virtually ignored by the American press. The Liberation Committee for Africa and all other African friends of African freedom must take the speeches and resolutions of the Cairo conference as a direct challenge to demonstrate solidarity with the Freedom Fighters of Africa by opposing and exposing the racist, imperialist policies of the foremost Neo-Colonial power not only in the Congo and Liberia; in Laos and the Philippines; in Cuba and Brazil; but in Alabama and Mississippi as well."[14] The relationship of the civil rights struggle of black people in the United States to the anti-imperialist struggle in Africa and across the globe positioned the LCA as a direct beneficiary of the internationalism inspired by Bandung and the upsurge of anticolonial fervor in the Congo. Its efforts to follow the developments at the United Nations, coupled with close attention paid to the African press and the relationships between Africans and African Americans in the United States, shaped its outlook and journalistic activism. Over the magazine's first five years, the *Liberator* published nearly one hundred articles and analyses dealing with African liberation movements and independence, and it would continue its coverage throughout the rest of the decade. *Liberator* dutifully watched U.S. government activity in Africa. Most articles dealt with the Congo, Ghanaian independence, and South African apartheid, while others covered political entanglements and cultural engagements in Angola, Tunisia, and Kenya.

The September 1961 issue of the magazine included a small note requesting financial support from subscriptions. Proud of its increasing circulation, which had just crossed fifteen hundred, it enthusiastically reported that readers throughout the country and in Africa were pleased with the efforts the small organization had displayed.[15] With the modest goal of doubling its circulation, the LCA headed into the New Year with the wind at its back. In December, the budding periodical resumed its coverage of the Congo Crisis. Included in this issue were reports on Northern Rhodesia and the experiences of African students studying in the United States. The editors also critiqued African Americans who lent rhetorical support for U.S. participation in undermining African independence. For example, in its coverage of Congo, the *Liberator* routinely criticized African American journalist

George Schuyler, who utilized his column in the *Pittsburgh Courier* as a launching pad for his conservative opinions, calling him "The Afro-Americans' Tshombe," and claiming he stoked, and then benefited from, Lumumba's fatal demise. They also shamed former CAA associate Max Yergan, and writer William F. Buckley as intellectual apologists of American empire.[16]

In particular, Beveridge provided a strong rebuke of *New York Times* coverage of the events unfolding in the Congo, while Watts made the rounds on local radio debating journalists and, when possible, media representatives of Tshombe's pro-western government. This particular article was a rebuttal to an ad placed in the *Times* requesting support for Tshombe under the name "American Committee for Aid to Katanga Freedom Fighters." Point by point, Beveridge challenged the positions expressed in the ad. Efforts to counter mainstream press accounts quickly became the magazine's *raison d'être*. Having decided to make his lot with leftist radicals at a young age, and having joined the Communist Party (CPUSA) as a young adult, his sense of internationalism drew him to the study of colonialism in Africa and Asia. His training in African history allowed him to develop a consistent critique of western influence in Africa. In 1953, while at Columbia University, Beveridge completed a master's thesis on the subject of white supremacy in South Africa.[17] He was therefore well equipped to discuss the particularities of western control over the continent. His deep interest in education and politics informed many of his *Liberator* writings.[18] Writers representing various African and Arab student groups were regularly featured in the periodical up to this point. One student spoke of the difficulty of having honest discussions with Americans about crises in Africa. When invited to parties and meetings hosted by campus organizations, the student noted that faces often turned sour when he would try to discuss "politics." So harsh had his experiences been that this student simply signed his article anonymously, "An African Student."[19]

The LCA's habit of monitoring mainstream press commentary on African affairs enhanced its credentials as a viable alternative site for news and information. Spending much of its early efforts countering press coverage of visiting African diplomats and a growing African student population, it began its 1962 series with a long critique of the Institute for International Education's survey and study of African students' educational experiences in the United States.[20] Its critique of that study initiated the LCA's own investigation into the experiences of African students, which reached beyond the personal contacts of Beveridge and others. Throughout the year, they would compile letters, personal biographies, academic success stories, and political commentary from African students around the country. An Arab student leader wrote to Watts in response to an article published in December 1961, wherein Watts identified the complicity of the United States and the state of Israel in undermining African independence through aid projects.[21] The student appreciated Watts's position and proceeded to recount his disdain for what he interpreted as the global influence of Zionism.[22]

Another writer, representing the Central African Students' Union of America, Inc., complained about the scholarship programs many of the international students received. He argued plainly that many scholarship programs for African students were but examples of "economic imperialism," as big business and private foundations underwrote many of the financial packages that students accepted. Financing international student education consisted of a complex web of government and corporate interests, he argued. "In this context, my argument points to the fact that a recipient of a scholarship receives financial aid from a business corporation which is posing for a Foundation," he wrote as he recalled his own experience in such programs. "I have myself been on such a scholarship program, and it has only been recently that I have realized that I have been accepting economic imperialism through the back door," he noted, calling attention through caution. Although he argued that students should keep their scholarships, they should at least know how they were funded.[23] These examples importantly help to show *Liberator*'s attention to the nuances of U.S. educational interests, which tended to follow its political investments in western-friendly outcomes.

The funding of African students' education in the United States continued to be a source of controversy. Editor Dan Watts penned a long article bemoaning the lack of adequate support offered to African students. Perhaps this was a dig at groups like ACOA and the African American Students Foundation (AASF), which boasted its support for a range of needs facing African petitioners and often students, but Watts took his chances nonetheless. It is interesting that he seemed to contradict the warning of economic imperialism through such funding programs, arguing that wherever it came from, African and African American students deserved financial support sufficient for long-term study. As an example, Watts recounted the experience of a Kenyan student who was placed on a "work scholarship" to attend Warren Wilson College, a small two-year college in North Carolina whose education model—reminiscent of Tuskegee—combined the development of skills through hands-on work, academics, and community service. According to Watts, the student had no inclination that "his work scholarship meant cleaning floors and toilets," and was surprised that he was not at a leading American institution of higher learning. For Watts, such was indicative of the failure of the scholarship programs to properly educate prospective students about their educational choices. Though he encouraged improved funding opportunities, he ultimately rejected the approaches taken by government-funded organizations or private foundations even if it meant that his own work suffered as a result.[24]

Accompanying the critique of students' financial aid entanglements, Beveridge reported on the formation of the Pan-African Students' Union of the Americas. This newly formed organization was established at a meeting of African students in Chicago in December 1961. This collective had grown out of an earlier organization, the All-African Students Union of the Americas, which Beveridge noted "was smothered to death by aid from the U.S. State Department and businesses."[25] Judging by its resolutions, this new organization took cues from Nkrumah's brand of pan-Africanism and explicitly aligned itself with the resolutions passed at the All-African People's Conference of 1958. Except for including student-specific concerns, the resolution appeared to be a carbon copy of the historic Casablanca-led meeting, a significant yet contentious indicator of the many attempts at global African unity.

The efforts to revive pan-African ideals through close attention and support for African independence would continue throughout *Liberator*'s existence. Throughout its first few years of publication, it continued to describe the rapid, ever-shifting pace of independence to its readers. The *Liberator* emphasized the distinctions between those leaders who pushed for full autonomy and those who were content to work within the existing colonial model. In March and June 1961, Beveridge paid tribute to two African leaders who lost their lives in the struggle for liberation.

Felix Roland Moumie, president of Union of Populations of Cameroon (*Union des populations du Cameroun* or UPC), who was assassinated in Geneva, Switzerland, in 1960, was given tribute in March. The UPC was an active radical organization made up of trade unionists, intellectuals, impoverished farmers and workers, nationalists, and Marxists. Active since the 1950s under the leadership of Um Nyobe, it had long been a thorn in the side of French colonialists. In the end, it took five military battalions between 1960 and 1962 to defeat Moumie and his associates.[26] The following month Beveridge eulogized Joao Baptista, head of military operations for the Angolan National Liberation Army, who had been killed in a battle against the Portuguese army in Bembe, Luanda Province, the previous year.[27] Further revealing its solidarity, *Liberator* reprinted Elisio Figueiredo's speech at the All-African Students Association meeting in Chicago the previous December, which appealed to readers for their support of the Angolan struggle against Portuguese colonialism.[28]

In May 1962 the LCA celebrated its one-year anniversary, though it had already surpassed this milestone. Its perspective in the ensuing years would be shaped by an expansive combination of left-wing radicals, Black Nationalists, artists, and community organizers. This commemorative issue listed the names of advisory and editorial board members for the first time. With critical assistance from their comrades, Watts and Beveridge had plans to grow both the organization and the magazine. An advisory board was established, whose members included Ossie Davis, Len Holt, Louis H. Michaux, Richard B. Moore, Willard Moore, Hugh Mulzac, George B. Murphy Jr., Uthman A. Salaam, Florence Shervington, Selma Sparks, and Paul Zuber. Editorial board members included Watts, Beveridge, Evelyn Battle, and Joan Stokes. Collectively, this group was poised to make a contribution to the liberation of African descendants around the world. "After one year," *Liberator* had successfully established a foundation on which to expand its reach and sharpen its repertoire. "This issue of *Liberator* marks the beginning of its second year of regular monthly publication," they stated, marking the significance of the feat. "This achievement in the face of increasing monopoly of the press and consequent decline of independent publications in this country gives us some pride and determination to keep going. It also gives us a sober awareness of the obstacles ahead if we are to grow in scope and influence," they continued.[29]

The support they had received from concerned readers, college students, local activists, and sister publications such as *Freedomways* inspired the editors to keep up the fight. The community that began to form around the magazine was reason enough to try to do more with the little resources they possessed. "We attribute our success to date to three factors," they wrote. "We are too poor to be sued; we are too small to be attacked; and too challenging to be ignored. During the next year we expect to remain too poor to be sued; we hope we become too big to be attacked; and pledge to expand and sharpen our challenge." This declaration of struggle demonstrated the resilience of the small, eclectic group of individuals concerned with the plight and future of black people around the globe.

The anniversary issue was celebratory, but it kept to the business of social justice advocacy and awareness. Moving past the aplomb, several articles kept readers' minds fixed on the task at hand: one detailed police brutality at Talladega College in Alabama, another recounted the police murder of Muslim member Ronald Stokes in Los Angeles, a third article protested the nuclear arms race, and a fourth, by attorney Len Holt, argued that the Freedom Rides were in part inspired by African independence movements across the Atlantic. Though these struggles would receive close attention in ensuing issues of the publication, the remaining contents were congratulatory and encouraging remarks from students and political luminaries. A letter of congratulations from Egyptian leader Gamal Adbel Nasser spoke of the need to stave off colonialism at all costs since "the colonial bag holds no end of devices," and "therefore, prudence and experience suggest that, in the struggle for national development, African solidarity is a vital urgency, not only to increase development efforts, but also to safeguard African newly-won freedom." Nasser's endorsement of "African solidarity" reflects the political alliances shaped in this early period of African independence. As far as the LCA was concerned, his words of support ("wishing the Liberation Committee for Africa all success in every endeavor in the noble causes of humanity") revealed the promising impact of this small organization though only two and a half years old, their way of showing what a little determined outfit could do.[30]

Alpheaus Hunton, the longtime associate of W. E. B. Du Bois, welcomed the LCA's contributions to anticolonialism and the promotion of African unity. In his view, the organization was making "a most valuable contribution to the fight for the final liquidation of racism, colonialism, and imperialism in all their manifold shapes and disguises." Though he spoke favorably of trans-Atlantic solidarity, writing that the struggles of Africans and African Americans were "inseparably linked," he sounded the alarm of neocolonialism, warning of, "Black men who can be bought off and used to help maintain old or new forms of domination and exploitation of black people."[31] Hunton, alongside his wife, Dorothy, spent a lifetime agitating and mentoring generations of young radicals, including Beveridge, who had encountered Hunton in the 1950s while working with Paul Robeson's *Freedom* newsletter as well as the CAA publication, *Spotlight on Africa*.[32]

Further exploring the tensions emerging in independent Africa, *Liberator* published speeches of Ghanaian leader Kwame Nkrumah, reports on South African apartheid, and articles condemning South Africa's domination of South West Africa. Like events in the Congo, Ghanaian independence loomed large in the minds and hearts of black activists of all stripes. For radicals in the United States, Ghana represented the first stage in the independence of the continent as a whole. At least one LCA associate had traveled to Ghana to witness the practice of independence. Selma Sparks, a *Liberator* advisory board member and labor rights activist, mailed a letter to the magazine from Accra detailing her attendance at "The World without the Bomb" conference convened under the direction of Nkrumah. For her, the conference signified "the awareness of the African people that they will have to take leadership in this struggle to keep man from blowing himself to kingdom come." Sparks explained key agenda items discussed at the conference, including nuclear disarmament and building economies based on peace rather than on war, writing, "It seems such a waste to spend billions of dollars per year learning bigger and better ways to destroy man." Quoting from Nkrumah's plenary speech, Sparks noted that all humanity had a role to play in the creation of a peaceful world.[33] The enthusiasm displayed in Sparks's letter was shared by a number of African American expatriates, including Alphaeus and Dorothy Hunton, Julian Mayfield, St. Clair Drake, and others, who moved to Ghana, temporarily or permanently, under Nkrumah's idealistic diaspora-wide invitation to assist in the development of the young nation.[34]

Correcting and countering mainstream press coverage of the African liberation struggle spurred *Liberator*'s intense interest in happenings on the continent. Stories and reports from radical journalists William Worthy and Julian Mayfield were often reprinted in the *Liberator* having been culled from other news sources, including the *Baltimore Afro-American*, where Worthy wrote; the *Ghana Evening News*, where many of Mayfield's articles were published; and the *Voice of Africa*. Worthy noted that the U.S. press coverage of Africa was decidedly pro-western. Speaking at the Negro Newspaper Publisher's annual conference, held in Baltimore on June 23, 1962, he argued that Americans were ignorant of the struggles being waged in Africa, Asia, and Latin America because of the press's willingness to simply report the "quasi-official party line" of the U.S. government. Lock-step reportage unnerved Worthy, who commented, "Our daily papers, our giant weekly magazines, our radio and television networks, with notable exceptions, are not going to report the anguish of an Africa struggling to rid itself of American-supported colonial wars."[35] Worthy's critique reflects an early effort at media integrity.

According to Worthy, the black press had a responsibility to fill this void and "rise to the great historic need," of accurately reporting the global struggle against colonialism, even if it meant placing blame on the U.S. government. Good journalism required valuing truthful reporting over dinners with state department officials, he added. "The First Amendment does not say that the press is supposed to be an instrument of national policy," he reminded his fellow journalists, before once again expressing their duty to speak truth to power: "Let's keep in mind that if U.S. support of colonialism is to be brought to an end, we must relentlessly keep the news spotlight on the crucial decisions of the policymakers."[36] Worthy's crusading journalism endeared him among radicals, and his personal entanglements with U.S. governmental policies were an indication that he was no mere objective observer, but rather an active participant in the struggle for justice.[37]

Liberator's coverage of Africa seemed to heed Worthy's advice. Providing an alternative to mainstream press coverage with comparably limited resources, however, forced it to rely on its informal networks. In addition to covering the independence movement, the periodical also reported on Du Bois and Hunton's *Encyclopedia Africana* project, giving readers a glimpse of the massive study that would occupy Du Bois for the remaining days of his life in Ghana.[38] Throughout the remainder of 1962, the magazine paid close attention to American and European activities in South Africa, Kenya, Uganda, Nigeria, and the Congo, and continued coverage of Ghana, watchful of traceable evidence with which it could continue to indict western oppression. In Ghana's case, Nkrumah's bright glow began to dim amid reports of assassination attempts on his life, which *Liberator* interpreted as another neocolonialist weapon.[39] Individuals such as Worthy, Mayfield, Selma Sparks, and others contributed to *Liberator*'s coverage of African affairs and added to the information Watts and Beveridge gathered through rigorous archival research, informal networks, and formal associations with African students and government ambassadors.

In addition to the journalism of a faithful few, the magazine also linked to African news dispatches for on-the-ground coverage of national news. The *Voice of Africa*, the Nigerian Information Service (NIS), and other outlets enhanced *Liberator*'s reportage. A press release from the NIS reported on Nnamdi Azikiwe's response to negative press coverage in Britain.[40] In a letter Azikiwe mailed to *The Guardian* editor H. A. Hetherington and published in *Liberator*, Azikiwe stated plainly that the western press was "dabbling too much in Nigerian problems about which you are so fundamentally ignorant and on which you are least qualified to pontificate." Azikiwe's letter inventoried news publications and magazines that were so enthralled with African independence, he argued, that it bordered on meddling. Accusing the West of "racial arrogance and social impertinence," Azikiwe placed such news coverage in the context of a dying colonial project.

· · · · · ·

Lumumba's assassination and the gap it left in Congolese leadership remained a concern for the LCA. Antoine Gizenga's brief stint as elected vice-premier to Lumumba's government added but another dimension to the crisis. Gizenga's incarceration late in 1962 gave *Liberator* an opportunity to revisit the Congo Crisis, offering a sobering account of the country's struggle for independence.[41] Jailed by the same forces that ensnared Lumumba, Gizenga had been imprisoned since January, according to *Liberator*, for holding "firm to the national and centralist principles of Patrice Lumumba and has the political following to make his opinions felt as if he were a free man."[42] Even before Lumumba was viciously and tragically removed from the political scene, the Congo had plunged into crisis. If anything, Lumumba's assassination exacerbated the turmoil, leaving the mineral-rich country susceptible to the rapaciousness and militarism that ensued.

Though Lumumba's death loomed large over the era, the *Liberator* struggled to provide thoroughgoing coverage of events on the continent. In 1963, Beveridge was able to place Nelson Mandela's struggle against apartheid in the context of the domestic freedom struggle waged in America's cities. In a similar manner to William Worthy who had his passport revoked due to his effort to write about subjects of which the United States did not approve, Beveridge argued, Mandela was trapped by policy protocols that made it illegal to travel without a passport. In addition to violating restrictions against organizing strikes, Mandela was sentenced to five years. For his supporters, this represented a heightened stage of struggle against apartheid; Beveridge quoted a member of Mandela's group as saying, "The arrest of Nelson Mandela opens a new chapter in our struggle. It is a demand for new and untried methods in South Africa."[43]

By 1963, the specter of neocolonialism haunted independent Africa. This reality forced many interested African Americans to come to grips with the limitations of national independence. Independence was but an important first step but was by no means the end of liberation struggle. In this year's January issue, *Liberator* ran a short article that portended ensuing struggles throughout Africa. One of its reports covered the South West Africa National Union (SWANU) battle for independence and autonomy. SWANU's statement on this struggle, issued by its publicity secretary, Gerson Veii, pointed to the limitations of the United Nations in supporting national liberation struggles. Petitioning the United Nations, however, was a critical first step in securing the rights of a sovereign nation, a strategic site of protest that *Liberator* writers would themselves exploit. Namibia (which had been known as South West Africa under colonialism) was a trustee territory of the United Nations, which nominally controlled the country after its long history as a German colony. Yet apartheid prevailed over Namibia, as it had in South Africa.[44] Though Veii and others sought pressure from the international community, applying economic sanctions would only lead to African peoples' further impoverishment, he argued. "The alternative is an armed conflict. This is now the only alternative facing the Africans." However, the report stopped short of calling for an all-out war.[45] Though it was Namibia's first and oldest political organization, the South West Africa People's Organization (SWAPO) would eclipse SWANU. Sam Nujoma, head of SWAPO, was the country's first president by the time independence belatedly arrived in 1990.[46]

Throughout the 1960s, many people continued to view the United Nations as a platform on which oppressed communities (i.e., nations) could seek redress. *Liberator* writers, however, were skeptical about the degree to which this was an effective point of view. Even as a strategic site of open debate and newsgathering, many perceived the U.S. role at the United Nations as too large; although the United Nations stood for international governance, U.S. policymakers greatly influenced its decisions. Subsequently, many perceived the United Nations as ineffective in holding the U.S. government responsible for its treatment of African Americans and any other marginalized political constituency.

With *Liberator*'s assessment of African American progress since emancipation dominating the contents of its January issue, its editors still sought to depict black struggle in a global context. Dan Watts had attended the American Negro Leadership Conference on Africa (ANLCA), which was held at the end of the previous year, and his initial reactions were published in the January number. Though he did not present all his points of contention in the article, he did express his displeasure with the dearth of knowledge many middle-class, professional, and elite African Americans had concerning Africa.[47] Watts was pleased, however, that the LCA's efforts had attracted the attention of some African leaders, such as Eduardo Mondlane, leader of the armed struggle in Mozambique, who had studied in the United States and had been courted by ACOA. Mondlane, who presented a paper at the conference on African Americans' involvement in African liberation struggles, distinguished the LCA as "about the only group who have managed to combine any active interest in the American Negro struggle for equality with an intense interest in African freedom."[48] With such comments, Mondlane observed a key distinction. Interests in global African liberation were at odds with support efforts that delinked ties throughout the black world. Watts used Mondlane's comments as a springboard to pinpoint a general frustration with African American leadership. To Watts the conference was not genuinely concerned with African liberation, but rather with how Africa would maintain western political and economic ties. Watts argued, "If our brothers and sisters in Africa are waiting or depending on the American Negro Leadership Conference on Africa for aid and support, they might just as well make their peace with Verwoerd, Salazar and Welensky. We Americans of African descent have long ago given up on our 'Negro Leaders.' "[49] This portended the deepening of fractures to come. Watts followed up his critique of ANLCA with an article in the February issue.

"What is the significance of the American Negro Leadership Conference on Africa which convened last November?" Watts asked.[50] Here, Watts again showed his disdain for the African American leaders who attended the conference, with few exceptions. Watts appreciated the paper presented by St. Clair Drake, entitled "Negro Americans, the African Interest, and Power Structures in Africa and America."[51] However, he took issue with the overall tone of the conference: "This conference . . . was called by and dominated by those who are ideologically committed to a non-revolutionary program of integration into the United States as it is presently constituted."[52] Watts had made a full turn away from the bourgeois lifestyle of a high-profile architect, shaping himself into an aggressive and bombastic documentarian of black liberation struggle. He, like many others, argued that the U.S. policy in Africa meant little more than the continuation of colonial policies and practices. By eschewing an open revolutionary program, the leadership conference, as far as Watts could see, was dangerously complicit in U.S. political and economic intrusion in Africa.

Watts, in tune with a growing sense of the political interdependence of these forces, coupled the program of integration at home with a neocolonial agenda abroad. He perceived a contradiction between African Americans' attempts toward social integration in American society and the demands for African liberation. "How can Afro-Americans, on the one hand, say to their African brothers, 'Let us fight together the battles for economic, political and cultural freedom,' and on the other hand say to those who would deprive them of that freedom, 'Let us work together to build a society of plenty here at home based on the blood and sweat of our African brothers'?" he asked.[53] Watts argued that many African American leaders concerned with Africa simply wanted to change the rules of the game rather than change the game altogether. African Americans and Africans on the continent could not beat back colonialism, Watts charged, because "the rules are fixed, so they can't win." He and others realized that African independence, like the achievement of Civil Rights at home, was only the first step toward what they imagined as total liberation. Later in this issue, *Liberator* reprinted the conference resolutions, which seemed to provide the evidence for Watts's assertions.[54]

In the spring of 1963, three years after the Sharpeville Massacre in South Africa, which left 72 people dead and 186 wounded, a group of South Africans led by Nelson Mandela and Walter Sisulu organized an underground group called Umkonto we Sizwe (Spear of the Nation). Naming South Africa a racist police state, *Liberator* reprinted an article from the Algerian-based magazine *Révolution Africaine*, the international periodical to which Richard Gibson was connected, was which told of this groups' formation and its efforts to overthrow the regime of white supremacy in the country.[55] Though this organization was raided this same year, leading to the imprisonment of Mandela, Sisulu, and others, it was an indication that white supremacist South Africa would rather enhance its violent police state than face extinction.[56] As a periodical charged with confronting the forces of colonialism head on, journals such as *Liberator* effectively demonstrated their worth early on. The space *Liberator* created and the voices it represented reveal the critical concern of everyday citizens for the political, economic, and cultural spatial and power relationships remapping the world. Moreover, these everyday agitators revealed a deep and principled investment in the future of western power and the fate of those who stood in its way.

・・・・・・

Liberator's expertise covering Africa continued throughout the early 1960s, offering columns that struck hard at the rhetoric and behavior of colonialism, but it was not necessarily through ideological convictions. Through the journalism of Richard Gibson and Charles P. Howard, *Liberator*'s coverage of Africa was more than an ideological defense of African independence, as it might have been expected following the Lumumba action. Howard, a longtime UN correspondent and top-notch journalist for the Baltimore *Afro-American*, had established a news syndicate named after himself (Howard News Syndicate), which fed the black press. He was also responsible for *Liberator* staff writer Ossie Sykes gaining access to the UN press gallery. Howard had long covered the project of independence in Ghana, interpreting the challenges of nation building plainly for a devoted audience. In the early 1960s Howard published articles in *Freedomways*. By the end of the decade his would be the words that much of black America read, as he carefully and critically reported on the coup that toppled Nkrumah and what it meant for the rest of the African world. This was as close to mainstream journalism that *Liberator* had come. Yet it was a view from the mainstream that it had long respected.

In the spring of 1963 the periodical published Howard's coverage of the assassination of Togolese president, Silvanus Olympio.[57] Olympio was shot outside of the U.S. Embassy in Togo in mid-January after three years in office. While the LCA may have taken exception with Olympio's ties to the West—he was one of the few to rise to the position of director at western soap giant Unilever and had studied at the London School of Economics—another political assassination painted an overall bleak picture for African independence movements, according to Howard. "The pattern of the killing of African leaders is beginning to cause alarm that borders on panic among African leaders," he reported.[58] Togo had been one of the countries that took a Monrovia-inspired pro-independence stance, which placed Olympio at odds with Nkrumah, who had been pushing for a united continent. This may help explain the lukewarm reception Olympio's death received in the *Liberator*. In contrast to the slaying of Lumumba, the champion of revolutionary independence, Olympio's assassination was not placed in a larger context of progressive African liberation. Howard reported that much had been made of the disagreements between the Togo leader and Nkrumah. However, as Ghana's immediate neighbor, there was more to consider between the two leaders than simply ideological disputes. Aside from sharing a border, Togo was also said to have been harboring dissidents in opposition to Nkrumah, though Howard noted that this was never proven.

Each month *Liberator* highlighted a different country's political struggle on the continent. In the April 1963 issue, the periodical published Richard Gibson's lengthy article on Ben Bella and the Algerian revolution.[59] Like Lumumba and Nkrumah, Ahmed Ben Bella was a highly regarded revolutionary leader. A photograph of the Algerian president was featured on the front page of this month's issue. While Carlos Russell reported on a Pan-African Student Union vigil in honor of Lumumba,[60] Gibson recounted the colonial background of the country and its anticolonial successes. The article spoke approvingly of Algerian independence and highlighted the plans set in motion by Ben Bella under his "Program of Tripoli," a program that essentially put Algeria on the path to Castro-style socialism.[61] Gibson's role as English-language editor of *Révolution Africaine*, based in Algeria, put him in close proximity to the Algerian struggle. Gibson left New York in 1962, arriving in Algeria just as it declared independence following nearly a decade of armed struggle, which left 1 million Muslim Arabs dead.[62] As already mentioned, Gibson's contacts and travels varied. In Algiers, he and his wife, Sarah, worked for *Révolution Africaine,* an organ of the Algerian National Liberation Front. As he recalled, he subsequently moved to Lausanne, Switzerland, to print the English-language version of the periodical.[63] While traveling, Gibson periodically sent articles to Watts for publication.

Also in the April 1963 issue, the magazine reprinted a statement by South Africa's African National Congress (ANC) leader, Oliver Tambo, denouncing apartheid in the region. The reprinted report was originally published in January in *South African Freedom News*, a London-based ANC publication; however, as that group was officially banned, it surfaced outside ANC ranks several months later. The report detailed the Bantustan policy of white apartheid rule and the struggles of freedom-seeking black South Africans. It recounted the atrocities of apartheid, UN moderation, and mounting resistance to the doctrine of white supremacy. "The Bantustan scheme involves the most ruthless intensification of all objectionable aspects of apartheid," argued Tambo. Encouraging the resistance against this action, Tambo argued that a form of guerilla warfare was a necessary outgrowth of that policy. "Bantustan in fact has the seeds for intensified resistance not only in the areas regarded as Bantustan," he argued, "but it can link both urban and rural people to attack apartheid and white domination from different angles and possibly using different methods." Tambo argued the timeless maxim that violence begets violence. He argued that the time had come for black South Africans to take their destiny into their own hands and that this might entail sacrificing one's life if necessary. In words that would become synonymous with the fiery rhetoric of Malcolm X, Tambo called for "the determination to meet the situation created by white domination on the basis of an eye for an eye and a tooth for a tooth."[64]

"The Plight of the Black Man Is Universal"

If total liberation was becoming a fading dream, small victories would have to suffice. Therefore, when Uganda's prime minister, Milton Obote, denied entry to racist segregationist senator Allen J. Ellender of Louisiana, *Liberator* writers cheered.⁶⁵ Obote was the first prime minister of newly independent Uganda. During the closing months of 1962, A. J. Ellender, a member of the U.S. Congress Appropriations Committee, planned a tour of Africa to see the continent for himself in hopes of influencing President Kennedy's Africa policy. Kennedy had shown avid interest in independent Africa. He had spoken favorably of Ghanaian independence and was pivotal in establishing the Kenyan Airlift, which brought eighty-one East African students to the United States. But he proved too liberal for the bullish Ellender. Ellender arranged travel to Mali, Zambia (then Northern Rhodesia) and Zimbabwe (then Southern Rhodesia) and was headed for Uganda when statements he made to the press during his travels reached the public. An arrogant southern segregationist, he stated that in none of the countries he visited were Africans prepared for self-rule. Black press outlets took note. The *Chicago Defender* reported that Ellender considered the transfer of power in Africa and western support to be "free handouts" and felt that "the average African is incapable of leadership without the help of Europeans."⁶⁶ Regarding Obote's snub of Ellender, *Liberator* writer Ernest Kalibala wrote, "Even peaceful integrationists hailed the move as guaranteed to show the segregationists the new order of things." For his part, the Afro-Panamanian writer Carlos Russell thought that Ellender's demonizing of Africans was demonstrative of his thinking about African descendants the world over. Therefore, Russell proclaimed, "The plight of the black man is universal. . . . The black man in Africa, the black man in Cuba, and the black man in Harlem are products of the same black stock, victims of the same white oppressors," he continued.⁶⁷ SWANU president Jariretundu Kozonguizi had the dubious distinction of sharing a panel with Ellender for a program sponsored by the Collegiate Council for the United Nations at the University of Maryland. There, Ellender commenced to once again discredit African independence. Defending the rights to self-determination, and calling Ellender's slanderous comments "nonsense," Kozonguizi pointed to Ghana, Guinea, and Nigeria of examples of the achievements of self-rule.⁶⁸ Indeed, *Liberator* writers perceived at least two less-than-favorable faces of American government attitudes—one that favored independence contingent on protection of American interests (Kennedy) and another that had no faith in self-rule at all (Ellender)—toward African independence.⁶⁹

In this same issue, the *Liberator* printed one of its most forthright defenses of pan-African ideals. African history scholar W. Ofuatey-Kodjoe wrote of the political and ancestral ties between African Americans and

Africans.⁷⁰ As much as small formations such as the LCA and similar organizations sought to evaluate and develop linkages between Africans and African Americans, a body of scholarship developed simultaneously that spoke against such connections, emphasizing the Americanness of black life in the United States. Massachusetts Institute of Technology professor Harold Issacs was but one of the many American writers who was skeptical about African Americans' relationship to Africa.

Liberator reviewed Issacs's book, *The New World of the Negro*, in the June issue of the periodical and warned readers of his dogged integrationist perspective toward African American citizenship in spite of the treatment African Americans faced when they sought to exercise and defend that citizenship. Worse, he spoke condescendingly of most African American efforts of self-determination from Garvey to the contemporary pan-Africanism of the 1960s, although he could admit that the world was changing and that outright, highly visible white supremacy was waning. Ofuatey-Kodjoe criticized such thinking as evidence of the enduring residue of white supremacy even in Issacs's liberal packaging. "It is therefore in the interest of the American white man to discourage any connection between the American Negro and the African," he wrote. Ofuatey-Kodjoe's article was written in response to an African American U.S. emissary who had recently returned from the Congo saying that he never felt more American in his life. Moreover, he is quoted as saying that the tribalism he witnessed in Africa far outstripped the racism found in America. Ofuatey-Kodjoe perceived an eager defense of American political interests in the emissary's report from his travel to Africa, and went on to highlight that the tribalism he lamented was the result of European and Euro-American political and financial interests in warring tribes. Appealing to a sense of brotherhood (and ostensibly sisterhood), he wrote as if speaking directly to the black community: "You see in spite of what *they* tell you, they recognize the fact that you and I have a great deal in common: that *we stand or fall together*."⁷¹ Despite these efforts, *Liberator* readers also heard about African ambassadors who, drawn to the American political elite, shunned pan-African ties.⁷²

If Harold Issacs needed confirmation of African influences on African American life and culture, he needed to look no further than Harlem. John Henrik Clarke, Langston Hughes, and Richard B. Moore, among numerous other writers, had for years identified a heightened African consciousness and celebration of African culture as salient aspects of Harlem life. Issacs had even interviewed Watts for his book.⁷³ Of the many formations concerned with African liberation that emerged in this period, *Liberator* noted the efforts of a small group that called themselves the Harlem Anti-Colonial Committee. Led by Bill Jones and Selma Sparks, the group also included writer and Clarke associate Sylvester Leaks, William Worthy, and local activist Pernella Wattley, who had been active in both the Fair Play for Cuba Committee (FPCC) and the Freedom Now Party. Following the example set by the 1961 UN protest, the Harlem Anti-Colonial Committee marched to the United Nations after a public meeting in Harlem Square. Located at 125th street and Seventh Avenue, this Harlem Square rally featured speeches by Conrad Lynn, Worthy, and Moore, who gave Harlemites the latest information on the fight of Robert F. Williams associate Mae Mallory fight against the Monroe frame-up, Worthy's passport case, and the police attack on the Nation of Islam in Los Angeles.[74] Pointing to the contradictions in American rhetorical support for African independence while keeping blacks in the United States colonized, they marched with pickets that read "Freedom Now" and "To Be Partly Free Is to Be Mostly Enslaved." The march culminated in delivering a wreath on the UN steps that included a note addressed to the U.S. government. The note read: "To the United States Government—For all black Americans who have died protecting the country which does not protect them."[75]

As apartheid raged in South Africa, that nation was increasingly viewed as the primary site for anticolonial agitation. *Liberator* ran a reprint of an ANC document presented to the United Nations in July 1963 that spoke of the U.S. role in upholding the apartheid regime. Presented to the UN Special Committee on the Policies of Apartheid of the Government of the Republic of South Africa, the document spoke to the financial collusion and military support provided by the United States and Great Britain. Moreover, the statement called for the release of political prisoners, a "blacklisting" of companies with business ties to South Africa, including trade, and finally, that the South African apartheid government be banned from the United Nations.[76] As ANC representatives Duma Nokwe, Tennysen Makiwane, and Robert Resha delivered the antiapartheid statement, members of the Harlem Anti-Colonial Committee, this time led by William Worthy, staged a small demonstration at the United States Mission to the United Nations. Including Pernella Wattley, Ora Mobley, Progressive Labor Party leader Bill Epton, and local activists Robert Fletcher and Jocelyn Jerome, the group numbered no more than seven total protesters. Yet, as Worthy noted, the group didn't "need numbers or big names, but passion." Worthy, who had suspected that his phone had been tapped, was confirmed in his suspicion when he witnessed police and undercover federal agents hop into formation upon seeing the small group approach the building. Upon entering, the group faced questioning authorities. There to meet with Adlai Stevenson, the group was forced to wait close to a half hour before they could be heard. After nearly two hours had passed, the group displayed a large banner that read in bold letters, "Expel South Africa from the U.N.," much to the dismay of Stevenson, who had hoped the group would quell dissenting Harlemites from similar or further protests. Worthy could not guarantee this was possible even if it was in his control. This small act of protest, Worthy intimated, effectively demonstrated the capacity of collective action.[77]

By 1964, *Liberator* coverage of Africa trailed off but had by no means ended.[78] *Liberator* reflected that the Lumumba protest was a beginning, but not the conclusion, of the challenges facing African independence. In May, the magazine returned to the coverage of Central African liberation struggles. The Burundi Mission to the United Nations sought to correct misinformation that had been reported about the country.[79] In July, two articles appeared that spoke to the role of the United Nations in supporting African and Third World sovereignty and the image of the United States in Ghana. Amid debate over the role of the United Nations in supporting antiapartheid efforts was also the continuing concern for the use of nuclear weaponry, specifically the use of the atomic bomb. Dan Watts, using his network of associates to gain access to the UN press gallery, reported that secretary general U Thant, who served for the entire decade of the 1960s, spoke out against the use of the atomic bomb, especially on populations of color. Speaking to reporters in Canada, Thant stated the glaring contradiction between the refusal to use atomic weapons on European nations such as Nazi Germany and the decision to employ such methods on nations of color such as Japan during World War II. He argued that there was a racially motivated use of nuclear weapons that should not be ignored. Watts also reported that the United States, France, and Great Britain continued to abstain from openly condemning South African apartheid, thereby continuing their complicity.[80] It is likely that Charles Howard also arranged for Watts to attend the UN meetings. The previous year, Watts was informed that his UN pass, which had been recovered after the Lumumba protests, had expired. When he requested Jacques Verges, editor of *Révolution Africaine*, to write on his behalf, UN press representatives balked.[81] Once again it seemed the U.S. government's containment tactics persisted uninterrupted. Other writers, such as T. D. Baffoe, editor of the *Ghanaian Times*, argued that in addition to perceiving it as a colonialist enabler, many people abroad soberly viewed the United States as a police state.[82]

In addition to its indictments of American government positions on Africa, *Liberator* also performed an educational function. Most often, this would be in the form of publishing histories that provided critical background information on a newly independent nation. In addition to its spotlight on Ghana, Nigeria, and Guinea, *Liberator* also covered Mali's importance to world history and its contemporary political moment. Tracing the rich history of Mali was hardly new for many Harlemites who read the magazine. Many had been introduced to the history of the great leader Sundiata and fourteenth-century Mali through the vibrant street-corner speaker tradition that had developed throughout Harlem. This historic background provided in *Liberator* was written as a political history of the rise of Modibo Keita, independent Mali's first president, who served from 1960 to 1968. Keita, along with Nkrumah and Toure, helped form the Ghana-Guinea-Mali union, with the hopes of sparking a greater continental union. *Liberator*, part of the contingent of U.S.-based radicals who supported independent Africa's push toward socialism, viewed Mali's pan-Africanism in a favorable light. Beveridge's immersion in African history and his active participation in the Association for the Study of Negro Life and History (ASNLH) lent consistency to *Liberator*'s educational function.

Watts's UN reports most often focused on events in Africa, though they often incorporated other international news. In January 1965, Watts reprinted portions of the speech given by the Ghanaian representative to the United Nations, Alex Quaison-Sackey, who had been elected as president of the Nineteenth Session of the General Assembly. Appointed by Nkrumah, Quaison-Sackey was an impressive and lively international diplomat. In his address, he spoke of the tremendous potential of the United Nations in protecting the sovereignty of newly independent countries such as Ghana. "Ghana has an unshakable faith in the United Nations, and has consistently supported the purposes and principles of the charter," he announced. An energetic figure with a large, bright smile, Quaison-Sackey was equal parts charmer and cunning politician. Following Nkrumah, he proclaimed the arrival of the African Personality on the UN stage and the role of the Organization for African Unity (OAU) in supporting continental unity. As if reading directly from the notebook of his country's top official, he emphasized that Africa's "future is now indissolubly linked up with the destiny of Asia, Latin America and the rest of the world." *Liberator* welcomed this new voice in the international arena, picturing him dressed in Kente cloth on the cover of the New Year's first issue, though the periodical had been one of the first to cover the significance of his UN role back in 1962.[83] Pictures of Quaison-Sackey seated next to secretary general U Thant and Ghanaian foreign minister Kojo Batsio, accompanied the text of his speech. *Liberator* also ran a series of photos of UN delegations from Malawi, Kenya, and Nigeria.[84] Though he had only recently been elected to the presidency, political turmoil in his home country tested his loyalty to Nkrumah. After the overthrow of Nkrumah the next year, 1966, Richard Gibson quipped derisively that Quaison-Sackey "was next heard of in Accra, loudly denouncing the 'tyranny' of his former master and, like the vast majority of Ghana's never-too-revolutionary diplomats, begging to keep his job."[85] Later in 1965, *Liberator* paid tribute to African women leaders at the United Nations. Though full reports on their participation were not provided, those pictured included Nancy Kajumbula of Uganda, Julienne Keutcha of Cameroon, Florence Addison of Ghana, Margaret Aguta of Nigeria, and Regine Gbedey of Togo.[86]

In June, *Liberator* staff writer Ossie Sykes penned a criticism of African Americans who represented government interests on the African continent, which was one of the magazine's penchants. African American leaders such as Martin Luther King Jr., Roy Wilkins, Whitney Young, James Farmer, and other, lesser-known figures, such as Arkansas attorney Wiley Branton of the Voter Education Project, were recruited as emissaries to African countries to convey the message that, although slow, racial progress was being achieved in the United States. Both the Kennedy and Johnson presidential administrations regularly recruited black leaders in the hopes of influencing international perceptions of racial progress. As Sykes pointed out, it was more than mere coincidence that Farmer's visit to Africa was scheduled just after Malcolm X's return from his long tour, which had effectively impacted African Americans' political consciousness. Though moderate to conservative African Americans were recruited to placate international concerns of American racism, Sykes was confident that Africans on the continent could see the true face of "United States business interest[s] and the milking of African wealth."[87] Internationally, it was clear to many people that America's image suffered. Donald Jackson, writing of the logic of anti–Vietnam War attitudes in the black community, spoke to American government efforts to protect its image: "A move to call America to question in the United Nations on the issue of domestic racism [via sympathetic African delegations] would be more embarrassing to America if the spillover of the racism into America's international affairs were also brought to light."[88]

Throughout the year, *Liberator* would continue its coverage of Africa through the pen of Gibson, who was following events from London while making occasional trips to the continent. In December he published an article on the struggle for liberation in Zimbabwe, which was then known by its colonial name, Southern Rhodesia. Gibson wrote of the meaning of this struggle for Britain, which had supported Rhodesia's white minority rule when it recognized settler self-government in 1923. Gibson wondered what this would portend for Britain's racial climate, and he wondered if Britons and Africans in Britain were on a collision course, as white settlers and Zimbabweans seemed to be in Southern Africa. Though he was convinced that Africans on the continent would decide the direction to take, his concern for the international reverberations of these conflicts pointed once more to the global impact of African independence.[89]

The overthrow of Nkrumah's government in 1966 was one of several signs of the instability African independence. African American activists interpreted the *coup d'état* as an American or western plot to stem the tide of left-leaning charismatic internationalism being embraced by many newly independent countries. Shirley Graham Du Bois, who had arranged for Nkrumah to meet with African American militant Malcolm X, tapped the reservoir of pan-African pride and resilience when writing to John Henrik Clarke after her expulsion from Ghana: "Many black heads are now bloody, [but] WE ARE UNBOWED and we are STILL ALIVE! Don't write us off."[90] Writing in *Liberator*, Gibson, who was now listed as editor of news on Africa, Asia, and Europe, considered the Ghana debacle as the first step in an updated western battle for Africa. In his own letter to Clarke, Gibson struck a more cynical tone than he had earlier expressed, perhaps disgruntled with evaporating hopes of a triumphant era of independence. "The situation in so-called 'independent' Africa is hardly very encouraging at present," he wrote to Clarke after updating him on a book project on Africa for which he had been compiling material in Tanzania. Gibson intimated to Clarke what the latter already knew: that the chief issue facing African leaders was to "liberate their country's economy from the neo-colonialist stranglehold." Yet, using Ghana as an example, Gibson interestingly expressed that Nkrumah and his followers were to blame, not the machinations of global capitalism. Gibson wrote: "In Ghana, there were many persons who understood what was wrong, but, once comfortably settled in various sinecures, they seem to have lost their vision and used their breath merely to add to the praises of Osaygefo. It was very sad, but only to be expected. And I don't think many people were really surprised by what happened on 24 February, except Nkrumah himself—which is the price you pay for listening to syncophants [sic] and Russian 'advisers.' "[91] It is not clear if and how Clarke, who had been compiling material for a book on Ghana, responded to Gibson's letter, but it is plausible that he would not have been too pleased with Gibson's dismissive attitude toward the coup. Yet Nkrumah's toppling and Ghana's transition typified a new phase in postindependence history. As Fitch and Oppenheimer observed following the coup: "The era of postwar colonial independence movements is over now. The political elites who mediated their way to power are giving way to new military/bureaucratic elites who function in the name of austerity and efficiency. But it must not be thought that, simply by acting in favor of the old colonial power, the new rulers have put an end to the contradictions which faced and defeated the departing political elites."[92]

If 1960 was dubbed the year of African independence, 1965–66 marked the coup in Africa. Following Gibson's report on Ghana and the assessments of a range of political observers, *Liberator* included an "African Scorecard," which listed the country, date, and name of each of the governments that had been undemocratically and violently overthrown. With five such coups occurring over the second half of 1965 and five more in the first two months of 1966, it seemed that wherever one looked, the more or less triumphant vision of African independence held by many had been shattered, compelling those who were interested to determine the next political vision.[93]

Charles P. Howard argued that the explosion of coups was not necessarily ideologically driven but rather was based on economic exploitation. In terms that recall Du Bois's "African Roots of War," written in the context of World War I, Howard argued that the West's belief that Africa's resources were open for plundering buttressed the support for *coups d'état*. Moreover, the West's political interests and hands-on influence bore as much responsibility for the coups as had local conditions. As had William Worthy, Howard castigated the American and British press for failing to investigate the role of the CIA and British Intelligence in these coups. Basing his analysis on the "sphere of influence" theory, which held that the world was in split into Western (capitalist) and Eastern (communist) spheres, Howard stated directly where he thought the blame should be placed. "There can no longer be any doubt that the rash of overthrows of governments in Africa, which are dedicated to the masses of African people, and opposed to the sphere of influence theory, and the continued exploitation of African countries, have been master-minded, financed, and directed, even though the hands that carried out the dastardly acts were black, by the American CIA and British Intelligence."[94] Howard was determined to provide his readers as clear a view of the issues as he could. Throughout 1966, Howard's News

Syndicate was almost entirely concerned with Ghana. On a weekly basis Howard sought to expose the corporate, neocolonialist, and U.S.-complicit agitation stirring the pot of African independence. One of his series put the matter squarely: "There is no longer any doubt that the overthrow of President Kwame Nkrumah of Ghana was engineered from outside Ghana, by and for the benefit of people who are not Ghanaians, not even Africans," he told his *Afro-American* readers. Commencing, he wanted to leave no doubt as to the certainty of the claim: "The wonder is that Nkrumah survived as long as he did. Of all the African leaders, past or present, he is the most hated and most feared by the former colonial power, the neo-colonialists and the present controllers of Africa's wealth who do not want to give it up."[95] Howard's writing, at once dutiful, opinionated, and direct, put in print what many African American activists felt was happening—African independence was being strategically, and tragically undermined. Howard, working to beat back the onslaught of western press accounts, used the space of the newspaper column as counterweight even if it was perceived as an open defense of Nkrumah.[96]

In July, Gibson's attention moved across the continent, writing ominously of the independence movement on the Horn of Africa. "No other part of Africa today is wracked by as many explosive tensions as East Africa," he began. Gibson's reportage showed Tanzania, Kenya and Uganda in the midst of political tug-of-wars between competing factions pushing for their own brand of nationalism and economic independence.[97] This was a far cry from the critical yet glowing reports of African independence that *Liberator* readers had come to expect. Nor did Gibson place blame for these political pressures on western shoulders. Perhaps Gibson was cynical about the future of African independence. It is not clear if Gibson saw himself as simply the bearer of bad news and therefore a teller of hard truths or if he was merely stating the obvious. In any case, around this time his credentials came into question after *Révolution Africaine*, the publication for which he had been the English-language editor, published a communiqué in one of its last issues to the effect of outing Gibson as "counter-revolutionary" for "disruptive activities."[98]

Though his reputation took a considerable hit, he continued to write and report on Africa. *Liberator* also suffered blows as a result of accusations against Gibson. *Soulbook,* published out of the Bay Area, openly challenged the magazine's connection to Gibson, who was listed on the editorial board. If *Liberator* consorted with such a questionable figure as Gibson, it could not claim to represent the best interests of the liberation movement, *Soulbook*

Spokespersons and Advocates   67

editors wrote.⁹⁹ The conflict over Gibson's credibility may explain the departure of Revolutionary Action Movement (RAM) activists from *Liberator*. Larry Neal's August report on the Detroit Black Arts Convention would be his last *Liberator* writing. It was also the last time Neal was listed on the editorial staff. Neal's two-year run (1964–66) as arts editor had ended, yet the impact he had made by this point could not be ignored. Muhammad Ahmad had never fully immersed himself in the *Liberator* because of Watts's interracial marriage, and Askia Touré left after the RAM analysis of Malcolm's assassination was published in 1966. It is not clear if Watts ever responded to the accusations against Gibson or if there was ever an official response to *Soulbook*. Their friendship appeared to have been more important to Watts than the charges being leveled against Gibson.

Charles P. Howard ended 1966 highlighting the assassination of South African racist apartheid architect Hendrik Verwoerd, who was stabbed to death in September. He reminded readers that the death of the chief engineer of apartheid did not mean the death of the system. Africans and African Americans still had a responsibility, he wrote, to undo the regime. Howard placed Verwoerd in the company of George Wallace of Alabama, Orval Faubus of Arkansas, Barry Goldwater, and others who practiced hatred toward blacks as official policy; in other words, he was a man who did not deserve public sympathy. Howard argued that much of the disunity throughout Africa could be traced to the practices institutionalized under Verwoerd and his ilk. As such, "Afro-Americans and Africans must identify, isolate and move against those whose only stock in trade is hatred of the Black man," he wrote.¹⁰⁰ The struggle to liberate South Africa would consume much of the *Liberator* reporting on Africa in this period. Alongside tracing the aftermath of a number of military coups, the dismantling of apartheid emerged as a central issue for radicals nationwide.

On November 6, *Liberator* cosponsored a lecture on the South African liberation struggle at the Abyssinian Baptist Church in Harlem that featured exiled activist Franz J. T. Lee. His trip to New York also featured an appearance on New York City radio station WBAI the morning of his Harlem speech. A number of Harlem-based organizations, including the Harlem Congress of Racial Equality (CORE), the Harlem Parents Committee, the Harlem People's Parliament, and the New York Student Nonviolent Coordinating Committee (SNCC), along with individuals such as Ossie Davis, Ruby Dee, Yuri Kochiyama, Lewis Michaux, James Forman, Floyd McKissick, and others, collaborated to bring Lee to Harlem.¹⁰¹

The following year, Gibson, who remained listed on the editorial staff although he was overseas, wrote of Israel's impact on African independence as a result of the previous month's Six-Day Arab-Israeli war. Gibson considered Israeli aggression against Arabs an extension of neocolonialism and white supremacy.[102] For many, the parallels were striking. As one writer put it, "By [a] strange twist of destiny, Israel and the apartheid regime of the National Party of South Africa were born in the same year—1948. As the Zionist state was coming into being in the Middle East, the Afrikaners were taking over power in South Africa. The historical interaction between these two troubled regions of the world would be long-lasting and sustained."[103] Gibson feared that Africa was considered open territory for Israel, writing, "All of Africa lies open, vulnerable to the political and economic penetration of Israel and the European powers."[104] Tracking a variety of incursions over the past ten years, Gibson's final tally pointed toward Israeli dominance over Africa. The only reaction to Gibson's article came several months later in the form of a letter to the editor written by a member of the Israeli Socialist Organization, though it did not reference *Liberator*'s coverage of Israel. Writing from Jerusalem, the author reported the case of Khalil Toame, a law student at the Hebrew University of Jerusalem and a leader on the Arab Students Committee there. Toame, who was known for his outspokenness against Zionism, was arrested in January 1968, following a solidarity protest with Israeli students who also opposed Israeli occupation. This letter may have been sent to Watts directly and not necessarily intended for publication in *Liberator*. However, publishing this letter may have been Watts's way of lending support to the cause of the jailed student. Although he was fond of adding editorial comments for issues he deemed of utmost importance, none appeared for this issue.

Gibson, Watts, Charles Howard, and Yahne Sangare would continue to string together news and analysis on Africa, but as events on the continent became more complicated, the magazine refocused its attention on the home front. In one of his last analyses, Gibson spoke to what he perceived as African Americans' distance from the complex realities unfolding in Africa. "Some Afro-Americans would rather avoid the necessary task of studying Africa's complex history and examining the Black Continent's political, economic, and social situation in the contemporary world," he wrote, "instead they prefer to sink into easy fantasies about the homeland of their ancestors." Gibson's critique of African Americans' waning pan-African political sensibility appears harsh when one considers the shattered hopes of many in the immediate aftermath of Lumumba, Malcolm, Du Bois, and Nkrumah's government, parties that had long been viewed as avatars and standard-bearers of pan-African ideals. Still, he believed that African Americans were out of touch with Africa's impoverished reality. By contrast, he thought, Africans were on the move. Gibson expressed hope in the five-year-old OAU to lead Africa to political prominence, though earlier he had seemed not at all disturbed by the flurry of military coups engulfing the continent. Although he makes no suggestions for how African Americans were to support the efforts of the OAU, he maintained that viewing "Africa through foggy, tattered myths," was of no use at all.[105] Though Gibson urged greater political solidarity with Africa, others clung to an idea of Africa as refuge from America.[106] Still others believed that solidarity between African Americans and Africans who embraced Black Power ideals meant very little without a clear program. Vernon Boggs, who taught at City University of New York's York College, argued that "being black is not enough" to build a program, though like many critics, Boggs, of course, did not offer a program. He did, however, identify the Los Angeles chapter of the Congress of Racial Equality (CORE) and the African American students who led the Columbia University protests against gentrification as signs of real movement.[107] Boggs's particular cynicism toward African American leadership is perhaps indicative of a growing impatience with the rhetoric of independence, despite its galvanizing appeal. Though solidarity with Africa was initially a core aspect of the *Liberator*'s activity, owing in part to the complexity and pace of events on the continent, and dissolving contacts, its attention on the continent dissipated toward the last years of the magazine.

Liberator readers were alerted to this trend in the spring of 1969, when Tom Mboya, then minister of economic planning and development in Kenya, visited the Countee Cullen Library in Harlem as part of the Morningside Lecture Series on Modern Africa, on March 18. Mboya's visit caused at least two separate but related disturbances in the black community. On one hand, Mboya expressed to the African Americans in attendance that their fight was in the United States, not in Africa, striking a markedly different tone than could be heard earlier. On the other, Selwyn Cudjoe's account of the incident has it that some audience members were forewarned of Mboya's position in a lecture given by then–Columbia University professor Immanuel Wallerstein earlier in the lecture series. Worse, according to Cudjoe, Wallerstein announced that Mboya's Kenya was heading into a financial relationship with apartheid South Africa, which was later denied by Kenya's UN Mission representative. Upon hearing Mboya's position, some members of the audience hurled eggs at him for what sounded like an anti-pan-Africanist position, though *Liberator* did not clarify what exactly they were angry about.[108] Later it was revealed that the black activists in the audience chafed at Mboya's support for the Kenyan government's rejection of the idea of guaranteeing automatic citizenship to African Americans who desired expatriation.[109]

In any case, Cudjoe's article sparked a less-than-productive debate. Over a month later, three articles appeared in response to his depiction of events at the Cullen Library. The first response came from Wallerstein, who sought to clarify his remarks during the lecture series, saying that Cudjoe had misinterpreted what was said. To say that Kenya was an economic target was clearly different from presuming that Kenya was about to engage in trade with the apartheid government, he responded. The second response came from a Kenyan student living in Harlem who deplored the treatment Mboya received, though he seemed generally aware of the pan-African proclivities many of his uptown neighbors held dear. Yet he questioned whether those who hurled eggs at Mboya had treated white officials similarly. "The treatment to which Mr. Mboya was subjected has never been experienced by [Mayor John] Lindsay or [former Mayor Robert] Wagner, or indeed, [Vice President Hubert] Humphrey, on the many occasions they visited Harlem. Perhaps Harlemites simply wanted to prove that brothers from the other side of the Atlantic must accept worse treatment than an American whitey," he wrote. Moreover, he challenged African Americans' "love" for Africa, emphasizing that only "2000–3000 Afro-Americans have become citizens" of African countries and most of those had occurred in Ghana at a time when dual citizenship was a realistic possibility for an educated or technologically elite group of trans-patriots. "All that is required is the will and spirit to *accept* rather than *romanticize* Africa," he stressed. Reflecting on the Harlem egg-throwing incident, Mboya struck a diplomatic note that urged similarities over sameness, underscoring that distinction did not mean disconnection, while holding out that "our struggle and goal[s] are the same, and we need a common understanding on strategy so as not to cancel each other out."[110] However, Mboya went on to pinpoint concerns and challenges that militated against an uncritical merging of political aspirations. Most of all, Mboya urged African Americans to assert American citizenship as leverage for racial justice struggle: "The black American should look to Africa for guidance—and for a chance to give guidance—but not for escape. He must merge his blackness with his citizenship as an American, and the result will be dignity and liberation."[111]

The third response in the debate took issue with two points in Cudjoe's telling of the story. Pointing to evidence of cultural continuity, the author argued that Cudjoe's argument that Africans in the Caribbean and the United States were Americans and not Africans was incorrect. Second, he questioned whether Wallerstein's comments were the reason for egging Mboya. He described Kenyan students' protest of Mboya's visit to Howard University on this same tour as an example of political astuteness that followed Mboya to Harlem. Howard students of Kenyan descent feared that Mboya, who was an advocate of American interests in Kenya, would give a distorted view of Africa. The writer concluded by stating, "We should not assume that the actions of Black people are always based on what the last white person said."[112] On July 5, 1969, as this issue of *Liberator* went to press, Tom Mboya was assassinated. Those in the debate could not have known that Mboya's visit to Harlem would be his last trek to the United States. The emotion of the debate had temporarily blinded some people to the stakes of African independence. Writers, activists, artists, and protesters alike would continue to be reminded just how tenuous were the circumstances, as assassinations seemed only slightly less common than claims to independence.

This debate highlights how frayed, and often petty, the discussion of African and African American political and cultural connections had become by the close of the decade. Between 1969 and 1971, a paltry ten articles with African politics as the subject appeared. Yahne Sangare's correspondence from the United Nations ended in 1969 with an overview of Zambia's struggles to throw off economic colonialism.[113]

Conclusion

Richard Gibson's monthly "Africa Report," Edith Sanders's historical overview and analysis of the importance of African history, and a review of an opportunistic, Italian-made *Afric-sploitation*[114] film entitled, *Africa Blood and Guts*, were the final three articles that dealt directly with African themes published in *Liberator*. Though it appeared that the magazine abandoned African themes and issues after its first few years of publication, there is ample evidence that considerable energy and attention to the subject continued throughout the entire decade. Although its coverage was at times inconsistent and certain issues required fuller and more detailed attention than it was able to provide, *Liberator* was one of the only radical, grassroots publishing vehicles that covered African issues in a newsworthy fashion.

Liberator writers chronicled African issues, reviewed books, highlighted official and otherwise notable political figures, and at the same time discussed African art and fashion. In this way the magazine offered a view of Africa that was at once critical in the political sense while it simultaneously embraced African aesthetics and political vision. Nonetheless, approaching the close of the decade, its original intentions of documenting and actively supporting African liberation had faded, the casualties of political turmoil, vastly complex issues, and needs too large for Watts and his committed bunch to effectively depict, much less organize around. Nonetheless, the explication of the contours of anticolonial black activism makes clearer the range of African American interests and attitudes. As we have seen, there was considerable debate among a host of concerned people, including deep awareness of monthly readers. It is important that *Liberator's* journalistic activism centered on Africa yet reveals a diaspora consciousness that was contingent on, and contested through, political debate rather than simplistic assertions of African cultural unity or depoliticized notions of blackness. The community spokespersons and advocates of black liberation would include radical activists, UN petitioners, and liberal scholars. The black liberation struggle in the United States swelled just as the "unevenness"[115] and uncertain futures of Africa-centered black internationalism were revealed. Chief among those who continued the fight toward a new day at home and abroad were African American and African women intellectual-activists who demonstrated their radical commitments throughout the decade and long after.

3 Radical Commitments
The Promise of Black Women's Activism

> It must also be pointed out at this time that Black women are not resentful of the rise of power of Black men. We welcome it. We see in it the eventual liberation of all Black people from this corrupt system of capitalism. Nevertheless, this does not mean that you have to negate one for the other. This kind of thinking is a product of miseducation; that it's either X or it's Y. It is fallacious reasoning that in order for the Black man to be strong, the Black woman has to be weak.
>
> —Fran Beal, "Double Jeopardy" (1970)

Women in the black liberation era performed an array of roles, held numerous positions, and were often as revolutionary and radical in their approaches and perspectives on racial justice as their male counterparts in this movement. Though often ignored in the histories of these movements, the radicalism of the black liberation movement in the 1960s must include the writing, debates, and organizing of black women. These women conscientiously worked alongside, independently of, and occasionally against their self-assured male peers eager to strike down white supremacy yet failing to see the inherent gender bias in the process. Though second wave black feminist activity surfaced fully from 1968 onward, as this chapter reveals, women writers, artists, workers, and activists had long asserted themselves and their ideas in the public political sphere. The central claim here is that the writings of women at the beginning of the decade, as found in *Liberator*, elucidate and anticipate more assertive and organization-driven feminist activity by the end of the decade. Though not exclusively so, *Liberator* was one of the spaces in the early 1960s that carried the perspectives and writings of black women as well as that of some radical white women with increasing regularity. As much of the organizational black feminist activity emerged later, it is safe to surmise that the magazine's representation of women's voices and issues was more pragmatic than ideological. And yet it was a consistent space where women's perspectives on movement work, aesthetics, and political economy could be found. Tee Beveridge's activist career is yet another example of women's work that ran the gamut from organizing behind the scenes to building transnational communities and advocating for African liberation. While *Liberator*'s coverage of women's perspectives and activism was relatively inconsistent, their radical commitments were as strident as those of their male counterparts, and often more so.

While lesser-known personalities shape the actual content concerning women, *Liberator* was influenced by the careers of established female activists and artists such as Lorraine Hansberry, Abbey Lincoln, visual artist Valerie Maynard, Sonia Sanchez, and, later, Toni Cade Bambara, and other women whose careers in black women's activist and literary work defines the era in important ways. However, a significant number of female writers whose work appeared in the magazine did not pursue literary or academic careers and therefore do not register in most histories of this period. Like Tee Beveridge, not all were writers. Odd as it may seem, Tee never published one piece of writing in *Liberator* through Pete's time as associate editor from 1961 to 1965. Many more were behind-the-scenes organizers. Yet their voices are equally central to the magazine's dissemination of women's ideas and radical politics. Moreover, these voices offer a view of radicalism as simultaneously concerned with political work that cut across gendered divisions, local communities, and global imaginaries. These lesser-known but important female voices also expand our understanding of the issues women were generally concerned with in the 1960s, what they deemed important, and what their perspectives were on the major issues of the day. Issues such as school integration, economic inequality, political autonomy, and the politics of the aesthetic were hotly debated issues of black women's theorizing in the magazine. As shown, though these were hardly exclusively women's issues, they were some of the subjects that women writers explored through poetry, political commentary, cultural criticism, reviews, and analyses in the pages of *Liberator*.

Liberator became one of the spaces where women could articulate, debate, and share concerns on a range of topics. Although the magazine never issued an explicit position statement on feminism, it served as a forum for black women's political agency, ideas, and perspectives. As this chapter shows, black women writing in *Liberator* took up issues of labor rights, public school education, black aesthetics, and community organizing; they also wrote fierce poetry and showcased their visual artistry. Black women's *Liberator* articles and poetry often contained critical remarks about the state of the black community, the health of black children, the function of public schools and the education of black youth, and the role of women in American society. The latter proved to be a kind of general, broadly conceived question that persisted throughout the decade shaping black women's articulation of citizenship, while they envisioned the radical possibilities found in struggle. As such, *Liberator* offers a record of the presence, role, and voice of women as part of a broadly defined black liberation struggle. Though the articles that dealt with women's issues were few in number in the early years of the magazine, by the mid-1960s, the voices of black women showed that men were not the only activists able to put word to deed and thought to page.

Women writers in *Liberator* form a trajectory connecting the heroic female leadership of the civil rights movement, militant advocacy of the Communist Party (CP USA), and organizational feminism of the late 1960s. Their activism critically informed their writings, and vice versa, weaving together their own form of theory and praxis as they shaped transformative activist practices. Through their writings, these writers and activists represent an extension of civil rights–era female activists, whom Crawford, Rouse, and Woods have labeled "trailblazers and torchbearers," while Gore, Theoharis, and Woodard have identified four overlapping and distinct aspects of black women's activism: "charismatic leaders, behind-the-scene-organizers, strategic thinkers, and long-distance runners."[1] As Benita Roth has similarly argued, such activities should be considered part of the "parent movements" that functioned as training grounds for many women, providing them with "the basics of organizing," which included critical dialogue, conferencing, publishing, and collectivist organizing as parts of liberatory practices.[2] The issues discussed in these early years of black feminist thinking form an important, if underrepresented, bridge between the heroic activism of women such as Fannie Lou Hamer, Ella Baker, Jo Ann Robinson, and others during the civil rights movement and Angela Davis, Kathleen Cleaver, the Third World Women's Alliance, and the Combahee River Collective during the Black Power and Third World era. As such, they offer a fuller reading of the evolution of feminist ideals and black women's activism in the second wave.[3]

Women Pioneers of the Black Left

The activist careers of Shirley Graham Du Bois and Dorothy Hunton, though mainly, and incompletely, viewed through the work of their husbands, indirectly contributed to the formation of the Liberation Committee for Africa (LCA). Other women such as Esther Cooper Jackson and Queen Mother

Audley Moore also shaped the *Liberator*'s radicalism, though they did not publish in the periodical.[4] Jackson's decades-long work guiding *Freedomways* impacted *Liberator*, though the latter's explicit endorsement of black nationalism placed these two periodicals on different tracks. And Queen Mother Moore impacted virtually every strand of black radicalism over this period and long after. Black left-wing feminists of the 1950s had, by the 1960s, become activist-mentors to a new generation of activists that would find expression in *Liberator*.[5] To be sure, these women had careers separate from those of their male companions. In evaluating the involvement of women in the production of *Liberator*, it is worth acknowledging that at least two women were fixtures on its staff: Evelyn Kalibala, who was listed on early LCA documents as social director and who remained in this capacity throughout the life of the periodical, and staff writer Rose Finkenstaedt. With the exception of these women and Tee's behind-the-scenes organizing with African nationals, the men in the organization led the production of the magazine.[6]

However, *Liberator* did not ignore the significant and growing questions being raised in the black liberation movement regarding the role of women. Nor could it. Though women such as Rosa Guy, Abbey Lincoln, Mae Mallory, and others played a critical role in the radicalism of this period, the question of "the woman's role" was a common one that urged explanation, discussion, and debate. Nearly all left-leaning publications ran issues that dealt with some facet of this "question." Though the heavy male presence was evident throughout the early days, on the advisory committee were Florence M. Shervington and Selma Sparks, secretary of the Negro American Labor Council. Ann Walker, a local illustrator, contributed artwork for the cover of the June 1962 issue, which featured assassinated Burundi leader Prince Louis Rwangasore. At its start the day-to-day operations of the magazine were largely in men's hands, while the social events sponsored by the LCA were often sponsored and underwritten by women and women-led organizations around New York. Yet as the decade progressed, these roles would be challenged and new roles recognized. The LCA gained some traction and visual presence by sponsoring a number of panels and ceremonies that attracted luminaries and dignitaries. Like most newly established organizations, especially ones with explicitly political ambitions, their social networks were crucial to its early success.

One of its most successful was the Afro-American Heritage Week series of events held during the second week of April 1962, which culminated in an African Freedom Day Observance celebration. The listed sponsors of these events included such figures as Audrey Johnson, Louise Patterson, Adele Glasgow, Lorraine Hansberry, Helen Jacobson, Ida Lewis, actress Beah Richards, and writer Rosa Thompson, among others.[7] Though she would come under the fierce and unrelenting criticism of Harold Cruse in *The Crisis of the Negro Intellectual*,[8] Hansberry was no less an important cultural and political figure, who lent her name and energies to many causes for freedom and justice and could be counted on to speak at a rally or soiree. At the LCA's Negro History Week Observance of February 1963 she was a featured speaker alongside Carlos Goncalves, who was then a representative of the Angolan National Liberation Front, and Diallo Tell, United Nations ambassador from the Republic of Guinea.[9] Beveridge wrote in glowing terms of Hansberry's speech, which was witnessed by over three hundred people at St. Luke's Episcopal Church in Harlem. Calling the speech moving and eloquent, he stated "it rocked the boat" on civil rights leadership by eschewing the token African American leadership represented by the likes of Ralph Bunche and Jackie Robinson.[10]

Hansberry's involvement was widespread and her sincerity was notable. Watts published a note she mailed in with her magazine subscription renewal fees, which read: "Enclosed find a two-year sub, part of which may be applied to three copies of the magazine which I have received since the expiration in January. Never meant to let it lapse. It is becoming an excellent publication."[11] Hansberry's note of validation was crucial to the fledging publication. In addition to her own literary success, she also sponsored (along with Langston Hughes and others) a series of Coffee Concerts (also called Coffeehouse Concerts), which featured a variety of singers and musicians playing classical and jazz arrangements. Classical singer Raoul Abdul founded and served as artistic director of the concerts.[12] An interpreter of poetry into musical forms, he made a natural associate to Hughes, and later served as literary assistant to Harlem's greatest poet.

The son of Hamid Abdul, who was born in Calcutta, India, and black American-born Etta Bernice Shreeve Abdul, he moved to Harlem in the early 1950,s where he found a home in the vibrant cultural and political uptown scene while studying music with the likes of Marian Anderson. He performed at Carnegie Hall, where he also helped Hughes stage a version of "The Negro Speaks of Rivers." Billed as "a panorama of Negro history in folk song and poetry," it featured Abdul alongside a local actress and a solo guitarist, which served as a fitting tribute to Hughes who died, just two years later.[13]

Though the early years of the magazine featured a sparse number of female writers and issues, in ensuing years, women's voices would be clear

Lorraine Hansberry, cover of *Liberator*, December 1964.
Courtesy of Pete Beveridge.

evidence of the magazine's expansion. One notable subscriber was Eslanda Robeson, the wife of the venerable activist and artist Paul Robeson who, like Hansberry, wrote to the editor with her subscription fee enclosed and remarked, "Shame on you for having such a magazine and not letting me know!"[14] With these endorsements in tow and a who's who of left-wing intellectuals and artists on its advisory board, the magazine had arrived.

The January 1963 issue included three articles written by or about women. Union organizer Selma Sparks led off the issue in her reportage on

Radical Commitments 79

the perils of African American and Puerto Rican garment workers in the International Ladies Garment Workers Union (ILGWU) as they fought for respectable wages commensurate with their labor.[15] In her article, Rose Finkenstaedt, reflecting on the topic of black voting nationally and locally, lamented that an increase in black voters did not necessarily mean an increase in black influence.[16] As one of the few white radicals associated with the periodical, she garnered support among her black comrades for her consistent analyses of the race, class, and gender matrix that routinely penalized blackness in any form. As this issue was dedicated in part to the 100 years since the signing of the Emancipation Proclamation, as a counter to popular attention on President Lincoln, the editors published a tribute to "General Harriet Tubman: The Real Emancipator," and her interaction with John Brown. To them, Tubman provided the radical example of the quest for freedom. Mocking Martin Luther King Jr., if not the general religiosity found in the black community, they wrote that her God was to her both an "intelligence system and tactical advisor," who did not insist on loving her enemies and did not mind her carrying a gun for protection.[17]

The next month's issue featured Ossie Davis and Ruby Dee on the cover. Selma Sparks penned the second part of her expose of garment workers' exploitation, and Rose Finkenstaedt wrote of the widening drug abuse in Harlem as an indication of domestic neocolonialism, "the diseased effect of injustice in America."[18] Later in the year, Sparks offered a scathing critique of the peace movement, which she chastised for being out of touch with African Americans and working-class whites. It rightfully called for disarmament without also linking this to an end to imperialism and colonialism, she noted. Having returned from the World without a Bomb Conference, which convened in Accra, Ghana, the previous June, Sparks argued that peace would only follow freedom. "How can you discuss peace without discussing what causes wars?" she asked. "A meaningful peace movement in the United States must not be afraid to deal with those forces which pose a threat to world peace: colonialism, imperialism and the profit motive, which rule here in this country," she continued. Sparks's article also placed the peace movement in a context of African and Third World liberation, connecting Cuba, Vietnam, Korea, and the Congo as examples of U.S. efforts to thwart peace in the protection of its economic and political interests.[19] Though her contributions to *Liberator* were sporadic, they were nonetheless timely and befitting of the tone and candor readers expected from the periodical.

The actor-activist Ossie Davis's role as an advisor to the LCA since its inception earned him a lasting reputation among *Liberator* staff. The magazine's editors honored his and Ruby Dee's contribution to the political and cultural life of New York and revered their long-distant commitment to justice throughout the early 1960s.[20] Rose Finkenstaedt wrote consistently for the magazine, and submitted one of the periodical's first articles on the Nation of Islam (NOI).[21] She also penned an important article that highlighted the local activism of black women in Harlem. In this article she emphasized the work of female leaders such as Evelyn Thomas, who led a block association. Additionally, women including Lucretia Lamb and Gladys Coleman headed a group called the Citizen Care Committee; and Lucille Bulger led the Community League on 159th Street, both early examples of women-led left-wing activism.

Formed in 1953, the Community League comprised over fifty black community workers and educators from the Washington Heights area who supported area youth and residents engaged in various community empowerment initiatives. Bulger, along with one of her associates, Pairlie MacWilliams, led a tenants' education effort after residents in three buildings along 159th Street complained to the city about the dilapidated conditions of the buildings in which they lived. First, the pair would conduct workshops on tenants' rights, followed by a letter-writing campaign to building landlords to pressure them to conduct building repairs. Effective responses to such demands most often came at a snail's pace if they came at all, but through a mixture of political engagement and social networking, groups such as the Community League showed the possibilities of organizing and mobilizing local communities for change. Though they did not win every battle with an intransigent building superintendent, they nonetheless attracted attention as an influential local organization.[22] Finkenstaedt's coverage of the local activism in New York City continued throughout 1963. When not documenting local struggles she wrote articles that questioned integration, critiqued white liberalism, and challenged white political power by echoing calls for an independent black political presence as perhaps the only path toward black liberation.[23]

Months later, in November 1963, the magazine profiled the activism of Cambridge, Maryland's Gloria Richardson, chairperson of its Non-violent Action Committee. A picture of Richardson, poised and defiant, at the speaker's podium at what appears to be a community rally graced the front cover of the magazine. Inside, Dan Watts editorialized Richardson's struggle

Gloria Richardson, cover of *Liberator*, November 1963. Courtesy of Pete Beveridge.

and called for a unified front of black community support for her "courageous and effective leadership."[24] In this same issue, *Liberator* published an ad announcing the Northern Negro Grassroots Leadership Conference, to be held in Detroit, Michigan, November 8–10, 1963, which Richardson, Watts, James, and Grace Lee Boggs and others attended, and where Malcolm X would make his famed "Message to the Grassroots" speech.[25] *Liberator*'s brand of radicalism then would increasingly incorporate the work of women writers and local activists, while necessarily acknowledging female mentors.

Writings by women were scattered throughout the magazine between 1963 and 1964, which included articles by members of the Women's Strike for Peace organization (ironically one of the targets of Sparks's criticism), highlights of Lorraine Hansberry's work and that of artist Valerie Maynard, and critiques of integration by black women. Throughout the decade black women chimed in, critiqued, and debated a range of issues.

In December 1963, Edith Schomburg's article, "The Crux of Black Non-Violence," was published. In that article, she questioned the adherence of the civil rights movement to a nonviolent philosophy. Couching her critique in her evaluation of the message of Christianity, she wondered if that religion prevented black people from defending themselves in the face of violence. "But non-violence is questionable as a technique for black America's attainment of peace on earth, and out of the question as the single major weapon in the black man's struggle for freedom."[26] Schomburg founded and directed a culture and education organization called the Common Sense Clinic, which emphasized what she called "positive action" through strategic use of black culture, education, and community organizing methods. The questions she raised in her article mirrored that of a number of activists who opted out of nonviolence as a strategy—in rhetoric and outlook—if not in fact. Merle Stewart, a community activist writing from Queens, echoed Schomburg's concern, as well as positions taken by Robert F. Williams and Gloria Richardson, when she wrote: "The proud and sane American tradition of self-defense does not mean aggression or violence. It stands for honesty—and it is time that we be honest with the whites and tell them they do not have a license to abuse or kill us, and that we will defend ourselves until death. The only thing the white racist mentality understands is power. To allow oneself to be abused and beaten is not a display of strength—but of weakness."[27]

Though attentive to grassroots leadership among women radicals not identified with an organization, *Liberator* also became a space where coverage of women's involvement in nationally recognized organizations such as the Student Nonviolent Coordinating Committee (SNCC) and Congress of Racial Equality (CORE) were hotly debated. For example, Mississippi native and actress Buleah (Beah) Richardson's account of SNCC organizing in Greenwood, Mississippi spoke to the determination of SNCC activists and the courage of local black, working class residents who defended their rights to citizenship by registering to vote. Partially written as a passionate call for increased support, the article was otherwise an explicit documentation of effective (or necessary) organizational methods. As exigencies in the North kept *Liberator* staffers busy, Richardson's was one of the few articles written by a direct participant in the southern freedom movement.[28]

On the West Coast, Louisiana-born Los Angeles resident Mildred Pitts Walker spoke emphatically against the practices of housing discrimination in southern California. "In our town, spaciousness gives the feeling of freedom to move," she began, "but the Negro soon learns that he is free to move only within the boundaries set for him by realtors." Walker discussed the campaign against residential segregation and intimidation waged by the Los Angeles chapter of CORE. She noted that black residents often faced the hostility of white residents, might have gunshots fired into their home, would certainly confront the "mushrooming" of for sale signs, and witness the resulting spread of the ghetto. Graffiti outside a local realtor's office read: "Niggers Give Up . . . Niggers Go Home . . . Niggers go back to Africa," she noted. Walker, a schoolteacher in the Los Angeles Unified School District and the wife of Earl Walker, then national Vice Chairman and Chairman of the L.A. chapter of CORE, spoke of the organization's determined efforts to reverse such practices.[29]

However these explicitly political questions expanded female activists' visibility, discussions of identity and aesthetics demonstrate nuance and an abiding concern for the body politics facing women. Even in this early period of inchoate feminist organizing, black women were not simply trying to "be down" with the men, though they often used rhetoric commonly associated with masculinist expressions of nationalism. Women took full advantage of opportunities to engage with multiple issues facing black women and black communities. Though an explicit feminist consciousness was still emerging, there was an inherent feminism in many of these women's perspectives in the early part of the 1960s.[30] While a range of issues and strategies were being debated and discussed, women writers in *Liberator* consistently engaged overlapping questions of identity, self-definition, protest politics, aesthetics, and education.

Forcing Us to "See Ourselves"

One of the earliest discussions of aesthetics came in Eleanor Mason's article entitled "Hot Irons and Black Nationalism," in the May 1963 issue.[31] This article stands out for its assertion of a separate beauty standard for black women. "As a black woman," she wrote, "I must have a worth separate and apart from the white woman. But there must be a system of values that embraces my physical and cultural possessions." The article spoke candidly about how black women were viewed by black men and American society and argued that though natural hairstyles may be reflective of a heightened consciousness, black women who did not wear their hair as such still deserved the utmost respect. Moreover, she intimated that in the quest for black unity, natural hair was not an end it itself. "Natural hair is not synonymous with nationalism," she argued, "But naturalness is an instrument for the implementation of nationalism, i.e. manifestation of group strength. Nationalism demands only one thing from the black woman—that is, that she think Black." Mason identified the intersection between black women's self-perception and the impact of denigrating "social forces" that contribute to a sense of black inferiority. In other words, beauty standards were reflective of delimiting social structures (especially mass media) black people faced as part of their political and economic struggle in the United States. In a letter to the editor included in the July issue, a reader named Mary Ann Bryant wrote to Watts that she appreciated Mason's discussion, but was upset that it didn't go far enough in explaining how black nationalism could effectively counter white supremacy. This reader thought black people should not only develop their own value system, as Mason had argued, but, in the best sense of economic nationalism,[32] should also "build our own marketplace and sell our own goods."[33] Economic independence has been a staple strategy at the heart of many black-led social justice efforts. African American political energies have been focused on black peoples' ability to provide for their families and participate in the available opportunities for respectable labor throughout the history of American labor struggle. Moreover, little in these sorts of efforts differed from that of other marginalized ethnic groups and social classes.

The debates on women's aesthetic practices sparked by Mason's article drew many more women into the discussion. Rose Nelmes's article "Natural Hair, Yes—Hot Irons, No," appeared in the July 1963 issue. Accompanied by two pictures of brown-skinned black women wearing natural hairstyles, Nelmes set out to expand on Mason's argument connecting black aesthetic beauty and values to questions of black nationalism. Nelmes went a step further and argued that natural hair was as important as abandoning the word "Negro" to an enlightened black consciousness. Asserting her African features and beauty ideals, the black woman would begin the process of destroying the negating impact of American society's attitude toward black people, according to Nelmes. Helene White, Clara Buggs, and Priscilla Bardonille were pictured alongside Nelmes's article wearing different African-inspired hairstyles. Nelmes, sporting a short Afro, was pictured on the front cover of the same issue purposefully indicating the politicized aesthetic environment *Liberator* was poised to interpret. Though the periodical leaned toward a full-fledged expression of black radical nationalist politics, it remained open to an array of equally potent cultural nationalist concerns.

The four women featured in the magazine were members of the Grandassa Models of Harlem, a group that "pioneered creating a beauty standard for black women" through open identification with, and affirmation of, African-derived styles of dress and appearance.[34] "Thru Women's Eyes," a column signed by a writer named Jeannette, explained to readers where they could find the latest African fashions along 125th Street.[35] The Grandassa concept was developed and espoused by staunch black nationalist Carlos Cooks, who, through research, had determined that Grandassala was a more appropriate name for the continent of Africa.

Cooks, a lively and visible member of Harlem's street-corner speaking tradition and leader of the African Nationalist Pioneer Movement (ANPM), considered himself a direct ideological heir to Marcus Garvey. The ANPM took its cues directly from Garvey's Universal Negro Improvement Association (UNIA), organizing members into military formations and assigning its leaders important-sounding, elaborate titles. In an effort to affirm black beauty and African consciousness, Cecil Elombe Barth and Ronald Barth staged beauty pageants (called the Miss National Standard of Beauty Contests) and fashion shows each year on Marcus Garvey's birthday (August 19), which featured the women of the Grandassa group, drawing fanfare and admiration equally from average Harlemites as well as from those of various ideological stripes.[36] The *Liberator* was a significant aspect of this political and cultural milieu. Its coverage of these issues in its pages was a matter of depicting the details and insights of New York's black communities. The approaches to black unity and aesthetics by the likes of Cooks and his ANPM, as well as the NOI, are as central to the emergence of Black Arts expressions as they are to the explicitly black radical political efforts developing in New York at this time. As evidenced by *Liberator* and other publications, black women were far more than models in a beauty pageant.

In 1964 the magazine's coverage of women dipped, though this was perhaps unexpected. With the spike in coverage in the previous year, this year belied expectations. In the January issue, the magazine featured an article written by the dynamic jazz couple Abbey Lincoln and Max Roach.[37] Roach supplied the bulk of the text, which was interspersed with stanzas from a poem written by Lincoln. The two were not strangers to politicized aesthetics. Lincoln, the renowned vocalist, and Roach, the world-class drummer, had been part of the early 1960s protests in the wake of Lumumba's assassination. And the classic recording entitled *We Insist! Freedom Now Suite,* which debuted in 1960, combined the richness of the jazz tradition—highlighted by Roach's collaboration with Oscar Brown Jr. on the writing of the album—with the militancy of African American protest, thus epitomizing the early Black Arts Movement. With songs entitled "Freedom Day," "Tears for Johannesburg," and "All Africa," this album symbolized the merging of the civil rights struggle in the United States with the struggle for independence on the African continent.[38] As musicians, they stood at the forefront of an internationally conscious black nationalism in this period. Having recently returned from a concert tour in Japan in the middle of October 1963, Roach found that he had been paid a level of respect as a man and an artist there that he could only dream of in the United States. "There have been rare and very few times when I have really enjoyed life," wrote Roach, intimating the delimiting effects of being born black in America. He rarely went to bed at night, he wrote, "without feeling literally attacked by the United States of America and its racist society." Japan offered a brief reprieve from the hostile treatment Roach received back home. While there, Roach and Lincoln, who had married two years prior, were treated as dignitaries and shown a sense of appreciation and recognition foreign to them in the United States. They were received warmly by everyone they met, causing Roach to note candidly: "It also became apparent to me that as an African American I was obviously starving for simple acceptance, because to the people of Japan this kind of treatment was no big thing!"[39] This was especially true of the Japanese press, which displayed a deep interest in the race problem in the United States.

While consorting with Japanese jazz musicians and enthusiasts, the group had found a vibrant scene that Roach thought might one-day eclipse its U.S. counterpart. Accompanying Roach and Lincoln on their cultural sojourn were such accomplished musicians as saxophonist Clifford Jordan, pianist Ronnie Mathews and bassist Eddie Kahn. The five-person group performed at Sankei Hall, the famed Japanese concert hall that had featured many African American jazz musicians, including Thelonious Monk, Cannonball Adderley, Yusef Lateef, and numerous others, many of whom had recorded concert albums there. The trip proved abundantly successful for the group who, as a result of their concerts, were contracted to score a film entitled *Black Sun*, produced by Nikkatsu Studios, Japan's oldest film and television production company.[40] On the title track, Lincoln's drawn-out lines are matched by Roach's up-tempo rhythm, providing a balance of the blues and jazz that was the couple's signature.

Lincoln firmly believed in celebrating African customs and worldview, a position she continued to hold throughout her extensive career. Her leading participation in the Lumumba protest, her organizing of the Cultural Association for Women of African Heritage, her leading film roles in *Nothin' But a Man* (1964) and *For Love of Ivy* (1968), as well as her music, especially the *Freedom Now Suite* (1961) and *Straight Ahead* of the same year, all tell of a dedication to ancestor veneration and spiritual commitment. An interviewer once asked whether she channeled her ancestors while on stage, to which Lincoln responded: "Of course I am. How else you gonna live? We live through one another. We live through our ancestors."[41] Though by all accounts their marriage was tenuous, finally ending in 1970 on cordial terms, their union made a lasting imprint on black expressive culture and politics in this period.[42] In an interview conducted on the set of *For Love of Ivy*, in which she starred alongside leading man Sidney Poitier, Lincoln commented on the impact of Roach on her life and career. In working with him, she "found out how wonderful it is to be a black woman. And I learned from Max that I should always sound how I feel, and that whatever I do, I should do it definitely."[43]

Abbey Lincoln's career in this period set a tone for the radical cultural work in which many female activists and artists were engaged. She and Roach had been active supporters of the LCA long after the UN protest. For example, the group's Negro History Week commemoration of Lumumba's assassination featured Lincoln and Roach's *Freedom Now Suite* along with Ruby Dee and Ossie Davis, who had recently staged *Purlie Victorious*. Including speeches from the UN ambassadors of Ghana, Guinea, and the United Arab Republic, guests at the Hotel Belmont Plaza experienced both the best in African American cultural expression and a contemporary view of the liberation struggles in Africa.[44] Though hugely important, Lincoln was among a number of lesser-known (or lesser-acknowledged) women who dedicated their talents to confronting issues facing black communities throughout the country.

A central issue that required urgent attention in the community at large was police brutality. Mildred Thomas and several other women of Harlem formed the Mothers Defense Committee as a result of unsubstantiated interrogations and frame-ups of their teenage sons who had been charged with murdering a white shopkeeper in Harlem in late April 1964. Thomas spoke defiantly of the inspiration and responsibility of organizing. After witnessing police bust into her home and handcuff her son without letting him put on as much as a coat before rushing him off to the precinct, she knew that it was time to organize. Trying to imagine what the parents of Denise McNair, Carole Robertson, Cynthia Wesley, and Addie Mae Collins (the young girls killed in the 16th St. Baptist Church in Birmingham, Alabama, church bombing the previous year) must have felt, Thomas noted that the police stopped just shy of killing the boys while in custody. "They are being beaten, spit upon and kicked daily," she reported. Seeking to channel the feeling of helplessness and defeat, she and the other mothers decided to organize to voice their concerns collectively and publicly.[45] Emphasizing the urban setting of these examples of black female organizing, *Liberator* staff writer Clayton Riley wrote not of the grassroots but the "cement roots." In addition to lobbying for educational reforms and speaking out against excessive police force, women such as Lucille Bulger also led clean-city campaigns around Harlem. Since the city government showed little initiative in keeping black communities clean, local organizations such as Bulger's organized to address the urgent need.[46]

Other women debated the prospects of integration. Writer and poet Kattie Cumbo sarcastically asked whose interest social and educational integration served besides whites, who were seemingly already in control over key aspects of black civic life. From her vantage point, integration offered little to African Americans. Integration was responsible for white teachers and principals in schools, white storeowners and cashiers, white mail carriers, white insurance and bill collectors, and white welfare investigators, so how could black folk benefit from increased integration? If it was the panacea it was purported to be, she questioned, why did her mother send her down South each summer to visit family members who still lived in rural areas with few if any white neighbors? She recalled her southern aunt sharing a dream of integration—integration of black people with black communities, who were autonomous and free.[47] Cumbo followed this article with a bleak assessment of the state of ghetto youth. After recounting a litany of perils befalling and awaiting black youth, she wrote: "We can't continue to let this happen again and again, this sickening continuous cycle of poverty, self destruction in our people and our children. We must start now to save our children and we must work to prepare something worth our toil and troubles in trying to save them." She spoke in terms that echoed earlier radical positions that called for a total restructuring of society so that black children would have the opportunity to grow and learn in healthy environments: "We must revolutionize if necessary. We must do what we must at any cost. Death is a mere price to pay to eliminate this continuous waste of our people, our children."[48] It is important that these issues were not simply relegated to the pen of women staff writers and contributors. Male writers such as C. E. Wilson and Larry Neal, for example, also wrote articles that mirrored women's concerns about education, health, and welfare.[49]

Liberator closed its 1964 volume with a tribute to Lorraine Hansberry, who graced the December cover and had been a guiding light of the magazine since its inception. Hansberry, who died of cancer on January 12, 1965, at the frighteningly young age of thirty-four, had already made a lasting contribution to the political and literary experience of African Americans. The first African American to have a play staged and run on Broadway in 1959, she was indeed a rising star in the art world.[50] Writing on the twenty-fifth anniversary of *Raisin*, Amiri Baraka wrote that the play "typifies American society in a way that reflects more accurately the real lives of the black U.S. majority than any work that ever received commercial exposure before it, and few if any since. It has the life that only classics can maintain."[51] Reflecting on Hansberry's life, writer Julian Mayfield, who had still been living an expatriate life in Accra, Ghana, spoke of her strength, commitment, and courage. "Genuine artists, toughened by a society hostile to creativity," he wrote, "are often impractical enough, brave, imaginative and uncompromising enough, to walk into the face of hell where principled objectives are to be won."[52]

Magazine coeditor Pete Beveridge and arts-editor Larry Neal each wrote pieces praising Hansberry's life and work that spoke to her lasting presence among many. Beveridge, a longtime friend of the playwright, wrote with admiration about her commitments, highlighting that she shunned her bourgeois upbringing in favor of radical political work, first as a member of the Young Communist League in Chicago, then as an assistant to Paul Robeson at his *Freedom* newspaper and finally as a commercial artist. That was already more than most had contributed. Beveridge spoke also of her willingness to speak out in the face of injustice. "To the extent that her health permitted, she appeared on the speaking platform for many organizations and causes," he recalled, "and spoke her mind in a blunt and straightforward way . . . yet she never sought the limelight or tried to pose as a 'leader' or 'spokesman.'"[53] For his part, the revolutionary nationalist art critic Larry Neal provided a favorable view of Hansberry's *The Sign in Sidney Brustein's Window*. Though her play *A Raisin in the Sun* had received critical acclaim and was more sharply focused than *The Sign*, the latter "shows Lorraine Hansberry as essentially the same humanistically-minded person" she proved to be in the first play. Accordingly, Neal noted that both black nationalists and mainstream critics missed the significance of the play's commentary on the reality of human survival amidst daily life and death circumstances.[54] As theater historians Errol Hill and James Hatch have noted, Hansberry's career represented the starting point of an arc of African American women dramatists that prefaced Ntozake Shange's work, for example, as well as that of most playwrights of color in the 1970s. Like many of their male counterparts black female artists along this arc emphasized the creation of institutions that would preserve and extend black theater. Black female writers such as Marjorie Moon, Cynthia Belgrave, Hazel Bryant, and Vinnette Carroll headed significant theater companies in this period and well into the 1970s.[55] In addition to its coverage of Hansberry, *Liberator* included an article by domestic worker Louise Moore, who spoke of the need for domestic workers to organize throughout the country to demand the pay they deserve.

By 1965, *Liberator* had achieved a level of consistency that readers had come to respect. Throughout the New Year it would continue expand its readership. Having grown closer to the ideological positions espoused by Malcolm X, while opening its pages more fully to younger writers such as Muhammad Ahmad (Max Stanford) and Askia Touré (Rolland Snellings), *Liberator* had emerged as a critical voice, if not *the* voice of black protest, as it had earlier proclaimed across its masthead. Malcolm's death reminded activists of the urgency of organizing. Women, too, remembered Malcolm's words and public persona and saw in him a leader men should emulate.

While *Liberator* dedicated its efforts to more fully analyzing the direction of the liberation movement, its writers kept their eyes set on issues facing the global black community through the United Nations. Harkening back to its coverage of the Grandassa Models, in May the periodical published a number of UN photographs of African women from around the African continent, including the Sudan, Burundi, Mali, Togoland, and Somalia.

However, the spread was not solely about the aesthetic performance of African women. The publication also published photographs of African women ambassadors to the United Nations. Featuring Nancy Kajumbula of Uganda, Julienne Keutcha of Cameroon, Florence Addison of Ghana, Margaret Aguta of Nigeria, and Regine Gbedey of Togo, these women are shown seated in session at the United Nations. *Liberator* again underscored the view that African and African American political fortunes were intertwined, if not wholly interdependent.[56] The Africa-inspired internationalism on display would stay throughout the life of the magazine.

On the home front, a particularly sensitive issue for many of the black women who wrote for the periodical was interracial marriage. Mirroring a more assertive Black Nationalist stance, which strengthened in the wake of Malcolm X's assassination and a growing sense of disillusionment toward liberalism, these black women writers often expressed fierce disagreement with the explicitly integrationist approaches in this period. Many of these women challenged black men for their public Black Nationalist rhetoric though some were in intimate relationships with white women in their personal lives. For example, in July 1965, *Liberator* published a "Letter to Black Men" by Katy Gibson, which singled out "the 'angry' Black Nationalist intellect who has chosen a non-Black mate." She continued by stating, "The fact that they have chosen non-Black mates to love, honor, cherish and to bear their off-spring, leaves little doubt in my mind that their pro-black, nationalistic, angry writings, speeches, etc. should not be taken seriously."[57] A male magazine subscriber from Brooklyn appreciated Gibson's chastising article, writing, "I certainly hope that to those whom it applies will straighten themselves," or at least cease making Black Nationalist pronouncements in public. In contrast to the type Katy Gibson identified, men like him were "earnest" Black Nationalists who took seriously "the destiny of Black people and other people of color throughout the world."[58] In some way *Liberator*'s decision to publish these contrasting views served as a counterweight to Hansberry's impact on the periodical. Having long been in an interracial relationship (as had Dan Watts), Hansberry was hardly the champion of an increasingly forthright expression of black nationalism. *Liberator* would have to attempt balancing its political advocacy with the personal relationships of its staff members and the larger community of support. This would remain a source of some tension through the periodical's career.

In the fall of 1965, *Liberator* sponsored and organized a small yet well-attended writer's conference, which centered around four panel discussions about the role and function of artists, writers and activists in rethinking

American society. By this time, the magazine's masthead declared, "*Liberator*: is the voice of the African-American." Accordingly the conference sought to encourage debate among black (and a few white) writers and community members in attendance. Each panel contained a separate theme: "Black Woman in the White Society"; "Is a Dialogue Desirable between Black and White?"; "Is Pro-Black Necessarily Anti-White?"; and "Must the Black Writer Lead?," and excerpts of the conference proceedings were subsequently published in the magazine.

The panel entitled, "The Role of the Black Woman in a White Society" featured Myrna Bain, Vinie Burrows, Edwina Johnson, Edith Schomburg, and Virginia Hughes. Openly distancing themselves from "the insidious, castrating, feminist concept that now pervades America," one of the panelists stated, "The role of the Black woman in this period of revolution is to help the Black man reject that society has attempted to destroy him and exploit her."[59] Based on the published account, it appeared that this position was more about distinguishing black women's perspectives from those of white women rather than an endorsement of black women's secondary position behind men, as some nationalists would have it. This panel demonstrated that many women sought a feminist concept that would speak to what they perceived to be the needs of black women and men. However, they did not all share the same approach toward social justice or the liberation of women. Vinie Burrows, an actress who starred in local theater productions, emphasized the role of the arts in community revitalization and consciousness-raising efforts. Edwina Johnson, a schoolteacher, drove home the importance of teaching African history in elementary school. And Edith Schomburg thought black women were the avatars of revolutionary spirit. Writers, activists, and educators, these women represent a range of black women's art and activist outlooks even as these perspectives were being sharpened.[60] Though an effective demonstration of black women's thinking in this period, this writer's conference was but a small fraction of women's overall impact in the liberation movement. In the same issue that featured the women writer's panel, Beverly Van Cortland spoke of the "War on the Poor" despite President Johnson's declaration of war on poverty.[61] Speaking about the contrasting realities in New York City, for example, Van Cortland asserted, "It is shameful in the richest city of the world where French poodles are dressed in mink coats with golden lockets thousands of humans are reduced to living like the lowest of animals."[62]

From Abbey Lincoln and Maya Angelou to Toni Cade Bambara and Sonia Sanchez, women in this period played crucial roles in the political expressive culture of the day. Additionally, *Liberator* featured female Black Arts visual artists such as Valerie Maynard. Maynard's work appeared to carry on a tradition of radical art in the vein of Elizabeth Catlett. Writing of Catlett and other early black women sculptors and visual artists, such as Edmonia Lewis, Meta Vaux Warrick Fuller, and Augusta Savage, Bonnie Claudia Harrison has argued for the recognition of their contributions as representations of "Diasporadas." Employing a term that synthesizes the word "Diaspora" with a feminized version of "desperado," she notes that "these black women created images that asserted black identity and independence, in part by de-centering traditional European subjects and centering subjects of African descent [while they also] supported, worked within, and sought transnational black activist communities."[63] Maynard, who served as coordinator of Project Uplift Gallery along 125th Street in Harlem, fits within the tradition described by Harrison.

Maynard's work was celebrated in *Liberator* as "one of the finest on the scene today," and was indicative of the "spiritual and social search for meaning" that African Americans seemed to face collectively. Her subjects were often depicted with penetrating eyes that seemed to peer out from the canvas. "Valerie forces us to see ourselves, our bodies and faces, and to understand the beauty of spirit that is in every black person." A depiction of black humanity that registered high among the best of Black Art, Maynard's work was a visual exemplar of what Askia Touré had termed the repudiation of western values applied to art. Maynard's work was powerful for "what it can do to inspire Black people towards making the outer world of Western society fall, and give way to the inner spirit of the Black man which demands and will have a better world," read the *Liberator*.[64] Accompanying the description of Maynard's work and impact were several images from her series of charcoal drawings that seemed to depict both the rage and resilience of the African American community, which was still reeling from Malcolm's assassination and the West Coast rebellion in Watts.

Like their male counterparts, many women grew tired of the slow pace of the civil rights movement, characterized by marches and nonviolent direct action—especially considering that violence meted out against civil rights demonstrators went without punishment. Even if caught and tried before juries, more often than not whites who committed violent crimes against African American demonstrators were acquitted. A woman from Brooklyn, Jacqueline D. Woods, wrote the magazine to express her frustration regarding a recent Lowndes County, Alabama case. Her letter, addressed to Dan Watts, is worth citing at length:

> Dear Sir:
>
> It's over. All the shallow promises, meaningless laws, fragmented revolutions (shades of Watts), poverty pacifiers, walk-ins, sit-ins, and the most popular of all—the crawl or shuffle-ins can now stop. For there is *no cause*, and we know where we stand!
>
> On October 4, 1965, A.D. in Lowndes County Alabama, Mr. Thomas L. Coleman who was being tried for the senseless, I mean by the standards of the so-called civilized world, wanton murder of Reverend Jonathan Daniels, age 26 (a demonstrator with the Students' Non-Violent Coordinating Committee) was summarily acquitted.
>
> With this action, Mr. Coleman and the State of Alabama put the final nail in the cross, and shattered the "I have a dream," illusion. They showed us, all of us—I mean you too [sic] my Afro-American brothers and sisters, just where we stand: firmly and securely at the bottom of the 'herring' barrel. Let the words of one of Coleman's defense attorneys now become our motto:
>
> *"These were not men of God (the slain reverend) as we know them in Alabama . . . Where can WE Draw the line? Where MUST WE Draw the line? We've GOT A RIGHT TO PROTECT OURSELVES."*
>
> Once more we have heard it. The illusion is over. We must begin. The lines are drawn.[65]

The disappointment that fueled this subscriber's frustration exemplified the growing disenchantment many African Americans felt. Ten months after Malcolm's brutal assassination, and with the war in Vietnam raging on with no end in sight, black people wondered what their future would entail if left up to government and white liberals to decide. The Great Society envisioned by President Johnson, whose implementation up to this point revealed serious cracks at its core, being dogged by the Vietnam War abroad and social protest for expansive racial justice at home, now appeared to be heading steadily to an unceremonious death.

By 1966 other female *Liberator* writers would ask: "Will the real Black man stand up or will the Black woman have to make this revolution?"[66] Anticipating the more formal emergence of black women's radicalism, Betty Frank Lomax's article "Afro-American Woman: Growth Deferred" offered a poignant critique of masculinity and the dilemma many women and men struggled with. "The Black man frustrated by white America," she wrote, "turns inwards to a perverted form of male supremacy in his relationship with the black woman. Male supremacy is just as immoral as white supremacy, in that it prevents the female from developing and realizing her full potential." However, she did offer an example of manhood that stood as a model of what the black man should be: "Brother Malcolm did more for her Black womanhood than any other so called leader. At last, at long last, there he was, a man, a Black man whom she could really be proud of."[67] Later in the year, Louise Moore, who had more than thirty years' experience as a domestic worker and who served as vice president of the Domestic Personal Service Workers (a group of unionized domestic workers), anticipated Frances Beal's "Double Jeopardy" by locating black women's oppression in the context of American politics and economy, commenting, "We are tired of being cheated of our womanhood by Black men, white men, white women and a whole capitalist-military system."[68]

In the late sixties, such issues would continue to receive coverage in *Liberator*. These topics ushered in a renewed sense of identity for many black women, informed their consciousness, and served as an early platform on which black women's collectives and organizations were formed. Evelyn Rodgers, writing in March 1966 reminded readers of the aesthetic questions that pervaded this period when she asked: "Is *Ebony* Killing Black Women?"[69] *Ebony* magazine, the creation of powerhouse publisher John H. Johnson, had experienced twenty years of successful publication history up to this point. However, a quick perusal of its magazine covers in this period reveals that it catered to a middle-class clientele and privileged, lighter-skinned African American women. "*Ebony* has been a highly successful magazine because it has mirrored the values and standards of the larger dominant white society," asserted Rodgers. Aping white standards of beauty, with ads for skin lightening creams and hair straighteners, *Ebony* seemed to eschew the diversity of black people and culture. Rodgers spoke to the potentially negative psychic effects of the magazine on black peoples' sense of themselves. Rodgers, along with an ad hoc group, which called itself Concerned Black Women, formed a picket line outside *Ebony*'s Rockefeller Center office. The women, all sporting their natural hair styled into Afros, carried pickets that left no confusion as to what was at stake. One picket put the matter in grave terms, asking, "Has *Ebony* Murdered the Black Woman?" Past issues of the periodical whose covers evidenced a clear pattern of light-skinned privilege were displayed as evidence, justifying their protest. While most pickets identified the problem, others posed solutions and advertised upcoming events that promoted brown and darker complexioned black women, such as the "Naturally '66" Grandassa Model Showcase.[70]

Evelyn Rodgers, Dona Humphrey, Lois Chinnery, and *Liberator* contributor Eddie Ellis requested and were granted a meeting with *Ebony* vice president William Grayson to discuss the flagrantly offensive article that was published in February 1966 issue of that magazine entitled, "Are Negro Girls Getting Prettier?" Rodgers argued that *Ebony*'s intent was not to promote the overall mental and physical health of African Americans, but "to push and even drag us into the image of whites. What they (*Ebony*) would really like to do is make us all look more and more like whites." Connecting *Ebony* to the machinations of western capitalist mass-media practices through its slavish dependence on ad revenue (what she called "blood money"), which evaluated all of humanity from the perspective of whiteness, Rodgers indicted *Ebony* for its failures to be truly independent and for abandoning African Americans' "cultural and historical roots."[71] Rodgers's article, in its attack on Johnson's magazine, displayed the centrality of media criticism in black liberation politics. Rodgers's historical, psychological, and sociological critique was a stinging rebuttal to the glorification of white aesthetic standards that permeated popular culture.

Though these women led the charge, men also supported the claims against *Ebony* and had separate critiques of the article. Frederick Bell, writing from Alabama, wrote a letter to *Ebony* after reading the "Negro Girls" article. In turn, *Ebony* published only the last paragraph of his letter. He wanted the letter read in its entirety, so he sent both the edited version and the original letter to Dan Watts. "Are you ashamed of your Black sisters? Well I'm one brother who is not. I love and respect them all no matter what complexion they are," he wrote. After reminding *Ebony*'s editor that black people came in all complexions "from near white to blue black," Bell stated "Frankly I thought the article was quite silly." Pleased that he had yet another reason to stick it to the black middle-class mainstream, Watts' editor's note read: "It has been obvious to us at LIBERATOR, that *Ebony* is not concerned with the question of Black Revolution and our search for identity."[72] Certainly the high-class magazine tried to steer away from any ensuing protests. In an effort to stave off a potential dip in readership *Ebony*'s June 1966 cover pictured a brown-skinned young black woman sporting a short Afro hairdo, with a caption that read, "The Natural Look: New Mode for Negro Women."[73] And to avoid readers thinking the June issue was a onetime deal, the magazine ran a special women's issue that sought to cover a variety of black women's experiences in August.[74]

Challenging Orthodoxy

Encouraged by a range of activity led by women throughout the urban North and South, *Liberator* editors decided it was time to focus singularly on issues affecting black women, dedicating the entire May 1966 issue of the magazine to their voices and approaches to racial and gender justice. What is important is that these women challenged orthodox religion, demanded equal if not superior education for their children, and vocalized opposition to U.S. imperialism, which in their view had led to the war in Vietnam. Expressing deep commitments to justice that cut across race, class, gender, and region, radical women writers forged a broad version of intellectual-activism throughout the 1960s. All five of its lead articles in May 1966 were written by, about, and ostensibly to black women.[75] Included was a photo essay that sought to capture the diversity of black women's physical appearance, along with several poems, including two by Black Arts exemplar Sonia Sanchez.

Louise Moore's article, "When Will the Real Black Man Stand Up?," spoke of what she perceived as African American's childlike state in relation to the U.S. government. "We are in the position of children to parents—parents who dislike children," she wrote. While Moore's claim might be read as a denial of African American maturity, her comments accurately described the hierarchal structure of American society. African Americans were to assert their rights as citizens while simultaneously pressing the government for employment protections and increased opportunities for advancement. Yet, her claim might also be read as a critique of black men's stature in American society through her emphatic call for black men "to be men." Speaking from her experiences as a longtime domestic worker, Moore stressed the need for cultural awareness and a sober look at the history of black people in the United States. She spoke of white supremacy, the god complex, and the failure of integration. Even going so far as to label Martin Luther King a traitor to his race, Moore asserted, "We have no future in this society the way it is today."[76]

Juanita Poitier, then wife of the black actor Sidney Poitier, who was most known for breaking the racial ceiling of the film industry, was far less bombastic than Moore in her appraisal of the future of black people in the United States and stressed the importance of identity, education for black children, and the need to uphold to their greater humanity.[77] Amelia Long raised the question of the role of the black women not only in revolutionary struggle, but also in American society at large. "Is there any special role for the Afro-American woman in this decadent society?" she asked. Long believed it was up to women to lead the action toward social change. "Based on America's unwillingness to deal with the Afro-American on the human plane," she asserted, echoing Malcolm's refrain advising against integrating into a burning house, "I'd say it is time NOW for women . . . to spearhead a single program geared to alleviate the continuation of this anti-human treatment."[78] In order to rectify the inhuman treatment of the black community, black women played a central role in shaping independent economic practices in New York's black communities, using their creativity in the service of community pride and, most of all pressed the need for action. This sense of urgency exemplifies much of the writing by black women writers in this issue. Their assertiveness often registered as a declaration of survival amidst a domestic war of attrition.[79]

Sonia Sanchez's "Poem at Thirty" and "Blues" were also featured in this spring 1966 issue of *Liberator*. She, like many of her contemporaries, believed art and politics (both imbued with an explicit concern with the well-being of African descendants) to be inseparable.[80] Sanchez's poem spoke to both individual and communal concerns facing African American women. Published on the same page as Amelia Long's contribution to the issue, this poem reiterated the theme of the personal as political, an effective motto of second wave feminism that awakened discussion of women's bodies as well as their politics.[81] Sanchez's poem told of women's personal maturity and childhood recollections, about traveling without knowing exactly where she was going, and about a sense of shared struggle between black women and men. Her "Blues" poem seemed to pick up where her "Poem at Thirty" left off and expressed her sensuality ("he put the bacon in and it overflowed the pot"). In these poems, Sanchez demonstrated what she described as both the "poetry of ethos" and "functionary poetry": the former was rooted in personal reflections, while the latter revealed aspects of the world in which the individual poet functioned.[82]

In this special issue, the writings of Amelia Long, Juanita Poitier, Betty Frank Lomax, Louise Moore, and Evelyn Rodgers, along with the poetry of Sonia Sanchez and Denise Nichols, captured a diverse range of African American women's political and cultural outlook and opinion. This political outlook ranged from assertions of black feminine identity and policy questions concerning the need for cultural education, to the role of women as individuals, as mates and as concerned members of local communities. Several of these women would continue to publish in the magazine, effectively commenting on the direction of liberation politics in New York and nationwide. In this issue women expressed opinion on national issues and revealed the pulse of local activism. In this sense, these black women served as both commentators and activists, who not only organized on the ground, but like the men, wrestled with the major issues of the day—integration, nonviolence, segregated education—that faced the black community nationwide.

Louise Moore's evocation of Malcolm X as an exemplar of black masculinity was perhaps a demonstration of a form of revolutionary nationalism embraced by black women, what historian Ula Y. Taylor has called "community feminism."[83] Her arguments, while often painted in broad strokes, were no less important to understanding the attitudes that women radicals held toward male leadership. Her writing was also indicative of advocacy for a particular style of public leadership many felt was necessary in order for black humanity to be accorded the respect it deserved. She argued that women should assert their human rights as women, wives, and mothers, and that as women they were deserving of respect from white society and from black men who did not value women's worth because they did not value their own personal worth. Expanding on the self-help ethos present in the ideology of the Nation of Islam and other Black Nationalist groups such as Cooks' African Nationalist Pioneer Movement, Moore argued that women were responsible for holding men accountable for their actions. Her critique ranged from discussions of black male indolence and inertia to the masculinist construction of American society. Lecturing her female readers and any males that cared to listen, she wrote: "I want to try to explain how we Black women got into this bind. The man's society is a masculine one that builds itself around the male and *his* masculine organ. His penis is played up at every opportunity. We see it in the skyscrapers of the cities, the military missiles, the church steeples. He even has one God, one sex, in fact a holy trinity of one sex. Poor Mary was given the business. Here's a woman who has a child and can't explain how she got it. She took a screwing from the 'get-go.' "[84] Moore's sarcastic tone notwithstanding, her statement leveled a dual critique. It took aim at black men for not living up to the example of manhood she perceived in Malcolm X, which left both black women and the black community worse off than before. And she couched her critique of black men in a critique of American capitalist society's practice of patriarchal dominance that relegated women to an inferior status. At the same time she explored the gendered coding inherent in Christian religious belief, a theme she returned to in later writings. Yet, this did not lead to an automatic embrace of feminism as practiced by white women, defined by an unwillingness to work in solidarity with their male counterparts. Her occupation as a domestic worker (most often with white women as her employers) countered any wishful thinking about solidarity among black and white women. In November 1966 Moore's writing returned to the problem of manhood in the black community.[85]

In this instance she offered a sprawling account of black history, evoking David Walker, Marcus Garvey, Du Bois, Robert F. Williams, and Malcolm in the telling of a courageous black masculinity. What is important is that she held these men up as examples of those who stood up but who were also ignored, banished, repressed, or killed because they took unpopular stands. Echoing Malcolm during his days in the Nation of Islam, Moore wrote, "There is still within us today a race hatred for each other. I, myself, fear negroes more than I do whites, especially if they proclaim to be Christians."[86] Her use of hyperbole, saying she feared blacks more than whites, can be attributed to her staunch advocacy of independent black politics. As had nineteenth-century abolitionist Harriet Tubman, Moore intimated that black Christians willfully participated in their own oppression; that Christianity kept them from forcefully asserting their rights. Her distrust for the church was also reflected in African Americans' joining the Nation of Islam or embracing other esoteric, eclectic, or non-Christian religious and spiritual practices, eschewing the Christianity many practiced as youth who were brought up in religious households.[87] Debates about the role of Christianity in the progression or regression of black liberation politics were frequent. Many opponents of Martin Luther King Jr. and the Southern Christian Leadership Conference blamed their nonviolent philosophy on Christianity's teaching of "love thy neighbor" and its lessons about receiving rewards for earthly toils in heaven. For many, this approach was inseparable from integration as a social strategy toward achieving equality between African Americans and whites.

Years after the *Brown v. Board* decision, public school integration remained an explosive issue throughout the country. Patricia Robinson, head of the Mount Vernon/New Rochelle Women's Group, penned an article in *Liberator* that spoke of New Rochelle's experiment with integrated schooling.[88] Robinson explained that African American children and their families were often hopeful about the prospects of attending integrated schools, but that the schools had a long way to go toward ensuring that black students were given the same opportunities to succeed as white students. Robinson's story reported a fight that broke out between two young female students, one African American and one white. She noted that prior to being asked for her side of the story, the black child was given dramatically harsher treatment by administrators. Teachers and administrators, as well as the white child's parent, immediately scolded the African American student. The white parent even went so far as to ask, in condescending fashion of course, whether the black student was native to New Rochelle or from out of town. She must be from out of town, the parent claimed, since black children from New Rochelle knew how to act. The white child was automatically assumed to be the victim by both teachers and administrators— some of which were themselves African American—and not given the slightest reprimand, according to Robinson.

Robinson's concern in this article with the process of integration, with the ways that schools exercised a double standard for white and black students was often lost amidst the din of the "integration versus separation" debate. What good was integration when African American children would not be treated with the same level of respect and care that white children received, she intimated, recalling similar concerns raised in *Liberator* by Kattie Cumbo. "But slowly these black parents who had struggled so hard for integration so their children could get a 'decent education' were learning that their children were in mental agony and had developed ways of fighting back these grown-ups who said they were not prejudiced and took such pride in teaching them about Booker T. Washington and non-violence," she wrote.[89] Here Robinson adeptly inserted black elementary school students in the evolution of African Americans' developing radical consciousness based on the treatment they received by school administrators. As a result, she argued, black parents were paying closer attention to the treatment of their children in schools, and some began to visit classrooms, much to the chagrin of many white faculty members.

According to Benita Roth, Robinson's Mount Vernon/New Rochelle Group was an early example of feminist politics as an outgrowth of earlier civil rights struggles. Formed in the early 1960s out of concerns for welfare rights, housing conditions, improved education, and the condition of poor women, Robinson and others also had connections to Planned Parenthood and sought to address teenage pregnancy. Key aspects of their work lasted throughout the 1960s and into the mid-1970s. Education was a central issue to many of the women in Robinson's activist circles. As a result "freedom schools" were offered as weekend opportunities to instill culturally aware education in children and parents alike. Robinson's group also played a significant role in shaping the debate around the politics of reproduction in an atmosphere where birth control was frequently interpreted as antirevolutionary.[90]

Some of the "study papers" of Robinson's group were later published in Toni Cade's *Black Woman* in 1970 as an example of the practice of black female activism. Women were engaged in serious, critical analysis of a range of issues facing the African American community and their participation in struggles for liberation and equality being waged nationally and globally. These study papers were communal documents that drew input from a community of women and were not therefore the perspective of a single individual. These efforts tell us a great deal about the ways black women organized and offer a critical backdrop for the establishment of more formal feminist organizations that formed from 1968 onward.[91]

As it turned out, the May 1966 issue of *Liberator* would be its last full-length dedication to women's issues. Nonetheless, female activists, community workers, and artists continued to issue timely contributions to the periodical. It is not clear why, after having convened a small conference with a significant and well-attended panel devoted to women and after publishing several widely read articles written by black women, that the magazine did not seek to place more women alongside Evelyn Kalibala on the periodical's staff or why no other were opened to a full-length discussion of women's concerns.

"War Is Hell": Battlefronts Abroad and at Home

While the politics of aesthetics and integrated education occupied much of women's writing in *Liberator*, equally important were international questions concerning Africa's place at the United Nations, and the war in Vietnam. Female *Liberator* scribes engaged these questions forcefully, rebuking government pronouncements while crafting ideological positions that bespoke a transnational and radical liberatory vision. In February 1967, Gwendolyn Patton, a former Southern Christian Leadership Conference and SNCC activist from Detroit, wrote of the effects of the Vietnam War on black people in the United States. Echoing Malcolm X's most memorable statements against U.S. imperialism and anticipating Martin Luther King Jr.'s famous speech denouncing the war in Vietnam in the context of the domestic civil rights struggle a few months later,[92] Patton opened her short article boldly, stating, "War is hell, and nobody knows it better than Black people in this country."[93] Like Malcolm and King, she perceived gross parallels between the American government's reluctant embrace of civil rights at home while carrying out human rights abuses abroad. Black people, she noted, began to make the connections between the war and their situation: "As time progressed and as the escalation for black soldiers increased and as the black death toll got higher, black people saw that they had to be concerned about the Vietnam war." Black people, she astutely emphasized, had begun to see that the war against the spread of communism in Vietnam as distracted the government from the domestic battle against poverty. Instead of expanding low-rent housing in Washington, DC, she noted, that area was turned into a staging ground for war. America's attention on Vietnam physically sapped young African American activists and students who, rather than educating themselves and organizing in their communities were being conscripted to the battlefront. "When we Black people began to analyze this war," she continued, "it became very clear to us that it is a racist war." The victims of U.S. imperialism throughout history were people of color, she argued, therefore African Americans were political allies of the people of Vietnam who struggled under napalm attacks.

Patton wanted to present the matter to the reader in the clearest terms possible: "The country is built on racism and imperialism. This country has constantly been building a world empire through exploitation and capitalism." Then she provided a statement that is perhaps best interpreted in the context of the African American prophetic tradition. Referring to Vietnam she warned: "We *know* that this country is not going to stop that war because we know that Vietnam and wars like it are inherent in the very nature of this country. After Vietnam, we know there'll be another." Patton's statements were a bitter indictment of the practice of war throughout American history. Black people's protest against the war required a long-range vision of the future. In her view, black people needed to think past the war and ask themselves where they were headed. Rethinking the structure of American society was perhaps the best way to perceive the struggle going forward. "Therefore, the course of action to take is not to simply stop the war in Vietnam, but to radically change this country so that no more horrors and atrocities will exist in this country and abroad."[94] Patton's broad and sweeping, yet penetrating, indictment recalled Du Bois's essay, "African Roots of War,"[95] in which he made the prescient argument that World War I was a battle over Africa's physical resources. Echoing Du Bois's analysis of global white supremacy, Malcolm's internationalism, and King's intellectual courage, Patton's short article (it was only two columns in length) extinguished any doubt about black people's embrace of an international consciousness. It was, however, a staple of *Liberator*'s content throughout its career. Moreover, Patton's writing stands as a stellar example of a black women's transnational political consciousness that would also be found in activist-literary practices from those of Fran Beal to those of Toni Cade Bambara.

Arguably, the war in Vietnam had a disproportionate impact on the black community indirectly as many were drafted into service and placed onto distant battlefields, leaving thousands to return with irreparable wounds, mental shock, or suffering from drug addiction. black males were drafted at twice the rate of white males. And though black soldiers made up roughly 11 percent of the troops, they accounted for over 22 percent of casualties. No single figure represented a rebuke of the Vietnam War more than prizefighter and Nation of Islam disciple Muhammad Ali, who made headlines for his February 1966 stance against the war, to the concern of many in the black community and the admiration of some. Many African Americans worried that Ali's athletic career was being jeopardized as a result of refusing the draft. Others celebrated and were ecstatic that a black man with his level of public visibility had stood up against this country's march to a war that cost millions of dollars and thousands of lives. A number of celebrities were asked their opinion of Ali's decision. Like the black community generally, some supported his efforts, while others wondered why he was involving himself in "politics" since he was an athlete.[96] John Cosby Jr., writing in the pages of *Liberator*, singled out the singer Nancy Wilson for her comments against Ali's antiwar stance.[97] To be fair, however, Wilson was among a number of mainstream African American celebrities who thought it wise to publicly exude an air of patriotism during the war effort. Prior to his death, Malcolm X had been in a heated debate with Jackie Robinson over this issue, as were national organizations such as the NAACP and SNCC.[98] Though Ali would eventually be exonerated, the conflict over the Vietnam War became yet another example of African Americans' stand on global issues.

The work of several writers often accompanied *Liberator*'s coverage of political debates. For example, in May, Rashidah Ismaili Abu Bakr, a resident poet and playwright of the Lower East Side artist scene (which included Askia Touré, Ishmael Reed, Tom Dent, Archie Shepp, Sarah E. Wright, and Tom Feelings), published "Scenes of Home"—a poetic remembrance of her West African roots. Recalling this period, she wrote of her affection and admiration for Feelings, who as longtime illustrator for the magazine, she credited for getting her poem published in *Liberator*.[99] Sonia Sanchez lamented some black men's pursuit of "those grey chicks parading their asses" in front of them in her poem "To All Brothers" in the November issue of that year.[100] Don Lee (Haki Madhubuti) provided a counterpart to Sanchez's concern in his "A poem for Black Women," in which he lamented the "Blackmen ain't shit" refrain believed by some black women. His dreams of doing better and being a better mate to a black woman ("i even hit on her a couple of times") and getting himself together were dashed when he saw her "on the other side / natural & all / smiling those words: "Blackmen ain't shit" / & holding that white boy's hand."[101] Other poets spoke to the black women's perceived mothering role in the building of a black nation: "You are my strength, the Nation is my glory, you are the Nation."[102] Though such a perspective of womanhood in the service of black nationalism within the United States was readily apparent in this period, it would subsequently and slowly come undone with the burgeoning black feminist movement, which included eschewing a solely racial analysis that ignored the intersectionality of women's oppression.

Aside from a few articles, female voices in the magazine were sporadic throughout 1968, despite this being a watershed year in feminism's second wave.[103] In April of that year, *Liberator* published a poem by Irma Princeton that addressed the distrust between white storekeepers and black customers and how working class black men were often the hired help to secure white property.[104] A similarly skeptical view of structural power was expressed in Barbara Butler's evaluation of urban renewal plans under New York governor Nelson Rockefeller. Recalling the Poor People's March led by King, Butler wrote: "What the Governor has given us is a Rich People's March—right through the ghetto."[105] Butler saw the governor's plans as a power grab. The bill that would officially grant operation to Rockefeller's Urban Development Corporation had no real solutions for the black poor, but explicitly defined the power the corporation would wield through eminent domain. Earlier in the year the *New York Times* reported the governor's plan would start with "$50 million in 'seed money' to be passed on to the private corporations."[106] Anticipating the negative impact of this measure on local communities, Butler wrote: "This particular bill is the most dramatic demonstration of local disenfranchisement. It is total."[107] Highlighting key provisions in the plan, she quoted directly from the legislation showing precisely where power was being wrested from local communities and placed in the auspices of a nine-person corporate committee.

Butler's article provided an in-depth look at the reactionary response of state and federal government to urban rebellions. Government funding to corporations was the answer to demands for economic power in America's ghettos. A people who rebelled against their powerlessness remained powerless and financially dependent on temporary short-term job creation with no structural changes to facilitate community empowerment.[108]

In June, Butler offered another view of urban renewal that translated into urban removal for the local black community. Here she pointed out how Columbia University contributed to the further erosion of community empowerment. Labeling the school an "arrogant giant," she spoke to the institution's "deal to take over 2.1 acres of Morningside Park to build a gym in exchange for the annual payment to the city of $3,000" as nothing short of a coup. She also pointed out how some mainstream African Americans such as Kenneth and Mamie Phipps Clark, local clergymen, and at least one federal official endorsed this uptown expansion project.[109] New York City resident M. P. Johnson wrote to *Liberator* arguing that Butler had only told a fraction of the real story of Columbia's land grab. Johnson argued that the school's chief business partner, Percy Uris, along with First National Bank and the Uris Building Corporation, was linked to a number of influential legal and financial firms and facilitated a network of capitalist developers in a quest to dominate the city at the expense of the local community.[110] Like Rockefeller's urban renewal policy, the Columbia project accepted little direct input from the student body and community members, which led to student and community protests and demonstrations, countered by trespassing charges and arrests.[111]

In addition to the political analyses by women writers like Butler's, women continued to publish poetry and analyses of culture throughout the decade in the pages of *Liberator*. These articles dealing with a range of issues from prescribed gender roles and independent organizing to community challenges directed at government programs, often mirrored and spawned public debates off the page. For example, Sonia Sanchez's concern about white women parading in front of attentive black men was a continuation of a debate about relationships between black men and women, and the specter of interracial dating. Undoubtedly, such discussions of black female experiences emerged in the context of organizational battles, controversial governmental perspectives on the black family, as infamously embodied in the Moynihan Report (1965), and the white feminist movement.

Like Sanchez, Gail A. Stokes's essay, "Black Woman to Black Man," was a personalized account of the challenges of reconstructing harmonious relationships between black men and women. Writing in *Liberator* in December 1968, she perceived that the treatment black men received under structural racism often made black women the easy targets of their aggression in the home. However, hostile behavior toward women was no longer tenable, if it ever was. "For each blow the man rains on your head, you come and rain triple blows upon my already weary and battered skull," she wrote defiantly. Nor did she accept the effort by some cultural nationalists to reconstruct gender roles based on African traditions. "You greet me with 'My Black goddess,' but you don't know how goddesses are treated. Can you really expect me to believe that you can treat me that way? No sir, I will not accept your humble, feeble offerings," she stated before continuing, "No, not now. It's too late; I'm broken beyond repair."[112] An exasperated Stokes painted a glum picture of male-female relationships, though her statements could also be viewed as a challenge to the notion that black women were the inevitable victims of a dejected black masculinity.

Here she distanced herself both from what many perceived to be the racist assertions encoded in the Moynihan Report and the masculinist responses that ensued in its aftermath. As Benita Roth has written, "Black nationalists condemned the report as racist, but many responded that the patriarchal family had to be reinstituted so as to right the historic wrongs done to the black male."[113] Not all agreed with Stokes's demands for respect. Edith Hambrick responded to Stokes's article with one of her own, stating that women need to support men seemingly at all costs. The logic in her rejoinder suggested that men were indeed castrated and emasculated. To her, the male revolution was intended "to defy that emasculation and grow new balls!" Telling black men to "take your rightful place ahead of me," Hambrick appeared to enable a masculinist hierarchy that was out of step with a growing effort to critique and challenge masculinist revolutionaries and to create equally fulfilling relationships.[114] Hambrick's position, however, was cultivated and urged in a number of ways. Aside from patriarchal partners, some groups circulated "Truth Posters" that pictured a black woman's profile with a bronze colored Afro above the statement: "I am the Black Woman, Mother of Civilization, Queen of the Universe. Through me the Black Man produces his Nation." On sale for $1.25, these images could be found in local bookstores, organizational meeting spaces, on college campuses and hung on bedroom walls.

Through the reassertion of black manhood, some men reinforced a gender hierarchy that handicapped black women. Though many male activists had been mentored by female radicals such as Queen Mother Audley Moore, Grace Lee Boggs, Shirley Graham Du Bois, and Abbey Lincoln,[115] many women were aware that activism did not always translate into respectful intimate relationships with black men. These gaps provided space for women to assert their own ideas about their family responsibility, their contribution to community organizing, and their opinions on the politics of affection, perspectives that coalesced into formal black feminist organizations toward the latter end of the decade.

Liberator subscribers might have juxtaposed its coverage of this debate with the growing sense of political independence that women throughout African society were seeking in this period. UN correspondent Yahne Sangare's essay praising African women provided a detailed view of African family life and customs. The explanation of matrilineal customs, village life and the pulse of the marketplace offered African American readers a deeper knowledge of everyday life in West African nations. In the context of growing identification with Africa as a core expression of black nationalism, the article served a dual purpose: to bring African lifestyles closer to African American's global consciousness and to provide a traditional definition of family and community that countered American sociological arguments about dysfunctional matriarchal black families. What is important is that the long article gave readers a sense of African women as political actors, thus demonstrating the capacity of female leadership. Sangare, an accomplished journalist–beauty model from Liberia, countered notions of African backwardness, instead revealing dynamic and complex traditional systems of government and familial relationships.[116]

Though accounts of her time in the United States differ, Sangare arrived in the United States initially with her father in 1955, returning again in 1966 with her husband, Louis Sangare of Mali, who was then completing a Ph.D. in economics. She received training in journalism in Switzerland and Paris. In Monrovia she was women's editor of one of the local newspapers and when she arrived in the United States, began making radio appearances on the Voice of America and publishing in U.S. government–controlled publications that featured stories on politics, fashion, and lifestyle in Africa.[117] Watts, who had obtained United Nation credentials as a correspondent for his magazine as well as for Jacques Verges's *Révolution Africaine*, seems to have used what little influence he had to attract Sangare to write for *Liberator*. In this way, he was able to keep some semblance of the original intent of the magazine—coverage of African liberation. However, hailing from U.S.-dominated Liberia, Sangare was a far cry from the type of radical women writer the magazine had attracted over the years. Nonetheless, she continued to publish stories on African women and African independence in the magazine intermittently throughout 1968–69. Though Sangare and female writers represented an attempt at a greater recognition of black women's thought, liberal policy wonks and government spokespersons seemed to willfully ignore the range of their ideas, lifestyles, and perspectives.

Curious Allies and Moynihan's Gordian Knot

In 1965, U.S. assistant secretary of labor Daniel P. Moynihan published an essay that purported to analyze the social predicament of urban black communities, with special focus on black family life. In what became known as the "Moynihan Report" or the "Moynihan thesis," *The Negro Family: The Case for National Action* essentialized African American family structures and froze them as matriarchal, fatherless, pathological entities while supposedly making a case for increased government attention.[118] Almost immediately, black women countered the report's assertions, and perceptively interpreted Moynihan's attempt to explain *their* problem as an absurd affront to the complexity of their lives. From their vantage point his explanation had come at their expense. Expectedly, the criticism and ire the report drew lasted well after its publication. Numerous formal and informal groups of black women met to discuss and refute the report. While many women in and around movement circles had already begun to develop a critical analysis of the social and economic forces affecting their lives, the Moynihan Report was but another example of the government distortion of black realities. Years after it was published, the specter of the report haunted virtually every public discussion of black family life, and especially that of black women. Moynihan would survive this debacle considering much of the animus toward his report came from black communities still clamoring for power.

Perhaps one of the least expected voices to weigh in on Moynihan's liberal paternalism was none other than Dan Watts himself. Watts's editorials tended to veer away from the current of thinking at times, while at other moments he stood in concert with the radical voices of the magazine's pages. Watts had grown increasingly cynical toward all forms of leadership. If asked, he may have even bemoaned the *Liberator*'s lack of sufficient impact. Yet his rather large ego motivated him to keep pounding the drum even if he chose to take an unpopular position. In the December 1965 issue of *Liberator*, Watts penned an editorial titled, "The Negro Is Obsolete." The editorial acknowledges changes in technology and infrastructure that would make conditions close to impossible for black people, especially the working classes, to thrive. As he had often done, Watts reserved his staunchest criticism for black leaders and communities themselves. The editorial opened with remarkable bombast: "The so-called american negro (nigrah or nigger for those who have difficulty with the word negro), is obsolete. In fact this pitiful product of 4 centuries of American racism and slavery is dead." He then resorted to a series of slights hurled at civil rights leaders who had convened in Washington the month prior attending the White House Conference on civil rights. Calling Dr. King the "Self-Annointed One," and A. Phillip Randolph the "Pullman Porter Chief," he reserved perhaps his basest discourtesy for Bayard Rustin, labeling the civil rights organizer "Madame Socrates." Watts had grown deeply dissatisfied with those leaders, a sentiment that increased following the March on Washington, which some *Liberator* writers called the "Farce on Washington." To his mind, they were content and well adjusted, "part of the game of hustling the man for more guilt money." Curiously enough, however, Watts's editorial praised Daniel P. Moynihan as "the one man at the conference possessing a possible blueprint for meaningful change."[119] Watts did not explain what Moynihan's program entailed in this editorial or later, but in this instance he seemed all too prepared to cozy up in rhetorical alliance with the liberal politician in ways that must have drawn the chagrin of those Watts intended to represent. It is unclear what Watts saw in Moynihan's understanding of the plethora of issues befalling black people. Yet, according to longtime associate Richard Gibson and his former wife, Marilyn Watts, Watts considered Moynihan a trustworthy liberal and perhaps a cordial adversary.[120]

Moynihan was well-known for speaking broadly about the need for more jobs at a time when the black working force eroded under the punitive traction of corporate globalization, otherwise known as deindustrialization. It is likely that the two met during the time that Moynihan ran an urban studies institute jointly established by Harvard and MIT in the mid-1960s. As evidenced by a 1966 CBS News Special, "Black Power/White Backlash" however, it is clear that the two knew each other. Moynihan referenced Dan Watts and Kwame Ture (Stokely Carmichael) in an answer to reporter Mike Wallace about urban rebellions. Moynihan expressed a shared understanding between himself and Watts, and also Carmichael, for that matter. He could admit the fact of urban rebellion as a response to brutality, neglect, and structural isolation, though he opposed violence toward the police or any governing agency. In Moynihan's view, Watts was a credible witness in this instance because of his Ivy League training (Watts graduated from Columbia University) and the fact that he had helped plan and build the international wing of Kennedy International Airport in New York in his days as an architect. That a former middle-class aspirant such as Watts had begun to cosign urban rebellion as an expected response to the structural violence of white supremacy affected Moynihan's sense of what black people needed. Though he seemed to understand the roots of this problem, he characteristically distanced himself from black activists' claims of revolution.[121] Moreover, as Stephen Steinberg has written, Moynihan's clever rhetoric and liberal maneuvering allowed policymakers, from the Johnson administration on down, an opportunity to shift blame away from the state and onto the shoulders of black people themselves.[122] If Watts intended to put stock in Moynihan's perspectives on the race problem, he was certain to come up empty. This was clearly one of Watts's more contradictory associations. Earlier he was providing moral and energetic support future leaders of African independence, and recruiting some of the most radical voices of black America to his magazine, and now he was cozying up with one of the chief architects of state-sponsored patriarchy.

Years later, Watts continued his inspired foray into the large topics of the day. As editor, he felt it his obligation to comment on whatever issue passed his desk. In May 1969, although he was not noted for his discussions of feminism and issues pertaining to women, Watts joined the debate over women's use of birth control and its potential impact on both female fertility choices and the African American community. His knack for drawing headlines was on full display. In a lead editorial boldly entitled, "Birth Control," Watts spoke of the systematic extermination of Native Americans, the diminishing value of black workers, and Japanese internment as warning signs of his fear that "white Americans will not hesitate to try and phase us out of the American scene." For Watts and many others, black people were already in a life and death struggle for survival. For years he had argued in favor of armed self-defense, for example, though it is uncertain whether or not he himself carried or owned a weapon. Since black folk were in a war "our safety, our survival literally depend [sic] on our ever increasing numbers," he argued. Echoing an argument radical thinker James Boggs had asserted in the *Monthly Review* and later in *Liberator*, Watts maintained that the concentration of African Americans in the urban centers of America could and perhaps should lead to increased control of these "Chocolate Cities."[123] Yet, by his count, African Americans had little time to waste. Haunted by professional setbacks and profoundly disgusted with liberalism (perhaps excluding Moynihan in this instance), Watts perceived that racial annihilation was not only possible but also imminent. Fueled by such logic, Watts argued: "For us to speak in favor of birth control for Afro-Americans would be comparable to speaking in favor of genocide. . . . So, if Black people are to survive," he argued adding emphasis to the point, "one of our best guarantees would be a more vigorous effort on our part to reproduce our own."[124] The reproduction argument served to be one of the most controversial issues the black feminist movement was forced to engage. Though Watts was a father by this time, he appeared way out of his league considering the politics of birth control. Most obviously was the seeming contradiction in his casting of this issue in black race survival terms considering he was the father of a biracial child. It would take a number of heated debates to clarify for concerned women and men that the practice of birth control was not a sacrifice of revolutionary principles but an essential feature of black women's efforts to achieve greater control over their lives.

If the title of Watts's editorial did not grab readers' attention as they passed the newsstand, passersby could not ignore the headline just below: "Has the Black Man Been Castrated?" These words hanging above a close-up photograph of a dark-skinned young black woman staring out from the page with an expressionless intensity left no doubts about its female issue-related content. In many ways, this was *Liberator* picking up where it left off following its writer's conference that featured women artists and activists. In a lengthy lead article, freelance writer Jean Carey Bond and Minnesota city planner Pat Peery penned what would become one of the seminal articles of the decade.[125] Bond and Peery argued plainly that black male emasculation was a myth. In one of the boldest and forthright critiques of the Moynihan thesis, they argued that white specialists had it all wrong and that many African Americans (including Watts) were wrong for buying the myth as fact. What boiled down to a rather negative gender blame-game could be attributed to the disappointing success of the myth.

Black men blamed black women for being domineering and therefore stripping them of manhood. Black women blamed black men for not protecting them from the onslaught of poverty, worsened by the economic opportunities available to black women, largely in the form of domestic work. Or so the argument went. Bond and Peery argued that rather than buy the myth "hook, line and sinker," all black people needed to do was analyze white society's continuous *attempts* at emasculation to see that black manhood and black people's humanity were still intact. In other words, social constraints on black life were mere indications of the strength of African American will. "The enduring manhood/humanity of Blacks, burning bright despite all efforts to extinguish it, is the nemesis of Western civilization," they wrote. Were black people really downtrodden and weakened, why the insatiable need for white individuals and institutions to control black life? "We contend that as a whole people," they maintained, "Afro-Americans lack neither spirit nor strength nor vigor, for it is they who have given this nation the only culture it has, the only humanity it has." If any one entity was responsible for black emasculation, it was capitalist America. Their textured feminist argument at once sought to rescue black women from an untenable indictment while also drawing on the themes of historic survival that reaffirmed the black liberation struggle.[126]

Moynihan's thesis was only "consistent and logical in racist terms," they argued, which gave rise to the mythical Black Matriarch, who embodied "a kind of folk character largely fashioned by whites out of half-truths and lies about the involuntary condition of Black women." In other words, the creation of the Black Matriarch was but another falsification and distortion of black life. Taking their thesis one-step further, they argued that rather than ask if the black male has been castrated, why not ponder the emasculation of white males? "Just who is the emasculated person in this society?" they asked. "Surely it is the white man, whose dazzling symbols of power—his goods, his technology—have all but consumed human essence. Yes, he is effective because his power enables him to rule; but he is emasculated in that he has become a mere extension of the things he produces." Here, Bond and Peery not only challenged the flawed theory of emasculation theorized by Moynihan, but they also challenged black males who bought that argument. Their analysis openly contradicted Watts's editorial. Perhaps, this was Watts in his editorial capacity attempting an open dialogue, his effort to provide readers with both sides of the issue. In any case, the Bond and Peery article was so effective that it attracted Toni Cade, who republished the article in her seminal anthology the following year.[127]

· · · · · ·

Sonia Sanchez's "A Poem for My Father" seemed a fitting segue into a new decade of debate regarding intimacy between black men and women. In this short poem published in *Liberator*, Sanchez was the observer of her father's appetite for "so many perfumed Black bodies weeping underneath" him and was saddened by what had become a routine. Her father's "makeshift manhood" was in fact a "deformity" leading him to take a sixth wife who was destined to meet the same fate as the previous five. In this poem Sanchez captured a triangular relationship between father, daughter and her father's companion, a scenario infrequently discussed in the much-debated issue of gender roles. From this vantage point readers were urged to question the potential impact her father's actions would have on her relationship choices. Concluding the poem thusly: "I guess that is why on meeting your sixth wife, I cross myself with her confessionals," Sanchez is painfully in solidarity with her father's women.[128] In a few short lines Sanchez demonstrated the complexity and dynamism of sisterhood.

By the end of 1969, *Liberator* articles on women were in short supply. However, one of the emergent voices that found a temporary publishing outlet in Watts's publication was Toni Cade Bambara. Her book and movie reviews as well as her short stories published in the magazine were at once an indication of an emerging literary talent, an affirmation of women's thinking and expression, and an assertion of political agency that would continue in various formal and informal ways through the mid-1970s. A look into Bambara's writings at the end of the decade is instructive to understanding the role of the magazine in the shaping of an intellectual community even in its declining years.

Critical Communities: Toni Cade Bambara's *Liberator* Writings

Under Watts's stewardship, the magazine continued to devote ample space to historical and cultural analysis as it had done throughout its career. As the movement began to spin further away from a discernable direction, Watts consistently editorialized that what was needed was a specific program. The search for a program for black material advancement remained just out of reach for black activists of Watts's generation. From his viewpoint this was the most important issue facing what was left of the movement. Watts was concerned with how African Americans could achieve effective political participation. Though black men were most often the ones holding forth in its pages, as I have shown, women around the magazine also played a no less significant part in the shaping of its political and cultural perspectives. Though the establishment of more formal feminist organizations emerged in 1968 and continued to flourish long after, *Liberator*'s coverage of women's issues and the publication of women writers was sparse by that year. Still, in addition to the writings of Toni Cade Bambara, Watts published Sonia Sanchez and Evelyn Rodgers Neal (who published an article on surgical methods in West Africa), and others for whom the magazine remained an indispensable space to circulate their work.

As we have seen, women were as eager as their male counterparts to determine a way forward. A clear difference, however, was in their search for internal answers as well as external ones. Whereas the male activists were chiefly concerned with state-sponsored violence and political invisibility, women activists often couched those concerns within a vocalized rebuking of the masculinist exclusions of women. One of the women writers who stood out in this regard was Toni Cade Bambara who published short stories and cultural analyses in the form of book and film reviews in *Liberator* from 1968 to 1970. Two of her short stories first published in the magazine were republished in her collection of fifteen short stories entitled, *Gorilla, My Love*.

Toni Cade Bambara's consistent publishing career began in the late 1960s and early 1970s, though she published her first piece, "Sweet Town," in 1959, at the age of twenty.[129] Between 1970 and 1977, she edited the seminal anthology *The Black Woman* (1970), and published *Tales and Stories for Black Folk* (1971), *Gorilla My Love* (1972), and *The Sea Birds Are Still Alive* (1977). By the early 1970s, Bambara had established herself as a dependable and fierce literary voice among a tradition of black writers. Indeed, by the time *The Salt Eaters* was published in 1980, Bambara had etched her place among the pantheon of legendary community-centered writers and thinkers. Her work influenced a number of feminist scholar-activists. One clear example is Barbara Smith's anthology *Homegirls* (1983), which clearly owed a great deal to the space first carved by *The Black Woman*. With its focus on the dynamics of black female sexuality, it can be said that *Homegirls* extended conversations about black women's lives that began in *The Black Woman*. What is important is that the critical attention paid to sexism and sexual politics in Bambara's text inspired the multifaceted analysis of homophobia and black lesbian politics in the black community that are on display in *Homegirls*. Bambara (known only as Toni Cade at this time) was developing her voice on the page with greater effectiveness in this period and had composed work for *Liberator* as well as *Negro Digest/Black World*, among other periodicals in this period.

Writing in *Liberator* in 1968, Bambara published a short story entitled "The Manipulators" (August issue) and two book reviews; one of Austin Clarke's *The Meeting Point* and another of Joseph Viertal's *Monkey on a String* (November and December, respectively). In the first, Bambara presented a narrative of young, graduate-school-aged black women conversing about the different ways they had to manipulate circumstances with their youthfulness, wit and beauty to ensure both their personal safety and their academic success in order to maintain their humanity and self-esteem. Having just completed graduate studies in 1965, Bambara seemed to be reflecting on her own experiences through the young women in the story.

Aside from Larry Neal and Clayton Riley, few literary critics of the period seemed as at home with nationalist and transnationalist ideas about community and political vision without sacrificing their craft than Bambara. Her commitment to community justice was demonstrated in another review she wrote for the July 1970 issue of *Liberator*. Fixing her critical gaze on the semiautobiographical novel *Defender of the Angels* (1969), which was based on the experiences of a retired black police officer named Jess Kimbrough, this review is telling of Bambara's attention to, and compassion for, all aspects of black life. Referring to the dearth of information on African American police officers she wrote, "On Black cops we haven't got much and that's too bad." Though she was quite aware and sensitive to state violence at the hands of police officers, she was also critical of the offhanded dismissal of black police officers as mere agents of the state. She wrote: "We've fallen into dangerous thinkin' that a cop or a university teacher or Madison Avenue ad man or Pentagon janitor or most anybody who ain't doin' what we're doin' is necessarily a Tom, or in current coin, a counter-revolutionary, and therefore an anathema." She wanted to give readers a more nuanced interpretation of officers as people, writing, "In day-to-day life, a Black cop can save a Black life, can protect us from a white cop, a white gun . . . and probably has more often than we know." Although this may be perceived as naïveté at first glance, Bambara briefly explained her disgust at "the sort of things that currently plague us—infiltrating agents, bloods participating in the murder of Panthers and such like," which could mean either that even the cop's story deserved to be heard, or that he too was a part of the destructive forces debilitating African American communities and corrupting their political efforts.[130] As evidenced by her positions, Bambara was not an ideologue. She was a pragmatic black female transnationalist who was able to keep her eye on what was possible without losing sight of her present reality. She appreciated the complexities that comprised black life rather than expecting black communities to conform to or perform certain expected roles.

On May 27, 1971, *Third World News*, a student-run paper at the University of California, Santa Barbara campus, published an article on Bambara who had recently visited the university to participate in a campus celebration of Black Family Day. Bambara's stardom among the students was evident. "How does one describe Toni Cade Bambara?" asked student writer, Tansey Thomas. "I can say dynamic energetic and vivacious intellectual fountain of information. Also, classy, shapely, petite and good looking—a sister whose got her head and everything else together and Toni is described."[131] Bambara, who was a professor of English at Rutgers University at the time inspired a number of female activists, her intellectual acumen, and her conceptualization of critical community work drew admiration from many. Moreover, people who came into contact with her were undoubtedly impressed with her passion and conviction. Bambara held forth on a number of topics, both individual and communal, inspiring those in her company during her stay. Over the course of two days, Bambara "rapped" about black preschools and nursery schools, the future of Equal Opportunity Programs at colleges and universities throughout the country, black women's organizations, black parenting, and media images of African Americans. Bambara's idea of community relationships and preschool-to-college education comprised much of her political vision. Through her emphasis on autonomy, determination, sacrifice and responsibility, central tenets of Black Nationalist thought, it was clear that these were not merely clichéd concepts in Bambara's work. They were themes by which she lived her life.

Conclusion

Liberator was not known as a space that appealed to black and some white women radicals exclusively. However, women held forth on the top political and cultural concerns of the day in its pages. As had many of the male-led organizations of the era, the women's issue was deemed important only as far as it was second to the primary concern of rescuing black masculinity from the dustbin of American capitalism. Those kinds of blind spots and often intentionally narrow politics were not lost on the radical black women who began using the space of this periodical to express concerns and to galvanize public opinion on issues that pertained to them, their children, their friend's children, their communities, and the formal and informal institutional spaces they navigated. A reappraisal of the impact of women on the periodical reveals that these women's analyses located anti-imperialism and antiracism at the center of their gender critique. Women writing in *Liberator* provided a keen sense that radical theorizing and community struggle was not simply the domain of the revolutionary man, no matter the providential perception men had of their own work. Nor was women's work merely that of caretaker and behind-the-scenes organizer and strategist. Oftentimes it was all of these and more. The writings, political activities, and the biographies of the women who saw in the magazine an opportunity to advance their own ideas, reveal that there was virtually no space in the liberation struggle where women were not a critical part. Black women writing in *Liberator* shared the heady intellectual work and the heavy community protest work in equal measure. Their radical commitments vehemently opposed the spatial isolation of the ghetto, segregated education, and narrow articulations of nationalism. These women showed prescribed gender roles as eminent from attempts to maintain power though this was often overshadowed by the rhetoric of tradition. By the 1970s, black women radicals had built on the work of earlier generations and continued to organize collectives; issue demands on the state for recognition of diverse structures of identity, family, and community; and directly challenge the intransigence of many black male leaders who clung to an exclusive notion of nurturing ("You take care of the kids, we'll do the politics") as women's work. Such views and approaches would be dismantled by such formations as the New Rochelle Group, the Third World Women's Alliance, and the Combahee River Collective, to name a few in existence throughout the 1960s and 1970s. They demonstrate, much like the women who held forth on *Liberator*'s pages, that not only does "revolution start with the self," as Toni Cade once put it, but that women and men had an equal ability (and responsibility) to challenge the discourses and discipline of white supremacy on all fronts.

4 Rebellion or Revolution
The Challenge of Black Radicalism

> Black Nationalism in America lapses into romantic and escapist moods so long as it depends on emotional slogans, the messianic complex for a leader, or empty militant aggressiveness. Nationalism the world over is being expressed and must be expressed through economic, political, and cultural institutions to make them conform to nationalist aspirations. That these questions are not understood among Negroes is more than obvious. But the ability of the Negro movement to proceed beyond its present impasse depends on the solutions to these problems.
>
> —Harold Cruse, "Rebellion or Revolution, II" (1964)

Maintaining a handle on the tempo of African American, Afro-diasporic, and Africa liberatory energies was no small task. While numerous world events, notably the Vietnam War, loomed large over this period of political activities, African independence remained at the center of *Liberator*'s perspective toward global solidarity. Though uneven and often difficult to predict, African nations' efforts to thwart colonialism gained persistent support from the magazine's crusading, aggressive style of journalistic commentary. Coupled with its attention to the racial and class oppression faced by U.S.-based African descendants, the magazine's writer-activists amplified the contours of an internationalist-oriented black radicalism. In the mid-1960s, *Liberator* matured as a critical site of news, information, and analysis. It tackled as many of the major issues, campaigns, and personalities of the day as necessary to its relevance.

Alongside Dan Watts's furious efforts to establish broad circulation for the *Liberator* and Pete Beveridge's passionate consistency to the cause, the timely additions of Askia Touré, Larry Neal, Harold Cruse, and others to the core staff of writers would help catalyze the magazine into a periodical regarded with high esteem in these years. Cruse would emerge as a major theorist of black revolutionary thought in this period, though he, like most, posed more questions than answers to the challenges of black liberation. His discomfort with the organizational approaches taken by both civil rights and radical groups fueled Cruse's efforts to develop fierce, unapologetic, and often-scathing critiques of any and every one claiming justice work as their vocation. *Liberator*'s pivotal role in advancing debates, staging panels, and above all publishing a monthly magazine demonstrates the sheer amount of energy devoted to black radical futures, and yet it also reveals how deeply contested definitions and practices of radicalism were in this period.

Pete Beveridge would play a signature role in figure prominently in the first half of *Liberator*'s run. Though he helped establish the magazine with Watts, by 1965 he had left the editorial staff due to growing tensions in the liberation movement concerning the reliability of interracial alliances. His departure resulted in the placing of all aspects of the magazine's production under the direction of Watts. The middle years of the 1960s also witnessed other shifts that would impact *Liberator*'s diverse clientele of supporters and associates, if not its reputation. Ossie Davis and James Baldwin, early associates who supplied the periodical with moral support and institutional credibility, would eventually sever ties as a result of growing controversy surrounding the magazine's hard-charging radicalism. Their relationship with the periodical indicates the ways *Liberator* sometimes strained friendships, and drew the scorn of critics, often as a result of its unpopular (and sometimes unwieldy) positions. At the same time, it was one of the few outlets for both up-and-coming radical authors and seasoned activists who were critical of the political mainstream represented by civil rights leaders and disenchanted with or distrustful of the Communist Party, even as it can be viewed as part of a New Left milieu. In this way, *Liberator* crafted a unique black radical politics that at times converged with and diverged from the radical perspectives available in this period.

In some ways the arc of James Baldwin's association with *Liberator* is instructive of the trajectory of the magazine during the mid-1960s, when its momentum steadied. Baldwin's return to the United States was just in time to be reenlisted in the social justice struggle. Having been an associate of the magazine at its inception, Baldwin later distanced himself from *Liberator* and its main staff writers amidst charges of anti-Semitism leveled at the magazine. Though that controversy hampered the magazine's public reception for a moment, it did not derail the magazine's significant articles on black nationalism and black peoples' economic development by well-known political commentators such as Harold Cruse and less known but equally capable writers such as C. E. Wilson. By the end of the decade, many of the magazine's writers would find themselves looking for other outlets, though for myriad different reasons.

These years would also prove especially significant for Cruse as he utilized the *Liberator* network to publish his tour de force, *Crisis of the Negro Intellectual*, the book that would define his legacy. In it he leveled his heaviest criticism against black leadership, especially those on the left. *Liberator*, its editors and staff, also drew Cruse's scorn. *Liberator*'s iconoclastic politics made it a natural fit for Cruse for a time, though in his search for a successfully autonomous radical politics, the periodical, like all others, fell far short of his vision. Cruse's other important collection, *Rebellion or Revolution?*, an assemblage of his writing on African American politics and culture dating from the early 1960s, included articles that he had first introduced in *Liberator*.

Malcolm X's political evolution also loomed large in this period, significantly influencing the publication. Malcolm's separation from the Nation of Islam in 1964 was intriguing for many and portended his broader political engagement with the civil rights movement. His assassination a year later, however, left many—especially radicals—angered and disillusioned. The founding of the short-lived Organization of Afro-American Unity (OAAU), Amiri Baraka's Black Arts Repertory and Theater School (BARTS), the radicalization of Student Nonviolent Coordinating Committee (SNCC) and the Congress on Racial Equality (CORE), and the emergence of the Revolutionary Action Movement (RAM) comprise significant organizational signposts for the flowering of black radicalism in this period. *Liberator* writers were equal partners in these struggles to articulate and activate black radical politics. Not content with merely expressing their dissent from the mainstream, these writers searched diligently for an analysis of structural changes that would undermine racism and colonialism in the United States and abroad.

・・・・・・

In January of 1963 the Liberation Committee for Africa incorporated as the Afro-American Research Institute, nearly two years after it circulated its "Liberation" pamphlet denouncing U.S. complicity in Lumumba's assassination. That the *New York Times* would publish such an announcement in perhaps indicative of the lingering attention paid the organization following the 1961 UN disruption.[1] The organizational name and structure changed but the radical outlook and content it began to fashion remained. Over the next the four years, *Liberator* would prove to be a defining voice of black radical politics and culture.

As a collective of thinkers engaged in both political and cultural (but not necessarily popular) discourse, *Liberator* writers exemplify what Grant

Farred calls the vernacular intellectual tradition.[2] Farred's description of vernacular practices informs my discussion of the role of the *Liberator* magazine as a site of critical dialogue concerning the strategies of black liberation politics. Yet the black radicals who defined the period were not merely intellectuals. Many were also cultural producers, namely, critics, playwrights, novelists, poets, singers, musicians, vocational education specialists, public school educators, and in Watts's case, even architects. Nearly all *Liberator* associates had day jobs, as the magazine was never in a position to financially compensate writers for their submissions or energy spent circulating the magazine around New York City.

These writer-activists combined both politics and culture in a practice of antiracist, anticolonialist, and antiwestern intellectual discourse and activism. As Farred writes, such intellectuals "vernacularize. [They] explore and explicate the links between the popular and the political. [They] never underestimate the capacity of the popular to elucidate the ideological, to animate the political, [they] never overlook the vernacular as a means of producing a subaltern or postcolonial voice that resists, subverts, disrupts, reconfigures or impacts the dominant discourse."[3] Though he employs language commonly found in postcolonial studies,[4] his description is useful in examining the relationship between culture and politics, as demonstrated by the *Liberator* staff writers and the social milieu in which they operated. Moreover, it draws attention to the very political culture the magazine grew out of and helped to shape. As Farred asserts, "Within the terms of the vernacular, no minority or anticolonial struggle can be sustained if it does not contain in it a cultural element."[5] Indeed, Farred's description helps contextualize the political nature of cultural work, highlighting the dialectic between theory and praxis that fueled the political labors of many black radicals. *Liberator*'s brand of what can be called political expressive culture adds to the understanding of how the *Liberator* emerged in this period as a formidable site of radical Black Arts politics and arts criticism.

James Baldwin, Harold Cruse, and *Liberator*: Allies into Adversaries

The *Liberator* began 1963 with an unsigned editorial, likely written by Beveridge, announcing the nationwide expansion of the magazine's distribution. Liberator's print number of 15,000 may have seemed small, but its impact and reputation were far outpacing concerns about circulation. Watts tirelessly advocated for the magazine, using his editorial page as a bully pulpit, while planning and speaking on a number of panels and conferences. Transforming the magazine from a local outfit addressing the concerns of a loose collective of radicals to a nationally circulating publication would require a lot of support.

It is important that the magazine was deemed valuable enough that it could assemble an advisory board that included local and national radical and left luminaries, including Ossie Davis, Richard B. Moore, Lewis Michaux, George B. Murphy, Selma V. Sparks, and former Garveyite, Hugh Mulzac. Of all these figures, perhaps none were as nationally renowned as James Baldwin, who was listed on the magazine's advisory board up to June 1966. The cover of the 1963 centennial issue displayed a close-up photo of Baldwin looking intensely in the direction of the camera shot. Above his right shoulder were the words, "Not 100 Years of Freedom," marking the title of Baldwin's article in this issue, and signaling to readers the continuation of African Americans' struggle for justice in the ten decades since the signing of the Emancipation Proclamation.[6] At the height of the civil rights movement, two years after the Freedom Rides and one year after the Supreme Court ordered the University of Mississippi to desegregate, African Americans wanted to remind the American mainstream of its captivity. Baldwin, who by this time was arguably the most important and widely known African American writer having eclipsed Ralph Ellison and Richard Wright,[7] began the article with a personal reflection of the meaning of the hundred-year anniversary of the Emancipation Proclamation. "I myself do not feel that the nation has anything to celebrate this year—certainly not one hundred years of Negro Freedom," he wrote. "Rather, I feel that we should use this year, which so harshly illuminates our failure either to end the Civil War or to recognize the Negro as a human being, as an opportunity to take a delicate and arduous inventory."[8] Baldwin, ever holding up a mirror to the country, suggested that America take a long, close look at itself.

Like many avid black internationalists of his day, having participated in the Negro Writers conferences of the late 1950s, he located African Americans' struggle for dignity and rights in the context of the struggles around the world.[9] As did a host of other homegrown activists, he wanted the government to honor African Americans' right to live free as human beings. "Is it too radical to hope that a statement can come from the White House saying, flatly, that desegregation is right and that ignorance, violence, and bloodshed are wrong?" he asked. Baldwin's words captured the sentiments of many. Why was it so difficult for the government to protect the lives of its African derived citizenry? Baldwin contrasted the rhetoric of progress with America's unwillingness to change, and argued that the country lacked the courage to deal with the demand of the moment to change.

A towering literary figure of his time and product of Harlem, Baldwin was well versed in the literary and political culture of New York City. Baldwin lent his name to *Liberator*'s advisory board throughout the first seven years of the magazine, though it is not clear if he had any specified role in the magazine's production.[10] Baldwin had previously spoken at events sponsored by the magazine's parent organization, the Liberation Committee for Africa, as early as 1961. He was scheduled to speak at a Negro History Week event at St. Luke's Church in Harlem in February 1963, which was also sponsored by the Liberation Committee for Africa (LCA), but writer Carlos Goncalves and literary comet Lorraine Hansberry spoke instead.[11] It is interesting that, for all of the early support Baldwin provided the LCA, the only article he published in the magazine was, "Not 100 Years of Freedom." Though he was an early supporter of the magazine, by 1966, a controversy over a series on black-Jewish relations written by Eddie Ellis would strain Baldwin's ties to the periodical. Nonetheless, throughout the remainder of that year, Baldwin or his writings and public speeches would continue to be the subject of debate, evaluation, and critique by *Liberator* writers and subscribers.[12]

Eddie Ellis was an original member of the New York chapter of the Black Panther Party and former Harlem Youth Unlimited (HARYOU) staff worker.[13] It appears his article was intended to provide a thoughtful if critical analysis of the resentment brewing between African Americans and Jews, with a focus on Harlem. Yet, the tone of the articles he composed—indeed, the tone of the *Liberator* generally—was decidedly provocative and unapologetic. As a forewarning, he penned a short article to announce the series and provided an explanation of his reasons for initiating "a discussion of Semitism in the ghettoes," which appeared as a three-part series in January, February, and April 1966. The series was Ellis's and, perhaps, Watts's attempt to publicly discuss the resentment developing between African Americans and their Jewish neighbors and no doubt provoke debate no matter the cost.

In January 1966 the series began with Ellis explaining a general sense of distrust that increased as a result of the recent killing of an unarmed black man named Nelson Erby by a white policeman named Sheldon Liebowitz. Though a case was brought against the officer, the grand jury found that he had "acted in justifiable self-defense." To worsen matters, the Shomrin Society, a Jewish fraternal organization within the New York Police

Rev. Albert Cleage, Man of the Year, *Liberator*, December 1963. Courtesy of Pete Beveridge.

Department, shortly thereafter named the presiding judge "Shomrin Man of the Year" in November 1965. From Ellis's vantage point this was high-level collusion that warranted public criticism and protest. Such events overshadowed Jewish solidarity with civil rights struggles. It was but a short step to connect such incidents to a history of economic control and political powerlessness.

Many people perceived the Jewish community to be complicit in the economic colonialism that black people felt was practiced at their expense, an issue Ellis took up in the second part of the series in February. Contentiously, in this segment of the series he sought to distance African Americans from any guilty feelings regarding the Holocaust. "Black people did not build or operate the labor camps . . . or operate the concentration camps," he contended. Therefore, it followed that "if there are any people free of guilt on the Jewish question, it is the Afro-American." In April, the third part of the series appeared and identified several Jewish foundations that underwrote the activity of the major civil rights organizations. According to Eills, this example of economic control over black political agency at once spoke to African American economic dependence and fertilized the need for political and social autonomy. In his view black people did not even control the defense of their own civil rights.

The Ellis series is indicative of several turning points in the liberation movement as a whole in this period. On the one hand, African American radicals were engaged in a general reevaluation of the roles whites would play in and around black organizations. On the other hand, black activists who had worked or had personal relationships with whites began to reconsider these relationships as part of the imperative of an increased awareness of one's black heritage. At the same time, for many people, the lived experience between African Americans and Jews was generally one of tension and distrust, even though there were plenty of examples of interracial marriage, especially on the left and a long history of Jewish membership in civil rights organizations. As far as personal examples stand, Dan Watts was married to a Jewish woman of Russian heritage.[14] These facts did little to curtail the magazine's critique of Jewish-black relations, however.

On February 28, 1967, *New York Times* reporter Homer Bigart penned a column announcing changes to the *Liberator* advisory board. The article "Baldwin Leaves Negro Monthly," announced the formal and final separation of Baldwin and Ossie Davis from the magazine.[15] The article explains the departure of the two cultural and political stars as a result of the magazine's alleged anti-Semitism stemming from the Ellis article series. That

Baldwin chose that moment to distance himself is ironic considering his own outspokenness on the so-called Jewish Question that put him at odds with many intellectuals and writers, black and white, at various points in his career. According to biographer Herb Boyd, who dedicates a full chapter in his work to Baldwin's associations, confrontations, and perspectives on black-Jewish interactions, Baldwin was at times empathetic and at other times scathing in his recollection of personal interactions with Jews. This issue is arguably one of the defining aspects of Baldwin's legacy as a writer and social philosopher. According to Boyd, the Ellis series was a turning point in Baldwin's struggle with the Jewish Question as it forced him to apply greater nuance in his analysis of such ethnic tensions.[16]

For his part, Ossie Davis submitted a letter to be published in *Liberator* stating the reasons for the separation and fully disclosing his dissatisfaction with the anti-Semitism series. Watts, however, refused to publish it, stating in an interview that he was not going to let Davis and Baldwin disassociate themselves from the controversy so easily. "Now I refused to publish the two letters of protest that Mr. Ossie Davis and James Baldwin wanted me to publish on the grounds of principle," he argued in an interview, indicating that their protest to the series stemmed from pressure from the American Jewish Committee. He continued stating in an expectedly stubborn manner: "But under no circumstances was I going to rescue James Baldwin and Ossie Davis from the Jewish community wrath because Baldwin and Davis and people like that—they have made it and they have not turned back one penny, one dime to the black community to help their brothers and this was the reason why I refused to publish their articles."[17] Watts's stance on Baldwin and Davis partially stemmed from his impatience with accepted civil rights leadership. Although these two stars of the Harlem community and American cultural landscape had provided support to Watts's efforts to distribute an alternative view on black liberation, Watts exhibited little tolerance for their efforts to distance themselves in the face of controversy. A man of Watts's personality relished the conflict.

A year earlier, Ruby Dee and Ossie Davis graced the cover of the Negro History Week issue of the magazine and its editors wrote glowingly about them and their contribution to the arts. Praising Davis's 1961 play, *Purlie Victorious*, and even quoting lines from it, the *Liberator* celebrated Dee and Davis for their black pride. And for the December 1963 issue, Davis sat for an interview with staff writer Charlie Russell.[18] The anti-Semitism series (it was entitled "Semitism and the Black Ghetto" but described what he perceived as "anti-Semitism" in Harlem), however, challenged Davis's support for the magazine. Though Watts refused to publish Davis's letter, the longtime radical journal *Freedomways*, then edited by former LCA associate John Henrik Clarke, was willing to do so. In the letter, Davis wrote that he felt the series "went beyond the bounds of Black nationalism."[19] Davis, who had long considered himself a Black Nationalist, thought the article failed to critique structures of exploitation that communities like Harlem suffered under but instead used the Jewish community as a scapegoat.[20]

Baldwin was quoted in the *New York Times* article saying Watts's decision to publish the series was "incredibly naïve." Ultimately, Ossie Davis asserted: "I felt it was racist and said so to the editor, a man whom I still respect, Dan Watts. But 'Semitism in the Ghetto' blows it for me, but good and definitely."[21] It is important to note that Watts, the magazine's editor in chief, though considered by many to be a curmudgeon, had a very generous publishing policy. This is not to excuse his axe grinding of issues relating to Jewish Americans, however. Known for his intransigence, Watts was quoted saying, "The object of my publishing the articles, was hopefully, to start a dialogue between Jewish leaders and the black community. The chief exploiters in the black ghetto are the Jewish merchants and landlords."[22] Though he stood by these and other comments, he was by no means alone in expressing such views. This was a popular line of critique that circulated with great frequency among those with nationalist proclivities, and who questioned existing power relationships governing urban communities. Some would later fine tune their analyses or recant them altogether, but Watts was hardly the lone voice on this issue.

Yet, Watts's personal anguish over this issue probably stemmed from his interracial marriage, which seemed to contradict his staunch defense of militant black political agency and must have weighed heavily upon him. As Muhammad Ahmad recalled, Watts's marriage kept many young radicals from developing a closer relationship with Watts even as he, unlike many of his generation, sought and took seriously their perspectives on black political struggle.[23] This incident was forever burnished into Watts's memory, and affected the legacy of the magazine. Writing in the spring of 1969—roughly two years after the series—he recalled the conflict in a lengthy editorial where he expressed his contempt for black and white forms of liberalism and provided a play-by-play account of the episode.[24] Labeling both Davis and Baldwin "house negroes," he argued that they saved their careers at the expense of a truthful dialogue about black-Jewish relations. He asserted that "a lot of 'good brothers' were being squeezed by publishers, producers and editors" who objected to the Ellis series, leaving some black writers to pressure Watts into retracting the articles. Watts, who was by nature intransigent and blusterous, would not budge. In his mind, pressure from the Jewish community was the chief reason many of the more famous writers ceased their relationship to the publication. The lone exception, Watts indicated, was Langston Hughes.[25] Watts believed that the magazine's penchant for discussing controversial issues inspired the attack on the magazine, which he took personally. As such, he would continue to fight the good fight regardless of anyone he had alienated or offended. He was not he concerned with the bridges that turned to ash as a result of his crusading brand of journalism.[26] It should also be pointed out that Watts had also spoken about the historic oppression of the Jews. In the editor's note to an earlier article discussing whether Germany would gain nuclear weaponry, Watts wrote, "I believe it is important for us to remember the horrors of the concentration camps and gas ovens which the efficient Nordic supermen used for the extermination of 6 million Jews."[27]

Ellis's articles on anti-Semitism among black urbanites should be viewed in this context of freethinking black political expression, which was held in high regard by *Liberator* contributors and readers alike. The *Liberator* series is indicative of that sentiment. Yet the debate had actually started years before. The radical historian and *Liberator* advisory board member Richard B. Moore penned an article in the July 1963 issue, entitled, "Criticism Is Not Anti-Semitism," in which he lent support to Selma Sparks's articles on discrimination in the Jewish-led International Ladies Garment Workers Union. In a vein similar to that taken by Baldwin and others, Moore sought to focus on the issue of discrimination rather than charges of anti-Semitism. Rather than belabor the distinctive histories and experiences shared by African Americans, Puerto Ricans, and Jews in New York City, Moore sought to use the occasion to raise the question of whether a sense of common struggle could be fashioned out of the particular ethnic history of each group. "We should all recall and reflect deeply upon the atrocious repression and wholesale massacre of Jews in Hitler's Nazi Germany. Similarly, we should ponder upon the frightful lynchings and mass murders which have been perpetuated against Afro-Americans in this country . . . obviously then, unity of all oppressed minority groups, classes and peoples is their only sure hope for salvation and liberation."[28] In the August issue of that year, a writer named C. Black (likely one of Watts's pseudonyms) noted that the charge of anti-Semitism was an aggressive weapon used against black people "to avoid dealing with problems of common interest, housing, education, political appointments, [and] city services."[29]

Several scholars have examined historical relationships and points of contention between the two groups, often highlighting that African Americans and Jews have had a long history of interaction, sometimes as allies and at other times as adversaries. In the heated atmosphere of the late 1960s, these tensions were heightened due to the exigencies of the day.[30] Again, Baldwin's departure from the *Liberator* on this issue is somewhat ironic considering that he himself, as a Five College Consortium professor at the University of Massachusetts, Amherst, and affiliated institutions, would be at the center of a controversy concerning the historic relationship between black and Jews in the mid-1980s.[31] It is interesting that this controversy came over a decade after Baldwin edited a book that sought to address and ameliorate tensions between Americans of African and Jewish ancestry.[32]

Watts regularly offered space to the letters to the editor that were compiled in the final pages of each issue, and he often published his own responses or the responses from the author of the article that the letter referenced. In this way he encouraged open community engagement with the relevant and often controversial ideas cast in the periodical. One of the letters to the editor that Watts published appeared in July under the heading, "Anti-Semitism in the Black Ghetto." It was not written in response to the Ellis series, but rather to Baraka's incendiary poem, "Black Art," which was published in the January 1966 issue, the first appearance of one of the poet's most memorable work.[33] The author of the letter, Frank Smith, who was writing from California, suggested that Baraka reconsider the language in the poem that depicted Jews, for fear that its hostile stance be used "as a pretext for discrediting you and the struggle that all true libertarians are engaged in, namely to end the reign of the white power structure and bring about the dawn of a New Day."[34] Throughout the remainder of the year, *Liberator* seemed to have escaped the vitriol that would come as a result of the Semitism series, as no other letters to the editor were published in response that year.

In May 1967, Watts published a letter from a New York City reader named Umoja Kwanguvu, whose response to the Semitism series cut to the core of the matter. He wrote: "As for most of the inmates (voluntary and involuntary) of the black ghettos, their feelings aren't really anti-Semitic, but anti-exploitation and anti-domination which are not any more plausible just because they are kosher."[35] Though Baldwin's arc from ally and advisor to adversary shows how charged racial politics were, he was hardly the only intellectual concerned with openly debating interracial alliances. Harold E.

Cruse, the equally controversial theorist of black nationalism, also wrestled with this issue throughout his writing career.

In his tour de force, *Crisis of the Negro Intellectual*, Harold Cruse came down hard on the *Liberator* for a variety of reasons, with a central point of his criticism being its alleged lack of ideological coherence.[36] Yet perhaps the writer Carlos Russell's recollection is more palatable in evaluating the impact of the magazine than Cruse's boldfaced dismissal of the publication and its crew. As a longtime member and staff writer, he argued that the *Liberator* was "eclectic."[37] By this he meant that though they all shared the commitment to black liberation, its writers consisted of people of divergent backgrounds, experiences, motives, aspirations, and ideological perspectives. Their coherence came through a commitment to first understand the transnational situations black people faced and their sharing of an acceptance of the responsibility to black liberation struggle through a commitment to antiracism, anti-imperialism, and deep critiques of capitalism. The resulting eclecticism was arguably its most significant attribute as it called into focus the diversity of black radical thought among activists and intellectuals in this period, although in the heat of a raging movement for justice, this may have been a nuisance for some. As the publication grew in popularity throughout movement circles and at bookshops, it thereby attracted more up-and-coming writers.

As mentioned, many of the writers in *Liberator*'s heyday, including Amiri Baraka, Larry Neal, and Askia Touré, would become major theorists of the ensuing Black Power/Black Arts Movement. These figures played increasingly significant roles in affirming and emphasizing African Americans' nonwestern cultural heritage and values.[38] What is important is that their work in many ways reflected and extended Harold Cruse's call for cultural revolution. For Cruse, culture provided the soil on which liberatory politics would emerge. Cultural institutions would not only reflect black aesthetics, they also would protect and reinforce the desires and political vision of autonomy and independence. Highlighting some of the generational differences that surfaced among *Liberator* staff, Askia Touré commented, "Larry and I were 'young Turks' working with our elders. So from time to time minor differences would occur, as in any family."[39] Touré, for example, published a number of influential articles employing ideas from Cruse's writings, but also developing his own analyses. These include, "The New Afro-American Writer," published in October 1963; "Toward Repudiating Western Values," published in November 1964; "Afro-American Youth and the Bandung World," published in February 1965; and "Malcolm X: International Statesman," in February 1966. These articles highlight Touré's contribution to the internationalism at the heart of black radical politics among younger activists in this period. In 1964, Touré had written to John Henrik Clarke asking whether his report on the National Afroamerican Student Conference would be published in *Freedomways*. Clarke does not seem to have been able to convince his associate editors to publish the piece, replete as it was with denunciations of "Bourgeois Reformists" who failed to see black people as "colonial subjects or slaves," as opposed to "second-class citizens." Touré's attacks on existing civil rights organizations may have been a bit too heavy-handed for *Freedomways* but it is a clear indication of important transitions that underscored changing attitudes.

Touré's report from the Nashville convening summarized speeches made by Max Stanford, Donald Freeman, Obi Wali, of the Pan African Student Organization in America, and Len Fraser Jr., of the Angolan Refugee Rescue Committee. According to Touré, the conference left attendees with four essential points: (1) bourgeois reformism (their description of civil rights efforts) must be repudiated; (2) African descendants in the United States should openly espouse "Pan-African Socialism" or "Revolutionary Black Nationalism" as their philosophy; (3) they should adopt former NAACP leader Robert F. Williams as "the leader of militant Afroamerican youth"; and (4) there should be black solidarity with revolutions in Africa, Latin America, and Asia.[40]

While ambitious in scope, this platform would largely remain the operating outlook of small collectives of radicals than the governing vision of a general black community. These issues would be hotly contested in the weeks, months, and years following the student conference. Though he had almost single-handedly influenced a host of young radicals, the figure at the center of nearly every dispute concerning black nationalism was Harold Cruse. Despite his disagreements with Dan Watts, Cruse offered penetrating analyses on the state of African American progress and published several seminal articles in *Liberator* from 1963 to 1964. His three-part series, "Rebellion or Revolution?," was published from October 1963 to January 1964. In this series Cruse called for a cultural revolution in which black people would acquire ownership of the American cultural communication infrastructure, "i.e. films, theatres, radio and television, music performing and publishing." Most nationalists, including Malcolm X, promoted a similar desire as critical to liberation and power. This, Cruse argued, was the only way that African Americans could move the struggle from a civil rights–based rebellion to a full-fledged revolution. As had occurred in revolutions throughout the Third World, the revolutionists seized ownership of the communication technologies. Cruse held that the same would be required of revolutionary-minded African Americans fighting for freedom in the United States.

In the November 1963 issue he wrote an article entitled, "Third Party: Facts and Forecasts," which analyzed the viability of forming an all-black political party and the possible effects on the American political landscape. "The Roots of Black Nationalism" was published in two parts in March and April 1964. Cruse also penned the two-part series, "Marxism and the Negro," in May and June of that year. And his last series, "The Economics of Black Nationalism" was published in July and August. In these articles, Cruse attempted to provide a critical appraisal of the movement as a whole, both thematically and systematically. He also intended to give the black intellectual community a historical context of its predicament. Cruse's *Liberator* analyses of American society and black liberation formed the skeletal structure of his book, *Rebellion or Revolution?*[41] Yet his experiences working as a staff writer for the *Liberator* would form the basis of his discussion of the magazine in *The Crisis of the Negro Intellectual*, wherein he offered a highly charged historical analysis of the shortcomings of all black leadership.[42]

Though Cruse's *Liberator* contacts made *Crisis* possible, in the book he nonetheless excoriated the publication as a journalistic example of the failure of the movement as a whole.[43] According to Cruse, until the movement could resolve such questions as, "What is integration? What is nationalism? What is Marxist Communism, and how does it relate to the first two ideas?," the *Liberator* could not offer a program or direction of its own. Moreover, he claimed that the magazine did not maximize its ability to clarify these questions even while publishing Cruse's own theoretical work.[44] Ironically, his articles attempted to tackle the very questions he posed in the *Crisis*. And though these issues were discussed at great length, many of the questions remained.

By basing his critique of the magazine on Beveridge's pivotal relationship with the periodical, Cruse demonstrated his impatience with interracial coalition politics. However, he omits his relationship with James Finkenstaedt, who was an executive at Morrow Publishing and was responsible for *Crisis of the Negro Intellectual* seeing the light of day. It is not clear if he consulted Watts, or anyone else for that matter, before going to his editors with the manuscript. Nor did he have to. His credentials, political experience, and analytical sophistication made him an expert among amateurs. Although he could be exhaustingly argumentative and difficult to work with at times, Cruse commanded the respect of his peers, such as C. E. Wilson and Clayton Riley, and young upstart radicals such as Askia Touré and Muhammad Ahmad (Max Stanford). In this sense, Touré argued that too much is made of the generation gap in this period, as figures such as Cruse, Killens, Jimmy and Grace Lee Boggs, John Henrik Clarke, and Dan Watts often served as mentors in their own ways.

Touré recalled that these figures "nurtured young writers," affectionately calling them "radical mentors."[45] He described Cruse as a one-man "encyclopedia of the movement," who frequently took time to sit and talk openly with activists and intellectuals, young and old. Touré, unlike many people, appreciated Cruse's forthrightness. Many of the sections of *Crisis* were elaborations of conversations Cruse had with people around him. Cruse's outspokenness and intellectual boldness often drew the ire of colleagues. Killens, for one, did not take kindly to Cruse's no-stone-unturned analytical approach, and he was so upset that he challenged Cruse to a fistfight. Before it came to fisticuffs, however, it was suggested that a more respectable course be followed. Both men agreed to fight it out intellectually through a public debate, but such a meeting never took place. As far as Touré is concerned, Cruse won by default because no one was willing to stand up and issue a real challenge to *Crisis*.[46]

Like Baldwin, Cruse struggled publicly with black-Jewish relationships. His attitudes, which had been shaped by negative childhood experiences with people of Jewish ancestry that carried into his adult life, became a chief target of analysis as he matured as a self-trained scholar and committed theorist.[47] A related issue for Cruse was the *Liberator*'s ties to the Old Left. Though many in the *Liberator* circle interacted on some level with members of the Communist Party, only he, Beveridge, and Richard Moore had been members of the Party. Yet it is clear that some members of *Liberator*'s advisory board, such as former *Freedom* editor George B. Murphy, for example, had ties to the Communist Party at certain points in their career. Though Cruse decided that his tenure with *Liberator* was over by 1964, his writings made a lasting impression on the periodical's audience and on the theoretical formulations within black radical politics. His departure is not as unfortunate when one considers that he and Watts both had huge egos, which may have foreclosed any long-term association. When asked who influenced his intellectual approach to the movement, C. E. Wilson indicated that in addition to the work of Caribbean activist-theorist Frantz Fanon, Cruse's ideas were instrumental to his own understanding of history and political struggle.[48]

Several years after Cruse had left the publication to pursue other politically worthwhile projects, *Liberator* reviewed *Crisis* in its pages. Writer Lynn Wheeldin, who up to this point had never written for the periodical, authored the review. None of the feature writers or longtime associates saw fit to answer Cruse's monumental undertaking. Wheeldin, then, played the part of untainted, nonpartisan analyst who could at once attempt an objective reading of the book and dodge Cruse's fiery response. After reviewing and summarizing the main sections and points raised in *Crisis*, Wheeldin noted the "smell of vindictiveness" in Cruse's book, which, she argued, could only come from direct participation in the movements and organizations that came under his stiff rebuke. Though she urged readers to read the book for its "historical tie-ins," his proximity to his subject detracted from the effectiveness of the critique. To cite an example of Cruse's vindictive stance, Wheeldin states, "One glaring example in point is his ridiculous attempt to discredit *Liberator* by giving completely erroneous information as to that magazine's circulation—information 'gleaned' from a conversation with an uninvolved white man. The black editor/publisher was never consulted." Here the reviewer reveals herself as a partisan critic, though her allegiance is balanced by her suggestion that the book be read: "It is a long book, but for the historical tie-ins alone it is worth reading." Concluding, she added, "Although Harold Cruse does not offer any creative program of his own, he does point some directions."[49] Cruse would remain a controversial figure throughout his lifetime, and though many have critiqued certain elements of *Crisis* or disagreed with his thesis entirely, the book has, on the whole, maintained its status as a seminal text of the period for raising important and difficult theoretical questions of black politics, even if he himself could not provide the answers.

Expanding Circles and the Angry Generation

As a site of radical black politics *Liberator* carried stories of protests and local movements taking shape nationwide as well as those it followed that were occurring internationally. But most important, this period is one that witnessed the explosive fusion of cultural and political work. Artists and writers held forth on a number of explicitly political issues and were perhaps better suited than the activist to move into the popular realm.[50] The periodical approached national events with a sense of dedication that held allowed a consciousness of simultaneous struggles internationally. In the spring of 1963 the magazine featured a West Coast organization known as the Afro-American Association. And in the fall of that year it carried a short write-up on director and playwright Frank Greenwood's Afro-American Cultural Center Committee, a group dedicated to cultural awareness and African American history-inspired education, which was based in Los Angeles, California.[51] This marked the first occasion that *Liberator*'s coverage of the national racial justice struggle that was occurring on the West Coast.

Enthused by civil rights protests around the country and especially in the South, the Afro-American Association began as a study group in 1960 on the campus of the University of California at Berkeley.[52] In his article, "The California Revolt," organization leader Donald Warden wrote about the emergence of the group and its perspective on the civil rights movement.[53] Warden, who was educated at Howard University, identified several aspects of the liberation struggle that help explain the radicalism in this period. The association, according to Warden, sought to buttress the reforms promulgated by civil rights leaders and organizations, which at this time hung on the acquisition of voting rights in the South. Warden and the association called attention to the equally important emphasis on history, culture, and economic development. The association interpreted social change along the lines of education and economic self-sufficiency. They viewed voting rights as one step toward meaningful citizenship, but by itself it would not end discrimination and hostility toward black life. "The extension of voting rights does not necessarily produce power," Warden wrote. Rather than focus on voting rights, Warden suggested an emphasis on education. But though education was central to Warden, he did not discuss it in relation to desegregation. Rather, education should instill pride, purpose and dignity. Desegregation, he submitted, would not guarantee that those sentimental aspects could be achieved. To achieve the pride, purpose, and dignity he envisioned, black people needed to recognize the importance of their African past. "Our sense of dignity must be based upon our African past, and now is a most opportune time to strengthen our ties with our African brothers."[54] A connection to African history is a central characteristic of most cultural forms of black nationalism. Here, Warden echoes a perspective popularized by Cruse, which tied black liberation to cultural revolution.

On the economic front, however, Warden's prescription was more conservative. Rather than calling for the construction of alternatives to capitalism, Warden asserted that black businesses should be created around the country. In all fairness, he sought to address the black community's inability to produce a thriving business class. Yet his plan did not move beyond the black business model that first emerged under Reconstruction, when such approaches circulated with some voracity following the Civil War. This part of his program can perhaps be compared to that of the Nation of Islam's effort to curb black people's spending habits by encouraging frugality and thrift. Warden wrote of the capital that could be created to build black businesses should black people use their funds wisely, stating: "The capital for such industries also is available from our own community, if it could be diverted from the consumption of alcohol, bleaching creams and preachers' Cadillacs."[55] It is interesting that Warden's analysis of black peoples' predicament was not focused on systematic inequality or systemic barriers to black peoples' ability to generate wealth, but rather on a notion of black pathology. "Most of the crimes we commit are against ourselves; with a feeling of real dignity and group respect we can attack our basic problems," he asserted.[56]

With skillful usage of the slogans "Buy Black" and "Act Black," Warden hoped to inspire a sense of direction and purpose toward the development of black communities nationwide. Though these slogans would be insufficient as corrective measures, they could be used to galvanize support for the more detailed program for change offered by the association. As historians Peniel Joseph and Donna Murch write, the Afro-American Association, with its emphasis on cultivating pride in African American history and culture, had a significant impact on the radicalization of black students in California, influencing black college students attending the University of California at Berkeley, Merritt College, and San Francisco State University and inspiring future Black Power–era radical activists such as Maulana Karenga and Huey P. Newton.[57]

That *Liberator* would publish the writing of a relatively small West Coast organization is a significant commentary on its outreach efforts. Fashioning itself as a meeting ground of black radical political ideals, the magazine used its meager resources to expand its circle of contacts to cover regional, national and international movements and events. It is uncertain how exactly the New York–based magazine knew of the Afro-American Association, or vice versa. The staff writers traveled widely, and many moved in and out of radical and/or Black Nationalist circles. One explanation may be found in the Robert F. Williams support committees that sprung up throughout the country in the early 1960s.

A related possibility is the formation of the Fair Play for Cuba regional committees, which were also represented on both coasts in the early 1960s.

It is likely that the globe-trotting of black left-wing journalists such as William Worthy may have led to the reception of the magazine in cities outside New York, since *Liberator* consistently reported updates on Worthy's legal battles. An additional explanation may be found in the strategic role that black bookstores and reading groups played in circulating black journals, publications, and newspapers. It appears that a combination of these factors contributed to the *Liberator* staff's plan for national distribution. Through its expanded distribution, it attracted more writers, many of whom were making names for themselves in other literary, political or cultural efforts taking shape in other parts of New York City or around the country. One such aspiring black writer was University of San Francisco (USF) graduate Charlie L. Russell.

Russell's writing, beginning with a short excerpt from a novel-in-progress entitled *Dark to Dark*, first appeared in *Liberator*'s May 1963 issue.[58] Born in Monroe, Louisiana, Russell migrated with his family to the West Coast, relocating to Oakland, California. For many black families leaving the South during the World War II era, Oakland was an attractive locale to find work and a relatively less hostile place to raise a family.[59] Russell then relocated to New York City to pursue his writing career. He had been encouraged to consider a career in writing by one of his instructors at Santa Rosa Junior College, about an hour north of Oakland, where he took classes before transferring to USF. His writing instructor pulled him aside one day after class and told him that he should consider taking his writing more seriously and possibly becoming a professional writer. As Russell recalls, "He said: 'go where writers go, and do what writers do.' In my mind I conjured up the image of New York."[60] An admirer of the writings of James Baldwin, Russell decided to write a story of his own after reading Baldwin's "Sonny's Blues." From that moment he began fashioning himself as a writer, though he found it was difficult adapting to the discipline it required. After attending Santa Rosa Junior College and then USF, he left the Bay Area for New York. Arriving in New York around 1960, he contacted John Henrik Clarke, who among his numerous activities was an editor of the widely read *Freedomways* magazine. Clarke, himself an anthologist of short stories, told Russell about the Harlem Writer's Guild after Russell sent him a sample of his writing.[61]

As did Russell, a number of writers cut their teeth in the pages of the *Liberator,* among other publications. One such young writer was Rolland Snellings, who later changed his name to Askia Muhammad Touré,[62] an indication of the personal and political transformations accompanying the period. In one of his earliest *Liberator* writings, Touré published a long poem entitled, "Cry Freedom," which he dedicated to two young activists named Matthew Meade and Mustapha Bashir who had participated in the Lumumba UN protests. Throughout the poem Touré uses the refrain. "I am not an invisible man," distancing he and his generation from the notion of invisibility and unseen marginality of Ellison's novel with broad streaks of nationalism. Indeed in the first full stanza of the poem he pronounces the emergence of a "fighting spirit" of determination, embodied by an

> Angry Generation, Lonely Generation, Black Renaissance,
> New Negro, Black Nationalist, etc., etc.
> Classify me, hypnotize me, ostracize me;
> Will me away from your sight
> Hide me from the watchin' world; the 3/5 colored watchin world
> They see and hear; they care . . .
> I'm not an invisible man
> My anger stalks on ghetto legs
> I'm not an invisible man.
> My song, like
> Rain, is universal.
> Listen while I blow my horn.[63]

Touré had enlisted himself as a standard-bearer for a new generation of radicals. Characterizing the new spirit described by John Henrik Clarke in his influential essay, "The New Afro-American Nationalism,"[64] Touré referenced Malcolm X twice in this poem, signaling the growing relevance of the Muslim leader to the liberation movement as a whole and his attractiveness to young black radicals. Although originally from North Carolina, Touré spent much of his youth in Ohio and was "reborn on Brooklyn's teeming streets," along with Tom Dent, Calvin Hernton, Sarah Wright, Ishmael Reed, Rashidah Ismaili-Abu-Bakr, Baraka, and others who belonged to the Lower East Side multicultural black artist milieu in the early 60s.[65] With the presence of Touré, Neal, Riley, and others, *Liberator* not only represented the New York City politics and arts scene but also symbolized the political and cultural linkages evident in the Black Arts Movement as a whole.

Though he is not always credited with being a key barometer of the transition away from civil rights protest and toward black internationalist militancy, Touré published several seminal pieces in *Liberator* that typified broad generational and cultural shifts occurring in this period. One such article was "The New Afro-American Writer," which was published in the

October 1963 issue. Here Touré identified the militant shifts taking place among a younger generation of writers who were college-educated and increasingly race-conscious, yet stuck between existing civil rights programs and organizations on one hand, and the militancy and radicalism of the Nation of Islam on the other. Arguing in favor of increased education about African Americans' African past, and opposed to liberal leadership, whether black or white, Touré wrote, "A militant new generation has arisen." Positioning his critique of liberalism, he argued against the general and generational fear of nationalism, and asked, "Why does nationalism seem to disturb and frighten the white applauded 'Negro intellectuals' and self-appointed 'spokesmen of the race'?"[66]

Born in 1938, Touré, like many of his political cohort, was a very young man when he decided to deeply immerse himself in radical politics. Politically precocious, he wrote articles that were at once critical, driven by pivotal moments in Afro-diasporic history, and celebratory. His report from the National Afroamerican Student Conference clearly identified the restless mood among young radicals. His article, "Unchain the Lion," which was published in *Liberator* in July 1964, struck an apocalyptic tone ("unchain your hero . . . and gird yourself to meet the gathering storm!") and warned of an ominous "final confrontation." In it he spoke favorably of the place of the *lumproletariat*, "who make up the angry, exploited masses," and their potential as a revolutionary force in the movement. Strengthening his critical stance toward American society, Touré penned the influential article, "Afro American Youth and the Bandung World" in the February 1965 issue.[67] In this article, he again imagined an inevitable war between white America and the colonized black nation within the United States. The piece contained several themes that mark the period and typify the militant tone that many younger activists advocated, including especially relating black suffering to patterns of colonialism.

Touré imagined a long, resilient line of radical activism whenever he put pen to paper. Pointing to the Garvey movement and the influence of the Nation of Islam as historic and contemporary exemplars, Touré stressed the urgent necessity of black nationalism. He surmised that black youth were more prepared than many of their elders to envision the relevance of the "multi-colored" anticolonial movements in places such as Vietnam, the Congo, Panama, Venezuela, and India for the situation facing black people in the United States. The youth—or as he called them, the "children of change"—saw the world as awash in anti-imperialist ferment. At once invoking the Du Bois, Hunton, and Robeson era of internationalist black radicalism, and anticipating Fred Hampton's Rainbow Coalition, which he expressed within the context of the Black Panther Party's position on the potential of multiracial and multiethnic alliances,[68] Touré spoke against the philosophy of integration, writing, "As brothers and sisters of the 'Bandung' peoples, it would be downright immoral for our people to seek integration into a society which thrives on their plundering; because in doing so, we would be asking for our 'share' of the loot."[69] Social transformation, he argued, involved more than African Americans fitting into an imperialist system.

Touré spoke of the need to revisit black history and provided a brief overview of the conflict between Marcus Garvey and W. E. B. Du Bois at the turn of the century, ultimately calling for a synthesis between the two approaches. The antiracist, anti-imperialist, anticolonial, anticapitalist, pro-black outlook espoused in the article captured a resurgent radical internationalist vision of black nationalism in the United States at a time when it seemed that domestic issues were viewed in isolation from the efforts of freedom struggles around the globe. The importance of this article can also be found in the influence of Harold Cruse on Touré's discussion of "the oligarchy of imperialism" that "controls the economics of the United States." Perhaps taking a cue from Cruse, he argued for an analysis of the economic structure of the country as the backbone of the political order. Yet it was Touré's advanced sense of black radical internationalism that distinguished him among his peers. His strategic invocation of Bandung as a template for a youth-led revolutionary vision was a unique contribution to black radical thought in this period. Though the signature contributions of his close friend and comrade Amiri Baraka may have overshadowed his own, Askia Touré played a catalytic role documenting, theorizing, and reworking an outlook of insurgency among his generation of writer-activists.

· · · · · ·

On both the cultural and political fronts, the magazine continued the diligent and prodding coverage of local, national, and international events that readers had learned to appreciate. Locally, the periodical took on issues of equal education, poverty (and government-sponsored antipoverty programs), youth (especially programs such as HARYOU), economic development, and police harassment of everyday working people. In addition to these policy issues, the magazine also examined the role of local elected black leadership, most notably Adam Clayton Powell Jr. Local leaders in cities outside New York, such as Detroit's Albert Cleage and Cambridge, Maryland's Gloria Richardson, also received special recognition. In fact, Cleage was named "Man of the Year" by the magazine in December 1963.[70]

Nationally, the chief concern of *Liberator* writers was how to make sense out of the direction of the black freedom movement. "Which Road to Freedom?" asked staff writer Rose Finkenstaedt in an article in which she examined several issues confronting African Americans' search for freedom, including interracial alliances, integration in residential communities, electoral politics, and the formation of an independent black political party. "In the frenetic crisis of this age," she wrote, "only the black man has endurance and depth to create inspired leadership for the lost and forgotten peoples of this land. If he has been the symbol of enslavement, he can be the world-wide symbol of the struggle of all men for liberty."[71] Though it is unlikely that she penned these words in prophetic anticipation of the historic election of the first African American president of the United States, she nonetheless seemed to endorse the perspective that black leadership could be instructive for the nation as a whole. Finkenstaedt's reasoning here reveals the contestation and frequent consternation among whites concerning black national leadership. She was one of the few people who insisted that nothing short of an upheaval of the status quo would bring about the necessary improvements in the lives of black communities throughout the country.

African American radical formations sprang up all around the country, defined by presence alone the multilayered elements of, and approach to, black liberation. It is important that many people began placing greater emphasis on the distinctions between an assertive black nationalism, revolutionary nationalism, and civil rights reformism. Outfits like *Liberator* knew which side it was on and directed its bully pulpit to shape alliances among radical Black Nationalist individuals and groups. It can be argued that this goal set the magazine apart from publications such as *Freedomways*, which were much more ideologically focused as an organ of the remaining black members of the Communist Party's militant integrationism. Part of the strength and relevance of *Liberator*, especially in the bridge years between civil rights militancy and Black Power (roughly 1963–1967), was its ability to accumulate and articulate a wide range of Black Nationalist thought.

As evidence of this approach, another group emerging outside New York that attracted the magazine's attention was the Afro-American Institute, in Cleveland, Ohio. This organization, not to be confused with either the Afro-American *Association* in Oakland or the Afro-American *Research* Institute, under which *Liberator* was published, was led by Donald Freeman and was essentially another front organization of the Revolutionary Action Movement (RAM).[72] Freeman's organization typified the radical coalition politics reflected in *Liberator*. Formed in Cleveland in 1962, the organization proudly based its approach to black liberation on "Awareness, Agitation and Action," which was reminiscent of Marcus Garvey's protest politics that instilled pride in African heritage in the 1920s. Like most other formations in this period, Freeman's Afro-American Institute was concerned with politics, education, economics, and what they termed "social independence and maturity" among African Americans. In many ways, the institute was a consortium of different groups and individuals working in solidarity.

Black activists from Cleveland's organized labor community, individuals who worked with Cleveland's Monroe Defense Committee, members of Cleveland CORE, as well as notable figures such as Max Roach and William Worthy all expressed support for the Afro-American Institute. Locally, according to Freeman, this solidarity contributed to the creation of "a Black United Front of Cleveland protest groups." The Soul Circle, which was the institute's policy-making unit, sought local alliances as a part of a vanguard strategy, though they were quick to distance these efforts from overtly Marxist or socialist organizations. "The Institute's Soul Circle declares that white socialists and Marxists do not possess the solutions to the ills of Black America," he wrote.[73] Instead, an alliance of black organizations could begin to address the political, social, and economic needs of black communities locally and nationally.

The emphasis on independent thought, strategy, organization, and action also contained traces of Harold Cruse's theories of autonomous leadership.[74] The alliance viewed "African American groups throughout the nation such as the Afro-American Association in California and RAM in Philadelphia as a potential vanguard in Black America's liberation, along with the Black Muslims." The institute placed great importance on developing "effective communication and cooperation between itself and similar oriented black organizations throughout the United States," as that would be in the best interests of African American political progress domestically, while also providing a basis for pan-African international solidarity globally.[75] The Afro-American Institute of Cleveland was among a number of radical organizations seeking to unify the black left and work toward collective goals. It is indicative of the many localized efforts to raise consciousness and empower black communities while fighting established structures of state power. Though Freeman's style of radical coalition politics gained some traction, the liberal and labor coalitions of civil rights organizations nationally overshadowed such efforts. And although numerous alternative political ideas, such as those found in *Liberator*, were heavily circulated in the early 1960s, for most African Americans and supportive whites, the main issue was how to gain political advances in the mainstream of American society without abandoning principles of black self-assertion, cultural awareness, and political autonomy in organizing. Such questions were center stage for *Liberator*'s radical writers as the mainstream leadership of the civil rights movement prepared to descend on Washington, DC, and announce their demands to the world.

The "Farce on Washington"

Talk of the March on Washington dominated the news that fall. The stand against nonviolence and civil rights gradualism on the part of *Liberator*'s staff writers and many of its associates placed the magazine at odds with civil rights establishment leaders such as Martin Luther King Jr., James Farmer of CORE, and Roy Wilkins of the NAACP. Mocking their leadership, *Liberator* pictured them on its August cover under the headline, "August 28th Will They March?" Though the magazine was critical of the march, the editorial penned by Beveridge and Watts was an endorsement of a march *on* Washington, as opposed to what they thought would be a march *in* Washington. Doubtful that the announced march would bring the significant change that many envisioned, and convinced that it would not move beyond its symbolic impact, the *Liberator* staff planned to attend the proposed march as witnesses to the affair. The editorial warned, "The integrationist, non-violent leaders of the major civil rights organizations in this country have grabbed a lion by the tail in committing themselves to mobilize 100,000 people in Washington, D.C. on August 28 in support of the Administration's admittedly inadequate civil rights bill." It criticized the announcement made by King, Farmer and Wilkins that the march would be orderly, stating that the leaders of the march were more concerned with order than getting African Americans' issues addressed.

Though they had a number of reasons to criticize the march, Beveridge and Watts nonetheless encouraged readers to attend. "In spite of all these negative factors, we say that Washington, D.C. is the place to be on August 28," they urged. "Let us make the March IN Washington into a March ON Washington in spite of 'our leaders' efforts." The march made a tremendous impact on the civil rights struggle if for no other reason than the large numbers of people, totaling over 200,000, who responded to the call to descend on Chocolate City. Indeed, the march was one of the watershed moments in American history.[76] Staff writers Carlos Russell, Charlie Russell, and C. E. Wilson; art critic Clebert Ford; photographer Leroy McLucas; and editor in chief Dan Watts traveled to Washington to witness the march. It is interesting that the September issue of the magazine did not include any reports or articles assessing the march as might have been expected. In this issue, they did, however, publish an article that spoke in contrast to the integrationist tone of the March on Washington by Progressive Labor organizer Bill Epton. Still, for the time being it was the only piece that dealt directly with the march.

• • • • • •

In his *Autobiography*, Martin Luther King Jr. characterized the March on Washington as "a shout which awoke the consciousness of millions of white Americans and caused them to examine themselves and to consider the plight of twenty million black disinherited brothers."[77] On the heels of President Kennedy's civil rights proposal and Medgar Evers's assassination, the March on Washington for Jobs and Freedom symbolized the desire of many people to end the brutality and violence toward African Americans and served as a collective protest against the federal government's unwillingness to protect black lives. He acknowledged the historic nature of the gathering. "The Negro Revolution in the South had come of age," King wrote. "It was mature. It was courageous. It was epic—and it was in the American tradition, a much delayed salute to the Bill of Rights, the Declaration of Independence, the Constitution, and the Emancipation Proclamation."[78] King's delivery of his "I Have a Dream" speech is arguably the most remembered event of the march. "To the extent that any single public utterance could," wrote Harvard Sitkoff, "this speech made the black revolt acceptable to America." Yet not all people believed in the brotherhood between white and black that King envisioned would transform America. Some defiantly opposed King's passionate belief that America could be made anew through black struggle. Nation of Islam leader Malcolm X, who was in many ways antithetical to King and his dream, famously referred to the march as the "Farce on Washington," putting voice to a sentiment of doubt shared by many. In any case, the march was not the power move many radicals envisioned.[79]

The *Liberator* gathered its coverage and criticism of the march in its October 1963 issue. In many ways, this issue was a turning point in the magazine's impact. A quick perusal of the issue's table of contents reveals a magazine of serious black politics and aesthetics. Boasting an eight-person executive board and a thirteen-member advisory board, it was a publication that commanded attention. Important as well was the magazine's coverage of domestic events and issues, alongside those occurring on the international scene (especially African political events and personalities), which demonstrated black radical politics and aesthetics. Articles in this issue included "Ghana Speaks Out" and "The Pilgrimage," both of which discussed the March on Washington; Askia Touré's "The New Afro-American Writer"; Cruse's "Rebellion or Revolt"; "Du Bois an African Patriot," which was written in tribute to the recent passing of the pan-Africanist writer, philosopher, and activist; "Thru Women's Eyes," which marked an emergent feminism in black radical politics; and "An All Black Party," marking the renewed search for an independent black political agenda. Also included in this issue was a review of Baraka's *Blues People*. Collectively, the articles indicated the wide range of subjects that the magazine would cover over its ten-year history and simultaneously identified some of the salient aspects of an emerging, broad-based black radical critique that encompassed issues of politics, economic, education, and culture.[80]

Following what had by now become a traditional pattern, the October 1963 issue opened with an editorial penned by Dan Watts. Recounting several murders that had occurred within weeks of the March on Washington, Watts called readers' attention to the fact that black lives remained in danger, despite the dream of a new America that was being celebrated as a result of King's speech. In addition to the murders of Cynthia Wesley, Addie Mae Collins, Denise McNair, and Carol Robertson, the victims of Birmingham's Sixteenth Street Baptist Church bombing, Watts pointed to Johnny Robinson, a sixteen-year-old black youth shot by Birmingham police, and thirteen year-old Virgil Wade, a black boy who was the victim of two white boys. Watts's editorial indicted several public figures for not protecting the lives of African Americans while they urged the African American community to maintain hope for greater inclusion and dignity in American society. Watts directed his "finger of guilt" at the perpetuators of the crimes, first and foremost, noting, for example that "as we go to press, there have not even been any arrests for the Church massacre." He then charged Alabama governor George C. Wallace, FBI director J. Edgar Hoover and "his racist cohorts," attorney general Robert Kennedy, president John F. Kennedy, and King "for false leadership of black people; for continuing to preach a policy of non-violence and love in spite of the daily toll of humiliation, blood and life which this policy has cost his people."[81]

Watts did not stop there, however. His last assignment of guilt was to "Afro-American people themselves," for their blind faith. Watts, like many others, believed that African Americans had given support to King and other civil rights leaders undeservedly. They were the tacit followers of leaders who had duped them into thinking American racial history could be overcome by sacrificing their bodies, dreaming, and loving their enemies. Watts believed that instead, black people should teach and practice strategies of survival, including most seriously methods of self-defense. "We must wake up to the fact that the issues of jobs, education, desegregation, and civil rights are only small parts of the basic problem of survival," he wrote. Watts's version of the crisis went counter to the peace doctrine practiced by King: "If we do not organize for survival, we will not be here to enjoy the fruits of equality. We must demand our leaders recognize the reality of our struggle and responsibly organize for physical self-defense and abandon all irresponsible reliance on the tragically demonstrated ineffectual powers of love and conscience." The caustic tone of Watts's editorial is indicative of Black Nationalist radicals' impatience with civil rights liberalism. Lives were at stake and government officials seemed to be taking their time in guaranteeing protection or capturing perpetrators if they were willing to do so at all.[82]

Editorial board member and staff writer C. E. Wilson penned an appraisal of the March on Washington in a four-page article entitled, "The Pilgrimage," which identified critical aspects of the march.[83] Wilson intended to critically examine the importance of the march, but like many on the left, he took the position that the march alone was not enough to bring about the desired change in African American experiences in the United States. Throughout the essay, Wilson, known for his wit, described the march as "a pilgrimage," a "picnic" replete with thermoses and lunch baskets, and "a commencement" exercise. He wondered why the police feared violence would erupt at the gathering since the army they anticipated was made up of aging mothers and their children. Of those gathered he wrote: "their uniforms—white shirts, ties and their frightening battle hymns were We Shall Overcome and Freedom." Though President Kennedy eventually endorsed the right of the marchers to assemble, it was only after King and others guaranteed that there would not be violence. With those assurances given, Wilson wondered why the police presence was so thick. Perhaps, he suspected, American authorities wanted violence to ensue so as to provide a reason for the assembled to be sent back to their homes, beaten, jailed or killed and then blamed for it.[84]

While admitting the importance of the march, Wilson took the position that the gathering left many of the pressing issues such as poverty and state sanctioned racial violence unaddressed in terms that would encourage structural changes. From Wilson's vantage point the march symbolized the hope of many African Americans in the Constitution and their assertion of citizenship. It was indicative of a growing impatience toward the pace of social change in the country. "America was given a bit longer to pay off the debt [to African Americans]," he wrote, "but was served notice that the debt will have to be paid." Echoing Baldwin's landmark essay, he wrote, "to wit: Negroes gave America the rainbow sign. They want payment or the fire next time." Wilson did not want to focus on the gathering alone, but also what the march actually stood for: the demand for freedom and jobs. He wanted to keep the focus on the socioeconomic demands that the march represented.[85]

Tellingly, he did not mention Dr. King directly in this initial write-up. If Lincoln's statue was honored by "the pilgrimage" and heavy police presence typified "the picnic," King was referred to as "the class valedictorian" of the commencement, who "eloquently spoke of the future and clearly enunciated what should be the dreams and hopes for the future of all Americans." Wilson, who was clearly wrestling with the meaning of the gathering, questioned the notion of appealing to America's conscience. As King's signature strategy aimed at changing as many hearts as minds, Wilson identified the contradiction inherent in such an appeal, when he asked: "Does a nation that thinks in terms of the fast-buck, misleading advertising and sloganeering have a conscience?" He, like many other radicals believed that America's conscience—if the country did indeed possess one—should have already been shaken at the number of fatalities that black communities throughout the country had suffered since emancipation, and therefore was impervious to such an appeal. It would not have been necessary to march in the first place if America possessed a conscience, he argued. Rather than the march standing as a symbol of progress as a nonviolent demonstration, Wilson intimated that the problem of jobs and freedom for African Americans was only getting worse not better. And though he could state that the march "was neither a complete triumph nor a complete bust," he noted somberly, "The pilgrims came back from Washington empty handed."[86]

Wilson was among a number of black radicals who were doubtful about the march's impact. For example, writing at the end of 1963, Baraka called

Rebellion or Revolution 149

Adam Clayton Powell, cover, *Liberator*, July 1964. Courtesy of Pete Beveridge.

the march a "sham gesture."[87] Recalling the deflation of swelling pressure on the government leading up to and during the march, former Student Nonviolent Coordinating Committee activist James Forman wrote, "Somewhere along the line, the church and labor people had been told that this was a march to support the administration's Civil Rights Bill, which was passed in 1964, after Kennedy's death. Who did this and how it happened, I do not know. But people all over the country thought they were marching for jobs and freedom when in actuality the sellout leadership of the March on Washington was playing patsy with the Kennedy administration as part of the whole liberal-labor politics of Rustin, Wilkins, Randolph, Reuther, King, the Catholic and Protestant hierarchy."[88] If this period represents the increased radicalization of black protest politics, the march also marked a generational shift of another sort. W. E. B. Du Bois, the esteemed scholar-activist, passed away on the eve of the historic gathering after having relocated to Kwame Nkrumah's Ghana. The *Liberator*'s October issue carried a dedication entitled, "Du Bois, an African Prophet," which was reprinted from the *Ghanaian Times*, and accompanied by a portrait by illustrator Leo Carty of a middle-aged Du Bois dressed in a shirt, tie, and vest.[89] And the brief article, "Ghana Speaks Out," which featured W. Alpheus Hunton, Julian Mayfield, Maya Angelou, Alice Windom, and others of the African American expatriate community in Ghana, recorded their support for the March on Washington and the simultaneous collective mourning of Du Bois' passing. The expatriates marched to the American embassy in Ghana and delivered a message to President Kennedy via the consulate. After Hunton delivered the letter, the marchers picketed with signs that read, "Remember Lumumba and Medgar Evers"; "Stop Mad Dog Attacks"; "Down with American Apartheid"; "W. E. B. Du Bois 20th Century Prophet"; and "Remember South Africa in Washington."[90] This is evidence of the wide support the march received and the balance of radicalism meant that activists supported the march on symbolic terms while marking the limits of relying on such a dramatization to generate the full range of black political and economic desires.

Though the expatriates and supporters around this group were largely more progressive in their political outlook, Mayfield reported on a certain type of expatriate he dubbed "homo tomo Americanus," who serviced U.S. interests in Ghana.[91] "Uncle Tom Goes to Africa" told of the aloofness of some black travelers to the continent, a type who was a self-made radical in Africa but would not take even the most basic stand against the status quo in America. As Mayfield put it,: "Back home you could probably not get his signature for a petition defending the right of women to have babies, but once on African soil he becomes a vociferous advocate of 'socialism,' not lowering his voice or even looking over his shoulder." Mayfield wanted to highlight the difference between the African Americans in Ghana working actively for African independence and opportunists merely exploiting the moment. Though the traveler in Mayfield's description used radical terms, he "never does or says anything that might annoy the local U.S. embassy." From Mayfield's point of view, the earnest supporter of African independence was not afraid to disturb government officials if that was what was required for change or at least to heighten government awareness of black dissent.

Charlie E. Wilson, the son of immigrants from Barbados, grew up in New York City. Though he had a sense of the importance of African independence, he did not travel to Africa until well after his *Liberator* days were over.[92] After serving a stint in the army, where he and Beveridge met, he made good use of the G.I. Bill and enrolled in classes at St. Francis College, located in Brooklyn Heights and later at City University of New York, Brooklyn. Around this time he joined the Brooklyn chapter of the NAACP and served a term as chapter president. After leaving the army in 1955, he worked at an industrial screw manufacturing company while taking civil service exams in order to apply for municipal jobs throughout New York City. These exams qualified him to take jobs at the New York State Employment Service and later the New York Department of Education, where he worked as a vocational education councilor for the physically handicapped. Later, he would enroll in New York University's master's degree program in audio communicative disabilities.[93]

Wilson remembers that Beveridge often worked closely with Rosetta Gaston (1885–1981). Mother Gaston, as she was affectionately known, was a local activist who served as president of the Brooklyn chapter of the Association for the Study of Negro Life and History, of which Beveridge was a member. Wilson and Beveridge lived around the corner from one another and often traveled in similar company. Beveridge, who by this time had connected with Watts on the idea of starting a magazine, asked Wilson if he would be interested in writing articles. According to Wilson, "I thought I knew a few things, so I started writing articles." One of the earliest members of the staff, Wilson would use his expertise in public education and New York City's civil service and welfare politics in all his *Liberator* writings. Beyond ideological commitments to a new social order, writers like Wilson brought the magazine an astute, in-depth criticism of government policies precisely because in some cases their day jobs required them to implement these policies. As such, when Wilson took up the subject of education or welfare policy he did not have to guess; his employment put the evidence right in his lap.

The *Liberator* brought together a number of individuals, each with their own area of interest and knowledge. In Wilson's words, "It brought together all these different strands; it represented the tremendous frustration of noncitizenship."[94] Though both he and Watts were born and raised in New York City, the immediacy of their Caribbean roots added a layer to their critique of the United States as an unwelcoming and hostile place for African descendants. The same can also be said of Carlos Russell, whose Afro-Panamanian heritage influenced his engagement in black radical politics in the United States, although he was not born in New York City.

Wilson argued that the magazine played a critical role in the civil rights discourse. "It gave a voice to the people who don't say 'yessah boss'" he contended. *Liberator* writers were "the ones who asked 'what is this democracy that they're talking about?' The *Liberator* asked the question: 'Can you work within to change these institutions?'" Like many radicals of the period, Wilson was greatly influenced by the writings of Frantz Fanon. Among his thirty articles and reviews published in the magazine, was a book review of the classic revolutionary text, *The Wretched of the Earth*, in the May 1965 issue. For Wilson, Fanon provided a clear definition of the evolution and function of racism. "He helped me put into perspective Ellison's invisibility."[95] In his review, he wrote, "Fanon's book is a radical document because it goes to the root of the problem. Western opulence is built on slavery. Nothing is legitimate about the murder for profit, brutality, or exploitation."[96] Radical anticolonial thinkers such as Fanon held particular importance for activists in search of theory to apply to their own analyses of the state of black life in the United States. His works were quickly added to the analytical arsenal of black radicalism. His searing, if at times clinical, diagnoses of colonialism, revolutionary culture, and African revolt struck a chord among an array of black activists. Fanon's theorizations were second only to the one-man battalion, Malcolm X.

Malcolm X as Quintessential Liberator

If Fanon was the theorist of the revolution, Malcolm X was the revolution's charismatic general. An important thread connecting the various strands of radicalism in the magazine specifically and in the period generally was the role of Malcolm X and the Nation of Islam (NOI). Beginning with religious scholar C. Eric Lincoln's pioneering work, *The Black Muslims in America* (1961), and followed by E. U. Essien-Udom's *Black Nationalism: A Search for an Identity in America* (1962), scholars have long noted the impact of the NOI on the cultural and political landscape in this period. The NOI was responsible for the radical transformation of many individuals and organizations, an impact also felt among mainstream civil rights and Christian organizations. More recently historian Jeffrey Ogbar wrote, "The NOI was the chief benefactor of the Black Power movement."[97] Its doctrine of race pride, economic autonomy, and self-defense proved a direct challenge to civil rights integrationist and nonviolent approaches. Although "The Messenger," Elijah Muhammad, provided the organizational and philosophical foundation on which the Nation stood, much of its historic impact can be attributed to Malcolm X. According to Ogbar, Malcolm's twelve-year tenure in the NOI (1952–1964) helped grow the organization from roughly 400 in 1952 to as many as 300,000 nationwide members by 1964, though the exact number of actual members is difficult to precisely quantify.[98] In his *Autobiography*, Malcolm states that he was directly responsible for the growth of the Nation from 400 to 40,000 members. According to historian Michael Gomez, however, scholars must also account for the "thousands (if not millions) who agreed with Malcolm, who enthusiastically received his message, and who regarded him as a leader while never formally joining his organization."[99]

Drawn to a variety of Harlem's local leaders and organizing efforts, the *Liberator* was one of a number of black publications that took notice to Malcolm X. In this sense its writers were among those "who regarded him as a leader," although they were uncomfortable with his specific role as representative of a religious organization and not an expressly political one. But because of their proximity to Harlem's Muslim Mosque No. 7, *Liberator*'s writers were in a position to witness Malcolm's ascendance. Though historian Harvard Sitkoff could write, "In death, Malcolm X achieved a far greater eminence and a larger following than he had in life," such statements fail to fully appreciate Malcolm's importance for black radicals in the early 1960s.[100] As the writers of *Liberator* would have it Malcolm was the quintessential liberator. Coverage of Malcolm in *Liberator* reveals his impact on an assortment of radical thinkers and activists in this period.

The earliest mention of the Nation of Islam in *Liberator* occurred in July 1961 when the *Liberator* was little more than a seven-page pamphlet. John Henrik Clarke, a friend of Beveridge through activist and educational circles, penned a celebratory review of Lincoln's *Black Muslims in America*. According to Clarke, Lincoln's book underscored the rapid and expanding influence of the organization and their historical importance, noting: "The Black Muslims in the United States have created what is essentially a proletarian movement. This is the largest movement of this nature to emerge among Afro-Americans since the heyday of Marcus Garvey and the collapse of his 'Back to Africa' dream."[101]

Discussion of Malcolm X first appeared in the magazine in May 1962. In an unsigned article culled from national news sources, the magazine carried a story about a young man named Ronald Stokes, the secretary of Los Angeles Mosque No. 27. Aptly calling it a "barbaric incident," the article pointed out the "brutal and unprovoked attack" on the mosque's members by seventy-five policemen, which resulted in the shooting death of Stokes and left at least fifteen other Muslims wounded. Malcolm was dispatched to Los Angeles to launch the NOI's own investigation of the killing. Stokes, who was only twenty-nine years old at the time of his death, was shot when a police-induced scuffle broke out between them and members of the mosque.[102] After a quick appraisal of the damage to both victims and police, the *New York Times* opened its report on the incident with police chief William H. Parker's comments that the Muslims "were a hate organization dedicated to the destruction of the Caucasian race."[103] Parker, who was well-known throughout the Los Angeles black community for his anti-black racist views, sanctioned the brutality, believing the NOI to be a threat to the white community.[104] Parker's views toward the NOI received support from the city's mayor, Samuel Yorty, who called upon the "fine leaders of our Negro community" to deal with the Muslims. Malcolm called a press conference to present the Nation's interpretation of the shooting. In his statement, Malcolm emphasized the fact that those who were wounded in the police-inspired melee went without medical treatment for hours, possibly worsening their injuries. Moreover, he denounced the "Gestapo tactics and false propaganda" of the police department and the mayor's office; and placing the responsibility on the city, Malcolm proclaimed Stokes's death a "police-state murder."[105]

According to historian Peniel Joseph, this event catapulted Malcolm into the center of heightening national debate over black militancy, police abuse, and civil rights protest although, under orders from the Nation's spiritual leader, Elijah Muhammad, he was not allowed to use this event to initiate a nationwide militant movement, as he had intended.[106] The *Liberator*, which (it must be noted) repeatedly misspelled Malcolm's name in this article, also saw fit to publish what it thought could be learned from this incident. "Malcom X [sic], as the most vocal and public figure of the Muslim movement must reconcile his militant talk with the non-militant action of his followers," they wrote, seemingly critiquing Muhammad's instruction not to retaliate. And continued: "If he wishes to continue fearlessly to speak the truth about the savagery and uncivilized nature of the white man—an activity in which we wholly support him, he should realize that his followers will need more substantial weapons than the truth of Allah to defend themselves against the wrath of the Los Angeles police—and others." At first glance, it appears that the Nation missed a golden opportunity to defend black humanity from the state power. Known for their willingness to defend their members at any cost, the Nation could and often would use whatever means at their disposal to retaliate against transgressors. In this instance, under orders from Elijah Muhammad, the Nation could not retaliate for the killing of Stokes. Whether The Messenger's decision hung on his belief that a war with the Los Angeles Police Department could not result in a favorable outcome, or whether he was pressured by Los Angeles mayor Sam Yorty to calm NOI members who were prepared to fight fire with fire remains unclear. We can be certain, however, that this incident, and especially the tepid response from Muhammad, left many NOI members disillusioned and angry. Many subsequently left the organization. For those who stayed on, every attempt was made to catapult Stokes's case to national, if not international, attention. This incident would remain an issue of tension between Malcolm and Elijah Muhammad.[107] And it was indicative of growing fissures between the two men, which would continue to widen over the next two years.

Though forced to stand down in the aftermath of the Stokes case, Malcolm's fiery rhetoric endeared him among those already critical of civil rights nonviolence. His increasing importance to radicals would place him alongside Fanon, Robert F. Williams, and Patrice Lumumba as pivotal figures in defining and reshaping black radical perspectives in this period. From 1962 through his assassination on February 21, 1965, the *Liberator* tracked Malcolm's evolution and growing alienation from the Nation of Islam, followed many of his speeches, invited him to debate, and pressed him to explain his ideas concerning the way forward for African descendants in the United States and abroad.

In the June 1962 issue, the black radical historian Richard B. Moore issued an open letter to the editor responding to the Stokes article. Moore, who had been involved in a number of radical circles dating back to the 1920s, was an advisory board member until its dismantling in the wake of the Eddie Ellis controversy. An active participant and observer in black radical politics, Moore told the editors of *Liberator* that he approved of the attention paid to the Stokes case and its catalytic potential. At the time of his letter, Moore had initiated a formation called the "Committee to Present the Truth about the Name 'Negro' " and urged the black community to embrace the term "Afro-American," which seemed a more historically accurate descriptor for African descendants in the United States.[108]

Moore urged black leaders and organizers to form a united front that would work toward the protection of the basic needs of the African descendant populace in the country. Once unity was achieved, he asserted, then collective policy decisions could be effected. The united front he envisioned included nationalist, labor, civil rights and religious individuals and organizations. He thought radicals could take a page from the black abolitionist Frederick Douglass, who in identifying the need for broad-based alliances toward abolition, stated, "I would help all and hinder none." Though he supported the *Liberator*'s editorial challenge to Malcolm, Moore argued against any insinuation of warfare against all whites. Striking a pragmatic note, he argued that the *Liberator* editors, and by extension the united front, should distinguish between "all European Americans" and "white supremacists." His letter also counseled against the Garveyite idea of repatriation to Africa. Though some African Nationalist and Black Nationalist groups might have been at odds with such an approach, Moore continued calling for a "basis of unity" among all groups concerned with the progress of the black community. Finally, Moore noted that the "separatism" versus "integration" dichotomy was "fruitless." He recommended that a Centennial Emancipation Convention be convened as an initial step toward collective organizational unity. Concluding his letter, he wrote: "To prepare such a Convention properly, we must urge the principal organizations and leaders, especially NAACP, CORE, Liberation Committee for Africa, and the Youth Movement, the followers of Elijah Muhammad, as well as the African and Black Nationalist Groups, the Negro Labor Committee, and other Afro-American labor groups, to take the initiative in the speedy setting up and capable staffing of broadly representative United Centennial Emancipation Convention Committee. We dare not fail to meet the present challenge; let us rise to the occasion!"[109] LCA chairman Dan Watts attached a small note of agreement below Moore's letter, which read, "We at LCA support the analysis and conclusion of Mr. Moore's open letter, calling for the uniting of all forces engaged in the civil rights struggle: To the liberal white community, we say join us, not lead us, work with us, support us." Though Watts appeared willing to work across racial lines, he grew increasingly distrustful of multiracial cooperation in subsequent years.[110] Moore continued to publish articles in the *Liberator*, and expanded his view of the importance of Douglass in a four-page article commemorating the Centennial of the Emancipation Proclamation and entitled, "Frederick Douglass and Emancipation," which appeared in the February 1963 issue.

As the NOI grew in public recognition and as Malcolm's public recognition increased, the *Liberator* grew in its support for his ideas. An equally important political figure to the Harlem community was Adam Clayton Powell, whose career in politics experienced a meteoric rise as well as an embarrassing demise. These two men and their outspokenness on questions of race and power struck a chord with Harlemites in search of identity and methods of resistance. Powell and Malcolm frequently shared podiums and pulpits, with their assertive denunciations of white supremacy, shocking their supporters and enemies alike. Additionally, they were both tragic figures: Malcolm suffered death by gunfire while Powell experienced political death in his expulsion from Congress.

Seemingly, as Malcolm's political philosophy evolved, he grew increasingly at odds with the apolitical position of Elijah Muhammad—a process that has been well documented. His evolution is perhaps the central theme of his legacy.[111] *Liberator* coverage of Malcolm reveals his increasing appeal among radicals. In the March 1963 issue, Rose L. H. Finkenstaedt, the wife of Morrow Books publisher James Finkenstaedt, penned an article entitled, "Never on Christmas: A Black Muslim Story."[112] Rose, a Columbia University graduate student, had been asked by Malcolm to schedule a speaking engagement at the school after she had contacted him.[113] Her subsequent article supported the Muslim struggle against the police and encouraged readers to support it as well. She also emphasized the religious importance of the group's existence in Christian white America. "The fact is that the Black Muslims are an indication of what can be done against another power structure in America," she wrote. A picture of Malcolm X sporting a scarf, long coat, and fedora accompanied the article. Malcolm, and at least a hundred other Muslims from his New York mosque, were pictured outside the courtroom where two NOI members, Hugh X. Morton and Albert X. Reese, were being arraigned following their arrest for "disorderly conduct and simple assault," while selling copies of *Muhammad Speaks* on December 25 of the previous year.

Liberator reported that the members of the Mosque attended the court hearing in hopes of insuring the protection of their brothers. One of the arrested men received forty-six days in jail and the other was let go. An attempt to arrange a meeting between Mayor Robert Wagner (who was in office from 1954 to 1965) and Malcolm X to discuss "police oppression against Muslims" was also considered as a result of the hearing.[114] In the publication's May issue, Malcolm is pictured on the cover seated on a rostrum smiling as Congressman Adam Clayton Powell is shown emphatically addressing the crowd at a Harlem rally. The editorial of this issue revealed appreciation to Powell for maintaining contact with his base of support in Harlem. However, Powell was a controversial figure throughout his career. As John Henrik Clarke wrote in the Introduction to one of several Harlem anthologies he compiled, Powell was "the creator of a political mystique and a dramatic enigma. This mystique and this enigma stand in the way of every attempt at making an objective appraisal of the adventurous career of Rev. Adam Clayton Powell."[115] Still, in the political history of 1960s Harlem, Malcolm and Powell are almost inseparable.[116]

Toward the end of 1963, with many people still pondering the impact of the March on Washington, others continued to push for substantive change. First introduced to mainstream audiences through Mike Wallace and Louis Lomax's documentary, *The Hate That Hate Produced*, which aired in 1959, the Nation began to receive more national attention in the vacuum left by the march.[117] Though viewed as a force to be reckoned with, if not feared, the Nation of Islam still carried the badge of uncertainty among some radicals. The *Liberator* writers paid close attention to the Muslim movement with a degree of skepticism even as they were drawn to Malcolm X. Doubt in the Muslim program was vividly displayed in Charlie Russell's article, "Black Muslims in Crisis," in which he strongly criticized the Nation, calling it an "intellectual wasteland" bordering on "naïveté" and "unable to present a concrete method for reaching [its] goals."[118] "Because of the growing disenchantment on the part of the black masses," the article began, "the Muslims, as potential leaders of the Negro movement, now find themselves in the unenviable position of a rookie on a last place team: they must produce quickly or be sent back down to the minors—in their case it would mean they would become just another religious sect."[119] Naturally, such a statement angered the Nation members and sympathizers who saw the article. Carlos Russell recalls being confronted on the street by members of the Fruit of Islam who mistook him for Charlie Russell after the edition had hit the stands. After some cajoling and explaining that the other Russell wrote the piece and that the two were not blood relatives, the Muslims backed down. Of course, it did not help matters that Watts and Beveridge mistakenly assigned Carlos credit for the piece in the table of contents.[120]

The title "Black Muslims in Crisis," written boldly across the front cover of the magazine, easily garnered the attention of passersby, much to the chagrin of both Russells. Though Charlie Russell's critique employed very provocative language that drew the ire of some Muslims, the article pressed for an increased role of the Muslim movement beyond the realm of religion and stopped far short of denouncing it. In any case, the misunderstanding did not sever the relationship between Carlos and Charlie; nor did it lessen the critical attention the magazine paid to Malcolm X and the Nation of Islam. Equally significant is the fact that Malcolm himself continued to stay in communication with the black radical press, including *Liberator*. This can partially be explained by Malcolm's growing weariness with the narrow platform of the Nation of Islam. His eagerness to join the broader civil rights fight with his presence, even while not fully accepting its philosophy, stemmed from an expanding interest in revolutionary politics that kept black peoples' needs front and center, leaving scholars to appreciate Malcolm's evolution from Black Nationalist to Revolutionary Nationalist.[121]

A significant turning point in Malcolm's career, prior to his "chickens coming home to roost" comment regarding Kennedy's assassination and the disciplining that ensued, was the Northern Negro Grassroots Leadership Conference in Detroit, which was held November 8, 9, and 10, 1963. This conference demonstrated the potential of a black radical united front to counter the civil rights established leadership headed by King.[122] Four months later, on March 8, 1964, the *New York Times* noted the occurrence of a split between Malcolm X and Elijah Muhammad. On March 12 Malcolm called a press conference offering the public portions of a letter he sent to Elijah Muhammad officially announcing the separation.[123]

In April 1964, *Liberator* pictured Malcolm on its cover with the heading: "Brother Malcolm X: Self-Defense vs. Submission." The majority of the magazine's contents, however, spoke to broader issues. An article by *Liberator* Man of the Year Rev. Albert Cleage entitled "Struggle for Survival;"[124] James Tillman's "Exiles No More," which critiqued American ideas of citizenship by arguing that African Americans were really exiles in America; and the second part of Harold Cruse's series, "The Roots of Black Nationalism," also drew readers' attention. The significance of Malcolm's presence on the cover pertained to a sympathetic editorial penned by Dan Watts, which briefly commented on Malcolm's position on self-defense. Watts, who had also attended the meeting of radicals at the grassroots conference in Detroit, had

Carlos Russell interviewing Malcolm X, 1963. Photographed by Al Hicks. Courtesy of Carlos Russell.

pushed for a viable alternative to the leadership of the civil rights establishment. Meanwhile, he remained wary of the Nation of Islam. Once Malcolm began to develop a political viewpoint independent of that of the Nation, many radicals, including Watts, perceived this as an opportunity to build a radical alliance. Watts's editorial referenced the March 12 press conference, where Malcolm had said "out loud what many Americans of African descent had been saying for years." Malcolm's mention at the press conference of forming "rifle clubs" to protect black lives was confirmation among the civil rights establishment of Malcolm's distance from their less outwardly confrontational efforts. Watts then turned his attention to Malcolm's exit from the Nation. Interestingly, Watts appeared subdued in his mention of the importance of the break. His editorial ended as follows:

> In splitting with the Brotherhood of Muslims, Malcolm X announced that he was going to pursue a more activist program by participating

in the civil rights movement in such areas as the political, economic and social arena. Nothing was spelled out by him, but the fact that he recognized the present struggle in terms of an all-out assault on the white power structure was a welcome breath of fresh air in contrast to the crawling, cringing, begging, pleading leadership of our present professional Negro leaders. One man cannot make a revolution; Malcolm is going to have to come up with a program and organization, if he is to take his place in the leadership ranks of the black revolution.[125]

Watts was not an easily impressed man. It is hard to know if there were ever any leaders whom he felt he could unconditionally support. An unwieldy independent skeptic to his core, his support of Malcolm's positions on self-defense, black nationalism, and civil rights criticism was as close as Watts came to fully and consistently endorsing any leader. Yet once Malcolm's break became public, the *Liberator*, like many other radical groupings, followed his efforts more closely. Many radical groups lined up to see who could create solidarity with Malcolm before another group might take advantage. This does not detract from the sense of genuine support that many radicals gave Malcolm; it only serves to suggest that many people were anxious to assess the type of evolution he had experienced and whether it confirmed or alienated their own appraisals of his trajectory. But it was clear that if black activists conjured up a prototype leading light, Malcolm X was it.

In another article, published in May 1964, Pete Beveridge noted the type of attention paid to Malcolm and other New York leaders by fearful authorities in New York City, including Harlem rent-strike leader Jesse Gray and Bronx CORE leader Herbert Callender.[126] Pointing to the fact that the police were more concerned with determining a black leader than they were catching real criminals (i.e., banking institutions and housing authorities), Beveridge wondered why white state and local officials were more frightened by a possible uprising than the concerns and conditions precipitating social unrest, such as the persistence of police brutality, poverty, and the denial of expansive political power. New York City police commissioner Michael Murphy's statements that publicly referred to Malcolm X as a threat to social order for refusing to follow a more "sincere" and peaceful course in favor of violence, caused Beveridge to remark sarcastically, "He is perhaps referring to the efforts to resolve job discrimination in the construction industry or educational discrimination and de facto segregation."[127]

The *Liberator*, being attentive to the ebb and flow of national civil rights politics and international anticolonial struggles, was one of the earliest radical publications to note Malcolm's transition. In the month following Watts's editorial endorsement, *Liberator* published Malcolm's interview with staff writer and editorial board member Carlos Russell, which sought clarity on Malcolm's program. At least one of Malcolm's writings was published in the magazine while he was on his second trip to Africa. Writing and references to Malcolm in the *Liberator* reveal the extent to which radicals identified with and incorporated aspects of Malcolm's vision and how much their insistent probing may have influenced his.

Sitting Down with the Minister

Following Malcolm X's much publicized, contentious departure from the Nation of Islam, Carlos E. Russell arranged for an interview.[128] In his subsequent article, Russell pressed Malcolm for a clear definition of his program. As his perspective evolved, Malcolm strained to give a precise explanation of the direction he was headed in. Russell seemed eager to get at the core of Malcolm's thinking. It is interesting that he did not ask him about the controversy with Elijah Muhammad. Russell probed Malcolm for a blueprint, raising questions about his definition of black nationalism, whether he had a position on socialism as a possible solution for black people's needs, and whether a coalition with the civil rights establishment was worth the effort.

Malcolm discussed the necessity for like-minded Black Nationalist leaders to come together and "formulate the best approach towards this end. It will not be unilateral." Finding himself unsatisfied with this answer in the transcribed version of the interview, after Malcolm's response, Russell editorialized his criticism: "It became apparent to me that the Minister, like all of the present Negro leaders, is caught in just this trap: the 'how' to achieve their aims. The problem of the black man in America has become a cliché, but the solution is still forthcoming. This is the real tragedy of the black struggle—it borders on futility."[129] Russell's comments indicate some of the rising expectations that came with Malcolm's separation from the Nation of Islam. Many people anticipated sweeping changes, a program that could be quickly implemented, or an organization that could begin the work Malcolm identified. Having just left the maelstrom of the Nation and facing the uncertainty of the future, request for a precise definition from Malcolm was a remarkably tall order.

During the interview, Russell, perhaps anticipating Malcolm's swift rejection of a socialist answer to black oppression, asked directly, "Speaking of socialism . . . how come neither you nor any of the other leaders ever use the term socialism as an alternative?" Malcolm responded by hinting that socialism might, in fact, be an answer, but one that people were not prepared to contemplate, much less organize toward. Russell went on to ask Malcolm why he saw fit to join the civil rights struggle and if this was contradicting his anti-interracialist perspective toward social transformation. Malcolm replied that he intended to demonstrate the ineffectiveness of fighting for civil rights in America, and since civil rights were denied in America, the United Nations perhaps afforded a better opportunity, a more appropriate stage on which to indict America's practice of procedural discrimination of black people. Malcolm's internationalist vision concluded that the condition of black people in the United States was a violation of human rights, that is, the rights belonging to people as human beings, and not merely civil rights, that is, those belonging to people as citizens of a given nation. This human rights approach was a hallmark of Malcolm's internationalist perspective; his worldview held that black people were a part of a world community of struggling people of color fighting for an end to their social, political, cultural, and economic subjugation under imperialism, colonialism, and American racism.

At the conclusion of his meeting with Malcolm X, Russell editorialized: "Reflecting on Malcolm's remarks, I felt that there was much truth in what he said; yet, somehow, something was lacking. He gave answers, but they were slogans, ready remarks. He knew the problem, but I felt that he was struggling with the solution. One thing is sure—Malcolm X is indeed a charismatic leader; if he were able to fully integrate all of the loose ends which, at the moment, seem to escape him, in terms of economics and politics, he would indeed become the most formidable leader black people have ever known. Secondly, he is badly in need of an organization; his mosque will not suffice."[130] These comments reveal that Russell, an admirer of Malcolm, was not afraid to call Malcolm's approach flawed. Malcolm was evolving but he had not formed a clear path toward liberation by this point. This interview also reflects the growing interest in Malcolm among many radicals. Many seemed to disparage his commitment to Islam, perhaps viewing such ties as a religious distraction from a broader fight for black liberation. At the same time, however, many also recognized the strength of Muhammad's movement. For example, writer Shelby Sankore wrote an article in the form of a letter directed to Muhammad Ali (who had recently changed his name from Cassius Clay), in which he displayed his appreciation for the transformative methods of the Nation. "Judging trees by their fruit," wrote Sankore, "America has produced nothing else to rival the Muslims in transforming people into well behaved citizens, and morally dedicated men and women—so often deriving these results from the most degraded elements in society, 'hate' or the lack of it notwithstanding."[131] As many writers have noted, considering the effectiveness of its recruitment activities, the Nation's success transforming the formerly incarcerated is perhaps its greatest and most unparalleled achievement.[132] Russell's interview with Malcolm did not discuss the Nation's "Fishing" program (as recruitment was called), however. Russell sought to extract a sense of direction for black liberation. The importance of this interview is that it is not a celebration of Malcolm's outspoken activism and charisma, but rather a serious attempt to understand Malcolm's approach to the substantive change that would lead to the respect and recognition of black humanity in America. Russell's conversational inquiry ran the gamut from prospects of socialism to definitions of black nationalism, from participation in the civil rights efforts to the role of the black middle class and questions surrounding African independence.[133]

Malcolm, who frequently referred to himself as a Black Nationalist, explained to Russell his view of the cornerstones of the concept: "I mean by Black Nationalism that the Black man must control his own community. We must control the radio, the newspaper and the television for our communities. I also mean that we must do those things necessary to elevate ourselves socially, culturally, and to restore racial dignity." Defining the concept broadly, Malcolm envisioned a united front of Black Nationalists to detail the specific program. Marking his break with the religion-centered program of the Nation, Malcolm, exhibiting a characteristic blending of religious and secular approaches, expressed a willingness to work with civil rights, but this too was a stage in a series of efforts to inspire a united front, and not an end in itself. It also did not signify a complete reversal. Malcolm genuinely wanted to meet the people where they were not where he hoped they would be. The master recruiter who had honed his skills in the leadership ranks of one of black nationalism's most polarizing organizations, relished this newfound aspect of his work though he was deeply uncertain about its outcome.

At once, measuring the distance between himself and King, Malcolm quipped that King's explanation of "Social Disruption" was more similar to his own frequent use of "Bloodshed" in describing revolution than many people were able to admit. King, according to Malcolm, used "big words" like "social disruption," whereas he is more "direct and to the point; this is what the white man doesn't like. I say violence and I mean violence," he told Russell. The united front was needed to make revolution real, Malcolm added, pointing up that black people at all levels of society had a role to play in overturning the power structure of America, emphasizing, "We need the alley Negro, the Harlem Negro, the middle class Negro; we need them all."[134] Having established the Muslim Mosque, Inc., two months prior to the interview with Russell, Malcolm seemed to relish his newfound latitude in participating more fully in the broader struggle for black liberation. This meant he could also redefine the principles and terms on which his political activities would stand, including identifying the tenets of his Black Nationalist political outlook.

Numerous scholars have traced the evolution of Malcolm's ideas.[135] According to chronicler George Breitman, Malcolm was evolving in his definition of black nationalism throughout the last year of his life and ultimately arrived at a more internationalist sense of black solidarity, in distinction from the more-or-less separatist philosophy of the Nation of Islam that he had espoused throughout much of his time in the public eye. A basic yet important shift that Breitman identified was the description Malcolm gave to his two organizations, the Muslim Mosque, Inc. (MMI), and the Organization of Afro-American Unity (OAAU). According to Breitman, when Malcolm founded the MMI in March 1964, he used the term "black nationalist," which was more in line with earlier definitions he held while a member of the Nation. In contrast, upon returning from his second trip to the continent and the formation of the OAAU in June 1964, notes Breitman, Malcolm significantly decreased his usages of the term. Breitman points out that no mention is made of black nationalism in either the organization's "Statement of Basic Aims and Objectives" or its "Basic Unity Program."[136] Equally significant is Muhammad Ahmad's description of Malcolm's evolving perspective. A founding member of RAM, a group for which Malcolm was to serve as international spokesman, Ahmad writes that Malcolm had "successively progressed from revolutionary Pan-Africanism to one of third world internationalism. At the time of his death he was moving to a position of revolutionary socialism."[137] Whether or not Malcolm had made a turn toward the civil rights struggle, he brought with him a firm sense of black political possibility, a feeling of black peoples' need to control their own lives and look with self-assured pride on who they were. These were real issues that impacted black peoples' ability to navigate American society with their wits intact. Moreover, Malcolm sought to bring all black people who were potentially drawn to the ideals of the civil rights movement closer to his vision of justice.

Although Russell expressed a degree of skepticism in his conversation with Malcolm X, he admired Malcolm and, like many other black radicals questioned the effectiveness of nonviolence as a practical philosophy in the face of violence. "It is time that the black man in the United States reevaluate the efficacy of non-violence," he wrote in August 1963.[138] "I say this in all honesty, for I believe that the practice of this doctrine is not the real means with which to combat racism in America." Russell's perspective on nonviolence placed him in agreement with Malcolm X and the Nation of Islam, and Robert F. Williams. It is clear from this article that Russell disagreed with the strategy of moral suasion: "One cannot morally persuade those who intend to enslave, for by definition they are devoid of morality." Russell saw the issue of violence and nonviolence as a matter of defending black dignity. Echoing the fiercest rhetorical moments of Williams and Malcolm X, Russell argued for "Dignity, love of self and people, cries for action. Action which the white racist can feel. He has to learn that he cannot strike and expect no retaliation; he must feel and smell his own blood, hot and sticky, mingling with the dust, the same as the black man whose skull he cracked."

The *Liberator* monitored Malcolm's radical moves with increasing support. Staff writers continued to refer, with a degree of admiration, to his break from the Nation of Islam and his public criticism of white and black liberals. Once his break was final, it gave many people the hope that an effective united front could be achieved. After padding his credentials as an international representative of African Americans fighting for freedom, Malcolm headed to Africa on July 9, 1964, traveling throughout North and West Africa until November. As would be expected, he sent many letters and postcards to family, friends and allies while abroad. One of the letters he mailed back to the states arrived in time to be published in the *Liberator*'s July 1964 issue after he had visited Cairo, Egypt, Beirut, Lebanon, Nigeria, and Ghana.[139] While in Nigeria, he wrote that a Caribbean visiting professor at the University of Nigeria, Ibadan, had publicly challenged his lecture and was summarily shouted down and thrown out by the students. Otherwise, Malcolm was treated with admiration wherever he traveled, meeting with and speaking to as many students as possible and at least fifteen ambassadors from Africa, Asia, and Latin America. The Muslim Student's Society of Nigeria welcomed him "home" and gave him the name "Omowale" which, he noted, means "a child has returned."[140]

Ecstatic about being on the ancestral soil of Africa, this time untethered and on his own itinerary, Malcolm's letter spoke of Nigeria's world power potential, owning to its abundant natural resources. He noted the rapid modernization of Ghana and spoke proudly of the "very progressive intellectual atmosphere" of the African American expatriate community there, which included Julian Mayfield, George Padmore, Maya Angelou, Leslie Lacy, Alice Windom, and Shirley Graham Du Bois, among numerous others invited from the diaspora by Prime minister Kwame Nkrumah to help build the new nation. While there, Malcolm spoke to members of the Ghanaian House of Parliament, lectured at both the University of Accra at Legon and the Kwame Nkrumah Ideological Institute at Winneba and had an hour-long private meeting with Nkrumah.[141] Though Malcolm spoke highly of the new country under the direction of veteran pan-Africanist Nkrumah, he could not have known the pressure the Nkrumah was under from constituents and adversaries alike.

According to Kevin Gaines, Malcolm's visit to Ghana was less exciting than the pan-Africanist leader from Harlem expected.[142] Still reeling from a public feud with his spiritual father, Malcolm longed for a community of activists aggressively defending African descendants' rights as human beings. While in Ghana, the African American expatriate community that formed there were Malcolm's natural hosts. Though a hero from home had returned home and there was much to celebrate, Malcolm also wanted an appraisal of the nation's progress. But the expatriate community, primarily through Julian Mayfield, informed him of the stiff, nearly impenetrable difficulties the new nation was experiencing. Moreover, they attempted to warn him of the corruption that appeared to have seeped into Nkrumah's government. Unknown to Malcolm, by the time he visited the country it was embroiled in turmoil. Nkrumah had survived an assassination attempt earlier that year and feared that the machinations of CIA disruptive activities were in full swing.[143] Malcolm, having been loosened from the weight of the Nation of Islam, had been sufficiently inspired by the formation of the Organization of African Unity (OAU), which was formed in 1963, to establish his own Organization of Afro-American Union (OAAU). In an effort to cement his organizational ties to Africa, he established a Ghanaian branch of the organization.[144] The *Liberator* reported that an information bureau of the OAAU had been established on August 27, 1964. This bureau would circulate information about the African American struggle to Africans and African Americans on the continent as a part of broader efforts to strengthen ties between Africans and their descendants around the globe.[145] Though the success of his organizational activities after his NOI membership would not come to fruition, Malcolm made a lasting effect on Ghanaian students, teachers, intellectuals, and workers.[146]

The politics of black international solidarity that Malcolm experienced demonstrate some of the challenges to building tangible linkages between African Americans and Africans on the continent. Notwithstanding these challenges, however, Malcolm's capacity to both inspire and frighten complicated his efforts to clarify his evolving perspective, distance himself from the NOI, and build a brand new organization. It can be argued that the *Liberator*, having been founded to highlight the political and cultural connections between African Americans and African descendants the world over, was brought back to some of its core ideas through Malcolm's renewed emphasis on and attention to Africa. In the first two years of the periodical's existence greater attention and space was paid to the continent. Exigencies occurring throughout the American South and North, however, drew its attention closer to home. Malcolm's assassination, coupled with the little organizational groundwork he was able to accomplish and the instability of African independence, inspired the *Liberator* to return some of its attention to the continent.

The *Liberator*, like most other formations on the left, paid close attention to Malcolm's political evolution. In the July issue, which featured Malcolm's letter from Ghana, the periodical also ran the first part of Cruse's seminal series, "The Economics of Black Nationalism."[147] Just below the first page of Cruse's essay, Watts published an editorial note that sought to locate Malcolm X in the context of Cruse's discussion of economics. The editorial pointed out that though Malcolm had split from the NOI to the applause and anticipation of many people, his economic perspective, at least as publicly stated, still included the buy-black strategies that had been staples of radical black protest since Reconstruction. As Malcolm could not offer a completely new program or a new set of economic ideas, Cruse's essay would therefore provide the explanation of the economic aspects of black nationalism, hence the editorial note accompanying the article. Cruse's article was not a critique of Malcolm's economic philosophy, however, but rather an attempt to situate Malcolm's black nationalism within a historic arc that reached back to the days of Marcus Garvey and W. E. B. Du Bois.[148] In this way, Cruse demonstrated that both Malcolm and the Nation of Islam belonged to a tradition of black radical protest thought, while at the same time careful not to glorify or discredit the philosophies wholesale. Though the split between Malcolm and the Nation partially recalled some of the larger fissures in the civil rights era, the Harlem Riots of the same year raised the stakes on the direction black political mobilization would take. While black internationalism remained high on the political agenda, the conditions throughout the United States were hard to ignore. As activists doubled back to concentrate efforts on the American scene, urban struggles for justice dramatized the urgent the need for collective organization.

The Harlem Riots, 1964

The Harlem Riots of 1964, which lasted for four long days, began on July 17 with the shooting death of fifteen-year-old James Powell by an off-duty police officer named Thomas Gilligan in the front of Senator Robert F. Wagner Junior High School. Gilligan alleged that the young boy lunged at him with a knife and he was therefore forced to fire three shots at him. One shot hit him in the hand, another in his abdomen, and a third bullet missed its target. When news of this killing reached Harlem, the black community there rebelled. Staff writer Ossie Sykes wrote of the riot as a rebellion by "the downtrodden, who . . . exploded in a fury of resentment against a society that hates them."[149] Accompanying Sykes's report on the Harlem rebellion was a cartoon of King dressed in a dark suit with a satchel hung across his chest illustrated by Leo Carty. Across the satchel were the words, "Dr. King's Tranquilizers: 'Bleed and Be Happy,'" and King is shown handing out pills on a path from Birmingham to Harlem, leaving black folk battered, bruised, and discombobulated along the way. Positioning the cartoon adjacent to Sykes's report, emphasized how *Liberator* perceived the question of nonviolence, a theme consistently poked at throughout the magazine. Moreover, it reminded readers that African Americans were victimized and in a perpetual state of war. Indeed, Sykes likened Harlem to South Vietnam and other war-torn sections of the globe, a point Malcolm also made often, though at the time of the rebellion he was still on his African tour.[150] Sykes's article also pointed at one of the flyers distributed during the rebellion. One such flyer, produced by the Harlem Defense Council (HDC), which was likely a front for the Progressive Labor Party, pictured Gilligan in a police uniform with the words "WANTED FOR MURDER" in bold letters above the photo.[151] Sykes's report also displayed a highly incendiary and controversial flyer that instructed how to make a Molotov cocktail, which was also circulated during the rebellion. Though the words, "Harlem Freedom

Fighters," were stenciled across the top of the handbill, it is uncertain if this was an actual organization, and it is more likely to have been an ad hoc group of agitators.[152]

The HDC was one of several groups that organized the United Council of Harlem Organizations, which consisted of Negro American Labor Council (NALC) members, Muslims, Christians, NAACP representatives, and African nationalist organizations, as well as Parent-Teacher Association members.[153] This loosely formed and politically diverse coalition, which was also known as the Unity Council, was headed by NALC leader Joseph Overton, and Livingston Wingate, chairman of the Harlem Youth Opportunities Unlimited (HARYOU) Executive Committee.[154] The Unity Council had several meetings with Mayor Wagner, at which they informed the mayor and his staff of their demands. The group, which represented a broad cross-section of Harlem residents' political opinion, urged the mayor to appoint black police captains to head up several key precincts servicing predominately black areas of the city and to promote other African American officers to ranking positions. They also called for the immediate suspension of Lt. Thomas Gilligan and the formation of a Civilian Review Board. And finally, they demanded the release of all Harlem residents arrested during the rebellion. Out of these the mayor accepted only a disappointing fraction of the group's proposals.[155] On August 15 the *New York Times* reported that forty-seven-year-old Capt. Lloyd George Sealy had been appointed as the first African American to head up Harlem's largest police precinct, #28, which was located at 229 W. 123rd Street. Sealy had been on the police force for twenty-one years. The pressure put on police commissioner Michael J. Murphy by Harlem residents accounts for the Sealy appointment. But despite these appointments there remained a heightened degree of tension between Harlem residents and "New York City's finest."

From this point on, the *Liberator* was full of reports and analyses on the crisis facing Harlem's African American community. The crisis there mirrored the crisis nationwide. The staff appeared energized by its charge to present the facts that were ignored in the mainstream press. C. E. Wilson penned an article in the September issue that, like many others, pointed to a crisis in black leadership. Clayton Riley, taking a break from his analyses of the arts, asked: "What's Next?" and echoed Wilson's critique of the impotence of civil rights leadership. Civil rights attorney and *Liberator* editorial board member Len Holt and Bill Mahoney coauthored an article that was equal parts appraisal and critique.[156] Focusing their attention on the police state that formed in the wake of the uprising, they told of the

Rebellion or Revolution   171

ineffectiveness of government strategies of control, which in addition to the fortress of police also included inept government agencies siphoning money and resources from the black community. They wrote of the many Harlems throughout the country:

Harlem—New York!
Harlem—Philadelphia!
Harlem—Detroit!
Harlem—Los Angeles!
Harlem—Birmingham!

Holt and Mahoney's article captured the view of many residents, activists, and organizations of Harlem as a northern example of neglect, depreciation, and blight, which were the byproducts of white supremacist attitudes and policies. As a global community, Harlem represented a domestic colony, a position advanced by Cruse, Robert F. Williams, Askia Touré, and Malcolm X, the limitations of the analogy notwithstanding. Indeed, Malcolm consistently urged that African Americans cease calling for civil rights, and instead advance a global-minded defense of human rights.[157] Holt and Mahoney concluded their article on a cautiously hopeful yet disturbingly visceral note, writing: "If the recent rebellion in Harlem can stimulate these and other self-help programs of improving Harlem life and making its residents less dependent on the Man and more dependent on each other, the deaths and bestialities will not have been in vain. Otherwise the anguish suffered by black bodies will have been but hot urine cast in the sour milk of Harlem life."[158]

In January 1965 the *Liberator* celebrated its fifth anniversary and received more attention and perhaps recognition for its role as the "intellectual voice" of the protest and liberation movement. Internal controversy also helped in the clarifying of positions. The editor in chief and staff writers were not afraid to jump into a fight, and they often provoked arguments among themselves. C. E. Wilson remembered the evening planning meetings where the contents, themes, and issues to be covered in forthcoming editions would be hashed out. "We would meet on Thursday nights. We would come and argue," he recalled fondly. "They would argue about what theme we would go for . . . that was to me a spectacular time."[159] While Watts and his rambunctious crew of scribes grappled with the question of which analyses and topics the periodical would interrogate, the captivating Harlem-based internationalist at the center of so many of their articles was gunned down.

Black Power and the Movement after Malcolm

Malcolm X's assassination on February 21, 1965, would spark a new level of intrigue in New York City politics and shook the radical community to the core. Immediately, residents asked why Malcolm had not received government protection, given that he had been under government surveillance night and day for the past ten years. This tragedy not only left the OAAU without its leader, it also left radical Black Nationalists without a public figure to relay their positions. Regardless of whether Malcolm was the sole international spokesman for all African Americans, he articulated and stood for many of the principles shared by radicals and nationalists of all stripes. Though many nationalists disagreed with him on the specifics of liberation politics, they generally supported his efforts to publicize the global plight of African descendants.

The March 1965 issue included a photo of a young brown-skinned boy with his hands gently clutching the gate behind which he is sitting. The photo, taken by Harlemite Roy DeCarava, depicts the child's gaze as one of bewilderment and uncertainty about life in the aftermath of Malcolm's assassination.[160] Dan Watts editorialized the "Unfulfilled Promise" of the slain OAAU leader. Watts used an 1848 remembrance of early abolitionist David Walker written by nineteenth-century emigrationist Henry Highland Garnett as an epigraph to his editorial remarks. "He had many enemies," it began, "and not a few were his brethren whose cause he espoused. They said that he went too far, and was making trouble, so the Jews spoke of Moses. They valued the fleshpots of Egypt more than the milk of Canaan."[161] Likening Malcolm to Walker was not difficult, for Malcolm had believed that black folk were still enslaved and frequently used slavery as a metaphor to dramatize their continuous struggle for freedom.

Pointing toward a conspiratorial explanation of the murder, Watts echoed the general confusion as to why there was no police protection at the time of Malcolm's death and blamed "the climate of hate and racism in the United States, a country that has been the graveyard of all the hopes and aspirations of 20,000,000 Americans of African descent" for the murder. He then went on to describe the ensuing void in black leadership. Though many people anxiously anticipated Malcolm's full entry onto the stage of black leadership occupied by King, many others, including Watts and other *Liberator* staff members, were as skeptical of the messianic style to which the African American community was drawn. Watts spoke somberly of Malcolm's slain potential: "It is not what he was but what he was becoming that was destroyed." Malcolm's death was a blow to nationalists of all stripes and Watts felt that a moment of unity could be achieved in view of Malcolm's general importance. He believed it was time to "close ranks" as black people and fight the racism and xenophobia of white America collectively.[162]

Other *Liberator* writers were equally moved by Malcolm's message and life's work. Ossie Sykes, for example, having met Malcolm through Phaon Goldman, a personal friend, recalls that he seriously considered joining the OAAU prior to Malcolm's death.[163] And Carlos Russell had relished being the first and only *Liberator* staff member to sit down with Malcolm for a one-on-one interview. Placing aside the critical journalism he had displayed in his interview with the minister, he penned a poetic eulogy whose last stanza read,

> Put a torch to the robes of mourning . . .
> For he would not have us weep.
> My brothers,
> Let not the Lion sleep!
> To fight, that he might live,
> Is a promise we must keep.[164]

In April, members of RAM (ostensibly Touré, Neal, and Ahmad) published their analysis on why Malcolm has been killed.[165] In this article they identified several reasons why Malcolm posed a threat to the U.S. government, which, they argued, was ultimately guilty of Malcolm's murder. The RAM scribes emphasized Malcolm's connection to Marcus Garvey and W. E. B. Du Bois through an undying love for Africa and for the reciprocal role Africans and African Americans played in each other's political fate. Here again, they stressed Malcolm's Bandung-inspired global vision, which revitalized the hope for pan-Africanism. They linked Malcolm to Patrice Lumumba and spoke of his efforts bridging an older generation of activists together with younger radicals. He was "going in a direction that would have consolidated both generations towards black liberation. In this context, he was to black America what Lumumba was to the Congo," they argued.[166] Most of all, they noted how Malcolm's efforts to take the cause of African American liberation to the United Nations also threatened the government's international image. By this time RAM played a central role on the magazine's staff, and had showed open support for Malcolm long before his departure from the Nation, if for no other reason than his advocacy of armed self-defense.

Malcolm X holding daughter, *Liberator*, April 1965. Courtesy of Pete Beveridge.

Back in the January 1965 issue, Ahmad had published the influential article, "Revolutionary Nationalism and the Afroamerican Student," which offered an explanation of the evolution of black youth consciousness.[167] The article is part sociological analysis and, judging by its conclusion, part apocalyptic essay. Ahmad provides an explanation of the contradictions faced by black college-educated youth. Picking up on E. Franklin Frazier's seminal study, *Black Bourgeoisie,* Ahmad argued that black college students were faced with the crisis of realizing that their educational attainment would not remedy the problem of racism and discrimination, and that, in other words, the student "leaves school only to find a hostile, savage, white world." As a result, black students would either withdraw into hedonism in an effort to be hip or would try to imitate whites, with the latter type represented by graduates of black colleges. Both groups refused to face the reality of their predicament. Ahmad and others saw a new consciousness and a new young intelligentsia emerging from the contradictions.

Ossie Sykes and C. E. Wilson penned an equally poignant piece in the May 1965 issue, which attempted a broader reading of Malcolm's meaning within the history of black political and religious leadership. They argued that Malcolm was a man ahead of his time, whose "death marked the end of prospects that the Negro revolution might become revolutionary. There will now be no spokesman for the wretched bottom."[168] In the same issue, Wilson compiled a number of Malcolm's sayings culled from press conferences and Carlos Russell's interview.[169] The June issue featured A. B. Spellman's article. "The Legacy of Malcolm X," which, echoing Wilson and Sykes, argued that going forward, the black community must organize rather than wait for another charismatic leader. Spellman's article sought to pierce the cloud of uncertainty after Malcolm: "What the assassination teaches us is (1), from here on it must be organization and not personality. And (2), there are elements within the black community which can be used to do the fascists' work."[170]

Despite the shock rippling through the radical community, during the summer of 1965 the magazine appeared to be at its height in terms of the attention it received. Its editorial board consisted of a combination of older and younger generations of male radicals including Clebert Ford, Len Holt, LeRoi Jones (Amiri Baraka), Larry Neal, Clayton Riley, Carlos E. Russell, Charlie Russell, Ossie Sykes, and C. E. Wilson. Tom Feelings, the esteemed visual artist, served as illustrator alongside Leo Carty, who had produced many of the hysterically satirical caricatures of civil rights activists, U.S. presidents, and others who appeared to stand opposed to *Liberator*'s brand of radicalism. Harlem stalwarts James Baldwin, Richard B. Moore, and Ossie Davis were still listed as members of the advisory board. As discussed earlier, although two women held staff positions—Kalibala as secretary and Kattie Cumbo as production advisor—the glaring absence of women reflected and anticipated black women's demands for more visible inclusion in the movement as a whole. The attention paid to the *Liberator* by a young set of radicals is exemplified by the presence of Neal, and to a lesser extent Baraka. As impatience with liberalism grew, black radicals sought out spaces to communicate their ideas and issue their demands. With Watts's intention to have the *Liberator* represent the nationalist and perhaps dissenting voices of the black left, Neal and others saw an opportunity to not only publish their work, but also to situate themselves in a position to move the magazine in a more radical direction.

Art critic Larry Neal shared Baraka's belief in the need to create a radical aesthetic practice and revolutionary vision. Neal would take full advantage of developing these themes as arts and culture editor of the *Liberator* from 1964 to 1966. Neal, like Baraka, Cruse, and others, was equal parts cultural critic, cultural historian, curator, artist, and political agitator. In summer 1965, Neal, at age twenty-seven, was an influential member of RAM which, according to Muhammad Ahmad, saw its role as influencing existing organizations toward a more radical direction from the inside.[171] Longtime staff writer and political theorist C. E. Wilson confirmed this stance, stating it as part of the reason he decided to leave the *Liberator* staff. He observed that Neal, Askia Touré, and Ahmad were attempting to use the *Liberator* as a platform for RAM-specific political ideals, rather than contributing to a collective of black political thought without specific ideological ties. Though he felt their critique of Malcolm X's assassination was timely and accurate, he did not believe their open advocacy of violent revolution was advantageous and felt it might do more harm than good.[172]

RAM represented a brand of black radicalism that it termed revolutionary nationalism, and which combined an unflinching analysis of the capitalist destruction of black life with an assertive embrace of African cultural identity. In line with the general dissatisfaction with liberalist notions of social change, *Liberator* consistently dedicated its pages to display the shortcomings of liberalism, whether espoused by black or white commentators, as when Neal penned an article sharply critiquing the ideology of integration espoused by longtime pacifist and March on Washington organizer Bayard Rustin. By 1965, the radical turn away from civil rights protest politics had revealed the failures of liberal-integrationism. In fact, many people on the left never believed integration could be a viable solution to political and economic inequality and exploitation. Yet it was mainly the critique of the rhetoric of liberalism and the appeal to international solidarity that distinguished black radicals from the civil rights leadership. For example, in the spring of 1965, the Detroit-based factory worker and radical theorist James Boggs wrote a letter to *Liberator* editors explaining the main differences between liberal-integrationism and revolutionary struggle. After providing a brief cautionary history of the absorption of the American working class into mainstream America, he concluded, "The more seriously the freedom struggle in this country becomes, both in terms of ideas and in terms of power, the more intimate must become its international ties; while the more integrationist it becomes the more fearful it will be of such ties."[173] Black Power's emergence at the middle of the decade would also benefit from the critical, historical analysis of Boggs. *Liberator* readers would become acquainted with Boggs through the widely circulated "Black Power: A Scientific Concept Whose Time Has Come" in two parts in the magazine. He offered a view that forced Black Power proponents to engage the structural, societal questions that went beyond "any special moral virtue in being Black."[174] In many ways, Boggs represented an intergenerational link between Touré's Angry Generation and longtime radicals who had come of age decades earlier. His would be one of the critical voices providing what he considered historical and dialectical insights into the emergence and expression of Black Power.

Moreover, the existence of religious and spiritual groups such as the Nation of Islam, the Yoruba Temple, and the Moorish Science Temple pointed to the cultural and spiritual alienation many African Americans felt toward western society. One of the key elements of Malcolm X's attractiveness among African Americans was the consistent attack he leveled at Christianity as the white man's religion. In the Epilogue to his critique of Rustin, which is entitled, "A Reply to Bayard Rustin: The Internal Revolution," Neal writes of a desire for spiritual renewal, indicting America as "a society which has abnegated both collective and individual responsibility, a society that is devoid of guidelines for bringing about the necessary internal or spiritual changes which will enable us to move forward towards control of our destinies."[175] Neal, a RAM member who advanced revolutionary nationalism, could equally be regarded as a cultural nationalist, owing to his explicit analyses of the role of cultural production in the black political struggle and RAM's embrace of African cultural heritage as a force in black identity. Neal's approach to both the material and spiritual desires of African American liberation politics reveals the fluidity of identity and the limitations of strict labels. "Therefore," he wrote, "the Muslims represented, at least initially, an important philosophical and religious thrust into the history of our struggle for survival in this graveyard of North America. Coming with a message of spiritual redemption and translating it into physical and objective terms was very inspirational to many of us who are both spiritually and culturally alienated in a society that basically has no way of relating to us."[176]

Neal's critique was in response to a recently published article by Bayard Rustin in *Dissent* magazine.[177] According to Neal, America was experiencing "upheavals . . . in a whole realm of spiritual, social, and cultural values." Rustin, who had been the chief organizer of the 1963 March on Washington, had criticized Malcolm X in a *Dissent* article for lacking a clear program for black people to follow. In reality, however, Rustin foreclosed Malcolm's program, which eschewed interracial coalitions as a panacea, while Rustin held that such alliances were essential to any program for black political, social, and economic change. Neal challenged Rustin and his co-author, Tom Kahn, for lacking a viable program as well. For Neal, Malcolm's rhetoric was far more effective than the integrationist program Rustin espoused. Moreover, in Neal's mind, Malcolm's vision for black liberation was closer to the "needs and aspirations of black people" than any strategy offered by Rustin. "Malcolm told the truth," argued Neal. "He made his commitment to a more soulful world by attacking the whole range of values and psychological barriers which have kept black people in a semi-colonized condition." "Malcolm's stance as a black man was *itself* a program," he contended.[178] For Neal, what distinguished Malcolm from "the Rustins and the Farmers who compete with each other for government favors and white acceptance" was, not, only his rhetoric, but also his efforts to "internationalize" black struggle. In Neal's words, the Organization of Afro-American Unity "was the first real step toward revolutionary black unity ever taken in this country." Neal argued that "civil rites" leaders failed to fully understand the global dimension of the domestic struggle against racism and economic colonialism. Referencing Du Bois, Garvey, Fanon, and the Kenya-based Mau-Mau rebellion, Neal argued that the internationalization of black liberation in the United States was the necessary next step in the movement. In other words, the black struggles underway around the globe "illustrate clearly what a people must do to liberate themselves." Neal concluded by returning to the cultural and metaphysical issues he pointed to at the beginning of his critique. "Malcolm knew that the only real program for black people lay in the area of black unity, black spiritual and intellectual awakening, black leadership and Mau-Mau-like commitment to change."[179]

Here, Neal points to the difficulty and limitations of certain labels used to describe the contours of black radicalism. Though Neal considered himself a revolutionary nationalist, a description he and many others believed Malcolm X personified at the time of his death, he also spoke of the spiritual and psychological elements that were often kept out of a strict interpretation of black political struggle. Malcolm therefore represented both an antiwestern spirituality and cultural outlook through his embrace of Islam and an anticolonial stance rooted in global black solidarity.

Like many nationalists of the period, Neal also espoused a masculinist attraction to Malcolm by emphasizing his quintessential manhood in the face of the emasculating features of American culture and global white supremacy, or as he claimed, "a world dominated by beasts of prey." Neal also expressed a negative concept of masculinity when he derisively claimed that the black community had "gotten bad vibrations from the *effeminate* projections of the Rustins, the flabby orientation of the Farmers and the shuffling acts of the Kings."[180] *Liberator* was, however, attentive to King's anti–Vietnam War position, even if Dan Watts's editorial still cast King as a peace movement opportunist.[181] The appearance of this statement is perhaps evidence of the threat Rustin posed to Neal's ideal conception of manhood, which was captured and immortalized by Ossie Davis's oft-quoted line from Malcolm's eulogy that "Malcolm was our shining manhood." By taking aim at Rustin's sexuality (Rustin was an openly homosexual man), Neal attempted to undercut his credentials as a public figure in the civil rights movement. Elsewhere in the article he comments, as if speaking directly to Rustin: "Yes, we remember you Bayard on that day [of the 1964 Harlem uprising] as you came off sounding remote and freakish, the nature of your alienation deeper than even James Farmer's." That he would describe Rustin as "freakish" appears to underscore not only Neal's contempt for Rustin's political outlook, but also his way of life.[182] In other words, Rustin was less of a man than Malcolm, which was one more reason not to trust his politics. To be sure, Neal was one among many in this period who coupled liberation with an ideal vision of black masculinity. Fearing for their survival in the wake of a violent white backlash to the civil rights movement, men and women in the movement often conceived of a nation of strong black men with strong wives raising strong black babies for the revolution. These notions persisted throughout the era, impacting the way black people envisioned community, shaped identity, and imagined revolutionary struggle, until a more pronounced and vocal black feminist movement surfaced in the latter end of the decade to challenge such idealized notions. Thanks in large part to Neal the pages of *Liberator* would continue the drumbeat Malcolm inaugurated with fervor. In particular, after his death, black radicals placed emphasis on his impact on culture. Neal, alongside Baraka, believed that it was the cultural realm where society was most porous, where Malcolm's ideas might filter in and inject the world of cultural production with an electrifying sense of commitment to liberation.

Throughout 1966 Neal penned a number of essays that influenced the reception of Black Arts aesthetics and radicalism. Establishing himself as cultural critic and literature expert, he published two essays in the January issue of *Liberator* that year, "Development of Leroi Jones" and "The Black Writer's Role—Ralph Ellison."[183] This issue is telling of the new focus on aesthetics and the critical role the magazine played in Black Arts criticism, as the writing of three central Black Arts figures, Neal, Jones (Baraka), and Snellings (Touré), were featured. Baraka was making his name known as a serious writer and standard-bearer of African consciousness and culture. Neal's article on Jones was important because of the way it situated the new generation of black writers. "Leroi Jones is Black, is thirty-one years old, is a man dedicated to the liberation of his people by any means necessary," it began. "In this latter he is not unique. There are many others like him. A significant part of the generation born in the mid-[nineteen] thirties feels the same way. That is, they have almost a cosmic desire to tear out of the value system that their parents had so much faith in," he continued, emphasizing not only the youth of the generation, but its worldview and inchoate system of values.[184]

Baraka's life and work are described as having reached a new plateau of critical awareness, of consciousness. Neal wrote that Baraka represented the type of African American writer who was college-educated, of middle-class origins, but who had no illusions about American society. "But for the Negro," wrote Neal, "education is full of interesting paradoxes. While the system exposes its good face, its ugly one also comes into view."[185] Neal described this educational experience as "spiritually destructive." Out of this destruction emerged increased awareness and a "unified identity" (perhaps as opposed to the Du Boisian Double Consciousness), which sought to blend spiritual needs with political (i.e., revolutionary) desires, the shared experiences of the African American community and the international community, and "a necessity to bring aesthetics in line with ethics."[186] Neal wrote of a commitment to militancy, especially in the aftermath of Malcolm X's assassination, which shook the black radical community and gave many people a sense of renewed purpose and dedication. And though Neal described Baraka as a poet who was also politicized, he perceived Baraka's approach to Black Consciousness as a useful spiritual concept to buttress revolutionary nationalism. "The Task, as Jones sees it," he wrote, "is to develop 'Black Consciousness' [into] a Black spiritual frame-of-reference based on the humanism of the Bandung world (non-white world)."[187] Eleven years earlier, the Bandung Conference was convened in Indonesia. American writer Richard Wright attended and was awed by the alliance developing among nonwestern nations gathered at the conference, and his account of the conference and its implications as far as he could discern was compiled in the book, *The Color Curtain* (1956). Though Wright was uncertain about the future impact such a formation could have on the dominating tendencies of the western world, he was at least inspired by the notion of nations of color attempting political autonomy. Neal, Baraka, and Touré (Snellings), among many other radicals of the period, held Bandung in high regard, no matter the limitations and complexity of building it into a more coherent alliance. For many, Bandung was a signal that the western world did not control the political destinies of nations of color. Though documented by Wright, Malcolm X was chiefly responsible for the popularization of Bandung as inspirational for black liberation. It represented a direct repudiation of the decadent society many believed the West to be.

The *Liberator* dedicated the February 1966 issue to Malcolm X's legacy, running articles by Len Holt, Neal, and Touré. Ironically, this issue seemed to be overshadowed by the anti-Semitism controversy discussed earlier in this chapter. Quoting from lines in Baraka's poem "Black Art," Dan Watts's editorial urged readers to carry on where Malcolm had let off and build institutions for "economic survival, political power and cultural inspiration." Significantly, Malcolm represented a bridge connecting spiritual commitments to political determination, serving to inspire the cultural production and worldview of Baraka, Touré and Neal among countless others.

The following year would witness critically important writing on Black Power. While mainstream press outlets scurried to fill its pages with the most incendiary definitions of the concept, had they wanted a firm and principled understanding of its emergence, they could have turned to James Boggs. In a series of searing articles beginning in January 1967 and continuing again in April and May of that year, Boggs provided perhaps the clearest description of Black Power and its attendant stakes. "Power is not something that a state or those in power bestow upon or guarantee those who have been without power because of morality or a change of heart," he cautioned. "It is something that you make or take from those in power." Approaching fifty years of age by this time, Boggs not only theorized revolution, but also welcomed opportunities to mentor younger radicals. He did not counsel against revolt; he wanted black people, especially young revolutionaries to possess a deep knowledge of its emergence in the bosom of racial capitalism. For Boggs, "people of color were not only the wretched of the earth but people in revolutionary ferment."[188] Boggs's analyses, alongside those of Cruse, cemented *Liberator* as a premier site where theoretical arguments were explicated as activists grappled with the challenges, opportunities, and political desires of a new day.

······

Larry Neal's impact on the *Liberator* was felt even after he left his position as arts and culture editor. Writing in the July 1967 issue, critic C. H. Fuller Jr. referenced Neal in his article, "Black Art and Fanon's Third Phase," in which he assessed the role and responsibility of black writers in the liberation movement through the lens of Frantz Fanon's *Wretched of the Earth*. Fuller, recalling a debate that emerged forty years earlier during the Harlem Renaissance, criticized black authors for their adoption of western values. Fuller argued that black writers were stuck in those stages, failing to arrive at their revolutionary purpose precisely because of their embrace of westernized concepts of individuality and free expression. "Should our individuality take precedence over their [the black community's] needs?" he asked. "Some will argue yes, but the fact of the matter is that only when we subordinate our individuality to the struggles of our people do we come to know them and their struggle." Neal, according to Fuller, correctly perceived the role of the artist in the black community. Rather than place an emphasis on individuality, he notes that an artist should "be one with his [or her] community." Moreover, "what is felt by the people begins to awaken them and ultimately becomes a part of their revolution."[189]

Conclusion

Black radicals were up against the clock. They felt the pendulum of the struggle for justice swinging in their direction and they worked to take full advantage of the moment as the stakes increased. While numerous debates were had and hundreds of public diagnoses of the condition of black communities were offered, black radicals were still shouting from the bottom of the well, as the late scholar Derrick Bell once put it. The talented, highly dedicated, and remarkably focused bunch that put mind to paper were unapologetically vocal agitators, yet they still possessed an extreme deficit in materializing their proposals for change. Yet, their persistent arguments nudged the black liberation effort further than it had ever gone before. Nonetheless, it was still a nudging. American society remained resistant to the prescriptions for a new society put forth by the choir of *Liberator* antagonists, insuring a bevy of frustrations for those who had dedicated themselves to pushing for social transformation. While many looked outward at an intransigent capitalist racial order governing American society, the movement also took its toll internally. As the environment of an outwardly male-dominant movement sharpened itself against the steel of American politics, it tended to overshadow the work of women who were equally fit and often better equipped to fight against the racial and economic status quo. *Liberator*, too, performed by a largely male-centered script, yet a cadre of female activist-writers would also mark its pages with their own liberatory vision, at once challenging and fueling black radical politics in this period.

Several other developments serve as critical signposts for the trajectory of the *Liberator* and the challenge of defining black radicalism in the mid-1960s. The March on Washington; the rise, assassination, and contested resurrection of Malcolm X; the radicalization of, and ensuing splits within, established organizations such as SNCC and CORE; the increased skepticism toward interracial alliances; heightened antipathy toward liberalism and gradualism; the advancement of Black Power in rhetoric and organizational vision; the blossoming of Black Arts expressive culture; the embarrassing demise of the once charismatic Adam Clayton Powell; and the persistence of neocolonialism in Africa, which dashed the hopes of pan-Africanist radicals are but some of the main instances marking the rise in expectations and the crushing disappointments of this period. More challenges lay ahead, and activists would have to count small victories along the way. *Liberator*'s role shaping of black radical thought left an imprint on a range of activist-intellectual activities. Though much of its work concerned explicit political debates, its openness to the radical cultural work of a class of professional and self-determined artists would perhaps be its lasting contribution to the black liberation era. It is to the radical aestheticians to which we at last turn.

5 New Breeds, Old Dreams
Liberator and Black Radical Aesthetics

....

> After Malcolm's death, thousands [of] heretofore unorganized Black students and activists became more radically politicized. . . . Never before had Black artists entered into such a conscious spiritual union of goal and purpose. For the first time in history there existed a "new" constellation of symbols and images around which to develop a group ethos. What was happening in Harlem was being repeated all over the United States. Black people were shaping a new concept of themselves both in the national and international sense. Where we were going, we did not know. But one thing was certain, we knew that, as James Brown says, we were a "New Breed."
>
> —Larry Neal, "On Malcolm X"

Larry Neal's description of the emergence of a new wave of black artists would be a clarion call only second to that of Amiri Baraka's Black Arts Repertory and Theater School (BARTS) manifesto. Similar to Michelle Wilkinson's use of "socio-aesthetics,"[1] black radical aesthetics include the cultural work infused with radical political visions, culturally independent formations, translocal and transnational in scope. *Liberator*'s demonstration of the search for a radical black aesthetic was central to its political vision. The political revolution would only be achievable through a demonstrable form of cultural remaking. In other words, culture was the soil on which politics were played out. In this sense, perhaps culture played a more central role in revolutionary imagining than it is given credit for through an explicit focus on political forms of campaigns, direct action protest, and electoral engagement. Moreover, stewardship in the realm of culture was as much about *power* as identity, empowerment, pride, and heritage.

Larry Neal's expertise as cultural organizer, aesthetician, scribe, and social philosopher would capture and catalyze the transformative purpose connected with the years preceding Black Arts Movement activity, and continued throughout the range of organizing and institution building fashioned by him and Baraka, among numerous others. This chapter turns attention to some of the contours that map the "new constellation of symbols" of which Neal spoke. Though Neal and Baraka loomed large over this period as driving personalities, they were by no means the only two figures imprinting the era with similar tools and strategies. Critics, artists, activists, and poets such as these were not merely social commentators. Instead, they saw their work as an effective tool in a larger political endeavor. This work was as much about personal transformation as it was about transforming society and reimagining a just society. As Robin D. G. Kelley wrote, "For many black radicals seeking justice, salvation, and freedom, the vision of socialism proved to be especially compelling, even if incomplete."[2] Exploring the political and aesthetic dimensions of the self in the world facilitated the passage of multiple strategies for political and cultural mobilization. Neal's espousal of black radical aesthetics would magnetize much of the activism espousing a specific, philosophical notion of black global identity in which art and cultural work played a pivotal role. Their productivity advocated an expansive diasporic, transnational knowledge of African cultures and a complex sense of the role of black culture in American contexts. As this chapter will show, artists and activists associated with *Liberator* saw their art and politics as two prongs in a singular black revolutionary project throughout the decade. As writer-activists, and torch bearers of a sort, cultural work of this new breed extended the long-held ancestral hopes of a liberated future.

Liberator's coverage of aesthetic life and practices in this period evolved from basic advertising of local community events and Africa-inspired soirees to providing sophisticated and detailed analyses of the capitalist control of black cultural production. As a period of considerable anxiety over the creation of independent cultural institutions, the debates in which *Liberator*'s writers and readers engaged in also reveal great complexity across a range of different activities and articulations. Artists doubled as critics and critics tried on new lenses through which to view black art. Writers such as Clebert Ford and Larry Neal echoed general calls for autonomous institutions to service the aesthetic needs of African American communities across New York and the entire United States, in particular Ford's advocacy of black theater production as instrumental to African American social progress. As a stage actor and theater activist, Ford's writing in *Liberator* anticipated more assertive claims for an autonomous black theater that emerged in subsequent years, though he is all but unknown in the cultural histories of 1960s black radicalism.

Neal's tenure as *Liberator* arts editor added seriousness and sophistication to the magazine's discussion of radical aesthetics. Many of Neal's most prominent and original articulations of black culture and politics in the mid-1960s were first published there. As the epitaph to this chapter indicates, Neal was one of many black cultural savants radicalized in the wake of Malcolm X's assassination. What Neal called the "New Breed" proved to be the cultural complement to John Henrik Clarke's announcement of "New Afro-American Nationalism" at the start of the decade. As key markers of black political and cultural life that came to fruition during the 1960s, both Neal's and Clarke's ascriptions contain the resurgence of an Africa-inspired militant nationalism and its impact on how U.S.-based African descendants challenged and interpreted the world around them. As the late scholar Richard Iton wrote,

> In their choices regarding whether to conform or transform, resist or embrace, confront or disengage, the distinct substantive dimensions of political and cultural existence become more salient and germane. Questions of geography and genealogy have less purchase on Black thought as the inside and outside; the local, transnational, and global; and past, present and future become conjoined and in some respects conflated. Moreover, beyond the cataloguing of geographical presences and genealogical connections, there is the possibility of approaching Black identifications conceptually: as a matter of indexing a related set of sensibilities that resist quantification, physical or temporal classifications, and corporeal boundaries.[3]

Liberator's advocacy of radical aesthetic practices in the 1960s includes black visual artists as well as jazz criticism, both key elements that help round out its approach to Black Arts, and one of its lasting contributions. It was the rare issue that did not include both cutting-edge cultural reviews and political analyses. Throughout the decade, *Liberator* interviews and commentaries covered the following areas: literature (especially novels and poetry), music (particularly jazz, but also blues and R & B), visual arts, theater, film, and sport. *Liberator*'s expansive analysis and explanation of these aspects of cultural life were as central to its overall influence on the period as its political analyses were. In this way, *Liberator* contributed to pivotal debates on black radical aesthetic practices that intersect with the politics of culture. Moreover, *Liberator*'s writers and subscribers took seriously the role of culture beyond mere artistic production and placed heavy emphasis on building independent institutions as part of a larger globally envisioned black radical project.

Afternoons in Africa: *Liberator* and the Celebration of African Culture

Attendant to the explosive interest in African independence was a growing attention paid to African cultures emanating from the African continent. Understanding and celebrating African culture took a variety of forms from the establishment of African cultural festivals in the United States and in Africa, and the production of new literacies about the numerous ethnic groups of a region, as well as its beliefs, habits, and of course, rituals.[4] African Americans were as drawn to this cultural search as anyone in the state department. As African Americans had long made assertions of their Africanness in heritage even if they were now of the West, many took the political independence movement as an opportunity to reappraise the meaning of their citizenship. No longer merely tied to the coerced or embraced patriotism demanded by U.S. citizenship, African Americans were looking to Africa for cultural as much as political inspiration. The early activities of the Liberation Committee for Africa (LCA) stemmed from their efforts to create and sustain tangible connections to African and Caribbean communities scattered throughout the United States. From 1961 to early 1963, activists closely associated with Dan Watts worked under the auspices of the LCA. However, as their publishing arm grew, their activities would fall under the umbrella of the *Liberator* from 1963 onward. As the LCA sought to influence U.S. policy toward newly independent Africa, most of its activities were directed at the United Nations. While it monitored U.S. relationships with African diplomats, LCA associates built friendships and alliances of its own. Cultural and social events were always a part of its networking activity. It frequently held celebrations for political figures as well as association members. Most often these social events were intended to raise awareness about the association's activities, gain allies, and, importantly, to raise funds to expand its efforts. They would host concerts, book fairs, lectures, and panels as ways to continue community outreach.

In the early period of the magazine, *Liberator* did not cover many arts and culture events, owing to its original targeting of U.S. imperialism by focusing on mainstream politics and observing and critiquing top-level government policies. However, attention to culture quickly increased as black consciousness began playing a more prominent role in black liberation politics. However, the pull of identification with Africa was frequently tied to issues of cultural proficiency. Through the writings of theater and social critic Clebert Ford, the socio-philosophizing of Larry Neal, and the poetic artistry of Askia Touré and others, the magazine emerged at the forefront of a new articulation of how cultural awareness and institution building served the global political needs of African Americans. These figures emphasized the role of culture in a newly awakening black consciousness and *Liberator* was the stage on which their analyses of the politics of black diasporic culture were first disseminated.

Though the theories of black art and aesthetics advanced by Ford, Neal, Touré, and Baraka had not yet arrived by early 1961, the LCA participated in the cultural life of New York City by sponsoring a number of events throughout the first two or three years of the magazine. Though not always driven by ideology, these events were efforts to inject a political perspective into the representation of African culture and African Americans' knowledge (or lack thereof) about the African continent. The magazine's earliest documentation of such events appeared in July 1961. At that time, LCA held an "African Night Festival," which was attended by over 200 people, including students and diplomats from Africa and the Caribbean. LCA thanked the attendees of the gala "for making it possible to add a net profit of $214 to our treasury."[5] In another effort to raise funds for the committee's work, the LCA announced an event entitled, "An Afternoon in Africa" that would feature an African fashion show and the music of Michael Olatunji that September.[6]

In the first month's issue of 1962, the program for the Negro History Week celebration included speeches by the Ghana, Guinea, and UAR missions to the United Nations, alongside the performance of their "Freedom Now Suite," by the dynamic jazz tandem, Max Roach and Abbey Lincoln. In honor of Lumumba, the night would also feature Ossie Davis and Ruby Dee who had recently staged Davis' play, *Purlie Victorious*, which garnered the praise of critics and activists alike.[7] Davis and Dee, who graced the cover of *Liberator*'s February 1963 issue, were part of a vanguard of black actors equipped with the talent that made them marketable to mainstream audiences to a degree. Yet their careers were also driven by an imperative to make art relevant to all aspects of black life. Black actors in New York, in particular, struggled against discriminatory practices that kept them off Broadway. Beveridge reported that black actors often picketed against tokenism in the theater industry. An ad hoc group, led by actor Clebert Ford and called the Committee for the Employment of Negro Performers, came together in an effort to organize this concern into a larger movement for equality on stage.[8] Davis and Dee's presence (even at this early point) added legitimacy to radicals and progressives, as they were as steadfast in their vision of racial and economic justice and African decolonization as they were established professional artists.

Though black actors struggled for marquee recognition, African musicians visiting or living in the United States often fared better. For example, the African Cultural Group of the U.S.A. was supported through the embassies of African countries at the United Nations. In the summer of 1962 this group sponsored an "African Symphony" at Carnegie Hall that featured Nigerian musical great Fela Sowande, then visiting the United States on a coveted Rockefeller fellowship. Sowande's concert was part of a several month effort to introduce the U.S. audiences to West African culture. Attendees were treated to African music, dress and, of course, food.[9] At these events guests were fed jollof rice, fish stew, and groundnut and palm nut soup, among other dishes. LCA encouraged families to serve staple West African dishes in their own homes and even published the recipes for groundnut soup and jollof rice in anticipation of an upcoming African embassy–sponsored event.[10] All the newly independent African UN delegates were featured at these events alongside American personalities representing New York state government and U.S. representatives at the United Nations.[11] It is important that these activists sought to maintain distance from U.S. government forces, which had their own designs on the relationship between African Americans and the African continent.[12] Though LCA associates sought to build relationships with African diplomats, oftentimes this hinged upon political expediency. As Beveridge put it, once many of these officials realized what little influence on government policy the group had, they ceased to socialize with the same frequency. With small resources and limited social cache, LCA realized that they could play a more significant role disseminating black thought rather than planning the next soiree.

Responsible Arts Institutions: *Liberator* and Proto/Black Arts Criticism

In 1963, Afro-Panamanian writer Carlos Russell (no relation to Charlie) joined the executive board of the LCA. In March, his interview with prizefighter Sonny Liston appeared as the cover story.[13] This was one of several interviews Russell conducted with notable cultural and political figures. His other interviewees included basketball star Bill Russell, Brooklyn minister

Reverend Milton Galamison, and his most prominent, sit-down with Malcolm X. Russell was a writer of many talents. In addition to covering a number of different issues for *Liberator*, ranging from politics to cultural affairs, he was also a poet. One of his earliest *Liberator* poems was entitled, "Negritude," in which he implored black people to "show thy soul!" and "let thy voice ring through the wistless [sic] winds."[14] Yet, another poem similarly implored African Americans to embrace rather than negate their black features: "Why can you not see that those things which God has given you—Black skin, hard and nappy hair . . . Are things for which you should be proud?"[15] Here, Russell anticipated the more assertive "Black is Beautiful" and "Black and Proud" pronouncements that achieved popular currency later in the decade.

When Russell arrived from Panama he enrolled at DePaul University. After completing his studies he served as a director of youth programs in Chicago before relocating to New York. In New York, he intended to focus more on his writing, and through a variety of connections found the Harlem Writer's Guild (HWG). Like many other budding writers who passed through the Guild, Russell honed his skills for a life committed to black global liberation. While young writers such as Carlos Russell, Charlie Russell and others cut their literary teeth under the tutelage of John Killens and John Henrik Clarke, elder literary giants, such as Langston Hughes continued to make their presence felt by mentoring and otherwise encouraging a younger generation of writers and activists. Hughes, for one, actively supported the efforts of younger writers and published several pieces of poetry in the pages of *Liberator*. For instance, inspired by an article on drug addiction in the ghetto, Hughes penned a poem entitled, "Junior Addict," whose opening lines began:

> The little boy who sticks a needle in his arm
> And seeks an out in other worldly dreams,
> Who seeks an out in eyes that droop
> And ears that close to Harlem screams . . . [16]

Several of Hughes's poems would be published in *Liberator* from 1963 until 1966, representing one of the last visible links between the Harlem Renaissance and the emergent Black Arts Movement. In the role of elder, Hughes's presence loomed large and he remained a touchstone for many young black writers throughout the 1960s and after. With connections to the artistic royalty found in the Harlem Writers Guild, Davis and Ruby Dee, and even Hughes, *Liberator* padded the institutional credibility it acquired as a key player in the radical aesthetic constellation of New York City.

In addition to the HWG role as a literary training ground, many young writers and activists were also drawn to the Umbra Poets Workshop, a critical proto-Black Arts collective, which functioned as a writing workshop more than as a political unit, although most of its members and associates were engaged in a range of political activity and were themselves self-styled activists.[17] Attentive to other formations throughout the city, *Liberator* reviewed Umbra's self-named 1963 publication in the April issue that featured Hughes's poem, calling it a marriage of "beauty and bitterness," and quoting a few lines of its poetry. Staff writer Clebert Ford referenced Umbra in one of his many defenses of black nationalism and artistic expression. Askia Touré, a founding member of Umbra, published his first piece of poetry in *Liberator* around the same time as the Umbra collection appeared in print. "Cry Freedom," a poem published in the May issue, introduced readers to a young fiercely political poet who would develop into a major figure of Black Arts. The Umbra review, though brief, reveals a growing interest in Black Arts consciousness in literature. These institutional sites of organized activity allowed die-hard activists and emergent writers to fashion a sense of duty to their craft and opened efforts to promote justice concerns simultaneously. These cultural workers exhibited an awareness of the world beyond their artistic production and imagined strategies that enabled the full array of their social claims.

While poetry and novels were suitable outlets for many, theater was also critical to the development of Black Arts in this early period. Though critics and artists such as Neal, Baraka, Bullins, and others are rightfully credited with shaping theater criticism, these figures overshadow lesser-known figures such as Clebert Ford who was first, in the pages of *Liberator*, to articulate the significance of the theater for African American artistic activity. Little is known of Ford, however; he seems to have receded into relative obscurity following the demise of the Black Arts Movement. Beveridge once described him as someone "who gave everything to the movement," implying that he had little to fall back on once the movement unraveled.[18]

Ford developed his career as a stage actor who gained some attention for his role in Jean Genet's *The Blacks* and had previously appeared on Broadway. Much as Robeson and Baraka were artists as well as critics and scholars of their art form, Ford wrote of the history of black people in theater while also establishing a fairly stable acting career. He was not simply an actor or a writer, but both, publishing reviews of plays and films, conducting interviews with artists, and theorizing black theater throughout 1963 until 1964. With Black Arts activity springing up among a host of U.S.

translocalities, many turned their attention to black artistic expression on the home front. As *Liberator* coverage indicates, as the rise of Black Arts attention on continental African culture waned it was replaced by a determined search for and defense of autonomous cultural institutions throughout the United States.

Ford wrote that the time had come for African Americans to assume responsibility for producing art that reflected reality in all levels of media production. White writers, producers and directors, it seemed, were incapable of rendering black life in all of its dynamism and complexity. He began and ended his assessment of problems facing black people in theater by pointing to current musical productions, one of which centered on the life of early twentieth century black vaudeville performer, Bert Williams, entitled *Star of the Morning*. This play, written by People's Theatre founder Loften Mitchell, directed by Edmund Cambridge, and produced by Houston Brummit, exemplified the kinds of roles black artists were to assume. "What is needed is total involvement in America's theatrical currents, and on every level from producer to backstage, from set designer to choreographer, writer and director," Ford wrote. He firmly believed that the ingredients were in place for such a transformation. White producers were incapable of accurately depicting black life, their token roles for black people did more harm than good, black audiences were ready to attend the theater, and there was a wellspring of talent waiting for greater exposure. Additionally, he claimed, black entrepreneurs were financially able to underwrite such projects. That these strides had not been made, that the "story of the Negro's true American experience" had not been told, was "a tremendous loss to the entire world, black and white," he argued. Ford's case for full representation of black life and American society in theater mirrored demands for political power in society at large. The kinds of advances sought in explicitly political spaces could also be applied to the world of theater.

Like many of his peers, Ford viewed the struggle for artistic representation as central to a people's expression of humanity. "Give the Negro an opportunity to truly express himself, not necessarily as a social problem but as a complete human being; not only as subservients [sic], singers and dancers alone, but as they truthfully exist in our society . . . the entire spectrum of human life as it exists in American life," he concluded. Ford, who played a leading role in the Committee for the Employment of Negro Performers (CENP), blended his acting prowess with activism off-stage. A photo from a CENP protest outside of the Broadway musical comedy "How to Succeed in Business Without Really Trying" showed marchers holding pickets using language that would be familiar to a public attuned to the fluctuations of civil rights protest that read "An Integrated Stage, An Integrated Theatre."[19] This May 1963 issue of *Liberator* signaled the magazine's emergence into a formidable presence on the art-criticism scene geared toward black audiences and forecast greater attention paid to the arts featured in future issues. Included with Ford's article was an excerpt from a forthcoming novel by Charlie Russell, poems by Rolland Snellings (Touré) and Desmond Victor, and Eleanor Mason's article on African American women's beauty standards. Yet, the sorts of appeals Ford offered were more in the mode of protest that politicized Black Arts writers came to reject. Soon after these calls for greater inclusion and exposure, Black Arts theater advocates would replace calls for integration with assertions of independence. However, Ford's overall view is in keeping with a transitory political space that many occupied in this period.

Clebert Ford carved out a solid career in theater and cinema. Ford played in *The Cool World*, based on the book by Warren Miller in the spring of 1960, and Lorraine Hansberry's *Les Blancs* (*The Whites*) in 1970 before starring in Melvin Van Peebles' *Ain't Supposed to Die a Natural Death* from 1971 until 1972. Back in 1963, Ford reviewed Jean Genet's *The Blacks* (*Les Negres*) in *Liberator*. *The Blacks*, arguably Genet's best-known play, was for Ford a tremendous success; indeed, the play became somewhat of a staple of proto–Black Arts activity and was staged in many of the theater houses opened to Black Arts productions. Among several notable African American actors, *The Blacks* featured Maya Angelou in a leading role. Prior to leaving the country for Cairo, Egypt and then to Accra, Ghana where she would work with other African American expatriates at the Institute of African Studies at the University of Ghana, Angelou had served as a Northern Coordinator for the Southern Christian Leadership Conference. In Ghana, Angelou wrote for the *Ghanaian Times* and the *African Review*, and also worked with Shirley Graham Du Bois at the Ghanaian Broadcasting Corporation.[20] About Genet's play, Ford wrote: "No play that ever has been presented on an American stage has given the Negro an opportunity to so completely express himself in both artistic and 'social' terms." For Ford, the play was an example of the direction black theater should take. Interestingly Ford also starred in the play. Yet, his review bears a certain degree of distance; he refused to simply praise the piece because he acted in it. In this way, he discussed the significance of the play's symbolism without hyperbole. Being an Off-Broadway production, his review does not appear to be a marketing strategy to sell tickets though he may have used it as such. The apparent objectivity is less important than the fact that as an actor, Ford also played the role of critic, thereby underscoring the calls for ownership over the reception of the play, and an effort to define the terms on which the play would be evaluated, a salient feature of emergent Black Arts criticism. Ford's dual function as artist and critic took him from the stage and into a discourse of black theater. In this arena his criticism symbolizes part of a larger dialogue or conversation rather than a manifesto, and allowed him to participate in a realm shared by other artists who also doubled as critics. There, he was but one voice among many.

Not all critics were as enthusiastic about *The Blacks* as Ford. Writing in *Freedomways*, *Liberator*'s estranged sister publication, for example, Jim Williams argued that the play took up space that could otherwise be filled by black playwrights. Making a case for the creation of a Harlem theater that would serve as a repertory for up-and-coming artists, directors and producers, he also challenged the play's meaning, arguing: ". . . If one play, *The Blacks*, can run for three years with its song of futility, its message of hopelessness, and cynical nihilism," then black audiences should be equally exposed to the work of Loften Mitchell, Langston Hughes, and William Branch, he argued.[21] Ossie Davis, the venerable pillar of the New York arts community once told Charlie Russell in an interview: "Genet is a wonderful writer, but he cannot speak for me. He is speaking of a decadent civilization whose sun is setting. My people's sun is on the rise. Where Genet negates, I affirm that which is human in man. My song is of hope, not despair."[22] Ford's essay "The Responsibility of Black Artists" bears traces of Hughes's 1926 essay "The Negro Artist and the Racial Mountain" and anticipated similar attempts to assign a specific responsibility to African American artists in the writings of Neal, Baraka and others such as Addison Gayle Jr. much later.

Ford, who had also been recently appointed to *Liberator*'s editorial board, saw in comedian Dick Gregory an example of how African American artists could participate in social justice efforts beyond their art. Highlighting Gregory's participation in civil rights efforts in Greenwood, Mississippi, Ford argued that it was the black artist's responsibility to not only create art that reflected social circumstance, but to physically enlist in doing the work required to bring about change.[23] Though Ford identified a role for artists beyond their specific craft, artists associated with *Liberator* had long connected their work to larger justice concerns. Yet, as a stage actor his comments anticipated discussions on the special role of the theater in addressing these issues. The following year he would extend his discussion, focusing on Baldwin and advocating the creation of black community theater.

In its September and October issues, *Liberator* featured Los Angeles–based actor and playwright Frank Greenwood and his Afro-American Cultural Center Committee (AACCC). Greenwood, who was originally from Birmingham, AL, moved to L.A. from Chicago. His ties to the Left on the South Side of Chicago fueled his arts-organizing efforts as he traveled. Upon relocating to Los Angeles he organized the Touring Artists Group, a traveling theater ensemble and the predecessor of the AACCC. The magazine printed an excerpt from Greenwood's play, *Cry in the Night*, which depicted a black man who is brutally beaten by police who suspect him a Muslim. It is not clear what inspired Greenwood's play, but the Ronald Stokes incident that occurred months prior, leaving several L.A. Muslims dead and wounded at the hands of the LAPD, seems to have been a partial inspiration. As a part of its community engagement, Greenwood's multi-talented group helped prevent the closing of Vernon Library (later renamed in honor of *Los Angeles Sentinel* founder and former *California Eagle* staffer, Leon H. Washington Jr.) by planning a craft fair, offering song-writing workshops, facilitating workshops on entrepreneurial strategies that might help counter staggering black unemployment, and offering cultural education courses for youth. These efforts reveal the depth of responsibility many black artists and cultural workers accepted. Greenwood and his wife, Vera, also appeared on local television, which helped to raise the profile of the group and its goals to hundreds of Los Angeles residents, many of whom called the station to ask how they could enlist their knowledge and skills.[24]

Though its artistic bent trickled through the early months of 1963, by October *Liberator* had discovered its footing and confidence as a journal of black politics and arts. As discussed earlier, this issue opens with an editorial questioning the purpose and stated intention of the March on Washington. Inside C.E. Wilson offered a detail review and criticism of the march. An opening article on the Ghanaian expatriate community was included alongside a tribute to the recently deceased W. E. B. Du Bois, just above a letter from British philosopher Bertrand Russell, expressing solidarity with the march. Underscoring the commitment to artists' political engagement, Clebert Ford interviewed Dick Gregory, "a man of the people," who had earlier been placed in a Chicago jail for "disorderly conduct" following a demonstration with CORE activists against school segregation.

Also included in this proto-Black Power/Arts-period October 1963 issue were Askia Touré's "The New Afro-American Writer," the first of three sections of Harold Cruse's "Rebellion or Revolution?," William Worthy's call for the formation of an all-black political party, and a review of Baraka's *Blues People*. Here, in one issue were central aspects of black radical thought and arts in this period, effectively revealing a coherence of black radical politics and aesthetics in progress. By this point the periodical boasted an eight-person executive board that included renowned artist Tom Feelings alongside Watts, Beveridge, James Finkenstaedt, Ford, Carlos Russell, Wilson, and Evelyn Kalibala. *Liberator* enjoyed an increasing readership, as well as subscriptions and encouragement from around the country. Longtime radicals such as Cyril Briggs (deceased in 1966) applauded the magazine's efforts and ordered a subscription after noticing the article "Criticism is not Anti-Semitism," by his "old friend, Dick Moore."

If there was ever a blueprint for the Black Arts and Black Power movements it can be found in this issue. Here was open identification with Africa, and a particularly anti-capitalist, anti-colonialist viewpoint, an exploration of alternative political models through the call for a third political party, the markings of a gender critique, and radical aesthetics in full view. The general mood of the militancy was expressed in Touré's article, which highlighted a new wave of young politically aggressive writers who embraced Black Nationalism. "These young people are mainly a thoroughly educated, politically sophisticated group," he wrote, a cohort "destined to play an increasingly dominant role in Afro-American affairs." While Touré's article was concerned with the present upsurge in youth militancy, Harold Cruse, one of Touré's intellectual mentors, argued for a radical appraisal of contemporary appeals for social inclusion and social change. Cruse urged a rethinking of both "integration" among liberals, and "revolution" among radicals. Published in three parts, Cruse sought to provide an explanation for why liberal ideals failed to create the change implied in the term, and why radical ideas fell short of their revolutionary potential.

Charlie Russell's review of *Blues People* noted the passion and scholarly appeal of Baraka's cultural history of black America. Its publication in this issue befitted the blending of arts, history, memory, liberated consciousness and politics *Liberator*'s reputation entailed. In Russell's words, "*Blues People* poses basic questions about the nature of the society the Negro so urgently seeks to enter, and the disdainful manner in which that society has viewed the artist." Baraka saw music as a mirror of black progress in much the same manner that Clebert Ford viewed the theater. After receiving mentorship by veteran Harlem Writer's Guild activists, Charlie Russell had found a home in *Liberator*. Over the next few years he would continue publishing on a number of subjects for the magazine, including analyses of current events or features on particular groups, but throughout his career Russell was most comfortable reviewing the jazz scene.

Taking a break from his acting career to write, Ford offered a review of recently produced plays with recommendations for future productions. He argued that the activity and agitation occurring throughout the country had also seeped into the theater. A member of The New Group, an ensemble that performed Off-Broadway productions, Ford again assumed the role of participant and critic, proudly asserting that over fifty African Americans had worked on this production. Though emphasizing the theater, Ford also evaluated the strides of black actors on television. He saw 1963 as a signal of changing times, eagerly identifying shows, films, and plays that cast black actors in specific roles or those that had all-black casts. Ford's concern was whether or not the performance world of mass communication could depict the reality of black life. Television shows as *East Side, West Side*, were criticized for the authenticity of its characters as was a show called *The Nurses*, which ran an episode featuring Ruby Dee and Carl Lee. Theatergoers got a chance to see Langston Hughes's *Tambourines to Glory*, as well as several productions by Jewish playwright David Merrick, which featured black actors. *The Ballad for Bimshire* (in which Ford played), *The Worlds of Shakespeare, In White America*, and *Walk in Darkness*, a play about black soldiers in World War II, were all featured on Off-Broadway stages earning the acclaim of a small but dedicated theatergoing audience.[25]

Ballad for Bimshire was a Barbadian-inspired musical directed by Ed Cambridge, starring Ossie Davis, Frederick O'Neal, Christine Spencer, and Jimmy Randolph.[26] Davis, speaking to Charlie Russell on the set of the play, discussed the seemingly contradictory impulses black artists endure. On one hand artists were driven by the desire to express themselves; on the other, their productions had to be financially successful.[27] Davis, who by this time had some mainstream success among African American theatergoers, still struggled to finance and distribute his own productions. His play, *Purlie Victorious* was well received, running for eight months between September, 1961 and May, 1962 for a total of 261 performances.[28] Much of the success of this play could be contributed to the efforts of John Henrik Clarke and Sylvester Leaks, who became the play's official marketing team, writing letters to churches, schools, and organizations and recommending group trips as fundraisers.[29] Featuring other left-connected cultural luminaries Ruby Dee, Godfrey Cambridge, and Beah Richards, the play was an Off-

Broadway success. Davis sought to expand the reception of the satirical piece, converting it into a film version under the title *Gone are the Days* in 1963. Yet, the film had a far shorter run than had the play, showing in only one theater and away from Harlem, as Davis begrudgingly remarked to Russell. According to film historian, Donald Bogle, were it not for Davis' association with the film, it would have been overlooked completely. This was evidence that for black artists moving from stage to silver screen was not as easy as it might have seemed.[30] Like many of the period, Davis believed that African Americans should produce art that reflected their lives. His open identification with strands of Black Nationalism, civil rights militancy, and socialism throughout his life established his credentials in an array of movement circles.

Embracing the black nationalist impulse developing in this period or perhaps influenced by the presence and writing of Harold Cruse, Clebert Ford penned the prescient article "Black Nationalism and the Arts." There, he entered the debate concerning the need for black-centered arts and institutions. Black Nationalist art, whether in theater, music (especially jazz), or dance, should not suffer a lack of skill, he argued. "On the one hand there is an absolute need for black oriented activity in the American theatrical scene, and on the other hand we as black artists must strive for professional excellence," he wrote. In addition to achieving professional respectability in performance, black artists must also begin to produce a collective of professionals, that is, black people should stage plays, hire and pay actors, and develop playwrights. "Once this is done on a community level and in the professional arena of Broadway and Off-Broadway there will develop a truly nationalistic expression in our theatre," he argued.[31] Placing institutional concerns slightly ahead of political sentiment would, he thought, preserve and extend black cultural expression. Institutions, he thought would reflect, cultivate, and encourage Black Nationalism. In this way, more openly nationalistic themes could be pursued independent of the pressure of white mainstream audience tastes, which feared the growing expression of an assertively anti-white artistic sentiment. Charlie Russell's article "Leroi Jones will get us all in trouble," which appeared in June, signaled white fears of an explicitly Black Nationalist theater.[32] Ford's pieces recall Cruse's discussion of the role of culture in instigating revolutionary change. Cruse's exploration of Black Nationalism's roots appeared in the two month's between Ford's articles at the start of the year and when his writings resumed, which helps explain Ford's downgrade of integrating theater and increasing emphasis on Black Nationalist themes, including a collective sense of empowerment and a shared political destiny. Ford took a break from writing while performing, and returned to *Liberator* pages in July and August of 1964.

Upon his return he reviewed James Baldwin's *Blues for Mr. Charlie*, in *Liberator*'s July issue. *Blues* debuted in April and ran throughout August 1964 at the American National Theatre and Academy Playhouse (ANTA) for a total of 148 performances under the direction of Burgess Meredith, and featured Al Freeman Jr., Rip Torn, and Diana Sands.[33] Though Ford was impressed, he argued that Baldwin placated white fears. Conversely, Baldwin, "the official angry Negro" of choice as approved by white critics and the general public, was met with "increasing disenchantment and disillusionment" in the black community, Ford noted. He calculated that "fully fifty percent of 'Blues' is devoted to a white point of view," and concluded: "if Baldwin finds himself becoming more alienated from the black community he has only himself to blame." Ford believed Baldwin was ultimately interested in white acceptance rather than autonomy and independence. Integration appeared to be Baldwin's goal, not liberation from white supremacy. In either case, Baldwin's talent, if not his perspective impressed Ford.[34] Roy Johnson reviewed *Blues* after its uptown debut at the Alhambra Theatre two years after it appeared on Broadway, and echoed Ford's concern, writing that "so many of Baldwin's works," lacking revolutionary sentiment, "can't go the distance."[35] Early on, *Liberator* looked to Baldwin as a burning flame in the liberation struggle. Yet, like most, he was not above criticism. The shifting view on Baldwin's work seemed to mirror larger shifts throughout the movement. Political desires of black artist-activists and intellectuals had moved past fomenting white liberal guilt. In the contested political space *Liberator* helped occupy, status quo white American worldviews were deemed wholly insignificant.

Baldwin's success (and failure) with white audiences was additional fodder for Clebert Ford's assertive call for an autonomous theater. He argued that a viable theater movement was the necessary next step in social progress as far as arts were concerned. In this regard, he believed that the community and the theater could reinforce one another to the health and longevity of both. "A reciprocal relationship may then be realized between the community and the black artist—the one providing audience and stage, the other giving of his talents, informing, educating, inspiring, entertaining," he wrote. He pointed to examples in the Jewish community and in the Free Southern Theatre among the black community of Jackson, Mississippi where successful community theater endeavors were underway. Actors and playwrights Gilbert Moses, Doris Derby and John O'Neal led the Jackson group, and Ford quoted at length from their mission statement. This southern theater movement signaled that black artists in the North frequently looked South for inspiration.[36] Above all, Ford wanted the full realities of black community life around the country reflected on stage and on film.[37] Yet, the experiences of black life in the United States mirrored in key ways black life around the world.

The reality of African experiences was left out of such period films as *Zulu*, directed by Cy Endfield, and starring British upstart actor Michael Caine in his first leading role as Lieutenant Gonville Bromhead. Ford reviewed the film, which debuted in the UK in January 1964. *Zulu* represented the negative stereotyping of the past, according to Ford. Here were tall, blond-haired, blue-eyed British soldiers fighting "black bodies falling at a ratio of 100 natives per 1 white bullet," he wrote. Though allegedly inspired by true events, Ford wondered what this subject matter would look like in the hands of black directors and producers. He pondered whether black women's bodies would have been as gratuitously exposed as they were in the film. Ford noted that black women's bodies were displayed as nude items of pleasure, whereas white women were always shown wearing clothes. "The white woman is still sacrosanct, while the black woman remains a tool of the western white man's sexual fantasy," he wrote, displaying a gender critique that had yet to fully emerge in film criticism by African American or white critics. *Zulu* was yet another example of the need for black controlled art.[38] Ford's review of *Zulu* proved to be his last published piece in *Liberator*. It is unclear why he stopped writing for the magazine; the demands of his acting career may be a partial explanation. He continued acting throughout the decade, but his time with *Liberator* had ended. He is listed on the editorial board for the last time in November 1965.

Ford's analyses of the theater in *Liberator* represent serious attempts to grapple with the direction of Black Arts. His writings are a bridge to the more assertively revolutionary nationalist writings of Larry Neal, Askia Touré and Amiri Baraka, who called for an alternative worldview that would catapult the creation of new arts institutions. Other theater organizers such as Woodie King, Barbara Ann Teer, Ed Bullins, would continue such efforts throughout the decade and long after. King, who relocated to New York from Detroit, and whose New Federal Theatre continues to produce plays to this day, was a persistent critic of the financial constraints that dogged black theater, and an unrelenting advocate of its independence.[39]

While Ford argued for true depictions of black life on the stage, stating that the struggle for black theater mirrored the struggle for African Americans generally, Baraka called for a theater that would completely do away with western ideals. Beginning with the 1964 presentation of *Dutchman*, Baraka stated unequivocally the new direction he thought Black Arts should take. Charlie Russell reviewed the play in the June issue of *Liberator* during its run at the Cherry Lane Theatre in Greenwich Village, starring Robert Hooks and Jennifer West.[40] Russell noted the new assertiveness in Baraka's vision revealed in the play. As one Baraka critic noted, the playwright successfully challenged the historical caricature and stereotype of African Americans as faithful assimilationists in *Dutchman*. In this way he utilized the metaphor of masking, a defining feature of African American cultural experience.[41] Baraka's no-holds-barred approach spoke to the intolerance of liberalism and prefaced his manifesto for a revolutionary theater a year later. As Touré recalled, even some white *Liberator* associates began to worry about the tone of Baraka's work.[42] While Baraka's ideas percolated, his seemingly vanguard role in Black Arts would grab the attention of even the most casual onlookers. Nonetheless, though many feared him, Larry Neal was one critic who seemed to immediately embrace him.

In addition to providing analyses of new directions in theater, *Liberator* also printed the work of playwrights it featured. One example is Douglas Turner Ward's one-act play, *Happy Ending*, which was published in two parts in December 1964-January 1965. Years later, Ward's group, the Negro Ensemble Company, would experience internal disagreements that resulted in new theater formations, most notably Barbara Ann Teer's National Black Theatre. Later, *Liberator* would publish Baraka's one-act *Black Mass*, as well as short stories by Woodie King Jr.[43]

Like Love at First Sight: Larry Neal, *Liberator*, and Black Arts Criticism

Though Larry Neal would emerge as a major theorist of Black Arts, he made his *Liberator* debut in an October 1964 review of the upcoming presidential election.[44] Askia Touré recruited Neal to *Liberator*. As Touré recalled, when Dan Watts met Neal "it was like love at first sight."[45] Watts was known for his acceptance of younger more politically militant, vocal writers. Neal, who had recently completed coursework for a Master's of Arts degree in Folklore at the University of Pennsylvania, quickly became a core *Liberator* associate. Watts appointed him to the position of arts editor, a key staff position, beginning in May 1965, though he had published several influential articles prior to that announcement. Touré jokingly remembered that Watts never provided *him* an official title though he was responsible for bringing Neal to the staff and had published in the magazine dating back to 1963, including a few cover stories.[46]

In December, Neal published two articles: a commentary on Lorraine Hansberry's play *A Sign in Sidney Brustein's Window,* and a review of Ralph Ellison's collected essays, *Shadow and Act.* Though he appreciated the many lines of inquiry Ellison pursued, what Neal called his search for truth, he intimated that younger contemporary writers were turning in a different direction. Having rejected the value system of western society and "its stuffy artiness" these younger artist-intellectuals were "trying to understand the values of what can be called African culture(s)," ostensibly choosing life over "the death-centered focus of Western culture." Neal appreciated Ellison's contributions, however. He believed Ellison was "one of the best novelists of our time," and that if one truly wanted to learn the craft of writing, they should look no further than *Invisible Man*. In this light, Neal identified Ellison's gifts, while embracing a new path. Though Neal displayed restraint in his critique of Ellison, he left no doubt about the Black Arts Movement's transitional and transformative new approach.[47]

The following year, Neal turned close attention to Baraka, focusing on two plays: *The Slave* and *The Toilet* as exemplars of new theater forms. Neal heaped high praise on Baraka's work and concluded that "Both plays are among the most socially-conscious literary works in the history of Afro-American and American drama."[48] Though Neal wrote on a number of subjects pertaining to black life in the period, his cultural analyses made the most significant impact, although as discussed previously he often provided straightforward political commentary. For example, he wrote passionately about the system of welfare, its parasitic qualities and of the need for fundamental change to that system. Though welfare could be understood in terms of class, he argued: "It is not merely, for us, a question of workers being exploited, but rather examining the role that this particular service plays in perpetuating oppression."[49] And though Neal could speak of the structural oppression of the welfare system, for him, the structure of American society was internally corrupt and morally bankrupt. "Black people are more and more the victims of a horrible delusion—democracy," he wrote, castigating civil rights leaders for their appeals to the American government. "Black people still have not recognized that the issue is state power and land. These things are not obtainable within the morality or the law that enslaves us," he continued.⁵⁰ In these articles, which dealt with social relations and state authority, Neal expressed a more assertive political voice than is often revealed in his cultural essays though a similar strategy can also be detected there. They demonstrate Neal's ability as a political thinker as well as a cultural critic and artist. Moreover, they hint at Neal's organizing abilities. He spoke in an everyday language that many could understand. As one of Neal's closest associates, Amiri Baraka remembered, "Larry came at a period of rising political intensity, struggle and consciousness. He passed it on, like the black baton of our history to any who knew him or was moved or influenced by him—by anyone who could read."⁵¹

Neal's writing on culture and the cultural aspects of revolutionary change are perhaps his most influential and memorable. As a critic, he set the tone for radical aesthetics of the period, second only to his good friend Baraka. Like his firebrand comrade, Neal took Malcolm X's assassination as a directive to exhaust every possibility to achieve black peoples' liberation employing whatever tools one had in their repertoire. Neal sense of radicalism was informed as much by Malcolm's aesthetic as his revolutionary vision. "What I liked most about Malcolm was his sense of poetry," Neal wrote, "His speech rhythms, and his cadences that seemed to spring from the universe of black music . . . My ears were more attuned to the music of urban black America—that blues idiom music called jazz. Malcolm was like that music."⁵² A political understanding of African Americans desires could only be achieved through black culture, he would argue, acknowledging a perspective that had been carried in African American thought since the turn of the century. According to Neal, Baraka's *Blues People* came the closest to a theory of culture Neal envisioned. Reviewing local events that foreshadowed the flowering of Black Arts, Neal identified a conference focusing on black culture whose theme was "The Role of the Afro-American Artist," which featured notable Black Arts figures and contributors, including Watts, Baraka, Patterson, Cruse, Baba Adefumi, Selma Sparks, Clayton Riley, C. E. Wilson, photographer Leroy McLucas, Queen Mother Audley Moore, A. B. Spellman, Max Stanford (Muhammad Ahmad), and Josef ben Jochannen (known as "Dr. Ben"). Convened at the Kappa Alpha Psi fraternity house, Neal noted with some hyperbole that this was the first meeting of its kind in Harlem.

In the same article, Neal announced the arrival of Black Arts with the opening of BARTS on 130th street and Lenox Avenue, and recalled the "explosive evening of good poetry" that kicked off the week culminating with theater school's opening. A small, but loud parade down Lenox Avenue led

Black Arts supporters and community members to the brownstone where the new theater was located. Neal, cocreator of this new wave of activity, celebrated the banner-carrying parade, saying, "It was Garvey all over again," as it recalled the Jamaican leader's penchant for elaborate parades through Harlem in the 1920s. A jazz concert and a panel discussion on "The Black Artist and Revolution" rounded out the inaugural events.[53] From that moment forward, Black Arts energy would continue to blaze across the Northeast and spark similar movements around the country. The evolving perspectives, theories and philosophies that help to define the movement would continue throughout the year and the remainder of the decade.

Carrying on a style of mentorship that Killens, Clarke, and others pioneered, Neal would continue to give definition to this movement through his reviews and analyses of black music, visual art, theater, and literature. Watts' eager acceptance of Neal into the *Liberator* ranks was beginning to yield positive results. For Neal, his work was no mere exercise in public intellectualism for its own sake. His was an earnest attempt at shifting the power of definition, that is, the capacity to define and to ascribe positive and negative meaning to aspects of black, and by extension, American culture. Neal believed that power should be in the hands of black people, artists, activists and community members. Writing of the Pulitzer Prize advisory board's failure to recognize the life achievement of Duke Ellington, Neal wrote that the black community should not be upset that a white cultural institution failed to recognize Ellington's genius. Black artists should not continue to seek praise from "a society that oppresses us, exploits us," for its "acceptance" would constitute but "another instrument of enslavement," he argued. Moreover, he added, American society lacked the ability to truly judge black artistry.[54] Here was Neal's attempt to delink the oppressive nature of the white cultural establishment through the strategic mobilization of African diasporic artistic and political desires. Black empowerment meant that "the Black public, Black musicians and artists," should set the standards for evaluating the quality of black art.

A similar perspective is found in Neal's approach to the history of black literature. In a three part series entitled "The Black Writer's Role," he evaluated the major black male writers of the day—Wright, Ellison, and Baldwin—and their approach to the question of the writer's responsibility. Curiously absent from this list is Langston Hughes, who Neal was likely to have the most in common with. Regardless, Neal believed that all black writers, and especially the supremely gifted among them, had an essential obligation in the shifting political climate of the period. "The writer must accept the responsibility of guiding the spiritual and cultural life of his people," he wrote. In his role as literary and cultural historian, Neal placed great emphasis on what can be called cultural genealogy.[55] That is, he located the present blossoming in black cultural and political expression within a history of black cultural activity. Turning first to Richard Wright, Neal saw some of the ingredients of a self-defined literary tradition that drew upon values germane to black experiences in America. Black writers were to embrace rural and urban regional experiences, as well as the ethos of the church and the street. Ultimately, Neal saw in Wright a defense of Black Nationalism, though simultaneously couched in Americana. Neal saw in Wright's work a value placed upon a uniquely articulated black worldview and pride based on experience.[56]

As he had done earlier, Neal turned again to Ralph Ellison. Spending the bulk of the essay on *Invisible Man* and a few of Ellison's articles written in the 1940s, Neal sought to examine the possible directions of black literature. Neal viewed Ellison as a "repository of Afro-American myth, folklore, rhymes and blues," and a "master of language, rhythm, irony and humor" who had not escaped black culture, as some had argued, but who had stopped short of utilizing his knowledge of black culture to inform black leadership. Neal viewed the writer's function as one that represented community outlooks, needs and desires, drawing upon a firm sense of African, Afro-diasporic, and African American history. "The writer's role is to articulate, not only, his perceptions, but those of his people," he wrote. "He functions in any capacity that the situation demands. His work is directed to black people, whites are incidental to it." Though Ellison assisted the general reception of black cultural forms, Neal was unsure whether his intentions were to help black people or to simply entertain whites. Though Ellison had earlier asserted the psychological utility of black culture, he had since moved away from that position, Neal argued. As such, Neal believed Ellison to be wasting his talents.[57] The space provided in *Liberator*, however, was inadequate to fully address this issue. In an article written toward the end of the decade, Neal expounded upon the issues he had raised earlier. Interestingly, Neal appeared in the process of deepening his understanding of Ellison. His self-reflection revealed to him that Ellison was the "most engaging" of all the African American male writers of his generation.[58] The picture accompanying his analysis of Ellison announced Neal's recent appointment as *Liberator* arts editor, though according to Neal his tenure in that role began sometime earlier.[59] A scholarly-looking Neal dressed in jacket and tie sporting dark rimmed eyeglasses with a neatly trimmed Afro and mustache evidenced the "sartorial splendor" he was known for.[60]

In between his studies of the craft of black writers, Neal's two-part series "Development of Leroi Jones" told as much about the generation of writers in their 30s (born in the mid to late 1930s) as it did about the fiery poet-playwright and lifelong cultural organizer. Neal described the tide in militancy that marked this younger generation of writers in a manner that recalled Askia Touré's 1963 *Liberator* article, "The New Afro-American Writer." As mentioned, Neal's "Black Writer's Role" series was arguably the most notable of his *Liberator* writings aside from his unveiling of Baraka. To use a sports analogy, Neal was both ring announcer and corner man for the new literary heavyweight champion Baraka was in the process of becoming. Though he at least mentioned Baraka in several of his writings from this period, in the January and February issues of 1966, Neal returned to discuss Baraka directly, rounding out his definition of the activist-intellectual's place in the new literary movement. He argued that Baraka, like others of his generation, were in search of what he called a "unified identity" that included spiritual development, an embrace of revolutionary principles, a concept of Third World unity, and an emphasis on a distinct aesthetics and ethics.

In the first installment Neal traced the emergence of Baraka, identifying key turning points in his personal and artistic life, particularly his Howard University education, his Greenwich Village lifestyle (although Baraka lived in Chelsea and the Lower Eastside mostly), which included numerous friendships with white writers and artists, and his marriage to Hettie Cohen.[61] In the second installment Neal sought further explanation of Baraka's development, expounding on his ideas and his art. In the preface to this article, Neal underscores the white literary establishment's disdain for Baraka's new direction and the overall attitude of Black Arts. Neal's discussion highlights Baraka's *Blues People*, juxtaposed by *Dutchman*, in an attempt to explain and justify the new approach of black artists to effectively break from the confines of western cultural norms, definitions and expectations. Though the full expression of Black Arts activity was still in its developmental stage, Neal anointed Baraka as "the most articulate spokesman" of the new revolutionary spirit. While Neal celebrated Baraka's talents, his criticism avoided becoming maudlin, primarily because the movement was so new that "it is too soon to predict where all of this is going."[62]

Neal observed that black writers around the world were essentially in the same predicament. In a supplemental article to the "Black Writer's Role" series, Neal reported on an American Society of African Culture (AMSAC) writer's conference that he attended. The conference featured Barbadian writer George Lamming who had been invited to speak on general themes addressed in African and Caribbean literature. Neal was not all that impressed with Lamming though he spoke favorably of *In the Castle of My Skin,* published in 1953. Neal believed Lamming was confused about for whom he was writing. Operating from within a Black Arts frame of reference where the politics of the writer should be discernable to the reader, Neal critiqued Lamming for his ambivalence, writing "Lamming had spent two hours discussing black literature with no discernable audience in mind." "Who is the Black writers' audience? Who are we writing for—our 'neocolonialist masters' or our *own* people?" Neal asked with some disgust. Ultimately, Neal came to a conclusion that typified the militancy of the period, marking a clear break with an earlier generation of writing. He concluded: "Essentially, we are a glorified proletariat accepting an occasional crumb from the tables of the establishment—an establishment which has yet to concede that our work has anything but *exotic* value. Under such conditions, the Black writer is another variation of the court jester—a literary Stepinfechit performing for an audience of white onlookers."[63] Here again Neal provided a sweeping history of black twentieth century literature from the Harlem Renaissance writers down to Ellison and John O. Killens. Neal argued that prior to Black Arts, black literature had not reached its full development as an art for the people in perpetual opposition to white literary standards and criticism. What he and others called the black revolution in literature was launched from two primary platforms: theater and poetry. Neal judged the novel as out of step with contemporary conventions: "the novel is a passive form," he wrote. With an overhaul in theater and poetry already underway, the novel, he argued, distanced a largely working-class audience from the urgency of the moment. Whereas the novel had previously epitomized the highest level of literary respectability, Neal argued that the immediacy of Black Arts required more direct forms. In theater, he identified Douglas Turner Ward, Baraka, and Ed Bullins. In poetry, there were David Henderson, Touré, Ishmael Reed, Marvin Jackmon (Marvin X), Ernie Allen, Hernton, Bibbs, Carol Freeman, Welton Smith, Ronald Stone, and others, according to Neal.[64] Though not all of these writers embarked on careers as poets, Neal was impressed with the frequency and force of their productivity. Moreover, that *Liberator* published Baraka's one-act play *Black Mass* in its June, 1966 issue, is further evidence of the salient role of black theater in this period.

Neal's view is instructive for demonstrating the exploratory nature of the Black Arts Movement. The artists were courageous and possessed with purpose. They often knew what they were eschewing but the result of that work was not always clear. In other words, the project was always the work of improvisation. In this sense, many looked to jazz for inspiration and in that regard they were closer to Ellison that they may have wanted to acknowledge.

Askia Touré shared Neal's vision and sense of urgency. He wrote to Neal of the importance of poetry, specifically the epic poem. Touré sought to "produce literature as well as social action," in a tradition of excellence that stretched back to the "supreme propagandists" of the early twentieth century. Though he was no stranger to the South owing to his North Carolina roots, he was forced to relocate to Atlanta from New York following Malcolm's assassination. Touré argued that epic poetry reflected "psychic changes and growth by which people come to self-realization," a critical but necessary stage in what he viewed as an emergent nationalism. He identified David Henderson's "Keep On Pushin'," Hernton's "Jitterbuggin' in the Streets," Neal's "Lenox Avenue Sunday," and his own "Sunrise" and "Cry Freedom" (the latter appeared in *Liberator* in 1963) as exemplars of the epic form.[65] Touré held a long view of history, mining African diasporic experience to discover a lineage of creative resistance and skilled navigation of some of the most difficult terrain of modern society.

The handwritten letter to Neal reveals Touré's determined search for a clear program and also of the growing impatience with nationalist claims that stopped short of a blueprint for change. In his view, the younger generation was not as clear about which direction to head next as the black writer-activist. Many of the younger radicals had argued that earlier movements had not moved far enough toward a revolutionary program. Here was Touré critiquing his own generation in a way that many, including Touré himself, had not stated publicly. Ranging from culture to politics and media criticism, its central thrust included a call to return South and a critique of the factions developing among nationalists, cultural nationalists, and Marxists, who all claimed to be in search of that all-illusive sense of power.

Though Black Arts/Black Power developed in various corners of the nation, Touré lamented the regionalization apparent in the movement, even as he imagined the South more open to the possibility of expanding Black Arts than New York City was at this point. He viewed regional divisions as a handicap; that activists were so spread out that their regions became more important than the widespread advancement of liberation politics. The lack of unity reflected the lack of coherence. "What did radicals want?" he asked. "If 'Charlie' asked most of us, or a group of us 'militants,' what we wanted, there'd almost be a fist-fight between the factions that would develop: 'Back to Mother Africa!' 'Separate states!' 'Black Revolution!' would be the factional cries, he imagined. He ended the letter stating that "I find that our people are more impressed by institutions than words." Touré and Neal were in constant dialogue about the future direction of black politics, often revealing a sense of frustration and vulnerability that was not easily expressed.

An older generation of writers still loomed large over the incipient Black Arts universe. Long after Baldwin's distance from *Liberator,* and his extended expatriate stay in Europe, Neal still sought to mark the stretch between Baldwin and the new movement. Before departing from *Liberator* ranks, Neal devoted his last "Black writers' role" commentary to an analysis of Baldwin. As had some, he had come to view Baldwin with mixed results. On the one hand, he appreciated Baldwin's sense of social commitment and held respect for the Harlemite's long-standing quest for racial justice. Yet, on the other hand, Baldwin seemed to be torn between his blackness and his American citizenship; a familiar concern held among a number of Baldwin's observers. Baldwin, according to Neal, wanted to save America by forcing the country to face the truth about the history and condition of African Americans, which in turn would reveal the true nature of the country.

In Neal's view, Baldwin's unresolved Du Boisian Double Consciousness prevented him from fully developing into an artist/writer of the people. In other words, from Neal's vantage point, Baldwin's yearning for America to face its true self betrayed his devotion to the black community generally, and left American liberalism unchecked. "His uncertainty over identity and his failure to utilize, to its fullest extent, traditional aspects of Afro-American culture, has tended to dull the intensity of his work," Neal wrote. Though as a critic he could highlight the limitations in Baldwin's artistry, Neal knew the Harlem-bred essayist and playwright could not be ignored. Though Baldwin's work was apparently "suffused with a[n] incisive sense of self-pity . . . it never fails to engage our attention, even when it is unsuccessful."[66] In July 1966, Neal returned to political analysis and offered up a stringent critique of liberalism. His writings on culture had consistently eschewed white liberal judgment of black art, but in this piece he turns directly to the question of liberal writers of African American experience, which he noted were, in the main, of Jewish heritage. Here, Neal joined the ranks of Baldwin, Eddie Ellis, Dan Watts, and other *Liberator* writers who sought to explain the contradictions in relations between Jews and African Americans.[67]

In what turned out to be his final *Liberator* article, Neal reported on the recently convened Black Arts convention, "Forum 66" held in Detroit the previous June. Earlier that month he was married to Evelyn Rodgers in a traditional or "neo-traditional" Yoruba ceremony, over which Baba Oseijerman Adefumi presided.[68] Adefumi also headed up Harlem People's Parliament and participated in the Detroit conference advocating the revolutionary potential of the Tanzanian economic philosophy Ujaama as a path forward. At the conference, Neal shared a panel with poet Dudley Randall, *Soulbook* editor Bobb Hamilton, and Detroit poet Oliver LaGrone. The conference also featured crusading journalist Charles P. Howard, RAM leader Max Stanford, Denise Nicholas, John Killens, and representatives from the Detroit-based theater Concept East founded by Woodie King. Neal noted the ideological tensions that surfaced at the meeting, particularly at the panel on black nationalism and politics, where Marxists, nationalists, and those advocating repatriation to Africa debated the merits of their positions.[69] As James Smethurst has written, Detroit proved to be a major locus of Black Arts activity in this period. More important, the Midwest was known for its institution-building activity, which was relatively more secure than its coastal counterparts.[70] Though *Liberator* was New York–based, it reached Detroit and as far west as California on a fairly consistent basis. It is quite likely that given his prominent role on the magazine's staff, Neal and others carried copies of the magazine with them on their travels around the country. Again, longtime Detroit-based radicals such as James and Grace Lee Boggs wrote letters to the editor commenting on articles published in the magazine. James published his analyses of Black Revolution in *Liberator* as late as 1970, and James and Grace Lee both were close to many of RAM's East Coast associates. Though separated by geography and local exigencies, such vehicles as *Liberator*, *Soulbook*, DRUM, and Broadside Press often closed the distance between cities and movements for many in and around black radical artistic and political circles. Moreover, these sites served as strategic organizing tools that linked translocal networks of activists and potential organizers.

Larry Neal would continue to write, publish, and participate in various efforts around the country years after his *Liberator* service expired. In subsequent years, he wrote for or appeared on a number of television projects focused on black experience. He wrote introductions for reprint editions of

Jonah's Gourd Vine and *Dust Tracks on a Road* by Zora Neale Hurston at the end of the decade.[71] He also lectured at City College of New York, Wesleyan, Yale, and Williams College. Two of his most lasting contributions, however, were the anthology *Black Fire* (1968), which he coedited with Baraka, and *Black Boogaloo*, published the same year. In the summer of the following year, Neal published a long article in *Ebony* magazine, wherein he further explained the major thrusts of the Black Arts Movement and its relationship to Black Power for a more mainstream black audience.[72]

Though Neal was the most notable and respected Black Arts intellectual on *Liberator*'s staff, it was theater critic Clayton Riley who announced the formation of Baraka's Black Arts theater to readers in April 1965 after attending a March fundraiser for the group. The benefit showcased a few plays, including Baraka's *The Toilet* and *Experimental Death Unit #1*, Charles Patterson's *Black Ice*, and Nat White's *The Black Tramp*. Though Riley promised to critically review the pieces in a future column, he encouraged readers to send what financial help they could to get this promising theater initiative off the ground.[73] In May, Riley reviewed the emergent Black Arts poetry scene in and around New York City. Baraka's BARTS, which was in the process of opening its doors in Harlem, staged a poetry reading that featured the standout male poets of the new movement. These included Jones and Neal, LeRoi Bibbs, Albert Haynes, David Henderson, Calvin Hernton, Charles Patterson, Lorenzo Thomas, Ishmael Reed, and Steve Young. Riley's article heaped critical praise on this gathering of poets, and expressed his delight in being part of the scene.[74] Poetry by Jones, Hernton and Thomas, along with Frederick Douglas Richardson, Eliot Black, Joe Johnson and Carlos Russell, followed Riley's rehash of the Black Arts poetry event. Also included in this May issue was Riley's long review of Baldwin's "The Amen Corner," which starred Bea Richards as Sister Margaret, the play's main character.

Debuting at the Ethel Barrymore Theatre, Richards' command performance in the play was its only saving grace, according to Riley. He thought that in the twelve years since Baldwin had first written the play, certain of its scenes should have been rewritten to make for better drama. Frank Silvera's direction and his acting in the role of Luke, Sister Margaret's estranged husband, were severely criticized by Riley. "More than anyone else in the cast, Silvera seems to need direction badly," he wrote, "and here again he bears responsibility for any inadequacies in that area—he is the director." Limping from one big moment to the next, he warned *Liberator* readers, "the play regularly becomes tedious." Writing in the *New York Times*, critic Howard Taubman, partially agreed with Riley's take, calling the play "sketchy" and "slow." Though he found more use in the supporting cast than did Riley, both critics agreed that "The Amen Corner" was a must-see, if for no other reason than to experience the talent of Beah Richards.[75] Though Riley berated his skills on the stage, Frank Silvera was part of a cadre of theater organizers whose workshops advanced black theater throughout the decade and into the 1970s.[76]

Following Neal's departure, the bulk of the theater criticism fell on the shoulders of Riley, yet another underrated cultural critic on the Black Arts scene. Again, Riley was one of the earliest *Liberator* witnesses to the flourishing of Black Arts consciousness. Lesser-known writers, such as Eddie Ellis, who would become a founding member of the NY chapter of the Black Panthers would also contribute to *Liberator*'s analyses of the theater, as seen by his piece "Is Revolutionary Theatre in Tune with the People?" published at the end of 1965. Riley, however, more than other writers emerged as the magazine's ambassador of the cultural scene following Neal's departure. He joined the *Liberator* staff in 1964. His writings focused on major aspects of black cultural life including sports, film, theater and literature. His musings on athletics, however, distinguish him among peer critics, with the exception of Carlos Russell, who also published a number of articles that featured black athletes. Riley's first two articles interrogated the world of athletics, specifically taking stock of the black professional athlete.

In his first essay, Riley offers an account of the importance of basketball to inner city youth. Their dreams and aspirations live and die on those courts, he wrote. At the uptown playground at 114th and Lenox, where "nobody plays for the exercise," Riley met two young men, one with the hope of one day striking it rich through his talent on the court, and another whose days of glory were behind him though he was relatively still a young man. Riley discusses the onlookers as well and the dreams they hold for the young men who run up and down the court in a "smooth, knowledgeable—almost dance-like" manner. In Riley's hands, what on the surface looked like an appreciation of God-given skills, was a thinly veiled critique of American society. Riley revealed the systematic roadblocks that dashed dreams and left young men ill-prepared for the reality that lay ahead. Riley noted the circumstances that many of the young men on the court faced: "Racing up and down the stone floor at 114th and Lenox are players who were making headlines as schoolboys a few years ago. Some came to rest on the block because nobody cared enough to tell them what subjects it was necessary to take in order to go on to college. Others drifted in and out of anonymous southern schools, earning degrees in a few cases which in turn earned them puzzled stares or patronizing smiles when they returned to the city and attempted to get jobs." And though he could acknowledge such iconic figures as "[Oscar] Robertson, [Bill] Russell, [Elgin] Baylor, [Wilt] Chamberlain, and [Walt] Bellamy [who] once ran on the stone, wooden or 'dust bowl' courts of Harlems all over this nation," he noted that most of the young men he witnessed that day, even if they made it, would merely be entertainment for "the vice-presidents, magnates, millionaires and rulers they must never think of becoming."[77] Through sports, Riley was able to critique America's treatment of black youth in a way that was far less polemical, but no less radical, than Cruse's or C. E. Wilson's overt critiques of liberalism or capitalism. Riley provided a view of black life unseen to many but no less important to analyzing the effects of deindustrialization and state restructuring in this period.

The following month, Riley turned his attention to the boxing ring. Similar to his analysis of playground basketball in Harlem, he encouraged readers to think of the sport of boxing in a political context. Boxing, especially at the professional level, necessarily carried with it an implicit commentary on race in American society, especially considering the careers of Jack Johnson, Joe Louis, Floyd Patterson, Sonny Liston, and later Muhammad Ali. Ali's brash in-your-face manner stoked fears in many, and his embrace of Islam in 1964 only worsened matters. Riley suspected that recent calls among mainstream sports writers to ban boxing had more to do with the fact that more black and brown boxers were not only winning championships—actually dominating the sport, especially at the heavyweight division—but were also taking home handsome purses, than a concern for the sport's brutal violence.[78] "It is becoming . . . increasingly difficult for the overseers of boxing's vast plantation to rob their chattel any longer," he wrote.[79] With a few articles under his belt, Riley was appointed to the editorial board in August 1964, thus providing the magazine a sense of stability in a crucial period of its transition.

Riley resumed his sports commentary the following month, writing on racism in American baseball in response to a derogatory statement made at black ballplayers by Alvin Dark, the manager of the San Francisco Giants from 1961 until 1964. According to Riley, Dark mentioned to a reporter that "his team's Negro and Spanish-speaking ballplayers were not as mentally alert as the club's white players." For Riley, such comments were not only indicative of the times, they also spoke to the core of America's racial fears and prejudices. As Adrian Burgos Jr. points out in his exemplary study of baseball and race, America's national past time offers up a case study in American race relations, patterns of racialization, and labor ownership, constituting a complex web of politics and sports.[80] And while writer Dave Zirin has argued against the exploitation of sports for political purposes, he acknowledges its political implications when he writes: ". . . we can pretend sports isn't political just as well as we can pretend there is no such thing as gravity if we fall out of an airplane."[81] Clayton Riley continued to analyze America's racial politics through the prism of sports. Analyzing the 1964 Winter Olympic games in Japan, Riley argued that the treatment black people received in their home country should have led them to boycott the games. Though Riley could not discern whether such a movement was afoot among black Olympians, his perspective would be confirmed at the summer games in Mexico four years later.

What advocate and professor Harry Edwards interpreted as the revolt of the black athlete was well underway in the spring of 1964, although their respective publications, written in response to the controversy surrounding the Mexico City games, appeared at the end of the decade.[82] As one example, *Liberator* editorial board member Carlos Russell interviewed basketball star Bill Russell, the brother of the magazine's staff writer, Charlie. Calling him "the bearded revolutionary of basketball," he spoke of his outlook on social change and political leadership. "I wear my Blackness as a badge of honor," Russell was quoted as saying. Shown on the cover of this month's issue dribbling a basketball in full Boston Celtics uniform, this brief conversation allowed readers a glimpse of the star athlete's thinking, which many were either unaccustomed to hearing or willfully ignored. Russell's outspokenness demonstrated that many black athletes were unafraid of using their visibility to convey the depth of their ideas and perspectives on social issues beyond the courts and playing fields.[83]

Riley extended his Olympic reporting in December, pointing out the number of black athletes who participated in the games as well as their state of origin. Emphasizing the racial climate of the period, Riley wrote that most of the players, whether they were from the North or the South, would be summarily walked to the broom closet for employment upon their return from the games. Their Olympic experience would be little more than a line on their resume, but would not open the doors of greater opportunity, he asserted, writing: "Now that they are home, many of them [are] forgotten already and all of them no more than second class golden, silvered, or bronzed colonials."[84] Riley brought a humility and passion to his articles, an additional quality that distinguished his writing from that of his peers. Whether analyzing the American Football League's decision to move the All-Star game from New Orleans to Houston because of racist treatment of professional players in that city, or when describing "Slug," a made-up youth game slightly similar to handball played in the ghettoes, Riley stressed the greater humanity and dignity of his subjects despite the conditions they faced. Yet, he could also be unforgiving and harsh in his criticism, especially concerning professional athletes.

Toward the end of 1964, Jackie Robinson published a partially biographical account of baseball's experiment with integration, entitled *Baseball Has Done It*.[85] Riley reviewed the book for *Liberator* and expectedly wrote the book off as "a badly written and frequently garbled tract" that sought to exploit to the climate of racial tension surrounding the civil rights struggle. Riley acknowledged that Robinson was for him a one-time hero, and wishes that it were 1947 again instead of 1964. However, placing aside his personal criticisms of Robinson's public life and baseball career, Riley asserts that the former Brooklyn Dodgers second baseman's analysis was flawed. Robinson, seeking to lend a voice of integrity to the integration debate, spoke of the benevolence and courage of team owners who hired black players. Riley, however, noted that Robinson should have been more honest by highlighting the financial incentives for ball clubs to integrate. In other words, it was revenues, not respect, that drove baseball to open its gates to black players.[86] In this regard, Robinson was the polar opposite of Bill Russell, who proudly wore his blackness, and perhaps as important, advocated a structural critique of the professional sports world of which he was a proud member. Robinson instead trumpeted his Americanness. Though Robinson often took controversial and unpopular political stances that brought disfavor from the black community, by the end of the decade his respectability was partially restored when he publicly supported St. Louis Cardinals outfielder Curt Flood's principled stance against major league baseball's trade policy in 1969.[87]

Though, with few exceptions, athletics are not always thought of as a major aspect of Black Arts and Black Power, sports and sports figures are no less significant as markers for the radicalism of the decade.[88] Black athletes not only responded with their own expressions of black consciousness, but many also participated in demonstrations or used their platforms to express solidarity with the larger movement for social transformation. Nowhere was this evident than in Muhammad Ali's protest of the Vietnam War. By the late 1960s, *Liberator*, like the rest of Black America, had forgiven Ali for his abandonment of Malcolm X during his crisis with Elijah Muhammad. Animus seemed to be replaced by an understanding. Malcolm's assassination forced many people to recalibrate their stances. By that time, Ali had arguably supplanted Malcolm at the pinnacle of a highly visible form of black masculinity. Whereas Malcolm stood for a renewed political vision, here was Ali, an exemplar of a celebrity with out-of-this-world talent who shunned the spotlight in defense of his principles and the values he developed under the guidance of the Nation of Islam. For *Liberator*, Ali represented the antithesis of Lyndon Johnson's Great Society. While the Vietnam War represented the struggle against communism in the eyes of mainstream Americans, to African Americans who eschewed the harness of the political status quo, it represented the unapologetic face of global white supremacy. In this sense, Ali was "the Establishment's Vietcong."[89]

Though a knowledgeable critic of sports, Riley's contribution to *Liberator* is also found in his film reviews. Throughout the decade Riley followed theater and film closely, reviewing such films as *Guns at Batasi*, a laughable portrait of postcolonial African nationalism, and *Nothing But a Man*, directed by Michael Roemer, which featured Abbey Lincoln, Ivan Dixon, and Yaphet Kotto. Riley enthusiastically endorsed the latter film with praise that seemed to anticipate the film's now classic status.[90] A month later, his review of the summer blockbuster *The Pawnbroker*, directed by Sidney Lumet, pointed out the stellar roles played by Raymond St. Jacques and Brock Peters, who would become cinematic fixtures throughout the decade and into the 1970s.[91]

An ad announcing the arrival of Felix Greene's film *China!* shared the page with Riley's *Pawnbroker* review. Billed as "the only major film by an American or British producer since the Communist revolution," the film made its New York debut at the Carnegie Hall Cinema. According to its billing it would be "a shattering eye-opener to all Americans!" Riley reviewed "*China!*" in his theater column in July 1965. Accompanying the film was a short that featured the Peking Symphony Orchestra. *China!* showed a nation on the move, a film whose every scene was an educational moment, according to Riley. "In scene after scene, activity fills the life of these people. No one loafs, no one drags [their] feet. The nation works, the nation learns, the nation moves," he wrote. It did not matter to Riley that the film could be considered Maoist propaganda. He welcomed a depiction of the country that countered the West's projection of the country "as a vast conglomeration of war machinery." Anticipating ensuing controversy, he recommended that readers go see the film and decide its value for themselves.[92] Toward the close of the year, Riley recommended that readers view theatrical presentations of German playwright Bertolt Brecht's *The Exception and the Rule*, and Langston Hughes's *The Prodigal Son*, both of which were staged at the Greenwich Mews in the Village.[93]

By 1966, *Liberator* writers epitomized radical aesthetic criticism found in virtually every corner of black thought. The writings of Ford, Neal, Riley and others shaped the magazine's criticism of U.S. popular and political culture. They searched for arts and criticism that spoke to and for the black community with a language and possessing the spirit of rebellion those communities would understand, as Neal maintained during his years on the staff. Though there was no set political or interpretive "line" these critics adhered to, there was a sense of a unified vision of how black cultural productions could advance the political and social struggles black people faced generally. Additionally, these artists and critics often communicated how different elements worked together such as when Riley reviewed four theatrical productions in jazz terms, imagining each of the plays as a different musician's instrument. In doing so, they often exceeded their own expectations. Critics such as Riley fashioned a distinctive style and form of politically informed cultural criticism and searched out the places beyond mainstream society's radius of newsworthiness.[94] While Ford, Neal, Touré, and Riley articulated the need for black controlled theater and literary institutions, photographer Roy DeCarava, painter Joe Overstreet, and others, carried these demands into visual arts.

Painting the Revolution, and Shooting it Too: Visual Artists and *Liberator*

Black Arts visual artists continue to escape wide scholarly attention. That a recently published book entitled *Art and Social Change*, does not include one artist of the Black Arts era working prior to 1968 is indicative of such neglect.[95] Appreciably, recent studies have begun to critically appraise Black Arts era visual artists, especially muralists.[96] Though this is a welcome addition to the much-needed appraisal of this movement, more is required. In this sense, then, I briefly turn attention to *Liberator* efforts to highlight the work of visual artists, who like their literary counterparts in the movement, helped articulate the radical aesthetic practices available in this period.

Included in its influential coverage of radical aesthetic activity, *Liberator* featured a number of visual artists, profiling their art and the galleries where they staged their works. In a previous chapter I review its coverage of Harlem-based artist Valerie Maynard. The magazine was equally attentive to visual artists such as Abdul Rahman, Wyndam Porter, Bedwick Thomas, Milton Martin, and Joe Overstreet, as well as photographers Leroy McLucas, Roy DeCarava, and even Dan Watts throughout its peak years. Illustrators Leo Carty and Tom Feelings also featured their work in *Liberator*. Feelings designed the *Liberator*'s logo, a sketch of a man in profile sitting at a restaurant booth in a dark suit that recalled a similar famous photograph of Malcolm X. Later, he and his wife, Muriel, would publish in *Liberator* an excerpt of their influential children's book *Zamani Goes to Market*, published in 1970.[97] Several of Feelings's drawings were prominently displayed in the November 1966 issue of the magazine under the heading, "African Impressions." Carty, along with Harold Esannason formed a publicity team that advertised local artist events and gallery openings. Carty and Esannason, who shared some of the magazine's distribution duties, also staged a viewing of their own work entitled, "Le Monde Des Noires" (The Black World) at the Kamoinge Gallery (also known as the Gallery), which was located uptown at 248 West 139th Street in the fall of 1964.[98]

Art historian Erina Duganne discusses the Kamoinge Workshop collective as standing both inside and outside Black Arts.[99] She argues that the Kamoinge photographers sought to represent both individual and collective standpoints, but that they were ambivalent about the depiction of their photographs as solely representative of black life, especially in regard to Harlem. Because many of the members did not live in Harlem (rather, many lived on the Lower East Side), she asserts that "while many Kamoinge members felt an emotional affiliation toward Harlem and often photographed there, defining their production solely in terms of generalized understandings of this locale fixed their images as the product of a collective expression, not unlike the one prescribed by supporters of the Black Arts Movement."[100] Another reading may suggest that there was much more of a fluid relationship between the Lower East Side and Uptown than is often accounted for.[101] It is likely that several of the Kamoinge members would have shared ideas and concepts with artists of other mediums beyond the workshop. That De Carava published work in periodicals such as *Liberator*, a critical site of activity of the proto-Black Arts and Black Arts Movement, is a noteworthy example of the fluid and transient nature of black artists spaces in this period.

Although Duganne argues that these artists were "transcending race," we might also appreciate the significance of the collective's decision to adopt an African-inspired title for the group.[102] The naming of the groups and individuals taking on new names are the earliest markers of the identity shifts in the period. They could have just as easily called themselves the Negro Photography Group, or the Black Photographers Workshop, but in choosing "Komoinge," they allied themselves with several registers of black self-assertion and an embodiment of black internationalism. Whether or not the Kamoinge Workshop members agreed on the evolving and often elastic tenets of the Black Arts Movement, there is no question that they operated within a black tradition of photography and art.

Roy DeCarava's photography captured the everyday sensibilities of Harlem. Often, his subjects were shown in the midst of everyday life activities. *Liberator* featured his work in its March and April issues of 1965. As early as 1955, he collaborated with Langston Hughes in *The Sweet Flypaper of Life*.[103] And by 1962, he had compiled material for a book that included his photographs interspersed with his own poetic descriptions, which was not published for nearly four decades. What eventually became *The Sound I Saw: Improvisations on a Jazz Theme* is DeCarava's photo diary of the New York jazz scene.[104] Keeping this in mind, it is clear that the revolutionary imagination was not only painted in vivid, robust colors, but also captured by the focus, snap and flash of radical, conscious and observant photographers.

Other groups, such as Abdul and Rose Rahman's 20th Century Creators, which also got its start in and around Harlem, issued a straightforward approach concerning the intended purpose of their work. The Rahmans worked out of the Universal Art Studio in the Bronx and, like many artists, offered workshops at schools, churches, and community centers to both make a living and extend their artistry to local communities.[105] Other affiliates of the 20th Century Creators, such as Virgin Island–born Brooklyn artist Bedwick Thomas, explicitly connected their work to Black Arts. Thomas, whose art was partially inspired by jazz, also associated with the jazz and art collective POMUSICART (a name that stood for "Poetry, Music, and Art"). "Besides my basic love of art, the desire to awaken and elevate the stature of my people will compel me to dedicate my life to art and the development of our culture," he told *Liberator*.[106] In this way, the magazine reflected an affinity for unknown community based artists, some of whom, such as Wyndham Porter and Milton Martin, were just beginning their careers. Yet readers were encouraged to look out for and support their work. In this way, *Liberator* played the role of popularizer, providing a space of imagination and improvisation, attempting to provide greater exposure to artists who might have otherwise had difficulty getting the public's attention.

Prior to his departure, Neal sat down in conversation with Joe Overstreet, a visual artist who taught painting at BARTS. Overstreet told Neal that like music, his art was intended to reflect a community vision of the world. Inspired by Romare Bearden, Jacob Lawrence, and small collectives such as Harlem's Yoruba painters, Overstreet's surname aptly connoted the centrality of community themes in his work. Though he saw the value of staging work in galleries, such as Harlem's Afra-Arts, which was located on Convent Avenue, Overstreet advocated "painting on billboards and fences where building construction is going up."[107] Interestingly, this view anticipates the call for an assertive street based visual art movement that blossomed in the 1970s. It can be argued that urban artists, some of whom became known as graffiti artists throughout the decade, find their roots in Black Arts visual culture. Black Arts muralists are equal partners to the musicians and poets of the period, and in their own right represent pioneers of art that "took it to the streets," in the popular vernacular of the day.

Groups such as the Organization of Black American Culture (OBAC) and Africobra were instrumental and innovative in community reclamation efforts throughout the 1960s and 1970s, though these and other outdoor artists suffered the general backlash against Black Arts/Black Power. Neal was determined to locate every facet of black life in relation to the project of liberation. His interviews and critical essays were central to his efforts to think through aspects of the movement that were more appreciated for artistry at the expense of possible spiritual meanings. Sites such as the Studio Museum in Harlem became a temporary home to Overstreet and similar-minded artists including Al Loving, Frank Bowling, Edward Clark, and Howardena Pindell.[108] By the 1970s, Overstreet and others were deploying art that exhibited more abstract tendencies, which some critics associate with the "new Black music," the musical, revolutionary jazz accompaniment to a radical liberation project.

Organized Freedom: Jazz Criticism and the Sound of Liberation

Thelonious Monk's appearance on the cover of the February 28, 1964, issue of *TIME* magazine inspired the feeling that mainstream attention was long overdue. According to Amiri Baraka, reviewing Monk's six-month residency at the Five Spot in *Down Beat*, the cover story was supposed to appear in November of 1963, but the assassination of President Kennedy pushed it back to a later date.[109] Baraka, like many, wondered what the mainstream attention would mean for Monk, and for the black community. He worried that widespread reception would reduce the quality of Monk's music. Monk, considered ahead of his time by some, if not from another universe altogether, came to represent an avant-garde class of artists by the time his gig at the Five Spot began. Baraka, Jayne Cortez and Ted Joans, among others viewed the eclectic pianist with reverence, hearing in his music a legacy of African American cultural experience, and its future. As Robin Kelley has posited, Monk simultaneously represented the avant garde, a new form of masculinity in music, and the nonconformity of the period. At the same time, however, Monk rejected the "avant garde" tag, and was sharply, and perhaps ironically, critical of artists such as Ornette Coleman who sought a freer expression of jazz. Though many appeared to appreciate Monk because he seemed to focus on the music rather than on race and politics, Kelley shows that Monk's social outlook and political opinions were often ignored by critics and in the mainstream press.[110] For one, *Liberator* guest critic Theodore Pontiflet was skeptical of Monk's newly found notoriety, viewing this as but another page in the history of exploitation of black musicians. Emphasizing the presence of Monk's white benefactor, Pontiflet feared a return of the white patronage that haunted black artists since the turn of the century.[111]

While many jazz artists of the 1960s embraced politics (here I mean that at various times they have participated in public demonstrations, played at benefit concerts for a given cause, or wrote and performed music in the name of a political figure or movement), white liberal jazz critics have more often than not looked with disfavor upon these efforts. Conversely, Black Arts artists and critics sought, in Larry Neal's words, "to link in a highly conscious manner, art and politics in order to assist in the liberation of Black people."[112] The avant-garde explosion in jazz complicated the Black Arts liberation project that dominated the period. Although liberals and radical critics could celebrate Monk—albeit for ostensibly different reasons—many asked if the "new music" brought the art closer to the people, or moved it away from the community altogether.

Charlie Russell and Larry Neal, along with a few guest writers, such as Marc Brasz, Pontiflet, Nadi Qamar, A. B. Spellman, and Robert Bowen, carried the bulk of *Liberator*'s jazz criticism and documentation in the mid-1960s. The magazine's coverage of the scene in and around New York accompanied a flourishing of new musicians and a new direction in the music. Its peak coverage lasted for roughly four years from 1963 until 1967, though it continued to publish jazz and music criticism throughout the remaining years of the magazine's publication. In the August 1964 issue of the periodical, Russell asked simply: "Has Jazz Lost Its Roots?" The article, a conversation with pianist Cecil Taylor, sought to locate the new direction in jazz and noted that the music had moved a long distance from the sounds of his father's day.[113] Russell acknowledged that the new music was often hard to listen to and recalled that once the "swing of the music left, the music left the people."[114]

Russell resumed his reportage on the jazz scene in November in conversation with Coltrane quartet bassist Jimmy Garrison. Garrison had previously played with Ornette Coleman, who is perhaps the musician most associated with the emergence of free jazz or the New Black Music.[115] The following month he included a write-up on trumpeter Calvin Strickland, founder of the Harlem-based twenty-five-member group, POMUSICART, Inc.[116] Russell placed the origins of this group in a kind of community needs assessment, as did Black Arts efforts broadly, justifying the arrival of black cultural institutions as earlier writers had done for the theater. POMUSICART sought to not only impact African Americans' cultural life, but intended to equally contribute to its educational livelihood through the building of a jazz library. Inspired by the tragic life of Charlie Parker, Strickland argued that musicians and other artists had to "perpetuate our own culture," in order for it to be sustained. Russell observed that POMUSICART members resembled "a Saturday Night prayer meeting," rather than an assemblage of cutting-edge artists. Without a building, they organized events at the signature meeting ground of the era, Hotel Theresa, though their efforts largely went unnoticed by critics and community alike, he wrote.[117] Yet POMUSICART's Harlem-based programs are an indication that not all artists were attracted to downtown clubs such as the Five Spot (of course, this was not even an option for many black artists).

Debates between black and white critics raged throughout the remainder of the decade.[118] Black artists and writers often issued strident critiques of the presence of white writers, who, they argued, did not understand enough about African American experience to effectively describe what they were witnessing. Some white writers, such as Nat Hentoff and Norman Mailer, both fixtures of the American cultural landscape in this period, were often perceived as intruders at worst and at best opportunists. Though this debate could also be found in the world of the theater, nowhere did this debate rage with as much ferocity as it did in jazz.[119] Music periodicals such as *Down Beat* often featured the strident opinion of black writers staking out their freedom claims, and white writers justifying their role as witnesses and interpreters. *Liberator,* as "the voice of the Afro-American" (as its masthead read) was one of the critical sites of this debate. That it dropped the "protest movement" end of its subtitle indicates a nuanced shift from earlier movements. Black artists were no longer appealing to white sensibilities and reward structures, as the term protest would suggest. Instead, they were in the process of creating a distinct self-reflective register "above examination by Western analytical methods," as Larry Neal once stated. To put it simply, protest, especially in a more or less liberal integrationist sense, was passé.

Echoing Neal's call for African Americans, especially cultural workers, to steep themselves in black folk culture, Charles Hobson, writing in January 1965, argued for increased appreciation of the gospel music foundation of much of the contemporary music, including jazz and especially blues.[120] The focus on cultural roots and ancestral identity among writers paralleled the equally aggressive drive toward the future among musicians. Ornette Coleman's music represented the drive toward a style of jazz free of the constraints of earlier approaches. As mentioned, Coleman influenced a number of artists, including Jimmy Garrison. Yet, he also alienated some older musicians such as Thelonious Monk who once argued that Coleman had not created anything new.[121] Charlie Russell resumed his critical appraisal of the jazz scene through an interview with Coleman. The subheadings of the interview reveal Coleman's many battles and tensions, and tell a story of their own: "Love and Hate Confrontation"; "Self-imposed Retirement"; "Records Sell, But No Money"; "Hostile Reception to His Music"; "Jazz Is Sound Put to Motion"; "White America Does Not Want Negro Artists"; "Old Musical Standards Must Be Discarded"; "Dares to Be Himself"; "Critics Fail to Accept Their Responsibility."[122] "Ornette Coleman's name belongs with other names like Archie Shepp, Cecil Taylor, LeRoi Jones, Sun Ra, Grachan Moncur III, Joe Overstreet," Russell wrote. For him these figures represented what he termed an "iconoclastic aggregate" that influenced the period, setting new artistic and political agendas and establishing a new horizon for black aesthetics.[123]

Neal's article, "Black Revolution in Music," appeared in September 1965 and featured drummer Milford Graves, who could also be situated in Russell's "iconoclastic" grouping. Neal argued that Graves had to be understood within a spiritual, explicitly nonwestern frame of reference. The spiritual aspect of Graves's playing, alongside that of the likes of Guiseppe Logan and

Don Pullen, was the connective tissue between musician and community, he claimed. However if these artists were to serve as representatives of community yearning, Neal still felt compelled to ask why it seemed that many in the community could not grasp the New Music, a subject he took up in a subsequent interview with saxophonist Archie Shepp.

Shepp was born in Fort Lauderdale, FL, moved to Philadelphia as a youth, and then, following undergraduate studies at Goddard College in Vermont, he relocated to New York City, residing mostly on the Lower East Side but also in Harlem. While many people saw their art as extensions of black community strivings, Shepp, like Charlie Russell, remarked that black artists were separated from the communities they sought to represent partially due to economic constraints that made it difficult to earn a living as a musician. Therefore, many of Shepp's peers played downtown rather than in Harlem. Shepp, who had released *Fire Music* in the spring of 1965, made music with the movement in mind, at once revealing historic specificity, ethics, and social justice aesthetics. The album included a dedication to Malcolm X, entitled "Malcolm, Malcolm, Semper Malcolm" (Malcolm, Malcolm, Always Malcolm). Yet he also believed there was a moment when playing music was not enough of an engagement with the tide of the movement.[124] In other words, the music could, and perhaps should, reflect the movement, but it was not the movement itself.

This larger dimension can be found in nearly all Shepp's albums throughout the decade. In 1969 he recorded such songs as "New Africa," composed by trombonist Grachan Moncur III, and "Bakai," (named after a Bangladesh village), which was first recorded by Coltrane in the late 1950s. And by the early 1970s, he would compose such politically themed albums as *Attica Blues*, which included the triumphant-sounding tribute, "Blues for Brother George Jackson," in January 1972, and *The Cry of My People* that September. The latter album is an example of the jazz–visual art synthesis at the core of radical aesthetics in this period. The album cover art for *Cry* featured the artwork of Africobra founding member Nelson Stevens, who also designed and directed dozens of mural projects in western Massachusetts in the 1970s as director of the Summer Public Arts program from 1974 until 1977. He is perhaps best known for his massive (26′ x 12′) mural, "Centennial Celebration of the Birth of Tuskegee," which was completed in 1980.[125] *The Cry of My People* is, in many ways, a sampling of black musical history, being steeped in the blues, gospel, and jazz, and thus offers up a musical legacy.

Baraka sat for an interview with Shepp around the time of Neal's conversation with the saxophonist. Here, ample space was provided for Shepp to expand on some of the ideas he offered in the Neal interview. Though the bulk of their conversation is devoted to a discussion of the technical or stylistic changes occurring in the music—differences in chord progression, melody, rhythm, and so on—they also discussed the social and political aspects of the music; the place of the sound in the world. "The Negro musician is a reflection of the Negro people as a social and cultural phenomenon. His purpose ought to be to liberate America aesthetically and socially from its inhumanity," he told Baraka, in terms that could be heard from most artists closely associated with Black Arts. Shepp believed that an artist was but a creatively gifted "reporter . . . an aesthetic journalist of America." In his view, jazz artists were cultural documentarians of an indigenous art form that bespoke present conditions while invoking an ancestral past, not merely gifted musicians.[126] Although Baraka had published several poems in *Liberator* and received ample attention there, he did not publish any of his seminal articles of jazz criticism in the magazine as he also had access to periodicals as *Kulchur, Negro Digest, Down Beat,* and later *Cricket* in this period.[127]

Neal's push for an aesthetic bereft of white influence often elicited debate. One such exchange occurred between him and jazz critic Frank Kofsky, who challenged Neal's interpretation of the black revolution in jazz. Yet Kofsky's problem was not that Neal had affirmed the Black Nationalist thrust of the New Music. Rather, he took umbrage with Neal's apparent eschewing of Marxism in his analysis of black cultural productivity. Again, Neal seized the occasion to emphasize the "spiritual reality" or, echoing Baraka, the "World Spirit" of jazz music and black culture that his writing sought to explain. In what may be an example of what theorist Gayatri Spivak has termed "strategic essentialism,"[128] Neal argued that the spiritual aspects of the music were drawn from the subjective experiences of African Americans.[129] The effort to challenge and dismantle western evaluative standards was at the heart of the Black Arts project. Though Kofsky would, by the end of the decade, show himself to be an astute critic of the jazz industry, at this point he, like Hentoff and Mailer, reminded Black Arts radical critics of the urgency of developing their own standards and tools to measure the social impact of aesthetic representation.[130] In any case, Neal left *Liberator* in the fall of 1966 after a short but impactful stint as associate editor of arts and culture. However, the periodical's engagement with jazz criticism would continue after his departure.

Though the spiritual dimension was difficult for some people to grasp, most admirers of John Coltrane allow the possibility of an otherworldly mission in his music. Upon hearing Coltrane at the Lincoln Center, Islamic instrumentalist Nadi Qamar imagined witnessing an "Islamic prayer chant echoing from marble mosque walls, or a giant oud or veena in the hands of a master." Reviewing that event, Qamar perceived the limitations of the term "jazz" itself. As he stated: "The indigenous music of exiled American-born Africans does not need (1) Europeans to name it JAZZ, which means 'to play around with,' and that is exactly what is happening to most of the artists involved; (2) to be dubbed 'the new thing,' because there is nothing new."[131] As shown in this example, for many, the very terminology used to describe the art form was constricting. The new identity shifts taking place in this period, whether in the form of embracing new religious practices, taking on new names, or blending nonwestern global influences into one's art, required, at least initially, a rethinking of the music. Coltrane's Lincoln Center performance would be one of his last. His death in 1967 at the age of forty was arguably as momentous as the passing of Malcolm X two years earlier.[132] As did *Liberator*'s writers in the wake of Malcolm's death, Paul Anthony's tribute alleged that Coltrane's early death was "a product of this racist system."[133]

Qamar followed up his commentary on the futility of applying European or western labels to black expressive culture in a June 1966 article aptly titled, "The Black Music Predicament." In this article, he arguably surpasses the critique of the business of the arts offered by Baraka and Neal, asserting that "only Black musicians can properly, and completely evaluate Black music." Whereas Neal played a pioneering role in Black Arts criticism and Baraka went to great lengths to wrest the critic's pen from white jazz scene observers, Qamar argues for the abolition of the nonartist critic altogether. Notwithstanding the limitations of such a claim, it is evidence of the frustration of many toward the exploitative nature of jazz record production and club promotion. For Qamar, the nomenclature used to describe this "indigenous music" was part of the seemingly colonial relationship artists had to the industrial side of the music. If jazz was but a reflection of black people's experience rendered in music, then the commodification of jazz—indeed its very packaging as such—could be an aspect of a larger controlling apparatus, he argued, asserting: "Jazz is a word coloring the contemporary expressions of black musicians with a melting pot ideology."[134] If Black Power represented the demise of liberalism in politics, the new music, as vague as that term may have been, symbolized a rejection of liberalism in the cultural realm. In this same (June 1966) issue, *Liberator* showcased the photography of Ray Gibson (no relation to Richard). The photography exhibit was entitled, "Spiritual Voices of Black America." Though this title may have conjured up visions of the Fisk Jubilee Singers, Mahalia Jackson, or the SNCC Freedom Singers, featured in the exhibit were torchbearers of the new movement in jazz: bassist Henry Grimes, the ethereal pianist and composer Sun Ra, trombonist Grachan Moncur III, drummer Sunny Murray, and saxophonist Marion Brown.

For its second annual benefit concert, the NYU chapter of CORE booked Cecil Taylor, the pianist who was hailed as one of the leaders of the new music. In the August issue of *Liberator*, critic Marc Brasz reviewed Taylor's performance, calling it "the ineluctability of Black." "Ineluctable," meaning "inevitable, not to be avoided or escaped," seems to have been the perfect description of the sound of liberation. As Scott Saul has written, for *Liberator*, "jazz was music that refuted the logic of the melting pot, music of unalloyed Black conception."[135] For Brasz, Taylor's work that night embodied "the torture of a death poem" recalling Baraka's 1965 poem "Black Art," in which he desires "poems that kill." The following month, poet and critic A .B. Spellman reviewed the budding career of Marion Brown (an Atlanta native, former Howard University student, and neighbor of Baraka on the Lower East Side), whose saxophone prowess helped fill the void left by Coltrane, if such was at all possible. Brown and his group had achieved what Spellman could not help but call "organized freedom."[136]

Spellman's 1966 book, *Four Lives in the Be-bop Business*, which critically examined the lives and careers of Cecil Taylor, Ornette Coleman, Herbie Nichols, and Jackie McLean, marked a career on the upswing. *Liberator* jazz critic Marc Brasz reviewed Spellman's book in December, arguing that it confirmed what he already knew: that Black Art was High Art. Brasz called on readers to embrace these recollections as their own, since their biographies were communal in nature. Their singular experiences told a collective struggle.[137] In many respects, jazz offered a similar generative quality derived from artists forming a union, a collectivity, with a shared purpose crafted out of their individuality. For the poets who emerged toward the end of the decade, this collective individuality would advance Black Arts into the 1970s with its similar stories of depressing limitations and brilliant achievements. If jazz artists and criticism occupied much of *Liberator*'s pages, it also gave as much space to the jazz poetry of the period.

Poetic Jazz Aesthetics on Stage and Off

The Original Last Poets' album *Right On!*, which was also the name of a film produced by Woodie King and directed by Herbert Danska, featured group members David Nelson, Felipe Luciano and Gylan Kain received attention by *Liberator* writer Clayton Riley. Danska had recently co-wrote and directed the film *Sweet Love, Bitter*, based on the 1961 John A. Williams novel *Night Song*, starring Dick Gregory and featuring Robert Hooks. The Last Poets were organized after a public poetry reading at Mount Morris Park in Harlem (now renamed Marcus Garvey Park) on Malcolm X's birthday in 1968. As Abiodun Oyewole recalled, he was in the original group along with Nelson and Kain. Luciano emerged as a replacement for Nelson, who eventually returned to the group years later. Personality differences between Kain and Oyewole, lead to Kain's departure. In any case, with all of the changes to their line-up, the album and the film of the same name would feature Nelson, Kain, and Luciano. Like their Black Arts mentors, the group was conscious of the need for community education and institution building. For a time they operated workshops and readings at a place they called East Wind, which was on 125th street between Fifth and Madison.[138]

In an interview with New Orleans-based Black Arts poet Kalamu ya Salaam, King spoke about the process and difficulty involved in making the film. King was one of the few artists and theater organizers of the period who successfully combined his creative prowess with business acumen. Up to this point he had earned a living acting in television commercials, which allowed him to sponsor a number of ventures. His multiple projects helped him put up $100,000 of his own money to produce the film, which showed at several venues throughout the city. At the start of the shoot Kain and Nelson refused to work with Umar Bin-Hassan and Oyewole, apparently owing to the latter's streetwise activities. Nelson, a former Detroit high school classmate of King's, would temporarily help mend the differences between the poets and eventually they were able to shoot the film. Unable to keep the peace much longer, the group broke into a fight during the three-month shoot, which resulted in the departure of Felipe Luciano from the group for full-time activity with the Young Lords, and the release of the group from King's management company.[139]

Yet the film had raised some eyebrows, despite the internal conflict exploding behind the scenes. A critic writing in the *New York Times* called the seventy-eight-minute film a "cinema-of-the-rooftops" and compared the performance of Nelson, Luciano and Kain to a "hard driving evangelical performance."[140] The critic's reference to the divine recalled Kain's Christian fundamentalist upbringing though he had long since left the church. Like many disillusioned with western religion, he once said that Christianity sapped black people's potency.[141] Though Umar's presence was left from the final edit of the film, he and King shaped a friendship out of the chaos. King later produced a play called *Suspenders* written by Umar, directed by Al Freeman Jr. and starred Clarence Williams III, two actors who would become fixtures in the post–Black Arts media landscape, carving out relatively successful Hollywood careers.[142]

Prior to their split, Nelson, Luciano, and Kain rendered their album for the theater under the umbrella of King's Concept East in the summer of 1969. *Liberator* theater critic Clayton Riley encouraged readers to bear witness to the three-man performance-poetry ensemble's unique "mixture of all recollection." The group's poetry wove together gospel music, street-alley brawls, beauty and barbershop therapy evoking "history [and] celebrations of forgotten other times," he wrote. Debuting downtown at the Paperback Theatre, which was located along Second Street, the group's performative gestures and linguistic cadences brought the dark realities of black ghetto life to the stage. Significantly, Riley also underscored the nexus between African American and Puerto Rican cultural life when he wrote that Luciano's role brought "the clearest marriage between Puerto Rico and Harlem we may ever see."[143] Luciano's "Puerto Rican Rhythms" vividly captures Riley's observation. Prefacing his recitation with the words: "taking you into el barrio now" at once located the poem in the physical landscape of Spanish Harlem, and also invited listeners to a review of Puerto Rican historic migration to New York City.[144]

After Luciano left The Last Poets (amid internal turmoil), immediately, and partially due to the encouragement of Amiri Baraka, he took up a leadership role in the Young Lords. *Liberator* carried a photo of the recently formed Young Lords Party on the cover of its February 1970 issue. The photo, which featured leaders Yoruba Guzman and Luciano accompanied a photo essay that featured another male leader, Raphael Viera, alongside minister of finance Juan "Fi" Ortiz and minister of education Juan Gonzales explained the formation of the group and its recent initiatives. In particular, *Liberator* highlighted their garbage collection protest against the deteriorating social ecology, as well as their infamous occupation of the First Spanish Methodist Church of East Harlem, which lasted for over ten days, from just after Christmas in 1969 through the first week of the New Year, and catapulted the group into the national spotlight.¹⁴⁵ *Liberator* coverage of this group is evidence of cross-cultural political and expressive activity. Indeed, Michelle Wilkinson has documented a shared history of socio-aesthetic parallel activity between the Black Arts and Puerto Rican Arts Movements in this period through the work of Miguel Algarín, Jeff Donaldson, Juan Sanchez, Faith Ringgold, and Miguel Piñero.¹⁴⁶ Though *Liberator* writers were attentive to the Young Lords' growing influence, this was the only coverage it devoted to that formation.

The recorded version of The Last Poets' *Right On!* revealed a sense of poetic democratization that jazz musicians, with their continuous sharing of the stage through alternate solos, had performed to great effect. Each of the poets composed or was the lead performer on six individual pieces, for a total of eighteen tracks on the album. And while one led, the other two would improvise, adding linguistic layers reminiscent of urban discursive communities that were bilingual and often trilingual, to a given piece. Though their ability to draw large, mostly black and Latino working-class crowds revealed The Last Poets' local celebrity, *Liberator* music critic and poet Ron Welburn, writing in November 1970, was not impressed with the labeling of their work as "the new Black blues" and, ostensibly, an extension of the description of jazz as the new black music. It is interesting that Welburn distinguished Luciano's political involvement in the Young Lords from his appraisal of the album, perhaps seeking to evaluate it on artistic registers exclusively.

What little positive acknowledgment he had for their self-titled album stemmed from the ugly truths it aired. "Black people will laugh at what the Brothers put down, and what they put down is a sad sad truth, and laughter becomes sad self-flagellation," he wrote. pointing out the bitter irony of their work. "The Last Poets mock, cajole, mimic, harass and insult, and blow away Niggers. So laughing to keep from crying about the hang-ups of Niggers is indeed the new blues," he lamented. Welburn was forced to conclude however that their poetry was indicative of the times, though the abrasive, brash style may have lacked a degree of sophistication he had come to expect (or desire) of black poetry. According to Welburn, The Last Poets, for all their urban revelations, fell far short of the tradition set forth by Langston Hughes, Melvin Tolson, Robert Hayden, Aimé Césaire, Derek Walcott, Wole Soyinka, Tom Dent, and others. Though David Nelson could proclaim, "Poetry Is Black," and assert that black people were poetry, blackness was not a strong enough aesthetic adhesive to link content and form. Instead, he accused them of straying from the legacy set by poets of an earlier generation and "legitimizing the worst kind of poetry."[147] Later, he compared Stanley Crouch's *Ain't No Ambulances for No Nigguhs Tonight* (FDS-105) to the debut of The Last Poets, praising the former for its "explanatory manner that paints surreal pictures" over the latter's blatant obscenity.[148]

Welburn's critique seemed to touch on the central recurring question and challenge of black artistic production in the twentieth century, that is, whether political subjectivity should overshadow form. Nonetheless, The Last Poets survived Welburn's criticism, in large part due to their ability to capture raw energy perhaps strategically at the expense of poetic integrity, though it is evident that they took their art seriously. In the future, Felipe Luciano would remake himself as a political leader, Gylan Kain would record the solo quasi-political jazz–street poetry albums *Blue Guerilla* and *Kain* (in the mid-1970s), and Abiodun Oyewole and Umar Bin-Hassan would continue recording albums throughout the decade as The Last Poets. Despite Welburn's critique there was an affective power in The Last Poets' style of performance poetry.

Though often hampered by the masculinist rhetoric of the era, these recordings add to the performance traditions of African descendants that reach back to West African griots and long-standing forms of ancestral veneration. The spontaneity of these recordings provides a clear connection to the advancement of Black Arts into the seventies. Much of Black Arts poetry, theater and jazz especially, mastered and utilized spontaneity and improvisation to great effect, providing a sort of movement punctuality that could only be achieved by being in the moment.

Conclusion

Liberator's radical aesthetic was expansive in its embrace of cultural production, critical analysis, and the envisioning of independent black cultural institutions. On the page and off, its role in shaping what I have called the black radical aesthetics of the period reflected an expansive pattern of translocality that linked sites of cultural and political struggle globally. Though African independence drove early debates about African diasporic identities and cultural integrity, as the decade unfolded, activists were concerned with mining the reservoir of African American cultural tradition as much as they expressed a revived interest in cultural practices exclusive to ethnic communities and national identity throughout Africa. While *Liberator* stood as an example of an independent black institution, its pronouncements on cultural revolution were largely drawn from the perspectives and tastes of individual writers as they wrestled with the purpose and direction of their work. Undoubtedly *Liberator* writers and subscribers were in constant conversation about the role of African American culture in black radical politics. These debates inseparably linked cultural and political autonomy.

As we have seen, culture arguably stirred community energies and passions to greater effect than explicit political demands. Reviewing the writing of Clebert Ford, Larry Neal, Clayton Riley, and others reveals an evolution, or at the very least an ebb and flow, of black perspectives toward the role of culture in black liberation politics. *Liberator*'s coverage of visual artists of the period included black muralists and photographers. One of the lasting aspects of radical politics in this period was in aesthetics. Though there were intense efforts to build alternative political parties as late as 1976, by and large, activists were unable to solidify the support required to construct and sustain a consistently autonomous black politics. The black radical cultural production—music, film, and literature, especially short stories and poetry—in this period forms a reservoir of aesthetic activities critically interpreted by Larry Neal, Amiri Baraka, Clebert Ford, Clayton Riley, and others that extended well into the 1970s. While many of the male radical aestheticians took to cultural criticism to express their political desires, women such as Abbey Lincoln, Sonia Sanchez, and Maya Angelou held forth on panels, at conferences, and in interviews, but most of all through their transcendent cultural work. Following the peak years of the mid-1960s, the *Liberator* staff dwindled down to a third of its original size, due to a combination of internal differences, effects of the liberation movement, and weakening financial support, as well as other factors. *Liberator* suffered debilitating changes to key staff positions, although some people were able to hang on despite the raucous shifts. Dan Watts proved to be a polarizing figure that alienated as many people as he had welcomed into the fold. With the publication showing serious signs of collapse by 1968 and experiencing obvious setbacks by 1969, the penetrating analysis of western imperialism, the sensitive treatment of working-class and poor black people, and the theorizing of imaginative radical cultural work that readers had come to expect from *Liberator* seemed to have faded away.

However, similar to its attention to the issues women faced in the movement, the *Liberator* made every effort to stay relevant by publishing articles on such groups as the Black Panther Party and the Young Lords Party and figures such as Angela Davis that were garnering national attention. Coverage of the Afro-Puerto Rican organization the Young Lords, which was based in Spanish Harlem although originating in Chicago, directly connected the *Liberator* back to its New York base, though it still strove—through a last-ditch effort at reorganization—to provide coverage of events occurring nationwide as well as those deserving attention internationally. Though the *Liberator* staff writers spoke with a defiant international consciousness, they were still largely New Yorkers who struggled in the communities in which they lived and worked. In short, its globally situated translocalism ultimately brought *Liberator* back to the home front.

Epilogue
Refusing to Go Quietly

....

By 1970 *Liberator* had begun to show the signs of a declining publication. After ten years of publishing, the former pulse of the radical scene had all the markings of transition into an uncertain future. Internecine differences among the staff left only a small number of committed individuals in the magazine's production ranks. Such struggles provide at least a partial explanation for the magazine's decline. By this time, many of the central activists and writers who helped shape and define black radical politics and expressive culture had left the scene (and the magazine), either voluntarily or by force of circumstance. Yet characteristic of Watts, *Liberator* refused to leave the scene quietly. The January issue of 1970 listed four main editors and four staff workers. Editors were also listed as regional representatives: Bill Mahoney was assigned coverage of the South; Richard Price covered events on the West Coast; Richard Gibson, who managed to keep some semblance of integrity despite the controversy surrounding him, continued to supply the bulk of the international coverage; and Clayton Riley continued to document the local arts scene. Tom Feelings and James Malone were listed as illustrators, James Connor handled photography, and longtime secretary Evelyn Kalibala remained a reliable staffer. A thinning production staff would encounter difficulty carrying the full weight of the magazine.

A second reason for the publication's decline was the variety of publishing opportunities that opened up to black writers in the latter end of the 1960s due to successful demands for social transformation. Watts knew, as he always had known, that with increasing popularity, black writers were beginning to receive critical acclaim in the white press, and it became more and more difficult to recruit and maintain a core staff of writers who could work on the cheap or for free, as they had done throughout much of the periodical's career.

Occasionally, with its remaining days numbered, the magazine would receive a spark reminiscent of its peak run. Longtime radicals such as James Boggs published influential articles on radicalism and nationalism in *Liberator* even as the magazine slumped.[1] And the emergence of newer voices, such as literary critic Addison Gayle and Toni Cade Bambara, alongside familiar writers, such as Riley, showed promise but would not be enough to keep the magazine alive. To a large extent, however, small, independent, radical black press outlets such as *Liberator* took a considerable hit in a climate dominated by ad revenue. The magazine's meager budget could not compete in such an environment. The periodical, and other publications and workshop spaces that had served as intellectual training grounds, were still available to young writers, but the older mentors, such as John Henrik Clarke, John O. Killens, and Harold Cruse, had moved into later stages of their careers as educators and public intellectuals, though both *Freedomways* and the Harlem Writer's Guild continued well into the 1980s. Although Watts needed as much community support as he could attract, he refused to place complete blame for the financial difficulties on publication costs alone. In addition, he had come to depend on the cadre of writers that, to his mind, he had helped popularize. No doubt envious of the white publishing world's ability to attract (and pay) black talent, Watts left little to the imagination when he lamented that some "revolutionary" writers had seen fit to publish their works elsewhere.

A Jamaica, New York, reader shared with Watts a concern for where the new leadership of the black community would come from and what would be offered beyond invoking "the name of Brother Malcolm to cover up their own lack of direction or program." The writer challenged Watts on the tone of an editorial, which questioned whether black revolutionary poets were offering a program toward liberation or simply spouting poetic obscenities to display their rage, ostensibly for white onlookers. The writer argued that Watts was disconnected from what was "happening in Black centers today," since, as he saw it, "there are many programs," although he did not identify any.[2]

Yet the radical content persisted despite the financial crunch and thinning staff. By the magazine's end, Watts seemed to be taking a cue from Cruse, hurling fiery and often personal insults at movement activists. In his March 1968 lead editorial, Watts had criticized what he termed "verbal revolutionaries" who were moving "from community to community with their Afro hairdos, a copy of Fanon under one arm and 'Quotations from Chairman Mao' under the other arm . . . seeking to confuse and divide the Black communities in the name of Black Power or Black Nationalism." This sentiment anticipated Gil Scott-Heron's song, "Brother," where a similar critique is made.[3] Watts argued that not enough time was being spent on building or developing a program for black liberation, an issue that almost all self-styled radicals raised, but whose answers remained elusive. Instead, some individuals (he refused to name them at times) had turned the movement into an experiment in entrepreneurialism. While black nationalists were jockeying for public attention, he claimed alarmingly, "Whitey is taking care of business . . . he is cutting back the so-called anti-poverty programs, and city Police commissioners are issuing daily news releases to the effect that they are ready to 'maintain law and order' by shooting down Black people in the streets."[4] Hyperbole aside, Watts's editorial effectively poked at the ways in which state power structures regrouped in response to urban rebellions rather than yield to assertive demands for political power, no matter how articulate, creative, or solidly based on clear evidence. Urban rebellions highlighted the search for new power arrangements in society. Yet by 1968, the rhetoric of law and order, and not the redistribution of political power and economic resources, ruled the day.

Dan Watts, who was proudly intransigent to his core, refused to belabor the fact that publication costs were far outpacing revenue. It didn't matter. The magazine had served its purpose. However, in the last few issues of the magazine, he was forced to tell readers how financially strapped *Liberator* had become. In February 1970, Watts published a letter addressed to readers asking for subscriptions and reminding them of the importance of independent black outlets such as his. Just below the table of contents appeared the lament that printing costs would drive an increase in subscription costs. Reminding readers that *Liberator* was one of the first publications to introduce such writers as Amiri Baraka, Nathan Hare, Eldridge Cleaver, Ed Bullins, Harold Cruse, Addison Gayle Jr., Toni Cade, Clayton Riley, and Malcolm X, he encouraged readers to support black thought through their subscription to the magazine. "*Liberator* is the only independent, completely Black-owned magazine today which regularly offers strong political comment," he urged. "Help us continue to print the inside truths on what's going on today in our Afro-American communities, the country, and the world by giving us your financial support."[5]

While Watts was still seeking to recruit new funding streams, he expressed bitterness toward the movement. Now that Black Power had stalled to a relative halt (although movement activities continued around the country), Watts took aim at leaders, as he had always done. However, as he had demonstrated with increasing velocity toward the end of the 1960s, the leadership class that found itself in Watts's crosshairs was one produced by Black Power specifically, and the Black Radical Tradition generally. As his conflagrations with Baldwin and Ossie Davis earlier in the decade had shown, Watts was far from gun-shy. Now, at the end of the decade, Watts had begun to express disillusionment with the slogans that had seemed to

Dan Watts and student Quinton Wilkes, Fordham University, from the 1971 Yearbook. Watts taught at Fordham from 1969 to 1971, the last two years *Liberator* was in circulation. Maroon Yearbook 1971, courtesy of Fordham University Archives.

at once stick to all forms of black organizing, and thereby stifle new ideas. By December 1970, Watts was no longer solely editorializing against the civil rights establishment. In this issue of *Liberator*, Watts revealed exasperation and deep frustration, perhaps with his own failed efforts to bring about a new political day for the struggling communities defended on the magazine's pages each month. As the magazine's tenth anniversary approached, Watts seemed to have little to celebrate. The magazine was thinning in size and revenue, although it could still attract talent, as seen in the writings of Toni Cade and Ron Welburn. It also kept ties to local community organizations based in New York City such as the Brownsville Community Council and the Young Black Political Action Committee.

In Watts's December editorial, which was blandly entitled "Big Brother," his exasperation surfaced all too clearly. In his mind, grassroots mobilization, the defense of workers, and coalition building had given way to top-down *only* organizing and self-aggrandizement rather than material improvements. His style would not allow him to placate those who still found some political refuge in what was left of movement politics, even if only as a marker of evaporated possibilities. "Black elites, while espousing endless and program-less rhetoric of Black Power, are discarding (in the name of revolution) the fundamental humanistic values that allowed us to survive the long ordeal of slavery. They are straying away from the people," he wrote. The people, in Watts's view, were being lost in the maelstrom of conference planning, speech making, conventions, and lecture circuits, he bemoaned. "So much of our rich African heritage is being dissipated in orgies of Blackness without providing one vehicle for the transfer of power from those who hold it to the powerless mass of Afro-Americans." Watts saw himself as part of this gap, but by calling attention to it in a manner reminiscent of the irascible Harold Cruse, he hoped he might also play some part in the solution. Watts had observed, and often stood at the center of, several divisions among black activists. He argued with many, and shared panels and press conferences with numerous others. As an editor of a decade-long radical publication, he knew, at least to his mind, exactly what he was talking about. Though one of Watts's last editorials concluded on a rather defeatist note, he saw it as his self-appointed responsibility to lay the facts bare and, true to form, to grind an ax or two in the process: "Today in the name of 'Power to the people' lives are being ripped off, bodies are being broken, thousands of eager young Black minds are being poisoned with the irrelevant claim of 'beauty and truth lie in conformity to the gospel of the self-anointed spokesmen of the moment.'" It is unclear if this was a veiled critique of Whitney Young, Amiri Baraka, or others. Though it appears that his attitude toward charismatic leadership had changed considerably from years prior, when he too was among those vying for the spotlight. Watts, now in his midforties, had grown disenchanted with the prospects of top-down leadership. Strikingly, Watts's final point must have caught faithful readers off guard. Urging an embrace of "diversity" within blackness, Watts discarded the singular call of unity that had long been a hallmark of black political thought across the board. "We are a proud and diversified people," he urged, adding, "Our survival lies in the very nature of our diversity and not in becoming slaves to an inhuman institution called oneness." This was a far cry from the hard-charging collectivist mindset that *Liberator* readers expected. Watts's editorial spoke volumes about *Liberator*'s future. If oneness or some semblance of unity within the race was an expired concept, then what would, or could, black solidarity mean? Perhaps this was the feeling of regret that was overwhelming Watts. Perhaps it was pragmatism tugging at his politically ambitious heart.[6] Watts's tone in this editorial suggests that he was looking ahead, and not necessarily back at the last ten years. In 1969, Watts had accepted a post at Fordham University as a lecturer in Black Studies (one of the first wave of such programs in the country) and director of the Higher Education Opportunities program, heading up a budget that included a grant of $684,000 from the New York State Department of Education to aid up to

700 economically challenged Fordham students.[7] He taught courses on the History of the Afro-American Press and Propaganda in the Black Community from 1969 to 1971.[8] Though it may have seemed odd that someone who had eschewed the corporate world of architecture would now take a position at a prestigious American university, Watts was in the same position of many former movement activists, in that they were looking to continue justice work when and where possible. For some this meant honing one's craft and marketing oneself to the mainstream, and for others, this meant going into some form of work in the academy.

At its tenth year, *Liberator* was still reminding readers of its pivotal role, listing its top reasons why readers should obtain or renew a $4 yearly subscription. Among the reasons provided, it boasted that its "compelling approach to journalism has made it the only magazine of its kind today." Proudly, Watts asserted, "We not only report the news, we help make news," with "penetrating analysis of trends in Afro-American communities and in Africa, Asia, and Latin America." Finally, *Liberator* was the place to turn to if readers wanted to "keep up with a changing world." In many ways, the periodical lived up to its bold claims. However, as a publication it was merely a vehicle of movement ideas, and could only accompany and document action. Though it could not bring about revolutionary change, it could represent a key role in how people understood revolutionary activity in the United States and around the world. Black communities needed as many outlets as possible to think out loud, argue, revise, strategize, and most of all, fight.

Watts's last editorial appeared in March 1971 and underscored the demise of Black Power rhetoric. Rather than lamenting the further misdirection of black leadership or bemoaning the lack of resources in the black community (or for his magazine), he simply reprinted a recent cartoon, in which a young man and woman who look like hippies are shown in front of a billboard advertisement for a gasoline company. The billboard features a man's hand gripping a gas pump, and written boldly across the top portion of the sign are the words: "All Power to the People!" The words from the couple ruefully express the co-optation of the once-popular and controversial phrase: "I guess it was bound to happen . . . sooner or later."[9] Though the remaining contents of this issue were potentially fecund, including the work of six new poets, two short stories, and a few timely analyses, this would be the last issue to hit the stands.

・・・・・・

Though *Liberator* made a critical impact on the period, it was by no means the only place one could find Black Arts and Black Power ideas being expressed and debated. Yet for its time, it recruited and disseminated some of the most cutting-edge radical black thought available. The periodical was an instrument of liberatory activist practitioners who were part of a larger global community of scholars, students, trade unionists, and everyday activists seeking to define, shape, and shake up the direction of black liberation. Publications such as *Liberator,* alongside peer-rival publications such as *Freedomways, Muhammad Speaks, Soulbook,* and *Negro Digest/Black World,* as well as lesser-known and short-lived journals, such as *Onyx,* were crucial to the creation and circulation of African American transnational ideas about culture, politics, economics, education, and religion and spirituality in the 1960s and 1970s.

These sites of radical thought are therefore of indispensable importance when evaluating this period. These periodicals were Black Studies departments before American universities and colleges were forced to embrace the Black Studies and Ethnic Studies movements. They were training grounds for numerous cohorts of activists, groups, and individuals. They were sites of strategy and planning. They were spaces of critical interrogation of governmental policies that anticipated the CNN network's all-day political punditry and the age of contemporary public intellectualism. On this score, they also serve as a marker for how much African American and Afro-diasporic cultural and political thought in the public domain has deteriorated; how far African Americans have moved from the demands for change vividly and eloquently expressed by Malcolm X and Martin Luther King Jr.

Houston Baker, who also published in *Liberator* just prior to its closing, has made a compelling argument that many public intellectuals—especially the wave of black conservative thinkers, but also so-called progressives who frequent the lecture circuit in our day—have betrayed the legacy of King and the entire period of heroic civil rights.[10] Taking a cue from Baker's critique, in some ways *Radical Intellect* asks what would Dan Watts, Larry Neal, Harold Cruse, Lorraine Hansberry, John Coltrane, Paul Robeson, Langston Hughes, and Malcolm X have to say about the election and reelection of the first African American president and our present cultural moment that marks a resurgence of white nationalist sentiment, xenophobia, and misogyny? What programs would they suggest African Americans follow? What would they have to say about the (limited) potential of electoral politics? What music would they create? What poems and plays would they write? What speeches would they give? In some ways we have recently witnessed the reincarnation of these voices in the form of the Black Lives

Matter movement, as well as Moral Mondays in North Carolina, and courageous fights against the disruption of Native soil through the building of a gas pipeline. These efforts are reminders that the voices and hearts dedicated to struggles for justice have not disappeared, but are rather given new life through the subsequent generations of activists, writers, and artists.

Radical Intellect is about an orbit of writers, thinkers, and activists who celebrated and fought with and often alongside one another while engaged in a politics of liberation. It is about how these activists grappled with history, politics, and culture as they were making history. History is often unkind to the lesser-known figures, such as community activists, artists, agitators, skilled debaters, collectors, bibliophiles, educators, lay historians, curators, and dedicated strategists. Yet these figures, as much as those who are better known, help to fill out and accurately represent attitudes not accepted in the mainstream, especially concerning black politics. *Liberator* was one such site for an assembly of voices that made history by not being afraid to openly challenge the status quo and publicly disagree with the expectations of respectable leadership. As the Palestinian scholar Edward Said once put it, "Every intellectual whose métier is articulating and representing specific views, ideas, ideologies, logically aspires to making them work in a society. The intellectual who claims to write only for him or herself, or for the sake of pure learning, or abstract science is not to be, and must not be, believed."[11] Called into activism by the requirements of the day rather than by vocation, *Liberator*'s intellectuals stretched the political and artistic imagination. As self-styled activists, few were concerned with recognition from political elites if such proximity did not generate the influence to enact their visions. Publications such as *Liberator* and the range of voices that filled its pages contributed to the creation of transformative political and cultural spaces and practices. *Liberator* writers, artists, and activists would have to navigate a hostile world not of their making and wholly indifferent to black suffering. But they did not go quietly. As both witnesses and participants, African American activists and budding intellectuals critical of the mainstream could speak candidly and critically about the major issues of the day as they saw them. For this reason, publications such as *Liberator* must ever be remembered for the example they set in providing courageous, innovative, imaginative, and unapologetic truth telling, a practice as urgently needed now as then. As Curtis Mayfield once sang, we must "keep on pushin'."

Notes

Prologue

1. Brenda Gayle Plummer, *In Search of Power: African Americans in the Era of Decolonization, 1956–1974* (Cambridge: Cambridge University Press, 2013).

2. C. Tinson, "Voice of the Black Protest Movement: Notes on the *Liberator* Magazine and Black Radicalism in the Early 1960s" *The Black Scholar* 37, no. 4 (Winter 2008): 1–15.

3. Though some scholars correctly assert that not all black international politics emanate from or are related to the African continent, for *Liberator* writers and readers, Africa remained central to black political outlooks and a source of cultural identity, as I discuss in chapter 2. For an example of scholarship on black internationalisms that are not centered on Africa, see Brent Hayes Edwards, *The Practice of Diaspora: Literature, Translation and the Rise of Black Internationalism* (Cambridge, MA: Harvard University Press, 2003).

4. John Bracey, August Meier, and Elliot Rudwick, eds., *Black Nationalism in America* (Indianapolis: Bobbs-Merrill, 1970).

5. Harvard Sitkoff, *The Struggle for Black Equality, 1954–1992*, rev. ed. (New York: Hill & Wang, 1993); Editors of *Black Issues in Higher Education*, eds., *The Unfinished Agenda of Brown v. Board of Education* (Hoboken, NJ: John Wiley & Sons, 2004); Thomas Wagstaff, *Black Power: The Radical Response to White America* (Beverly Hills, CA: Glencoe Press, 1969); James A. Geschwender, ed., *The Black Revolt* (Englewood Cliffs, NJ: Prentice-Hall, 1971); Robert H. Brisbane, *Black Activism: Racial Revolution in the United States, 1954–1970* (Valley Forge, PA: Judson Press, 1974).

6. A significant and well-known article dealing with the failures of liberals and liberalism is Loren Miller, "Farewell to Liberals: A Negro View," in *Black Protest Thought in the Twentieth Century*, 2nd ed., ed. August Meier, Elliott Rudwick, and Francis L. Broderick (Indianapolis: Bobbs-Merrill, 1971), 373–80. Originally published in 1962 in *The Nation*, "Farewell" spells out the sense of disillusionment and burgeoning dissatisfaction many African Americans began to have toward liberals. It is important that this article also explains the ascent of African American militancy and defiance in determining the very definition of freedom and the means by which freedom would be attained.

7. Robin D. G. Kelley, *Freedom Dreams: The Black Radical Imagination* (Boston: Beacon Press, 2002), 109.

8. This term was first employed by Harold Cruse in a 1962 essay first published in *Studies on the Left* 2, no. 3, entitled, "Revolutionary Nationalism and the Afro-American," and reprinted in *Rebellion or Revolution* (New York: William Morrow and Co., 1968), 74–96. It was subsequently embraced and further theorized by the Revolutionary Action Movement (RAM). See Ernie Allen (Mkalimoto), "Revolutionary Nationalism and the Class Struggle" (Detroit: n.p., July 1970); see also Bracey, Meier, and Rudwick, *Black Nationalism in America*.

9. Allen, "Revolutionary Nationalism and the Class Struggle." See also, Robert L. Allen, *Black Awakening in Capitalist America, an Analytic History* (New York: Doubleday, 1970).

10. My use of this term draws upon Ula Taylor's formulation of "community feminism" (*The Veiled Garvey* [Chapel Hill, NC: University of North Carolina Press, 2002]) to describe the relationship between black women and Black Nationalism. Though she employs this term in her study of Amy Jacques Garvey, I posit that it can be extended to late twentieth-century female activists such as Fran Beal, Toni Cade Bambara, Assata Shakur, Sonia Sanchez, and Elaine Brown, among others who made attempts to place their commitments to feminist ideals within the context of Black Nationalism. These are black women who at one time or another believed that Black Nationalism (race pride, black consciousness and identity, community control, pride in heritage) was a necessary strategy to assert political agency toward achieving equity in the United States and elsewhere in the African diaspora. Though they voiced their criticism of the sexism, masculinity, misogyny, and patriarchy inherent in nationalist organizations and movements, they maintained a commitment to black community struggle. See for example, Ula Taylor, "The Historical Evolution of Black Feminist Theory and Praxis," *Journal of Black Studies* 29, no. 2 (Nov. 1998): 234–53. See also Jean Smith, "I Learned to Feel Black," in *Black Power Revolt*, ed. Floyd B. Barbour (Boston: Porter, Sargeant, 1968), 207–18; Steven Ward sees Fran Beal as an exemplar of the expression of feminist consciousness as part of, not apart from, Black Power. See his "The Third World Women's Alliance: Black Feminism and Black Power Politics," in *The Black Power Movement: Rethinking the Civil Rights–Black Power Era*, ed. Peniel E. Joseph (New York: Routledge, 2006), 119–44.

11. These are terms that have been utilized by activists and writers of the period and after and are employed in an attempt to describe various identities, strategies, and perspectives in black liberation political thought. I use these terms to describe the diversity of political expression that was demonstrated throughout the decade of the 1960s.

12. See, for example, Edwards, *The Practice of Diaspora*; and Cynthia Young, *Soul Power: Culture, Radicalism and the Making of a U.S. Third World Left* (Durham, NC: Duke University Press, 2006).

13. For the most thorough historical treatment of *Negro Digest/Black World*, see Jonathan Fenderson, "'Journey toward a Black Aesthetic': Hoyt Fuller, the Black Arts Movement and the Black Intellectual Community," Ph.D. Dissertation, W. E. B.

Du Bois Department of Afro-American Studies, University of Massachusetts, Amherst, 2011.

14. James Smethurst, *The Black Arts Movement* (Chapel Hill: University of North Carolina Press, 2005), 92. See also Lisa Gail Collins and Margo Natalie Crawford, eds., *New Thoughts on the Black Arts Movement* (New Brunswick, NJ: Rutgers University Press, 2006).

15. Kimberly Springer, *Living for the Revolution: Black Feminist Organizations, 1968–1980* (Durham, NC: Duke University Press, 2005); Rhonda Y. Williams, "Black Women, Urban Politics, and Engendering Black Power," in *The Black Power Movement: Rethinking the Civil Rights–Black Power Era*, ed. Peniel E. Joseph (New York: Routledge, 2006), 79–104.

16. Benita Roth, *Separate Roads to Feminism: Black, Chicana, and White Feminist Movements in America's Second Wave* (Cambridge: Cambridge University Press, 2004), 17.

17. Ibid., 25.

18. Lauren Kessler, *The Dissident Press: Alternative Journalism in American History* (Beverly Hills, CA: Sage Publications, 1984).

19. An essay that places *Liberator* among a number of institutions at the center of radical activity in New York City in this period is James Smethurst, "Poetry and Sympathy: New York, the Left, and the Rise of Black Arts," *Left of the Color Line: Race, Radicalism and Twentieth Century Literature of the United States* (Chapel Hill: University of Carolina Press, 2003), 259–78.

20. See Robin D. G. Kelley, *Freedom Dreams: The Black Radical Imagination* (Boston: Beacon Press, 2002).

21. Beverly Guy-Sheftall, *Words of Fire: An Anthology of African American Feminist Thought* (New York: The New Press, 1995), 145–55.

22. Robert L. Allen, *Black Awakening in Capitalist America: An Analytical History* (New York: Doubleday, 1968), 246–73.

23. Jack Nelson, Kenneth Carlson and Thomas Linton, eds., *Radical Ideas and the Schools* (New York: Holt, Rinehart and Winston, 1972), 3.

24. Ibid., 3.

25. Ibid., 5–6.

26. See Cornel West, ed., *The Radical King* (Boston: Beacon Press, 2015).

27. Anthony Bogues, *Black Heretics, Black Prophets: Radical Political Intellectuals* (New York: Routledge, 2003), 7, 21. Cedric Robinson, *Black Marxism* (1983; reprint, Chapel Hill: University of North Carolina Press, 2000); Most recently at least one scholar has interpreted the evolution of black radicalism as foundational to a distinctive black radical worldview. See Reiland Rabaka, *Africana Critical Theory: Reconstructing the Black Radical Tradition, from W. E. B. Du Bois and C. L. R. James to Frantz Fanon and Amilcar Cabral* (Lanham, MD: Lexington Books, 2009).

28. For example, Ernie Allen's pamphlet, "Revolutionary Nationalism and the Class Struggle" (Detroit: n.p., July 1970) identifies the difference between "bourgeois nationalism," which aims to protect "material [and political] interests of

the Black petit-bourgeoisie," and "revolutionary nationalism," which viewed African Americans as an internal colony and called for a "world-wide revolution" against imperialism. See also Jeffrey O. G. Ogbar, *Black Power: Radical Politics and African American Identity* (Baltimore: Johns Hopkins Press, 2005).

29. James Boggs and Grace Lee Boggs, *Revolution and Evolution in the Twentieth Century* (New York: Monthly Review Press, 1974).

Chapter One

1. Mike Wallace, "Black Power/White Backlash," *CBS News Special*, 1966; American Archive of Public Broadcasting, WGBH and the Library of Congress, Boston, MA, and Washington, DC.

2. Harold R. Isaacs, "The American Negro and Africa: Some Notes," *Phylon* 20 (Fall 1959): 219–33. See also his book, *The New World of Negro Americans* (New York: Viking, 1963).

3. Walter L. Williams, "Black Journalism's Opinions about Africa during the Late 19th Century," *Phylon* 34 (September 1973): 224–35; C. A. Chick Sr., "The American Negroes' Changing Attitude Toward Africa," *Journal of Negro Education* 31 (Autumn 1962): 531–35; Adelaide Cromwell Hill, "What Is Africa to Us?," in *The Black Power Revolt: A Collection of Essays*, ed. Floyd B. Barbour (Boston: Porter Sargent, 1968), 127–35; James Reston, "Copper Sun, Scarlet Sea, What Is Africa to Me?," *New York Times*, March 12, 1961; John Henrik Clarke, "The New Afro-American Nationalism," *Freedomways* 1 (Fall 1961): 285–95; Richard B. Moore, "Africa Conscious Harlem [1963]," in *Harlem: A Community in Transition*, 3rd ed., ed. John Henrik Clarke (New York: Citadel Press, 1964), 77–96; Ernest J. Allen Jr., "Religious Heterodoxy and Nationalist Tradition: The Continuing Evolution of the Nation of Islam," *Black Scholar* 26, nos. 3–4 (Fall–Winter 1996): 2–34; George Shepperson, "Notes on Negro American Influences on the Emergence of African Nationalism," *Journal of African History* 1 (1960): 299–312; Shepperson, "Pan-Africanism and 'pan-Africanism': Some Historical Notes," *Phylon* 23 (Winter 1962): 346–58; Colin Legum, *Pan-Africanism: A Short Political Guide* (New York: Praeger, 1962); *Pan-Africanism Reconsidered*, ed. American Society of African Culture (Berkeley: University of California Press, 1962); John Bracey, August Meier, and Elliott Rudwick, eds., *Black Nationalism in America* (Indianapolis: Bobbs-Merrill, 1970).

4. James Meriwether, *Proudly We Can Be Africans: Black Americans and Africa, 1935–1961* (Chapel Hill: University of North Carolina Press, 2002).

5. J. Isawa Elaigwu and Ali A. Mazrui, "Nation-building and Changing Political Structures," in *General History of Africa, VIII: Africa Since 1935*, ed. Ali A. Mazrui (Berkeley: University of California Press, 1999), 435–67; Joseph Ki-Zerbo, Ali Mazrui, and Christophe Wondji, with A. Adu Boahen, "Nation-building and Changing Political Values," in *General History of Africa, VIII: Africa since 1935*, 468–98.

6. Kwame Nkrumah, *Africa Must Unite* (London: Heinemann, 1963); *Forward Ever: The Life of Kwame Nkrumah* (London: Panaf Books, 1977). For a comprehen-

sive look into the expatriate experience, see Kevin Gaines, *American Africans in Ghana: Black Expatriates in the Civil Rights Era* (Chapel Hill: University of North Carolina Press, 2006).

7. For a view of the post–World War II political contexts African Americans faced, see Martha Biondi, *To Stand and Fight: The Struggle for Civil Rights in Postwar New York City* (Cambridge, MA: Harvard University Press, 2003).

8. Liberation Committee for Africa, "Statement of Aims," circa 1960.

9. Ibid.

10. *Liberator* (December 1961): 2.

11. Advertisement, "What Africa Means to Americans," *The Nation*, May 13, 1961.

12. "Riot in Gallery Halts U.N. Debate," *New York Times*, February 16, 1961, p.1. See also Meriwether, *Proudly We Can Be Africans*, pp. 233–40.

13. Author correspondence with Richard Gibson, April 13, 2006.

14. Author interview with Calvin Hicks, June 13, 2007.

15. U.S. Blames Reds for Negroes Act, *Chicago Daily Defender*, February 16, 1961, 1.

16. Adlai E. Stevenson, "The New Africa: A Guide and a Proposal," *Harper's Magazine*, May 1960; Schomburg Clippings File, Amherst College.

17. Max K. Gilstrap, "Mr. Stevenson and Africa," *Christian Science Monitor*, July 7, 1955; Schomburg Clippings File, Amherst College.

18. Arthur Massolo, "Negro Leaders Deny Harlem Mad at Adlai," *New York Post*, September 9, 1956; "Stevenson Tells Negroes to 'Proceed Gradually' toward Desegregation," *Greensboro Daily News*, February 8, 1956; Schomburg Clippings File, Amherst College.

19. "Copy of Telegram Sent to Mrs. Patrice Lumumba, Leopoldville, Congo," dated January 21, 1961; Author's collection.

20. Ludo De Witte, *The Assassination of Lumumba*, trans. Ann Wright and Renee Fenby (London: Verso, 2001).

21. Liberation Committee for Africa, press release, dated February 13, 1961. Lumumba's murder proved to be one stage in a larger effort to protect Belgian interests in the Congo. Several months after Lumumba's killing, Hammarskjöld was killed in a curious plane crash on September 17, 1961. Scholars have discovered that competing economic, if not outright imperialist, interests were factors contributing to that death as well. For the best explanation, see David N. Gibbs, "Hammarskjöld, the United Nations, and the Congo Crisis, 1960–1, A Reinterpretation," *Journal of Modern African Studies*, 31, no. 1 (1993): 163–74. Even *Liberator* was urged to give the issue greater nuance than it had earlier, writing, "We mourn [Hammarskjöld's] death because he, like Patrice Lumumba, the man he betrayed, was a victim of colonialist greed in Africa"; *Liberator* (September 1961): 1; see also Meriwether, *Proudly We Can Be Africans*, 208–40.

22. Liberation Committee for Africa, press release, February 13, 1961.

23. Lorraine Hansberry, "Congolese Patriot," *New York Times*, March 26, 1961, SM4. See also Lawrence P. Jackson, *Indignant Generation: A Narrative History of*

African American Writers and Critics, 1934–1960 (Princeton, NJ: Princeton University Press, 2011), 507.

24. Liberation Committee for Africa, "Against Nuclear Testing: An Open Letter to President John F. Kennedy," *New York Times*, April 26, 1962, 16.

25. Gibson found himself at the center of several controversies in the late 1950s and early 1960s, the most significant perhaps being accused of serving as an agent provocateur by some in the liberation movement. In at least two publications from the period, Gibson's credibility is questioned, though no facts are provided in either account. See *Revolution Africaine* Fall 1964, n.p., and *Soulbook* 1, no. 4 (Winter 1965–1966): 233; and *Soulbook* 2, no. 1 (Summer 1966): 1. When I asked Gibson about this issue he responded by saying that the statement accusing him "appeared in the last issue of the *Revolution Africaine* when [publisher] Jacques Verges sought to insinuate that the financial ruin of his publication, no longer in Algeria and Switzerland, had been due to some sinister imperial plot. You will note that he did not mention the CIA because I would have sued him for libel. Eventually, I did that years later in London, and won my case and a substantial settlement"; author correspondence with R. Gibson, September 12, 2007.

Gibson is listed as a member of the editorial board of the *Liberator* beginning in March 1966, though he acknowledges that he merely sent articles to Watts for publication and had no hand in the actual production of the magazine. He had published only one article in the *Liberator* prior to that point: "The Algerian Story: A Million Lives for Freedom," *Liberator* 3, no. 4 (April 1963): 4. His name remained on the magazine's editorial staff list from 1966 until 1971, when the magazine ceased publication. He closed the correspondence quoted previously by referencing the long essay he had published, entitled "Richard Wright's 'Island of Hallucination' and the 'Gibson Affair,'" in *Modern Fiction Studies* 51, no. 4 (Winter 2005): 896–920. For an extended account of Gibson's time with the FPCC in New York, see Van Gosse, *Where the Boys Are: Cuba, the Cold War, and the Making of a New American Left* (New York: Verso, 1993), 137–74. And see also Besenia Rodriguez, "'De la Esclavitud Yanqui a la Libertad Cubana': U.S. Black Radicals, the Cuban Revolution and the Formation of a Tricontinental Ideology," *Radical History Review* 92 (Spring 2005): 62–87. (Thanks go to Anthony Ratcliff for providing me with the *Soulbook* documentation.)

26. John Henrik Clarke Papers. Box 2, Folder 46. Schomburg Center. New York Public Library.

27. Lawrence Jackson, *Indignant Generation*, 470–74; Peniel Joseph, *Waiting til the Midnight Hour: A Narrative History of Black Power America* (New York: Henry Holt: 2006), 42.

28. Jackson, *Indignant Generation*, 501.

29. Author correspondence with Richard Gibson, April 13, 2006.

30. Author correspondence with Gibson, December 10, 2007.

31. Author correspondence with Gibson, December 11, 2007.

32. *Liberator* (December 1961).

33. "Miss Evelyn Battle Engaged to Marry," *New York Times*, March 25, 1962, 101.

34. Author interview, April 8, 2006.

35. It is interesting that when I spoke to Beveridge, he mentioned that he never met Gibson, though they had been in the same room on occasion. He explained that Watts was a person who kept his contacts separate. Marilyn Lieberman Watts, Watts's first wife, confirmed this, indicating that she rarely knew fully all of the projects Watts had going or people that he knew.

36. Ibid.

37. Lowell P. Beveridge Jr., *Domestic Diversity and Other Subversive Activities* (Minneapolis, MN: Mill City Press, 2009), 277–78.

38. Hunter College, 149th Commencement Program, June 3, 1981, lists Hortense Sie Beveridge among the Class of 1981.

39. FBI File 100-90851. Outline of file contents concerning Hortense Sie in author's possession.

40. Beveridge, *Domestic Diversity*, 252.

41. Pete Beveridge, "Hortense Sie Beveridge, October 3, 1923–December 8, 1993"; unpublished biographical sketch.

42. See, *Africa-U.N. Bulletin,* American Committee on Africa (ACOA), 18 (January 13, 1960); African Activist Archive Project (online) Archive, Michigan State University.

43. *New York Age*, January 16, 1960, p. 10. This article lists Hortense "Tee" Beveridge as the president of the Brooklyn chapter of ASNLH.

44. Author correspondence with Pete Beveridge, April 12, 2006.

45. The use of the term "long-distance runner" to describe black women's activism is inspired by Dayo Gore, Jeanne Theoharis, and Komozi Woodard, eds., *Want to Start a Revolution? Radical Women in the Black Freedom Struggle* (New York: NYU Press, 2009), 13–14.

46. "Hortense Beveridge," International Movie Database, accessed on January 21, 2016, at http://www.imdb.com/name/nm0079708/.

47. African Activist Archive Project (online), Michigan State University, http://africanactivist.msu.edu/index.php.

48. Ibid.

49. Penny M. Von Eschen, *Race against Empire: Black Americans and Anticolonialism, 1937–1957* (Ithaca, NY: Cornell University Press, 1997), 143–44.

50. "Africa and the United States, Annual Report of the American Committee on Africa," June 1, 1960–May 31, 1961; African Activist Archive Project.

51. Ibid.

52. Ibid.

53. Von Eschen, *Race against Empire*; Wayne Urban, *Black Scholar: Horace Mann Bond, 1904–1972* (Athens: University of Georgia Press, 1992); Meriwether, *Proudly We Can Be Africans.*

54. See Larry Jackson, *Indignant Generation*, 478–79; see also Charles Henry and Tunua Thrash, "U.S. Human Rights Petitions before the UN," *Black Scholar* 26, nos. 3–4 (Fall-Winter, 1996): 60–73.

55. James Smethurst, *The Black Arts Movement: Literary Nationalism in the 1960s and 1970s* (Chapel Hill: University of North Carolina Press, 2005), 118–23. For the most complete coverage of the Harlem Writer's Guild, see Keith Gilyard, *John Oliver Killens: A Life of Black Literary Activism* (Athens, GA: The University of Georgia Press, 2010); in reference to Killens's travel to Africa, see 155–62.

56. See St. Clair Drake, "The American Negro's Relation to Africa," *Africa Today* 14, no. 6 (December 1967): 12–15.

57. P. Olisanwuche Esedebe, *Pan-Africanism: The Idea and Movement, 1776–1991*, 2nd ed. (Washington, DC: Howard University Press, 1994), 5.

58. Author correspondence with Gibson, April 13, 2006.

59. Although published works incorrectly mention that Dan Watts was the leader of On Guard for Freedom—see Komozi Woodard, *A Nation within a Nation: Amiri Baraka and Black Power Politics* (Chapel Hill: University of North Carolina Press, 1999), and Cynthia Young, *Soul Power: Culture, Radicalism, and the Making of a U.S. Third World Left* (Durham: NC, Duke University Press, 2006)—Calvin Hicks was the actual leader of this organization.

60. John Henrik Clarke, "New Afro-American Nationalism," *Freedomways* 1, no. 3 (Fall 1961): 285–95; Robert L. Teague, "Negroes Say Conditions in U.S. Explain Nationalists' Militancy: Negroes Explain Extremist Drives," *New York Times*, March 2, 1961, 1.

61. James Smethurst, "Poetry and Sympathy: New York, the Left and the Rise of Black Arts," in *Left of the Color Line: Race, Radicalism, and Twentieth Century Literature of the United States*, ed. Bill V. Mullen and James Smethurst (Chapel Hill: University of North Carolina Press, 2003), 259–78.

62. See for example, Robert L. Allen, *Black Awakening in Capitalist America: An Analytic History* (New York: Doubleday, 1969), 246–73.

63. Author phone interview with Marilyn Watts Lieberman, October 9, 2006.

64. Author correspondence with Rose Finkenstaedt, May 2007.

65. Author interview with Pete Beveridge, April 8, 2006.

66. *Liberator* (June 1961): 2.

67. Letter dated September 20, 1961. Robert F. Williams Papers, Microfilm collection.

68. Ibid.

69. Gibson, Correspondence with the author, April 13, 2006.

70. *Liberator* (May 1961): 1; Vusumzi L. Make, "NATO Countries Aid Military Preparations of Verwoerd Government to 'Shoot the Black Masses,'" *Liberator* 2, no. 4 (April 1962): 2.

71. "Freedom Riders Go beyond the New Frontier," *Liberator* 1, no. 6 (June 1961): 1–3.

72. Clarke, "The New Afro-American Nationalism."

73. Meriwether, *Proudly We Can Be Africans*, 233–40; Komozi Woodard, *A Nation within a Nation: Amiri Baraka (LeRoi Jones) and Black Power Politics* (Chapel Hill: University of North Carolina Press, 1999).

Chapter Two

1. Lawrence P. Jackson, *Indignant Generation: A Narrative History of African American Writers and Critics, 1934–1960*. (Princeton, NJ: Princeton University Press, 2011), 484.

2. Edward Said, *Representations of the Intellectual* (New York: Randon House, 1996), 52–53, 62–63.

3. John Henrik Clarke, "The New Afro-American Nationalism," *Freedomways* 1, no. 3 (Fall 1961): 285–95; James H. Meriwether, *Proudly We Can Be Africans: Black Americans and Africa, 1935–1961* (Chapel Hill: University of North Carolina Press, 2002).

4. St. Clair Drake, "Negro Americans and the Africa Interest," *The American Negro Reference Book*, ed. John P. Davis (Englewood Cliffs, NJ: Prentice-Hall, 1966), 662–705.

5. Brenda Gayle Plummer, *In Search of Power: African Americans in the Era of Decolonization, 1956–1974* (Cambridge: Cambridge University Press, 2013), 31.

6. Ibid., 343.

7. James K. Baker, "The American Society of African Culture," *Journal of Modern African American Society of African Culture* (Berkeley: University of California Press, 1962).

8. Editorial, *Liberator* 2, no. 1 (January 1962). *Studies* 4, no. 3 (Nov. 1966): 367–69; Colin Legum, *Pan-Africanism Reconsidered*, ed. The American Society of African Culture (Berkeley: University of California Press, 1962).

9. "Yankee Go Home: Nigeria Speaks to the Ford Foundation," *Liberator* 3, no. 4 (April 1963): 17.

10. *Liberator* 2, no. 2 (February 1962).

11. *Liberator* 2, no. 3 (March 1962).

12. Ibid.

13. W. E. B. Du Bois, *The World and Africa: An Inquiry into the Part That Africa Has Played in World History* (1946; reprint, New York: International, 1979).

14. *Liberator* 2, no. 3 (March 1962).

15. *Liberator* (September 1961), 4. As this was *Liberator*'s first full publication run, no volume numbers were provided for the year 1961. Beveridge indicated that the printer had mistakenly printed "October" on this issue of the newsletter.

16. *Liberator* (December 1961): 4.

17. Lowell Pierson Beveridge Jr., "The Theory and Practice of White Supremacy in South Africa, 1910–1913," master's thesis, Columbia University, 1953.

18. Interview with the author, April 8, 2006. In 1958, Beveridge and his wife, Tee Beveridge, sponsored a Ghanaian student named Eddy Gyando for study in the United States.

19. "America in the Eyes of an African Student," *Liberator* (December 1961): 3.

20. "The I.I.E. Report of African Students: An Exercise in Data Distortion," *Liberator* 2, no. 1 (January 1962): 2. For more on the educational issues and opportunities

for African students, see Julien Engel, "The African-American Institute," *African Studies Bulletin* 6, no. 3 (October 1963): 13–18; Gordon D. Morgan, "Exploratory Study of Problems of Academic Adjustment of Nigerian Students in America," *Journal of Negro Education* 32, no. 3 (Summer 1963): 208–17; Harold O. Lewis, "American Education and Civil Rights in an International Perspective," *Journal of Negro Education* 34, no. 3 (Summer 1965): 239–48. Seminal writings that include the subject of African and African American education are St. Clair Drake, "Diaspora Studies and Pan-Africanism," *Global Dimensions of the African Diaspora*, ed. Joseph E. Harris (Washington, DC: Howard University Press, 1983), 341–402; and Drake, "Negro Americans and the Africa Interest."

21. Dan Watts, "Israel, Arab Refugees and Africa," *Liberator* (December 1961): 1.

22. "Arab Student Comments on Arab Refugees," *Liberator* 2, no. 2 (February 1962): 3.

23. Skeva Soko, "An African Student Warns about 'Student Aid,'" *Liberator* 2, no. 2 (February 1962): 4. See also Julien Engel, "The African-American Institute," *African Studies Bulletin* 6, no. 3 (October 1963): 13–18. Engel identifies the African support programs overseen by the African-American Institute. One of the programs he identified, the African Scholarship Program of American Universities, sponsored upward of 800 African students studying in the United States from 1953 to 1963.

24. Dan Watts, "The Long Trip Home: Failure of the African Student Program," *Liberator* 2, no. 4 (April 1962): 1, 3. See also "Further Thoughts on African Student Programs," *Liberator* 2, no. 6 (June 1962): 2.

25. Pete Beveridge, "Further Thoughts on African Student Programs," *Liberator* 2, no. 6 (June 1962): 2.

26. "A Lesson in Cameroon History for President Kennedy," *Liberator* 2, no. 3 (March 1962): 1; Elikia M'Bokolo "Equatorial West Africa," *UNESCO General History of Africa*, Volume 3: *Africa since 1935*, ed. Ali A Mazrui (Berkeley: University of California Press, 1999), 192–220.

27. *Liberator* 2, no. 4 (April 1962): 1; M'Bokolo, 218–20.

28. Elisio Figueiredo, "Angolan Resistance to Portuguese Atrocities," *Liberator* 2, no. 4 (April 1962): 4. Though a student at the time of this speech, Figueiredo would eventually become the first ambassador to the United Nations from Angola, after the country gained independence in 1975.

29. *Liberator* 2, no. 5 (May 1962): 1.

30. "A Message from His Excellency Gamal Abdel Nasser President of the United Arab Republic," *Liberator* 2, no. 5 (May 1962): 4–5.

31. W. Alphaeus Hunton, letter addressed to Dan Watts, *Liberator* 2, no. 5 (May 1962): 13. See also Hunton, *Decision in Africa: Sources of Current Conflict* (New York: International Publishers, 1957). In the preface to this book, W. E. B. Du Bois wrote: "In all this, Dr. Hunton is fair and objective. He seeks his facts with the unprecedented fairness of the scholar; he does not try to foretell the economic path to happiness and justice for particular groups or states. He does insist, however, that social welfare and not private profit must be the goal of all people, and that black

Africans are people. This thesis his book supports with a wealth of material, and for this reason it is a notable contribution to African freedom," 10.

32. Beveridge, interview with the author, April 8, 2006.

33. Selma Sparks, "A First Hand Report from the Accra Assembly: 'The World Without the Bomb,'" *Liberator* 2, no. 7 (July 1962): 4–5. (Letter dated June 28, 1962.)

34. Kevin K. Gaines, *American Africans in Ghana: Black Expatriates and the Civil; Rights Era* (Chapel Hill, NC: Duke University Press, 2006).

35. "Bill Worthy Takes a Critical Look at the Treatment of Africa in the U.S. Press," *Liberator* 2, no. 7 (July 1962): 6–7.

36. Ibid.

37. Peniel E. Joseph, *Waiting til the Midnight Hour: A Narrative History of Black Power in America* (New York: Henry Holt, 2006), 45–48. See also "Black Unity Forces Concession in Worthy Case," *Liberator* 2, no. 8 (August 1962): 5.

38. "Encyclopedia Africana Outlines Proposed Plan of Work," *Liberator* 2, no. 7 (July 1962): 10.

39. "Assassination: A Weapon of Neo-Colonialism," *Liberator* 2, no. 8 (August 1962): 6.

40. "Zik Speaks Out on Anglo-Saxon Press Treatment of Africa," *Liberator* 2, no. 8 (August 1962): 2–3.

41. See editorials, "Gizenga Must be Freed" and "Lest We Forget: The Tragic Background of the Congo Story," *Liberator* 2, no. 9 (September 1962): 2–3, 8–9.

42. Ibid.

43. Pete Beveridge, "Nelson Mandela: Scourge of Apartheid," *Liberator* 3, no. 1 (January 1963): 5–6.

44. David Chanaiwa, "Southern Africa since 1945," *UNESCO: General History of Africa:* Volume 3, *Africa since 1935*, ed. Ali A. Mazrui (Berkeley: University of California Press, 1999), 272–73.

45. "SWANU Secretary Calls for Action," *Liberator* 3, no. 1 (January 1963): 16.

46. Sam Nujoma, *Where Others Wavered: The Autobiography of Sam Nujoma* (London: Panaf Books, 2001).

47. Daniel H. Watts, "View from the Top: American Leadership Conference on Africa," *Liberator* 3, no. 1 (January 1963): 14.

48. Ibid. See also Panaf Books Editors, *Panaf Great Lives: Eduardo Mondlane* (London: Panaf Books, 1978).

49. Verwoerd, Salazar, and Welensky were architects and agents of white supremacy in coalition to extend European rule over South and Central Africa. See Rosalynde Ainslie, *The Unholy Alliance: Salazar, Voerwerd, Welensky* (London: Anti-Apartheid Movement, 1962); and Matthew Hughes, "Fighting for White Rule in Africa: The Central African Federation, Katanga and the Congo Crisis, 1958–1965," *International History Review* 25, no. 3 (September 2003): 592–615.

50. Dan Watts, "The Reluctant Afro-Americans: American Negro Leadership Conference on Africa," *Liberator* 3, no. 2 (February 1963): 3, 22.

51. This paper was later published in the Davis, ed., *American Negro Reference Book*, under the title, "Negro Americans and the Africa Interest."

52. Watts, "Reluctant Afro-Americans," 3.

53. Ibid.

54. "American Negro Leadership Conference on Africa: Resolutions," *Liberator* 3, no. 2 (February 1963): 19–22.

55. "Three Years after Sharpeville: The Only Solution for South Africa," *Liberator* 3, no. 3 (March 1963): 3.

56. Chanaiwa, "Southern Africa since 1945," 249–81.

57. Charles P. Howard Sr. "The Assassination of Silvanus Olympio," *Liberator* 3, no. 3 (March 1963): 6–7, 18.

58. Ibid.

59. Richard Gibson, "A Million Lives for Freedom: The Algerian Story," *Liberator* 3, no. 4 (April 1963): 4–7, 20.

60. Carlos E. Russell, "All Night Vigil for Lumumba," *Liberator* 3, no. 4 (April 1963): 15.

61. Ibid., 20.

62. Author correspondence with Gibson, December 11, 2007. For a full account of the Algerian Revolution, see Alistair Horne, *A Savage War of Peace: Algeria 1954–1962* (1977; reprint, New York: Penguin Books, 1987).

63. Author correspondence with Gibson, December 11, 2007.

64. "The Hour Has Come: Report from South Africa," *Liberator* 3, no. 4 (April 1963): 12–13.

65. Carlos E. Russell and Ernest Kalibala, "Thank You, Massa Ellender for Your Contribution to African Unity," *Liberator* 3, no. 2 (February 1963): 4–5.

66. "La. Senator makes Visit to Mali Republic," *Chicago Daily Defender*, October 27, 1962, 3; "Dixie Senator Attacks African Nations," *Chicago Daily Defender*, December 3, 1962, 1, 2; "Uganda Bars Ellender; Rips Segregation Views," *Chicago Daily Defender*, December 4, 1962, 3.

67. Russell and Kalibala, "Thank You, Massa Ellender," 4.

68. Jariretundu Kozonguizi, "African Leader and Racist Senator," *Liberator* 3, no. 6 (June 1963): 11, 18.

69. Pete Beveridge (unsigned), "The Two Faces of America," *Liberator* 3, no. 6 (June 1963): 4. On the table of contents for this issue, Carlos Russell is credited for this article, but Beveridge authored it.

70. W. Ofuatey-Kodjoe, "My Unwilling Brother," *Liberator* 3, no. 6 (June 1963): 10, 19.

71. Ibid., 19. Emphasis in original.

72. "Dear African Brothers," *Liberator* 3 (November 1963): 3.

73. Issacs lists Watts as one of the fifty-five people he interviewed for his book. See Introduction, *The New World of Negro Americans* (New York: Viking Press, 1963), xvii.

74. Harlem Anti-Colonial Committee event flyer, dated June 1, 1963; William Worthy file, Schomburg Clippings file, Amherst College.

75. "Harlem," *Liberator* 3 (June 1963): 19.

76. "How U.S. Supports Apartheid," *Liberator* 3, no. 9 (September 1963): 3–5.

77. William Worthy, "Anatomy of a Sit-In," *Liberator* 3, no. 9 (September 1963): 6–7.

78. See Van Gosse, "More Than Just a Politician: Notes on the Life and Times of Harold Cruse," in *Harold Cruse's The Crisis of the Negro Intellectual Reconsidered*, ed. Jerry Watts (New York: Routledge, 2004), 17–40. Gosse argued that after 1964, *Liberator* abandoned coverage of Africa.

79. "Reporter Magazine Accused of Ignorance and Confusion," *Liberator* 4, no. 5 (May 1964): 5.

80. Daniel H. Watts, "U.N. Report," *Liberator* 4, no. 7 (Jul. 1964): 16.

81. Letters dated February 8, 1963, and February 15, 1963, between Jacques Verges, director, *Révolution Africaine*, and Osgood Caruthers, acting director, press, publications, and public services. In the author's possession.

82. T. D. Baffoe, "U.S. Image in Ghana," *Liberator* 4 (July 1964): 17.

83. "Quaison-Sackey Brings Afro-Asian Sanity to Security Council Debate," *Liberator* 2, no. 2 (November–December, 1962): 3, 12. His book, *Africa Unbound: Reflections of an African Statesman* (New York: Prager, 1963), details his participation at the United Nations. At the time of its publication, Nkrumah's government was still viewed as a shining example of African nationalism. Nkrumah wrote the Foreword for this book, praising Quaison-Sackey for his "force and clarity" in explaining "the political factors affecting the complicated process of evolution," and "the forces at work in Africa" (vii).

84. Daniel H. Watts, "UN Report: Africa Speaks Out," *Liberator* 5, no. 1 (January 1965): 16–19.

85. Richard Gibson, "Ghana and the Battle for Africa," *Liberator* 6, no. 4 (April 1966): 4–6.

86. "African Women at the U.N.," *Liberator* 5, no. 5 (May 1965): 18.

87. Ossie Sykes, "Playing the Game for the State Department in Africa," *Liberator* 5, no. 6 (June 1965): 6.

88. Donald Jackson, "Black People and Vietnam," *Liberator* 5, no. 12 (December 1965): 9–10.

89. Richard Gibson, "Race War Over Rhodesia?," *Liberator* 5, no. 12 (December 1965): 4–5.

90. Shirley Graham Du Bois to John Henrik Clarke, March 27, 1966; John Henrik Clarke Papers, Box 30, Folder 6, Schomburg Center, New York Public Library.

91. Gibson to Clarke, dated April 16, 1966; John Henrik Clarke Papers. Box 5, Folder 46. Schomburg Center, New York Public Library.

92. Bob Fitch and Mary Oppenheimer, *Ghana: End of an Illusion* (New York: Monthly Review Press, 1966), 129.

93. "African Scorecard," *Liberator* 6, no. 4 (April 1966): 7.

94. Charles P. Howard, "Africa vs. CIA," *Liberator* 6, no. 5 (May 1966): 8–9.

95. Howard, "Ghana Coup No Benefit to Africans," *Afro-American*, 8, 1966.

96. Some of Howard's articles over this run include: Charles P. Howard, "Eyewitness Doubts Ghana Coup's Appeal," *Afro-American*, April 2, 1966; "Outside Imperialist Make 'Greedy' Class Oust Nkrumah," *Afro-American*, April 5, 1966; "Says Nkrumah Overthrow Benefits Ex-Colonial Powers," *Afro-American*, April 16, 1966; "Sees Dwindling of Free Africa," *Afro-American*, n.d.; "Much Criticism Directed as Nkrumah Unfounded," *Afro-American*, n.d.; "Foreign Squeeze on Cocoa Hurt Ghana," *Afro-American*, n.d.; Kwame Nkrumah Papers, Moorland-Spingarn Research Center, Box 154–42; See also Gaines, *American Africans in Ghana*, 242.

97. Richard Gibson, "East African Timebomb," *Liberator* 6, no. 8 (August 1966): 10–11.

98. *Soulbook* 1, no. 4 (Winter 1965–66): 1.

99. Ibid. An additional statement on Gibson was included in *Soulbook* 1, no. 4 (Winter 1965–66); *Soulbook* 2, no. 1 (Summer 1966).

100. Charles P. Howard, "South Africa," *Liberator* 6, no. 11 (November 1966): 8.

101. *Liberator* 6, no. 11 (November 1966): 16. "Radio—Today's Leading Events," *New York Times*, November 6, 1966. The listing reads: "WBAI—The Making of a Rebel, an Interview with Franz J. T. Lee, South African Exile Living in Europe."

102. Richard Gibson, "Israeli Threat to Africa," *Liberator* 8, no. 7 (July 1967): 6–7.

103. Chanaiwa, "Southern Africa since 1945," 279.

104. Gibson, "Israeli Threat."

105. Richard Gibson, "African Unity and Afro-Americans," *Liberator* 8, no. 8 (August 1968): 16–18.

106. John Soaries, "Home IS Africa!" *Liberator* 8, no. 9 (September 1968): 15.

107. Vernon W. Boggs, "Slogans Are Not Enough!," *Liberator* 8, no. 11 (November 1968): 10–11.

108. Selwyn R. Cudjoe, "Taking Whitey's Word," *Liberator* 9, no. 5 (May 1969): 10–11.

109. Tom Mboya, "Africa and Afro-America," in *Black Homeland, Black Diaspora: Cross-currents of the African Relationship*, ed. Jacob Drachler (Port Washington, NY: National University Publications, 1975), 245–57.

110. Ibid., 246–47. Emphasis in original.

111. Ibid., 255.

112. Immanuel Wallerstein, "I Really Said"; Songha Wanyandey Songha, "Mr. Mboya in Harlem"; and Michael Knashie Searles, "It Ain't Necessarily So"; all in *Liberator* 9, no. 7 (July 1969): 9–11.

113. Y. Sangare, "Zambia: Towards Economic Decolonization," *Liberator* 8, no. 2 (February 1969): 14–17.

114. This is my term for the cinematic exploitation of African people. It's the counterpart to "Blaxploitation" in the U.S. context.

115. Robeson Taj Frazier, "Thunder in the East: China, Exiled Crusaders, and the Unevenness of Black Internationalism," *American Quarterly* 63, no. 4 (December, 2011): 929–53.

Chapter Three

1. Vicky Crawford, Jacqueline Anne Rouse, and Barbara Woods, eds., *Women in the Civil Rights Movement: Trailblazers and Torchbearers, 1941-1965* (Bloomington: Indiana University Press, 1990); Dayo Gore, Jeanne Theoharis, and Komozi Woodard, eds., *Want to Start a Revolution? Radical Women in the Black Freedom Struggle* (New York: NYU Press, 2009), 1–24.

2. Benita Roth, *Separate Roads to Feminism: Black, Chicana, and White Feminist Movements in America's Second Wave* (Cambridge University Press, 2004), 16. See also Kimberly Springer, *Living for the Revolution: Black Feminist Organizations, 1968-1980* (Durham, NC: Duke University Press. 2005), 1–44.

3. Roth, *Separate Roads to Feminism: Black, Chicana, and White Feminist Movements in America's Second Wave* (Cambridge University Press, 2004), 16.

4. Pete and Tee Beveridge counted both of these pioneering women among their friends.

5. For excellent historical treatment of black women's activism that predates *Liberator*, see Dayo Gore, *Radicalism at the Crossroads: African American Women Activists in the Cold War* (New York: NYU Press, 2011), and Erik S. McDuffie, *Sojourning for Freedom: Black Women, American Communism, and the Making of Black Left Feminism* (Durham, NC: Duke University Press, 2011).

6. Author correspondence with Rose Finkenstaedt, May 2006.

7. Liberation Committee for Africa, undated letter; Schomburg Clippings file, Amherst College.

8. Harold Cruse, *The Crisis of the Negro Intellectual* (2005 reprint; New York: New York Review of Books, 1967). Specifically, for the criticism of Hansberry, see the sections "Cultural Leadership and Cultural Democracy," 96–114; and especially, "Lorraine Hansberry," 267–84.

9. Liberation Committee for Africa, "Negro History Week Observance" invitation card, dated February 10, 1963; Schomburg Clippings file, Amherst College.

10. "Rock the Boat," (editorial), *Liberator* 3, no. 3 (March 1963): 2. Bunche and Robinson, though responding to different sets of historical circumstances, were viewed by many in the African American left community as out of touch with their political desires and far too eager to express patriotism or hold important government posts that extended, rather than challenge, American imperial and militaristic designs.

11. Lorraine Hansberry, Letter to the Editor, *Liberator* 3, no. 7 (July 1963): 16.

12. *Liberator* 3, no. 4 (April 1963): 22.

13. *New York Times*, January 17, 1965, X12

14. Letter to the Editor, *Liberator* 3, no. 7 (July 1963): 16.

15. Selma Sparks, "Dubinsky's Plantations" *Liberator* 3, no. 1 (January 1963): 3–4, 6.

16. Rose L. H. Finkenstaedt, "The Elections: No Choice for Black Americans," *Liberator* 3, no. 1 (January 1963): 8.

17. "General Harriet Tubman: The Real Emancipator," *Liberator* 3, no. 1 (January 1963): 10.

18. Rose L. H. Finkenstaedt, "Narcotics in the Ghetto: Neo-Colonialism at Home," 12–14; "Lumumba's Last Letter to His Wife," 15; Selma V. Sparks, "Dubinsky's Plantation, Part II," *Liberator* 3, no. 2 (February 1963): 16–18.

19. Selma V. Sparks, "Flight from Reality: The American Peace Movement," *Liberator* 3, no. 4 (April 1963): 8–9.

20. *Liberator* 3, no. 2 (February 1963): 22.

21. Rose L. H. Finkenstaedt, "Never on Christmas: A Black Muslim Story," *Liberator* 3, no. 3 (March 1963): 16–17.

22. Rose L. H. Finkenstaedt, "Upper West Side Story: Community League of West 159th St.," Liberator 3, no. 4 (April 1963): 10–11.

23. Rose L. H. Finkenstaedt, "Which Road to Freedom?," *Liberator* 3, no. 5 (May 1963): 12–14; see also "Equality Is Not Enough," *Liberator* 3, no. 8 (August 1963): 10–11.

24. Dan Watts, "Mrs. Richardson's Revolt" (editorial), *Liberator* 3, no. 11 (November 1963): 2.

25. Joseph, *Waiting*, 84–92.

26. Edith Schomburg, "The Crux of Black Non-Violence," *Liberator* 3, no. 12 (December 1963): 10.

27. Merle Stewart, Letter on Self-Defense, *Liberator* 4, no. 8 (August 1964): 11.

28. Buleah Richardson, "This Little Light of Mine," *Liberator* 3, no. 7 (July 1963): 6–9. *Liberator*'s connection to the South was limited. According to Pete Beveridge, aside from articles such as Richardson's, the magazine relied on figures such as civil rights attorney and SNCC associate Len Holt (who lived in the South and had participated in several demonstrations there) for their coverage.

29. Mildred Pitts Walker, "Nigger Go Home—Where?" *Liberator* 3, no. 7 (July 1963): 17–18.

30. Benita Roth, *Separate Roads to Feminism: Black, Chicana, and White Feminist Movements in America's Second Wave* (Cambridge: Cambridge University Press, 2004), 76–128.

31. Eleanor Mason, "Hot Irons and Black Nationalism" *Liberator* 3, no. 5 (May 1963): 21–22.

32. John Bracey, August Meier, and Elliott Rudwick, eds., *Black Nationalism in America* (Indianapolis: Bobbs-Merrill, 1970), 235, 486.

33. Mary Ann Bryant, Letter to the Editor, *Liberator* 3, no. 7 (July 1963): 16.

34. These models were also pictured on album covers from the period. Jazz musicians such as Lou Donaldson embraced this appreciation of black women's natural beauty. His albums, *The Natural Soul* (Blue Note BLP 4108), *Good Gracious* (Blue Note 45-1896), *Say It Loud!* (Blue Note BST 84299), and *Everything I Play Is Funky* (Blue Note BST 84337), all featured brown-skinned African American women in natural hairdos on the cover. For an expanded discussion of these strategies, see Tanisha C. Ford, *Liberated Threads: Black Women, Style, and*

the Global Politics of Soul (Chapel Hill: University of North Carolina Press, 2015), 51–58.

35. Jeannette, "Thru Women's Eyes," *Liberator* 3, no. 10 (October 1963): 15. It should also be mentioned that the magazine also showed African-inspired clothing for men as well. See "New Afro Fashions for Men," *Liberator* 7, no. 11 (November 1967): 12–13.

36. See for example, Robert Harris, Nyota Harris, and Grandassa Harris, eds., *Carlos Cooks and Black Nationalism from Garvey to Malcolm* (Dover, MA: Majority Press, 1991); Lorenzo Thomas, "The Shadow World: New York's Umbra Workshop and Origins of the Black Arts Movement," *Callaloo* 4 (October 1978): 53–72.

37. Max Roach and Abbey Lincoln, "Black Man in Japan," *Liberator* 4, no. 1 (January 1964): 12–13, 19.

38. Scott Saul, *Freedom Is, Freedom Ain't: Jazz and the Making of the Sixties* (Cambridge, MA: Harvard University Press, 2003), 93–96.

39. Roach and Lincoln, "Black Man in Japan," 13.

40. The film *Black Sun* was released in 1964 and was directed by Koreyoshi Kurahara. The soundtrack, which features Roach and Lincoln, was directed by Toshiro Mayuzumi; *Kuroi Taiyo (Black Sun) / Kyonetsu no Kisetsu (The Warped Ones): Original Soundtracks* (Think! Records SPFJ-10/11), Japan. Recorded by Norio Numakura; mixed at Nikkatsu Studio, November 7, 1963. http://www.japanimprov.com/indies/think/Blacksun.html (accessed on February 19, 2009).

41. LaShonda Katrice Barnett, *I Got Thunder: Black Women Songwriters on Their Craft* (New York: Thunder's Mouth Press, 2007), 15.

42. Eric Porter, *What Is This Thing Called Jazz? African American Musicians as Artists, Critics and Activists* (Berkeley: University of California Press, 2002), 149–90; Wayne Enstice and Janis Stockhouse, *Jazzwomen: Conversations with Twenty-One Musicians* (Bloomington: Indiana University Press, 2004), 195–214.

43. Nat Hentoff, "How Wonderful to Be a Black Woman," *New York Times*, January 14, 1968; Schomburg Clippings File, Amherst College.

44. *Liberator*, 2, no. 1 (January 1962): 1.

45. "Harlem Mothers Organize to Save Their Sons," *Liberator* 4, no. 8 (August 1964): 10.

46. Clayton Riley, "Cement Roots Action in Harlem," *Liberator* 4, no. 8 (August 1964): 10.

47. Kattie Cumbo, "Thru Women's Eyes: Integration—Who Needs It?," *Liberator* 4, no. 9 (September 1964): 20. Cumbo was also a poet, and her work was featured in *Black Sister: Poetry by Black American Women, 1746–1980*, ed. Erlene Stetson (Bloomington: Indiana University Press, 1981), 134–37. Another writer, who went by the initials S.A.L., shared Cumbo's questions about the value of integration. See S.A.L., "Thru Women's Eyes: What I Want for Junnie," *Liberator* 4, no. 10 (October 1964): 20–21.

48. Kattie Cumbo, "My People's Children," *Liberator* 4, no. 11 (November 1964): 9.

49. See, for example, C. E. Wilson, "Why Don't Public Schools Teach Our Children?," 4–6; and Larry Neal, "The Welfare Trap," *Liberator* 5, no. 3 (March 1965): 28.

50. Lorraine Hansberry, *A Raisin in the Sun: The Unfilmed Original Screenplay*, ed. Robert Nemiroff (New York: Plume, 1992). See especially Margaret B. Wilkerson's Introduction to this edition, xxix–xlvii.

51. Amiri Baraka, "A Critical Reevaluation: A Raisin in the Sun's Enduring Passion," in *A Raisin in the Sun/The Sign in Sidney Brustein's Window* (New York: Vintage, 1995), 9–20. See also Lorraine Hansberry, *The Collected Last Plays*, ed. Robert Nemiroff (New York: Plume, 1983); and Len Holt, "Not Our Lorraine" (poem), *Liberator* 5, no. 2 (February 1965): 16.

52. Julian Mayfield, Letter to the editor, *Liberator* 5, no. 4 (April 1965): 28.

53. L. Pete Beveridge, "Lorraine Hansberry's World," *Liberator* 4, no. 12 (December 1964): 9.

54. Lawrence P. Neal, "The Sign in Sidney Brustein's Window (Theater Review)," *Liberator* 4, no. 12 (December 1964): 25.

55. Errol G. Hill and James V. Hatch, *A History of African American Theatre* (Cambridge: Cambridge University Press, 2003), 375–429.

56. "Women of Africa" and "African Women at the U.N.," *Liberator* 5, no. 5 (May 1965): 16–18.

57. Katy Gibson, "Letter to Black Men," *Liberator* 5, no. 7 (July 1965): 29–30.

58. Curtis Hezekhiah Jackson, Letter to the Editor, *Liberator* 5, no. 8 (August 1965): 29.

59. Writer's Conference Report: "The Role of the Black Woman in a White Society," *Liberator* 5, no. 8 (August 1965): 4–5.

60. Ibid. See also Benita Roth, *Separate Roads*, 80–93.

61. For more on Johnson's policies, see Bruce J. Schulman, *Lyndon B. Johnson and American Liberalism: A Brief Biography with Documents*, 2nd ed. (Boston: Bedford/St. Martin's, 2007).

62. Beverly Van Cortland, "War on the Poor," *Liberator* 5, no. 8 (August 1965): 18–19.

63. Bonnie Claudia Harrison, "Diasporadas: Black Women and the Fine Art of Activism," *Meridians* 2, no. 2 (2002): 163–84.

64. "The World of Valerie Maynard," *Liberator* 5, no. 10 (October 1965): 12–13.

65. Alabama, Letter to the Editor, *Liberator* 5, no. 12 (December 1965): 18–19. All caps and italics are from the original.

66. Louise Moore, "When Will the Real Black Man Stand Up?," *Liberator* 6, no. 5 (May 1966): 4–6.

67. Betty Frank Lomax, "Afro-American Woman: Growth Deferred," *Liberator* 6, no. 5 (May 1966): 18.

68. Louise Moore, "Black Men vs. Black Women," *Liberator* 6, no. 8 (August 1966): 16–17; Frances Beal, "Double Jeopardy: To Be Black and Female," in *Words of Fire: An Anthology of African-American Feminist Thought*, ed. Beverly Guy-Sheftall (New York: New Press, 1995), 146–55.

69. Evelyn Rodgers, "Is *Ebony* Killing Black Women?," *Liberator* 6, no. 3 (March 1966): 12–13.

70. Ibid.

71. Ibid. Parenthesis in original.

72. "Is *Ebony* Killing Black Women?"; Letter to the editor, *Liberator* 6, no. 5 (May 1966): 19. Caps in the original.

73. *Ebony* 21, no. 8 (June 1966).

74. *Ebony* 21, no. 10 (August 1966).

75. *Liberator* 6, no. 5 (May 1966).

76. Ibid., 4.

77. Ibid., 10.

78. Ibid., 20.

79. Ibid.

80. *Liberator* 6, no. 5 (May 1966): 20; James Smethurst, *The Black Arts Movement: Literary Nationalism in the 1960s and 1970s* (Chapel Hill: University of North Carolina Press, 2005), 84–89.

81. Roth, *Separate Roads to Feminism*, 76–128.

82. Sonia Sanchez, "Ruminations/Reflections," in *Black Women Writers, 1950–1980: A Critical Evaluation*, ed. Mari Evans (New York: Doubleday, 1984), 415–18.

83. See Ula Yvette Taylor, *The Veiled Garvey: The Life and Times of Amy Jacques Garvey* (Chapel Hill: University of North Carolina Press, 2002).

84. Louise Moore, "Black Men vs. Black Women," *Liberator* 6, no. 7 (July 1966): 16–17. Italics in the original.

85. Louise Moore, "So Long Uncle Tom," *Liberator* 6, no. 11 (November 1966): 17–19.

86. Ibid., 18.

87. A number of African American writers have written about the impact of Christianity as a form of oppression. James Cone and Albert Cleague are most known for their analyses of Christianity. See Cone, "Failure of the Black Church," *Liberator* 9, no. 5 (May 1969): 14–17, 22. For other examples, see Nathan Hare, "Brainwashing of Black Men's Minds"; Marvin E. Jackmon (Marvin X), "That Old Time Religion"; Yusef Iman, "Show Me Lord Show Me" and "Love Your Enemy"; and Norman Jordan, "The Sinner" and "The Sacrifice"; all in *Black Fire: An Anthology of African American Writing*, ed. Amiri Baraka and Larry Neal (Baltimore: Black Classic Press, 1968). See also Gayraud S. Wilmore, *Black Religion and Black Radicalism: An Examination of the Black Experience in Religion* (Garden City, NY: Anchor Press, 1973), especially his chapters "The Dechristianization of Black Radicalism," 228–61, and "Black Power, Black People and Theological Renewal," 262–306. Also, for a discussion on the diasporic religious practices of African descendants, see Michael Gomez, ed., *Diasporic Africa: A Reader* (New York: NYU Press, 2006), 1–24.

88. Patricia Robinson, "School Integration: Westchester Style," *Liberator* 6, no. 9 (September 1966): 8–10. See also Rhonda Y. Williams, *Concrete Demands: The Search for Black Power in the 20th Century* (New York: Routledge, 2015), 234–66.

89. Robinson, "School Integration," 8–10.

90. Roth, 86–89. See also Kimberley Springer, ed., *Still Lifting, Still Climbing: African American Women's Contemporary Activism* (New York: NYU Press, 1999).

91. Kimberley Springer, *Living for the Revolution: Black Feminist Organizations, 1968–1980* (Durham, NC: Duke University Press, 2005).

92. King, "A Time to Break Silence," in *A Testament of Hope: The Essential Writings and Speeches of Martin Luther King Jr.*, ed. James M. Washington (New York: HarperCollins, 1991), 231–44. This speech was delivered on April 4, 1967, exactly one year before he was assassinated. It originally appeared in written form in *Freedomways* 7, no. 2 (Spring 1967).

93. Gwendolyn Patton, "Black People and War," *Liberator* 7, no. 2 (February 1967): 11.

94. Ibid.

95. W. E. B. Du Bois, "The African Roots of War," in *Black Titan: W. E. B. Du Bois, An Anthology by the Editors of Freedomways*, ed. John Henrik Clarke (Boston: Beacon Press, 1970), 274–85.

96. Mike Marqusee, *Redemption Song: Muhammad Ali and the Spirit of the Sixties* (London: Verso, 1999), 162–252.

97. John Cosby Jr., "Open Letter to Nancy Wilson," *Liberator* 7, no. 10 (October 1967): 16.

98. Marqusee, *Redemption Song*.

99. Rashidah Ismaili-Abu Bakr, "Slightly Autobiographical: The 1960s on the Lower East Side," *African American Review* 27, no. 4 (1993): 585–89.

100. Sanchez continued to publish in *Liberator* through 1968. Her "to blk/record/buyers" appeared in the July 1968 issue of the periodical. *Liberator* 8, no. 7 (July, 1968).

101. Don L. Lee (Haki Madhubuti), "A Poem for Black Women," *Liberator* 8, no. 8 (August 1968): 15.

102. Theodore, "You Are the Black Woman," *Liberator* 9, no. 3 (March 1969): 13.

103. Springer, *Living for the Revolution*, 7–10. This year marks the formal organizational phase of black feminism, as several core groups formed in 1968.

104. Irma W. Princeton, "The Uptown-Downtown Store," *Liberator* 8, no. 4 (April 1968): 20.

105. Barbara Butler, "Gov. Rockefeller's Plan for Harlem Removal," *Liberator* 8, no. 5 (May 1968): 11–13.

106. Sydney H. Schanberg, "Legislature Meets Today," *New York Times*, January 3, 1968, 1, 2.

107. Butler, "Gov. Rockefeller's Plan," 13.

108. Ibid.

109. Barbara Butler, "Columbia University: The Arrogant Giant," *Liberator* 8, no. 6 (June 1968): 10–13. Butler appeared to have a particular interest in the intersection of class and race. In the September issue, *Liberator* 8, no. 9 (Septem-

ber 1968): 18–19, she reviewed Ferdinand Lundberg's *The Rich and the Super-Rich: Who Really Owns America?*, which revealed "that practically everyone in this country is poor," (18).

110. M. P. Johnson, "Columbia University," Letter to the Editor, *Liberator* 8, no. 7 (July 1968): 22.

111. For extensive details and outcomes of this expansion effort, see Stephan M. Bradley, *Harlem vs. Columbia University: Black Student Power in the Late '60s* (Urbana: University of Illinois Press, 2009).

112. Gail A. Stokes, "Black Woman to Black Man," *Liberator* 8, no. 12 (December 1968): 17.

113. Roth, *Separate Roads*, 86.

114. Edith R. Hambrick, "Black Woman to Black Woman," *Liberator* 9, no. 2 (February 1969): 8.

115. Author interview with Askia M. Touré (Roland Snellings), February 26, 2009.

116. Yanhe Sangare, "The African Woman," *Liberator* 8, no. 7 (July 1968): 4–7. A website dedicated to Sangare, who died on November 8, 2004, states that she came to the United States with her father, Ambassador Charles T. O. King, II, in 1955, when he was assigned to represent Liberia at the United Nations in New York. The site states that Sangare attended high school at Riverdale Preparatory School, and college at Aldephi College, where she obtained her bachelor's degree in journalism. The United Nations published its own obituary of Sangare, honoring her contribution to the United Nations Association of the National Capitol Area (UNA-NCA) in its newsletter, *UN Vision*, 52, no. 1 (Winter 2005): 19.

117. E. Fannie Granton, "Africa's Famous Model: Mrs. Yahne Sangare," *Jet*, June 22, 1967, 40–42.

118. Lee Rainwater and William L. Yancey, eds., *The Moynihan Report and the Politics of Controversy* (Cambridge, MA: MIT Press, 1967).

119. Dan Watts, "The Negro Is Obsolete" (editorial), *Liberator* 5, no. 12 (December 1965): 3.

120. Author correspondence with Marilyn Watts Lieberman, October 9, 2006. See also, Daniel Geary, *Beyond Civil Rights: The Moynihan Report and Its Legacy* (Philadelphia: University of Pennsylvania Press, 2015), 122.

121. Mike Wallace, "Black Power/White Backlash," CBS video, 1968.

122. Stephen Steinberg, *Turning Back: The Retreat from Racial Justice in American Thought and Policy* (Boston: Beacon, 1995), 107–36.

123. James Boggs, "The City Is the Black Man's Land," *Racism and the Class Struggle: Further Pages from a Black Worker's Notebook* (New York: Monthly Review, 1970), 39–50.

124. Dan Watts, "Birth Control" (editorial), *Liberator* 9, no. 5 (May 1969): 3.

125. Jean C. Bond and Pat Peery, "Has the Black Man Been Castrated?," *Liberator* 9, no. 5 (May 1969): 4–8; reprinted in Toni Cade Bambara, *The Black Woman: An Anthology* (New York: Washington Square Press, 2005), 141–48.

126. Ibid.

127. Ibid.

128. Sonia Sanchez, "A Poem for My Father," *Liberator* 9, no. 8 (August 1969): 9.

129. Linda Janet Holmes and Cheryl A. Wall, eds., *Introduction to Savoring the Salt: The Legacy of Toni Cade Bambara* (Philadelphia: Temple University Press, 2008), 3–6.

130. Toni Cade (Bambara), review of "Defender of the Angels," *Liberator* 10, no. 7 (July 1970): 20.

131. Tansey Thomas, "A Very Black Sister," *Third World News*, May 27, 1971, 5; Bloom Collection, Amherst College Special Collections.

Chapter Four

1. *New York Times*, January 13, 1965.

2. Grant Farred, *What's My Name: Black Vernacular Intellectuals* (Minneapolis: University of Minnesota Press, 2003).

3. Ibid., 1.

4. See *Post-Colonial Studies: The Key Concepts*, ed. Bill Ashcroft, Gareth Griffiths and Helen Tiffin (London: Routledge, 2000).

5. Farred, *What's My Name?*

6. James Baldwin, "Not 100 Years of Freedom," *Liberator* 3, no. 1 (January 1963): 7, 16.

7. Lawrence Jackson, *Indignant Generation: A Narrative History of African American Writers and Critics, 1934–1960* (Princeton, NJ: Princeton University Press, 2011), 447–53.

8. Baldwin, "Not 100 Years of Freedom," 7.

9. Lawrence Jackson, *Indignant Generation*, 447–53.

10. Herb Boyd, *Baldwin's Harlem: A Biography of James Baldwin* (New York: Atria Books, 2008), 110–11.

11. *Liberator* 3, no. 3 (March 1963).

12. Baldwin was also referenced in a less kind light. W. Francis Lucas, for example, likened white writer William Styron's reimagination of Nat Turner to Baldwin serving as "American's conscience." See W. Francis Lucas, "William Styron: The Negro James Baldwin," *Liberator* 8, no. 6 (June 1968): 18–20.

13. See Thomas A. Johnson, "Black Panthers Picket a School," *New York Times*, September 13, 1966, 38.

14. Rose Finkenstaedt, correspondence with the author, letter dated May 4, 2007.

15. Homer Bigart, "Baldwin Leaves Negro Monthly," *New York Times*, February 28, 1967, 34.

16. Herb Boyd, *Baldwin's Harlem: A Biography of James Baldwin* (New York: Atria, 2008).

17. Dan Watts interview, circa 1971; UNC Library Media Resource Center Archives, call no. 65-CA80.

18. Russell, "The Wide World of Ossie Davis," *Liberator* 3, no. 12 (December 1963): 11, 22.

19. Ossie Davis, "Anti-Semitism and Black Power" (1967), in *Freedomways Reader: Prophets in Their Own Country*, ed. Esther Cooper Jackson (Boulder, CO: Westview Press, 2000), 207–9.

20. Ibid.

21. Ibid., 207.

22. Bigart, "Baldwin Leaves Negro Monthly."

23. Muhammad Ahmad (Max Stanford Jr.), interview with the author, March 4, 2009.

24. Dan Watts, "Censorship, Liberal Style" (editorial), *Liberator* 9, (February 1969): 3.

25. Hughes continued to support younger writers throughout the end of his life. He was also one of the few luminaries who lived in Harlem throughout his lifetime. *Liberator* published several of Hughes's poems throughout the decade, and staff writer Charlie Russell once wrote that Hughes was "in himself a literary tradition." This issue also featured Hughes on its cover. For a quote about Hughes, see Charlie L. Russell, "Langston Hughes: Citizen of Harlem," *Liberator* 5, no. 2 (February 1965): 15.

26. Ibid.

27. "Nuclear Arms for Racist Germany?," *Liberator* 4, no. 4 (April 1964): 9.

28. *Liberator* 3, no. 7 (July 1963): 14–16.

29. *Liberator* 3, no. 8 (August 1963): 16.

30. Maurianne Adams and John Bracey, eds., *Strangers and Neighbors: Relations between Blacks and Jews in the United States* (Amherst: University of Massachusetts Press, 1999).

31. See *The Black Scholar* 19, no. 6 (November 1988); see also "Action at Massachusetts U. Raises Censorship Cry," Special to the *New York Times*, May 29, 1988.

32. James Baldwin, ed., *Black Anti-Semitism and Jewish Racism* (New York: Shocken Books, 1970).

33. *Liberator* 6, no. 7 (July 1966): 22.

34. Ibid.

35. *Liberator* 7, no. 5, (May 1967): 22.

36. Harold Cruse, *Crisis of the Negro Intellectual* (New York: Morrow, 1967), 402–19; Van Gosse, "More Than Just a Politician: Notes on the Life and Times of Harold Cruse," in *Harold Cruse's Crisis of the Negro Intellectual, Reconsidered*, ed. Jerry Watts (New York: Routledge, 2004), 17–40.

37. Author interview with Carlos E. Russell, March 25, 2006.

38. Rolland Snellings, "Toward Repudiating Western Values," *Liberator*, 4, no. 11 (November 1964): 11–12; James E. Smethurst, *The Black Arts Movement: Literary*

Nationalism in the 1960s and 1970s (Chapel Hill, NC: University of North Carolina Press, 2005), 131–32.

39. Askia Touré, correspondence with author, May 15, 2006.

40. Rolland Snellings (Askia Touré), "Thunder from the South: A Report on the National Afroamerican Student Conference on Black Nationalism, May 1–3, 1964," unpublished ms., Clarke Papers, Box 30, Folder 47.

41. Harold Cruse, *Rebellion or Revolution?* (New York: William Morrow, 1968).

42. Harold Cruse, *The Crisis of the Negro Intellectual* (New York: William Morrow, 1967), 404–19.

43. Peniel Joseph, *Waiting 'Til the Midnight Hour: A Narrative History of Black Power in America* (New York: Henry Holt, 2006), 201–2; Gosse, "More Than Just a Politician."

44. Cruse, *Crisis*, 407.

45. Askia Touré, interview with the author, February 26, 2009.

46. Ibid.

47. Henry Vance Davis, "Harold Wright Cruse: The Early Years and the Jewish Factor," in *Black Scholar* 35, no. 4 (Winter 2006): 17–31.

48. C. E. Wilson, interview with the author, April 15, 2006.

49. Lynn Wheeldin, "Review of Harold Cruse's The Crisis of the Negro Intellectual," *Liberator* 9, no. 3 (March 1969): 17.

50. Richard Iton, *In Search of the Black Fantastic: Politics and Popular Culture in the Post–Civil Rights Era* (Oxford: Oxford University Press, 2008), 83–88.

51. *Liberator* 3, no. 10 (October 1963): 14.

52. Donna Murch, *Living for the City: Migration, Education, and the Rise of the Black Panther Party in Oakland, California* (Chapel Hill, NC: University of North Carolina Press, 2010).

53. *Liberator* 3, no. 3 (March 1963): 14–15.

54. Ibid., 15.

55. Ibid.

56. Ibid.

57. Peniel E. Joseph, "Black Studies, Student Activism, and the Black Power Movement," in Joseph, ed., *The Black Power Movement: Rethinking the Civil Rights–Black Power Era* (New York: Routledge, 2006), 259; Murch, *Living for the City*.

58. Charlie L. Russell, "Letter to a White Friend," *Liberator* 3, no. 5 (May 1963): 8.

59. Joseph, "Black Studies," 256; Robert O. Self, *American Babylon: Race and the Struggle for Postwar Oakland* (Princeton, NJ: Princeton University Press, 2003).

60. Russell, interview with the author, June 10, 2006.

61. Ibid.

62. Today he is simply known as Askia Touré.

63. *Liberator* 3, no. 5 (May 1963): 9–11.

64. John Henrik Clarke, "The New Afro-American Nationalism," *Freedomways* 1, no. 3 (Fall 1961).

65. *African American Review* 27, no. 4 (1993): 585–96.

66. Snellings, "Thunder from the South," 10.

67. Roland Snellings (Touré), "Afro-American Youth and the Bandung World," *Liberator* 5, no. 2 (February 1965): 4–7.

68. Jeffrey O. G. Ogbar, "Rainbow Radicalism: The Rise of Ethnic Nationalism," *Black Power: Radical Politics and African American Identity* (Baltimore, MD: Johns Hopkins University Press, 2004), 159–90; J. Smethurst, "Bandung World" in *The Black Arts Movement*, 247–318; Cynthia A. Young, *Soul Power: Culture, Radicalism, and the Making of a U.S. Third World Left* (Durham, NC: Duke University Press, 2006), 145–83; Fred Ho and Bill V. Mullen, eds. *Afro Asia: Revolutionary Political and Cultural Connections between African Americans and Asian Americans* (Durham, NC: Duke University Press, 2008); Michael L. Clemons and Charles E. Jones, "Global Solidarity: The Black Panther Party in the International Arena," in *Liberation, Imagination and the Black Panther Party: A New Look at the Panthers and Their Legacy*, ed. Kathleen Cleaver and George Katsiaficas (New York: Routledge, 2001), 20–39; Vijay Prashad, *Everybody Was Kung Fu Fighting: Afro-Asian Connections and the Myth of Cultural Purity* (Boston: Beacon Press, 2001), 126–49.

69. Snellings/Touré, "Afro-American Youth and the Bandung World," 6.

70. *Liberator* 3, no. 12 (December 1963).

71. *Liberator* 3, no. 5 (May 1963): 14.

72. *Liberator* 3, no. 6 (June 1963): 7, 18.

73. Ibid., 18.

74. Davis, "Harold Wright Cruse: The Early Years," 25.

75. Ibid., 18.

76. *Liberator* 3, no. 8 (August 1963): 1.

77. Dr. Martin Luther King Jr., *The Autobiography of Martin Luther King, Jr.* (New York: Warner Books, 1998), 218.

78. Ibid., 219.

79. Harvard Sitkoff, *The Struggle for Black Equality, 1954–1992*, rev. ed. (New York: Hill and Wang, 1993), 152–53.

80. *Liberator* 3, no. 10 (October 1963).

81. Dan Watts, "Dream and Reality," (editorial), *Liberator* 3, no. 10 (October 1963): 1. Interestingly, this editorial may have also been co-written or ghost-written by Beveridge.

82. *Liberator* 3, no. 10 (October 1963).

83. C. E. Wilson, "The Pilgrimage," *Liberator* 3, no. 10 (October 1963): 4–7.

84. Ibid., 4.

85. Ibid.

86. Ibid., 6.

87. Leroi Jones, *Home: Social Essays* (Hopewell, NJ: Ecco Press, 1998), 152.

88. James Foreman, *The Making of Black Revolutionaries* (Washington, DC: Open Hand Publishing, 1985), 335.

89. *Liberator* 3, no. 10 (October 1963): 12–13.

90. Ibid., 3. See Kevin K. Gaines, *American Africans in Ghana: Black Expatriates and the Civil Rights Era* (Chapel Hill, NC: The University of North Carolina Press, 2006), 167–68.

91. Julian Mayfield, "Uncle Tom Goes to Africa," *Liberator* 3, no. 3 (March 1963): 9–10. The *Negro Digest* reprinted this article in its June 1963 issue with permission from *Liberator*.

92. Wilson, interview with the author, April 15, 2006.

93. Ibid.

94. Ibid.

95. Ibid.

96. *Liberator* 5, no. 5 (May 1965): 30.

97. Ogbar, *Black Power*, 37.

98. Ibid., 38.

99. Michael A. Gomez, *Black Crescent: The Experience and Legacy of African Muslims in the Americas* (Cambridge: Cambridge University Press, 2005), 356.

100. Harvard Sitkoff, *Struggle for Black Equality*, 196.

101. *Liberator* 1, no. 7 (July 1961): 2.

102. *Liberator* 2, no. 5 (May 1962): 3.

103. *New York Times*, May 6, 1962, 73.

104. Gerald Horne, *The Fire This Time: The Watts Uprising and the 1960s* (Charlottesville: University of Virginia Press, 1995), 137–38.

105. *New York Times*, May 6, 1962, 73.

106. P. Joseph, *Waiting*, 63–65.

107. Frederick Knight, "Justifiable Homicide, Police Brutality, or Government Repression? The 1962 Police Shooting of Seven Members of the Nation of Islam," *The Journal of Negro History* 79, no. 2 (Spring 1994): 182–96.

108. *Liberator* 2, no. 6 (June 1962): 4.

109. Ibid.

110. Ibid.

111. See Malcolm X, *The Autobiography of Malcolm X* (1965; reprint, New York: Ballantine Books, 1990), 288–317; Karl Evanzz, *The Messenger: The Rise and Fall of Elijah Muhammad* (New York: Vintage Books, 2001), 270–82, 287–308; Gomez, *Black Crescent*, 331–70; Mattias Gardell, *In the Name of Elijah Muhammad: Louis Farrakhan and the Nation of Islam* (Durham, NC: Duke University Press, 2005), 76–85; William Sales Jr., *From Civil Rights to Black Liberation: Malcolm X and the Organization of Afro-American Unity* (Boston: South End Press, 1994), 53–95; Hakim A. Jamal, *From the Dead Level: Malcolm X and Me* (Springfield, MA: Masjid At-Tawhid, 1971); Peter Goldman, "Malcolm X: Witness for the Prosecution," in *Black Leaders of the Twentieth Century*, ed. John Hope Franklin and August Meier (Urbana: University of Illinois Press, 1982), 305–30; Reiland Rabaka, "Malcolm X and/as Critical Theory: Philosophy, Radical Politics, and the African American Search for Social Justice," *Journal of Black Studies* 33, no. 2 (November 2002): 145–65.

112. Rose L. H. Finkenstaedt "Never on Christmas: A Black Muslim Story," *Liberator* 3, no. 3 (March 1963): 16.

113. Rose Finkenstaedt, correspondence with the author, March 2006.

114. *Liberator* 3, no. 3 (March 1963): 16–17.

115. John Henrik Clarke, "Introduction," *Harlem: A Community in Transition* (New York: Citadel, 1964; reprint, 1969), x.

116. Clarke, "Four Men of Harlem: The Movers and The Shakers," in *Harlem USA*, ed. John Henrik Clarke (Brooklyn: A&B Books, 1964; reprint, 1971), 243–70. In an earlier anthology, Clarke considered Powell and Malcolm X two of the pivotal figures of Harlem history. A. Philip Randolph and Father Divine were the other two.

117. Joseph, *Waiting*, 21–23.

118. *Liberator* 3, no. 11 (November 1963): 12–14.

119. Ibid., 12.

120. Interview with the author.

121. See George Breitman, *The Last Year of Malcolm X: The Evolution of a Revolutionary* (New York: Pathfinder, 1967); and William Sales Jr., *From Civil Rights to Black Liberation: Malcolm X and the Organization of Afro-American Unity* (Boston: South End Press, 1994.)

122. Joseph, *Waiting*, 92–98.

123. For a chronology of Malcolm's life, see Clayborne Carson, *Malcolm X: The FBI File* (New York: Carroll & Graf, 1991), 70–75.

124. The *Liberator* expressed consistent support for the Michigan-based Freedom Now Party, which was headed up by Cleage and others. See Sterling Gray, "Architect of a Revolution," *Liberator* 3, no. 12 (December 1963): 8–9.

125. Dan Watts, "Malcolm X: Self Defense vs. Submission" (editorial), *Liberator* 4, no. 4 (April 1964): 3.

126. According to the *New York Times*, Herbert Callendar, president of the Bronx CORE chapter, was arrested and jailed for attempting a citizen's arrest of Mayor Wagner. Callendar accused Wagner of allowing public funds to be used on construction projects that discriminated against black construction workers. See "Callendar Jailed; Sentencing Put Off until Wednesday," *New York Times*, January 9, 1965, p. 17.

127. *Liberator* 4, no. 5 (May 1964): 4.

128. Carlos E. Russell, "Exclusive Interview with Malcolm X," *Liberator* 4, no. 5 (May 1964): 12–13, 16.

129. Ibid., 13.

130. Ibid.

131. Shelby Sankore, "Letter to Muhammad Ali," *Liberator* 4, no. 5 (May 1964), 7; see also Mike Marqusee, *Redemption Song: Muhammad Ali and the Spirit of the Sixties* (London: Verso, 1999).

132. C. Eric Lincoln, *Black Muslims*, 113–15; Essien-Udom, *Black Nationalism*, 191–92; Ernest Allen, "Minister Louis Farrakhan and the Continuing Evolution of

the Nation of Islam," in *The Farrakhan Factor: African-American Writers on Leadership, Nationhood, and Minister Louis Farrakhan*, ed. Amy Alexander (New York: Grove Press, 1998), 52–102; Jeffrey O. G. Ogbar, *Black Power*, 22.

133. Russell, "Exclusive Interview."

134. Ibid., 16.

135. For a listing of sources detailing Malcolm's evolution, see n. 105.

136. G. Breitman, *The Last Year of Malcolm X: The Evolution of a Revolutionary* (New York: Pathfinder, 1967); see also Sales, *From Civil Rights to Black Liberation*.

137. Muhammad Ahmad, *We Will Return in the Whirlwind* (Chicago: Charles Kerr, 2007), 124.

138. Carlos E. Russell, "A Question of Dignity," *Liberator* 3, no. 8 (June 1963): 15, 20.

139. Malcolm X, "We are all Blood Brothers," *Liberator* 6, no. 7 (July 1964): 4–6.

140. Ibid., 5.

141. Ibid.

142. Kevin K. Gaines, *American African in Ghana: Black Expatriates and the Civil Rights Era* (Chapel Hill, NC: University of North Carolina Press, 2006), 179–209.

143. Ibid., 164–65.

144. Ibid.

145. *Liberator* 6, no. 10 (October 1964), 16.

146. Gaines, ibid.

147. *Liberator* 6, no. 7 (July 1964): 8.

148. Ibid.

149. Ossie Sykes, "Harlem Report: After the Rebellion," *Liberator* 6, no. 9 (September 1964): 4.

150. Ibid. See also Joseph, *Waiting*, 112–13.

151. Ibid., 5.

152. Ibid., 6.

153. *New York Times*, August 7, 1964, 12.

154. For more on HARYOU and HARYOU-ACT see Kenneth Clark, *Dark Ghetto: Dilemmas of Social Power* (New York: Harper and Row, 1967); Clark, "HARYOU: An Experiment," in *Harlem: A Community in Transition*, ed. John Henrik Clarke (New York: Citadel, 1964; reprint, 1969), 210–13; Clark, "HARYOU-ACT in Harlem: The Dream That Went Astray," in *Harlem USA*, ed. John Henrik Clarke (Brooklyn: A&B Books Publishers, 1971), 80–85.

155. Theodore Jones, "Negro Boy Killed; 300 Harass Police," *New York Times*, July 17, 1964, 1, 31; John Sibley, "2 Harlem Demands Accepted by Mayor," *New York Times*, August 7, 1964, 1, 12.

156. Len Holt and Bill Mahoney, "Make Harlem Black—Therefore Beautiful," *Liberator* 6, no. 9, (September 1964): 10–11.

157. Malcolm X, *By Any Means Necessary*, edited by George Breitman (New York: Pathfinder, 1970, rpt. 1992), 84–89; Peniel Joseph, *Waiting*, pp. 1–34; 112–

117; Muhammad Ahmad, *We Will Return in the Whirlwind*, 23–33; Breitman, *The Last Year of Malcolm X*, 26–39.

158. Holt and Mahoney, "Make Harlem Black," 11.

159. Interview with the author.

160. *Liberator* 5, no. 3 (March 1965).

161. Dan Watts, "Malcolm X: The Unfulfilled Promise," (editorial), *Liberator* 5, no. 3 (March 1965): 3. This editorial was also likely ghost-written for Watts by Beveridge.

162. Ibid.

163. Interview with the author, June 1, 2006.

164. *Liberator* 5, no. 4 (April 1965): 8.

165. "Why Malcolm X Died: An Analysis by RAM," *Liberator* 5, no. 4 (April 1965): 9–11.

166. Ibid., 10.

167. Max Stanford (Muhammad Ahmad), "Revolutionary Nationalism and the Afroamerican Student," *Liberator* 5, no. 1 (January 1965): 13–15.

168. C. E. Wilson and Ossie Sykes, "Malcolm X: A Tragedy of Leadership," *Liberator* 5, no. 5 (May 1965): 7–10.

169. Wilson, "The Quotable Mr. X" *Liberator* 5, no. 5 (May 1965): 11–13.

170. A.B. Spellman, "The Legacy of Malcolm X," *Liberator* 5, no. 6 (June 1965): 11–13.

171. Ahmad, *Whirlwind*, 101, 137.

172. C. E. Wilson, interview with the author, April 16, 2006.

173. James Boggs, Letter to the Editor, *Liberator* 5, no. 3 (March 1965): 26.

174. James Boggs, "Black Power: A Scientific Concept Whose Time Has Come," Part 1, *Liberator* 7, no. 4 (April 1967): 8–10; and Part 2, *Liberator* 7, no. 5 (May 1967): 8–10. For an exhaustive collection of writings over Boggs's career, see Stephen M. Ward, ed., *Pages from a Black Radical's Notebook: A James Boggs Reader* (Detroit: Wayne State University Press, 2011).

175. Larry Neal, "A Reply to Rustin," *Liberator* 5, no. 7 (July 1965): 6.

176. Ibid.

177. Though Neal does not cite the specific article, see Bayard Rustin, Tom Kahn, et al., "The Negro Movement: Where Shall it Go Now?," *The Radical Imagination: An Anthology from Dissent Magazine*, ed. Irving Howe (New York: New American Library, 1967), 174–89. This article originally appeared in 1964. It is plausible that portions or variations of it were also published a year later, thus providing fodder for Neal's critique. *Dissent* was a quarterly magazine of some significance for many American leftists, liberals, and progressives from its founding in 1954 onward. Though it was primarily a publishing outlet of the white left, some black writers could also be found among the writing on its pages. The journal published political and social commentary from a range of intellectuals including Irving Howe (one of the journal's founders), as well as Norman Mailer, Rustin, Michael Harrington, C. Wright Mills, Richard Wright, Barbara Ehrenreich, Theodore Draper, Frances

Fox Piven, Todd Gitlin, Martin Kilson, and Claude Brown. See also Nicolaus Mills, ed., *Legacy of Dissent: 40 Years of Writing from Dissent Magazine* (New York: Simon and Schuster, 1994); and Nicolaus Mills and Michael Walzer, eds., *50 Years of Dissent* (New Haven, CT: Yale University Press, 2004).

178. Neal, "Reply to Rustin." Emphasis in the original.

179. Ibid., 6–7.

180. Ibid. Emphasis in the original.

181. Dan Watts, "Rev. King and Vietnam," (editorial), *Liberator* 7, no. 5 (May 1967): 3.

182. Ibid., 7.

183. *Liberator* 6, no. 1 (Jan. 1966): 9–11.

184. Ibid.

185. Ibid., 4.

186. Ibid.

187. Ibid., 5.

188. Boggs, "Black Power."

189. *Liberator* 7, no. 7 (July 1967): 14–15.

Chapter Five

1. Michelle Joan Wilkinson, "In the Tradition of Revolution: The Socio-Aesthetics of Black and Puerto Rican Arts Movements, 1962–1982," Ph.D. dissertation, Emory University, August 2001.

2. Robin D. G. Kelley, *Freedom Dreams: The Black Radical Imagination* (Boston: Beacon Press, 2002), 35.

3. Richard Iton, *In Search of the Black Fantastic: Politics and Popular Culture in the Post–Civil Rights Era* (Oxford: Oxford University Press, 2008), 22.

4. For a historical discussion of the revolutionary potential of African culture, see Sékou Touré, "A Dialectical Approach to Culture," in *Pan-Africanism*, ed. Robert Chrisman and Nathan Hare (Indianapolis: Bobbs-Merrill, 1974), 52–73.

5. *Liberator* 1, no. 7 (July 1961): 1.

6. *Liberator* 1, no. 9 (September 1961): 1.

7. *Liberator* 1, no. 1 (January 1962): 1.

8. "Black Actors Act against Broadway Producers," *Liberator* 2, no. 4 (April 1962): 4.

9. "African Cultural Group to Introduce 'High Life,'" *Liberator* 2, no. 10 (October 1962): 6.

10. "Big Turnout Expected for African Dinner and Dance on November 16," *Liberator* 2, no. 11 (November 1962): 13.

11. These events often attracted a wide range of support from the grassroots to the upper levels of state government. One advertisement for the event told of New York governor Nelson Rockefeller's endorsement for the African cultural nights, stating that these events rendered a "distinct public service" and declaring June 1, 1962, African Music Night throughout New York.

12. St. Clair Drake, "The American Negro's Relation to Africa," *Africa Today* 14, no. 6 (December 1967): 12–15; Drake, "Black Studies and Global Perspectives: An Essay," *Journal of Negro Education* 53, no. 3 (Summer 1984): 226–42; N.A., "African Studies in the United States," *African Studies Bulletin* 6, no. 1 (March 1963): 43–56.

13. Carlos E. Russell, "Sonny Liston: The Man behind the Myth," *Liberator* 3, no. 3 (March 1963): 4–5.

14. Carlos E. Russell, "Negritude," *Liberator* 3, no. 3 (March 1963): 10.

15. Carlos E. Russell, "Identity," *Liberator* 3, no. 9 (September 1963): 17.

16. Langston Hughes, "Junior Addict," *Liberator* 3, no. 4 (April 1963): 3.

17. James Smethurst, *The Black Arts Movement: Literary Nationalism in the 1960s and 1970s* (Chapel Hill: University of North Carolina Press, 2005), 148–50.

18. Beveridge, interview with the author, April 8, 2006.

19. Clebert Ford, "The Negro and the American Theater," *Liberator* 3, no. 5 (May 1963): 6–7.

20. George Goodman Jr., "Maya Angelou's Lonely Black Outlook," in *Conversations with Maya Angelou*, ed. Jeffrey M. Elliot (Jackson, MS: University Press of Mississippi, 1989), 7–9.

21. Jim Williams, "The Need for a Harlem Theatre," in *Harlem: A Community in Transition,* ed. John Henrik Clarke (New York: Citadel Press, 1970), 157–66.

22. Charlie L. Russell, "The Wide World of Ossie Davis," *Liberator 3,* no. 12 (December 1963): 22.

23. Clebert Ford, "Responsibility of Black Artists," *Liberator 3,* no. 8 (August 1963): 9, 20.

24. Ibid.

25. Clebert Ford, "Theatre: Review and Forecast," *Liberator* 4, no. 1 (January 1964): 17–19.

26. Errol G. Hill and James V. Hatch, *A History of African American Theatre* (Cambridge: Cambridge University Press, 2003), 282.

27. Charlie L. Russell, "The Wide World of Ossie Davis," *Liberator* 3, no. 12 (December 1963): 11, 22.

28. Internet Broadway Database; accessed May 23, 2009.

29. Clarke Papers, Box 2, Folder 7.

30. Donald Bogle, *Toms, Coons, Mulattoes, Mammies, and Bucks: An Interpretive History of Blacks in American Films,* 3rd ed. (New York: Continuum, 1994), 204–6.

31. Clebert Ford, "Black Nationalism and the Arts," *Liberator* 4, no. 2 (February 1964): 14–16.

32. Charlie L. Russell, "Leroi Jones Will Get Us All in Trouble," *Liberator* 4, no. 6 (June 1964): 10–11.

33. Internet Broadway Database; accessed May 22, 2009. ANTA was renamed in honor of playwright August Wilson in 2005.

34. Clebert Ford, "James Baldwin: Official Angry Negro," *Liberator* 4, no. 7 (July 1964): 7.

35. Roy Johnson, "Blues for Mr. Charlie," *Liberator* 6, no. 3 (March 1966): 22.

36. Smethurst, *Black Arts Movement*, 345–50.

37. Clebert Ford, "The Black Boom: Black Like Me; Cool World (Movie Reviews)," and "Towards a Black Community Theatre," *Liberator* 4, no. 8 (August 1964): 16–17, 18–19.

38. Clebert Ford, "Zulu," *Liberator* 4, no. 9 (September 1964): 21.

39. Woodie King, "Black Theatre: Present Condition," in *Black Poets and Prophets*, ed. Woodie King and Earl Anthony (New York: New American Library, 1972), 180–88. King also wrote and published short stories in *Liberator* throughout the decade.

40. Charlie L. Russell, "LeRoi Jones Will Get Us All in Trouble," *Liberator* 4, no. 6 (June 1964): 10–11.

41. Victor Leo Walker II, "Archetype and Masking in LeRoi Jones/Amiri Baraka's *Dutchman*," in *Black Theatre: Ritual Performance in the African Diaspora*, ed. Paul Carter Harrison et al. (Philadelphia: Temple University Press, 2002), 236–43.

42. Askia Touré, interview with author, February 26, 2009.

43. James Smethurst, *The Black Arts Movement*, 103–5.

44. Lawrence P. Neal, "A Black View of the Elections," *Liberator* 4, no. 10 (October 1964): 7–8.

45. Askia Touré, interview with author, February 26, 2009.

46. Ibid.

47. Lawrence P. Neal, "Review of *Shadow and Act* by Ralph Ellison," *Liberator* 4, no. 12 (December 1964): 28–29.

48. Lawrence P. Neal, "LeRoi Jones' The Slave and The Toilet" (Theatre Review), *Liberator* 5, no. 5 (February 1965): 22–23.

49. Lawrence P. Neal, "The Welfare Trap," *Liberator* 5, no. 3 (March 1965): 28.

50. Lawrence P. Neal, "Selma, Alabama: Black People in Crisis," *Liberator* 5, no. 4 (April 1965): 22.

51. Amiri Baraka, "Foreword: The Wailer," in *Visions of a Liberated Future: Black Arts Movement Writings*, ed. Larry Neal (New York: Thunder Mouth's Press, 1989), ix–xix.

52. Larry Neal, "On Malcolm X," in *Visions of a Liberated Future*, 125–32.

53. Lawrence P. Neal, "The Cultural Front," *Liberator* 5, no. 6 (June 1965): 26–27.

54. Lawrence P. Neal, "The Genius and the Prize," *Liberator* 5, no. 10 (October 1965): 11.

55. Though Neal worked from a different aesthetic foundation and sensibility, for a discussion of the term, see Walter Benn Michaels, "Race into Culture: A Critical Genealogy of Cultural Identity," *Critical Inquiry* 18, no. 4 (1992): 655–85.

56. Lawrence P. Neal, "The Black Writer's Role—Richard Wright," *Liberator* 5, no. 12 (December 1965): 20–21.

57. Lawrence P. Neal, "The Black Writer's Role—Ralph Ellison," *Liberator* 6, no. 1 (January 1966): 9–11.

58. Larry Neal, "The Black Writer's Role, II—Ralph Ellison's Zoot Suit," in *Visions of a Liberated Future*, 30–56.

59. Larry Neal Vita. Larry Neal Papers, Box 1, Folder 1.

60. Amiri Baraka, Foreword, "The Wailer," in *Visions of a Liberated Future*, ix–xix.

61. Lawrence P. Neal, "The Development of Leroi Jones, Part 1," *Liberator* 6, no. 1 (January 1966): 4–5.

62. Lawrence P. Neal, "The Development of LeRoi Jones, Part 2," *Liberator* 6, no. 2 (February 1966): 18–19.

63. Lawrence P. Neal, "The Black Writer's Role," *Liberator* 6, no. 6 (June 1966): 7–9. Emphasis in original.

64. Ibid., 8.

65. Rolland Snellings (Askia Touré) to Larry Neal, letter dated June 2, 1967, Neal Papers, Box 2, Folder 1.

66. Lawrence P. Neal, "The Black Writer's Role—James Baldwin," *Liberator* 6, no. 4 (April 1966): 10–11, 18.

67. Lawrence P. Neal, "White Liberals vs. Black Community," *Liberator* 6, no. 7 (July 1966): 4–6.

68. Larry Neal and Evelyn Rogers, Marriage Certificates. Larry Neal Papers, Box 1, Folder 4.

69. Lawrence P. Neal, "Report on Black Arts Convention at Detroit," *Liberator* 6, no. 8 (August 1966): 18–19.

70. Smethurst, *Black Arts Movement*, 179–246. In this chapter, "Institutions for the People," Smethurst focuses on the relationship between Chicago and Detroit Black Arts/Black Power activity. As he shows, these cities formed a hub of Midwest activity in this period. I mention the Detroit conference because *Liberator*'s ties to Detroit are demonstrable—including the Freedom Now Party, Albert Cleage, the Boggses, Grassroots Leadership Conference, Concept East, and so on—whereas I have not been able to determine the magazine's connection to Chicago as of this writing.

71. Larry Neal Papers, Box 1, Folder 1.

72. Larry Neal, "Any Day Now: Black Art and Black Liberation," in *Black Poets and Prophets: The Theory, Practice, and Esthetics of the Pan-Africanist Revolution*, ed. Woodie King and Earl Anthony (New York: New American Library, 1971), 148–65. This article originally appeared in *Ebony* magazine.

73. Clayton Riley, "The Black Arts," *Liberator* 5, no. 4 (April 1965): 21.

74. Clayton Riley, "Living Poetry by Black Arts Group," *Liberator* 5, no. 5 (May 1965): 19.

75. Clayton Riley, "Amen Corner," *Liberator* 5, no. 5 (May 1965): 26–27; Howard Taubman, "Theatre: The Amen Corner; Baldwin's First Play," *New York Times*, April 16, 1965, 35.

76. Errol G. Hill and James V. Hatch, *A History of African American Theatre* (Cambridge: Cambridge University Press, 2003), 420–24.

77. Clayton Riley, "More than a Game," *Liberator* 4, no. 6 (June 1964): 12–13.

78. Clayton Riley, "Boxing: Black Hope, White Cop Out," *Liberator* 4, no. 7 (July 1964): 12–13.

79. Ibid., 13.

80. Adrian Burgos Jr., *Playing America's Game: Baseball, Latinos, and the Color Line* (Berkeley: University of California Press, 2007).

81. Dave Zirin, *A People's History of Sports in the United States* (New York: New Press, 2008), 268.

82. Harry Edwards, *The Revolt of the Black Athlete* (New York: Macmillan, 1969); Jack Scott, *The Athletic Revolution* (New York: Free Press, 1971).

83. Carlos E. Russell, "The Rebellious Spirit of Bill Russell," *Liberator* 4, no. 2 (February 1964): 10–11.

84. Clayton Riley, "The Olympics: They Should Have Stayed Home," *Liberator* 4, no. 11 (November 1964): 19; Riley, "The Olympics: If They Stayed Home," *Liberator* 4, no. 12 (December, 1964): 23–24.

85. Jackie Robinson, *Baseball Has Done It*, with an Introduction by Spike Lee (1964; reprint, New York: Ig Publishing, 2005).

86. Clayton Riley, "Jackie Robinson Strikes Out," *Liberator* 4, no. 10 (October 1964): 22.

87. Zirin, *People's History*, 205–8.

88. William L. Van De Burg, *New Day in Babylon: The Black Power Movement and American Culture, 1965–1975* (Chicago: Chicago University Press, 1992).

89. Loyle Hairston, "Muhammad Ali vs. The Great Society," *Liberator* 7, no. 7 (July 1967): 18–19.

90. Clayton Riley, "Nothing But a Man," *Liberator* 5, no. 2 (February 1965): 20.

91. Clayton Riley, "Pawnbroker," *Liberator* 5, no. 6 (June 1965): 25.

92. Clayton Riley, "China!" *Liberator* 5, no. 7 (July 1965): 20.

93. Clayton Riley, Theater Review, *Liberator* 5, no. 10 (October 1965): 14.

94. Clayton Riley, "A Black Quartet," *Liberator* 9, no. 9 (September 1969): 21.

95. Will Bradley and Charles Esche, eds., *Art and Social Change, A Critical Reader* (London: Tate, 2007). This book covers art movements in four distinct historical periods, 1871, 1917, 1968, and 1989, which represent moments of watershed political activity in the U.S. and Europe. Though the editors include two *Black Panther Newspaper* articles by Emory Douglas, no other mention is made of the Black Arts Movement. Though Douglas deserves critical attention, he was obviously not the only black artist producing politically inspired art in the 1960s.

96. See, for example, Margo Natalie Crawford, "Black Light on the Wall of Respect: The Chicago Black Arts Movement," in *New Thoughts on the Black Arts Movement*, edited by Collins and Crawford (New Brunswick, NJ: Rutgers University Press, 2006), 23–42.

97. Muriel L. Feelings and Tom Feelings, "Zamani Goes to Market," *Liberator* 10, no. 3 (March 1970): 11–15.

98. *Liberator* 4, no. 8 (August 1964): 19.

99. Erina Duganne, "Transcending the Fixity of Race: The Kamoinge Workshop and the Question of a 'Black Aesthetic' in Photography," in *New Thoughts on the Black Arts Movement*, 187–209.

100. Ibid., 201.

101. See, for example, Smethurst, *Black Arts*, 147–52.

102. Ibid., 188.

103. Richard J. Powell, *Black Art and Culture in the 20th Century* (New York: Thames and Hudson, 1997), 118.

104. Roy DeCarava, *The Sound I Saw* (New York: Phaidon, 2001).

105. "Abdul Rahman Brings Art to His People," *Liberator* 4, no. 11 (November 1964): 13.

106. "Bedwick Thomas and the Black Art Movement," *Liberator* 5, no. 4 (April 1965): 26.

107. Lawrence P. Neal, "The Black Revolution in Art: A Conversation with Joe Overstreet," *Liberator* 5, no. 10 (October 1965): 9–10.

108. Powell, *Black Art and Culture*, 132–36.

109. Amiri Baraka, "Recent Monk," in *Black Music* (New York: William & Morrow, 1970), 26–34. This article originally appeared in *Down Beat*.

110. Robin D. G. Kelley, "New Monastery: Monk and the Jazz Avant-Garde," *Black Music Research Journal*, 19, no. 2 (Autumn, 1999): 135–68. See also Robin D. G. Kelley, *Thelonious Monk: The Life and Times of an American Original* (New York: Simon and Schuster, 2009).

111. Theodore Pontiflet, "The American Way: Monk in TIME," *Liberator* 4, no. 6 (June 1964): 8–9.

112. Neal, "Any Day Now," 149.

113. Charlie Russell, "Has Jazz Lost Its Roots?," *Liberator* 4, no. 8 (August 1964): 4–7.

114. Charlie Russell, interview with the author, June 10, 2006.

115. Charlie Russell, "The Evolution of a Jazz Musician," *Liberator* 4, no. 11 (November 1964): 14–15, 30.

116. Charlie Russell, "Minding the Cultural Shop," *Liberator* 4, no. 12 (December 1964): 12–13. See also Eric Porter, *What Is This Thing Called Jazz?* (Berkeley: University of California Press, 2002).

117. Ibid.

118. A recent study that explores some of these tensions in the production and criticism in music and popular films of the period is Amy Abugo Ongiri, *Spectacular Blackness: The Cultural Politics of Black Power Movement and the Search for a Black Aesthetic* (Charlottesville: University of Virginia Press, 2010).

119. John D. Baskerville, "Free Jazz: A Reflection of Black Power Ideology," *Journal of Black Studies* 24, no. 4 (June 1994): 484–97.

120. Charles Hobson, "Black Bourgeoisie and Gospel Music," *Liberator* 5, no. 1 (January 1965): 11.

121. Kelley, "New Monastery."

122. Charlie Russell, "Ornette Coleman Sounds Off," *Liberator* 5, no. 7 (July 1965), 12–15.

123. Ibid.

124. Lawrence P. Neal, "A Conversation with Archie Shepp," *Liberator* 5, no. 11 (November 1965): 24–25.

125. Robert L. Douglas, *Resistance, Insurgence and Identity: The Art of Mari Evans, Nelson Stevens and the Black Arts Movement* (Trenton, NJ: Africa World Press, 2008), 181–287. This chapter deals at length with Stevens' career as an artist, art organizer, and educator, including a gallery of images from his extensive oeuvre.

126. Amiri Baraka, "New Tenor Archie Shepp Talking," *Black Music*, 145–55. This article originally appeared in *Down Beat* under the title, "Voice from the Avant Garde."

127. A selection of these writings was compiled and published as *Black Music* (New York: William Morrow and Company, 1970).

128. Gayatri Spivak, *The Post-Colonial Critic: Interviews, Strategies, Dialogues*, ed. Sara Harasym (New York: Routledge, 1990).

129. Letters to the Editor, *Liberator* 6, no. 2 (February 1966): 21.

130. Baskerville, "Free Jazz," 492. See also Frank Kofsky, *Black Nationalism and the Revolution in Music* (New York: Beacon, 1970).

131. Nadi Qamar, "Titans of the Saxophone," *Liberator* 6, no. 4 (April 1966): 21.

132. Saul, *Freedom Is*, 260–68.

133. Paul Anthony, "John Coltrane: Beyond Genius, Night Trane," *Liberator* 7, no. 9 (September 1967): 19.

134. Nadi Qamar, "The Black Music Predicament," *Liberator* 6, no. 6 (June 1966): 19.

135. Scott Saul, *Freedom Is, Freedom Ain't: Jazz and the Making of the Sixties* (Cambridge, MA: Harvard University Press, 2003), 313.

136. A. B. Spellman, "Marion Brown: Growing into Gianthood," *Liberator* 6, no. 9 (September 1966): 20–21. In addition to recording several albums, Brown had also turned to writing about black culture. For example, he wrote an entry on the history of black painters and sculptors for the *American Negro Reference Book* the same year as Spellman's review. See Marion Brown, "The Negro in the Fine Arts," in *American Negro Reference Book*, ed. John P. Davis (Englewood Cliffs, NJ: Prentice-Hall, 1967), 766–74. Brown's article is a further example of the way in which many musicians often doubled as historians and critics documenting African American expressive culture.

137. Marc Brasz, "Four Lives in the Bebop Business (review)," *Liberator* 6, no. 12 (December 1966): 19.

138. "Interview with The Last Poets' Umar Bin Hassan and Abiodun Oyewole," in Darius James, *That's Blaxploitation: Roots of the Baadasssss 'Tude* by Darius James (New York: St. Martin's Griffin, 1995), 167–81.

139. Kalamu ya Salaam, "Black Theatre—the Way It Is: An Interview with Woodie King Jr.," *African American Review* 31, no. 4 (Winter 1997): 647–58. (No interview date given in the published interview.)

140. Vincent Canby, "Bland Exteriors and Madness Within," *New York Times*, April 9, 1971, 23.

141. Thomas A. Johnson, "Renaissance in Black Poetry Expresses Anger," *New York Times*, April 25, 1969, 49.

142. Kalamu ya Salaam, Interview with Woodie King Jr.

143. Clayton Riley, Theatre Review, *Liberator* 9, no. 7 (July 1969): 21.

144. Owing to labor opportunities and widespread impoverishment in Puerto Rico, New York City has been the largest destination of Puerto Rican migration since 1950. According to recently published statistics, in 1950 there were 252,515 Puerto Ricans in New York, but by 1970, that number had grown to 878,980. See *The Puerto Rican Diaspora: Historical Perspectives*, ed. Carmen Teresa Whalen and Victor Vazquez-Hernandez (Philadelphia: Temple University Press, 2005), 3.

145. "The Young Lords: Power to the People," *Liberator* 10, no. 2 (February 1970): 11–13.

146. Wilkinson, "In the Tradition of Revolution."

147. Ron Welburn, Record Review of *The Last Poets* (produced by East Wind Associates, distributed by Pip Records, New York), *Liberator* 10, no. 11 (November 1970): 20, 23.

148. Ron Welburn, Record Review of *Ain't No Ambulances for No Nigguhs Tonight*, by Stanley Crouch (Flying Dutchman, FDS-105), *Liberator* 10, no. 12 (December 1970): 23.

Epilogue

1. James Boggs, "The Final Confrontation," *Liberator* 8, no. 3 (March 1968): 4–8; "The American Revolution," *Liberator* 8, no. 10 (October 1968): 4–9.

2. *Liberator* 8, no. 4 (April 1968): 22.

3. Watts, "The Program" (editorial), *Liberator* 8, no. 3 (March 1968): 3.

4. Ibid.

5. *Liberator* 10, no. 2 (February 1970): 19.

6. Watts, "Big Brother" (editorial), *Liberator* 10, no. 12 (December 1970): 1.

7. "Former Chicago Priest Assigned New Post at Fordham 'U' in N.Y," *New York Times*, 12 Sept. 1970, 24.

8. Fordham University Archives and Special Collections.

9. *Liberator* 11, no. 3 (March 1971): 3.

10. See Houston Baker Jr., *Betrayal: How Black Intellectuals Have Abandoned the Civil Rights Era* (New York: Columbia University Press, 2008).

11. Edward Said, *Representations of the Intellectual* (New York: Vintage, 1996), 110.

Bibliography

Primary Sources

Manuscript Collections

Black Power Movement Microform Collection
    Amiri Baraka Papers
    Revolutionary Action Movement Papers
    Robert F. Williams Papers
Robert W. Woodruff Library, Atlanta University Center
    John Henrik Clarke Africana Collection
Schomburg Center for Research in Black Culture
    John Henrik Clarke Papers
    Julian Mayfield Papers
    Larry Neal Papers
Tamiment Library and Robert F. Wagner Labor Archives
    George Breitman Papers
    Harold Cruse Papers

Interviews

Muhammad Ahmed, March 4, 2009
Lowell Pierson Beveridge, April 8, 2006; July 14, 2006
Rose Finkenstaedt, July, 2006
Richard Gibson, April 13, 2006
Calvin Hicks, June 13, 2007
Marilyn Lieberman, October 9, 2006
Clayton Riley, April 15, 2006
Carlos E. Russell, March 4, 2006
Charlie L. Russell, June 10, 2006
Ozzie Sykes, June 2, 2006
Askia Toure, February 26, 2009
C. E. Wilson, April 15, 2006

Periodicals and Periodical Collections

The Black Scholar
Marshall Bloom Alternative Press Collection, Amherst College
Chicago Defender

Ebony
Jet
Liberator
The Nation
Negro Digest/Black World
New York Times
Révolution Africaine
Schomburg Clippings File, Amherst College
Soulbook
Third World News

Published Books, Articles, Chapters, and Dissertations

Books

Adams, Maurianne, and John H. Bracey, eds. *Strangers and Neighbors: Relations between Blacks and Jews in the United States.* Amherst: University of Massachusetts Press, 1999.

Ahmad, Muhammad (Max Stanford). *We Will Return in the Whirlwind: Black Radical Organizations, 1960–1975.* Chicago: Charles H. Kerr, 2007.

Allen, Robert L. *Black Awakening in Capitalist America.* New York: Doubleday, 1969.

American Society of African Culture, eds. *Pan-Africanism Reconsidered.* Berkeley: University of California Press, 1962.

Anderson, Carol. *Eyes off the Prize: The United Nations and the Struggle for Human Rights, 1944–1955.* Cambridge: Cambridge University Press, 2003.

Ashcroft, Bill, Gareth Griffiths, and Helen Tiffin, eds. *Post-Colonial Studies: The Key Concepts.* London: Routledge, 2000.

Austin, Algernon. *Achieving Blackness: Race, Black Nationalism, and Afrocentrism in the Twentieth Century.* New York: New York University Press, 2006.

Baker, Houston A., Jr. *Betrayal: How Black Intellectuals Have Abandoned the Ideals of the Civil Rights Era.* New York: Columbia University Press, 2008.

Baldwin, James. *The Fire Next Time.* New York: Dell, 1963.

Baldwin, James, ed. *Black Anti-Semitism and Jewish Racism.* New York: Shocken Books, 1970.

Bambara, Toni Cade, ed. *The Black Woman: An Anthology.* 1970. Reprint; New York: Washington Square Press, 2005.

Baraka, Amiri. *Black Music.* New York: William and Morrow, 1970.

Barbour, Floyd B. *The Black Power Revolt: A Collection of Essays.* Boston: Porter Sargeant, 1968.

———. *The Black Seventies.* Boston: Porter Sargeant, 1970.

Barnett, LaShonda Katrice. *I Got Thunder: Black Women Songwriters on Their Craft.* New York: Thunder's Mouth Press, 2007.

Biondi, Martha. *To Stand and Fight: The Struggle for Civil Rights in Postwar New York City.* Cambridge, MA: Harvard University Press, 2003.

Black Issues in Higher Education. Editors of *The Unfinished Agenda of Brown v. Board of Education*. Hoboken, NJ: John Wiley & Sons, 2004.

Boggs, James. *Racism and the Class Struggle: Further Pages from a Black Worker's Notebook*. New York: Monthly Review Press, 1970.

Boggs, James, and Grace Lee Boggs. *Revolution and Evolution in the Twentieth Century*. New York: Monthly Review Press, 1974.

Bogle, Donald. *Toms, Coons, Mulattoes, Mammies and Bucks: An Interpretive History of Blacks in American Films*. 3rd ed. New York: Continuum, 1994.

Bogues, Anthony. *Black Heretics, Black Prophets: Radical Political Intellectuals*. New York: Routledge, 2003.

Boyd, Herb. *Harlem: A Biography of James Baldwin*. New York: Atria Books, 2008.

Bracey, John, August Meier, and Elliott Rudwick, eds. *Black Nationalism in America*. Indianapolis: Bobbs Merrill, 1970.

Bradley, Stephan M. *Harlem vs. Columbia University: Black Student Power in the Late 60s*. Urbana: University of Illinois Press, 2009.

Bradley, Will, and Charles Esche, eds. *Art and Social Change: A Critical Reader*. London: Tate, 2007.

Breitman, George, ed. *Malcolm X Speaks*. New York: Grove Press, 1965.

———. *The Last Year of Malcolm X: The Evolution of a Revolutionary*. New York: Pathfinder, 1967.

Brisbane, Robert H. *Black Activism: Racial Revolution in the United States, 1954–1970*. Valley Forge, PA: Judson Press, 1974.

Broderick, Francis L., and August Meier, eds. *Negro Protest Thought in the Twentieth Century*. Indianapolis: Bobbs-Merril, 1965.

Brown, Elaine. *A Taste of Power: A Black Woman's Story*. New York: Anchor Books, 1993.

Buhle, Paul. *Marxism in the United States: Remapping the History of the American Left*. London: Verso, 1991.

Burgos, Adrian, Jr. *Playing America's Game: Baseball, Latinos, and the Color Line*. Berkeley: University of California Press, 2007.

Campbell, James T. *Middle Passages: African American Journeys to Africa, 1787–2005*. New York: Penguin, 2006.

Carmichael, Stokely (Kwame Ture), and Ekwueme Michael Thelwell. *Ready for Revolution: The Life and Struggles of Stokely Carmichael*. New York: Scribner, 2003.

Carson, Clayborne. *In Struggle: SNCC and the Black Awakening of the 1960s*. Cambridge, MA: Harvard University Press, 1981.

Carson, Clayborne, ed. *Malcolm X: The FBI File*. New York: Carroll and Graf, 1991.

Clark, Kenneth. *Dark Ghetto: Dilemmas of Social Power*. New York: Harper and Row, 1967.

Clarke, Cheryl. *After Mecca: Women Poets and the Black Arts Movement*. New Brunswick, NJ: Rutgers University Press, 2005.

Clarke, John Henrik, ed. *Harlem U.S.A.* Brooklyn: A & B Publishers, 1971.

———, ed. *Harlem: A Community in Transition.* 3rd edition. New York: Citadel Press, 1964.
———, ed. *Malcolm X: The Man and His Times.* New York: Collier Books, 1969.
———, ed. *Black Titan, An Anthology.* Boston: Beacon Press, 1970.
———, ed. *Who Betrayed the African World Revolution?* Chicago: Third World Press, 1993.
Cleaver, Kathleen, and George Katsiaficas, eds. *Liberation, Imagination and the Black Panther Party: A New Look at the Panthers and Their Legacy.* New York, 2001.
Cobb, William Jelani. *The Essential Harold Cruse: A Reader.* New York: Palgrave, 2002.
Collier-Thomas, Bettye, and V. P. Franklin, eds. *Sisters in the Struggle: African American Women in the Civil Rights–Black Power Movement.* New York: New York University Press, 2001.
Collins, Lisa Gail, and Margo Natalie Crawford, eds. *New Thoughts on the Black Arts Movement.* New Brunswick, NJ: Rutgers University Press, 2002.
Collins, Patricia Hill. *From Black Power to Hip Hop: Racism, Nationalism, and Feminism.* Philadelphia: Temple University Press, 2006.
Cook, Mercer, and Stephen E. Henderson. *The Militant Black Writer in Africa and the United States.* Madison: University of Wisconsin Press, 1969.
Crawford, Vicki L., Jacqueline Anne Rouse, and Barbara Woods, eds. *Women in the Civil Rights Movement: Trailblazers and Torchbearers, 1941–1965.* Bloomington: Indiana University Press, 1993.
Crossman, Richard, ed. *The God That Failed.* New York: Harper and Brothers, 1949.
Cruse, Harold. *The Crisis of the Negro Intellectual: From Its Origins to the Present.* New York: William & Morrow, 1967.
DeCarava, Roy. *The Sound I Saw.* New York: Phaidon, 2001.
De Witte, Ludo. *The Assassination of Lumumba.* Trans. Ann Wright and Renee Fenby. London and New York: Verso, 2001.
Douglas, Robert L. *Resistance, Insurgence and Identity: The Art of Mari Evans, Nelson Stevens and the Black Arts Movement.* Trenton, NJ: Africa World Press, 2008.
Du Bois, W. E. B. *The World and Africa.* New York: International Publishers, 1965.
Dudziak, Mary L. *Cold War Civil Rights: Race and the Image of American Democracy.* Princeton, NJ: Princeton University Press, 2000.
Editors of Black Issues in Higher Education. *The Unfinished Agenda of Brown v. Board of Education.* Hoboken, NJ: John Wiley & Sons, Inc., 2004.
Edwards, Brent Hayes. *The Practice of Diaspora: Literature, Translation and the Rise of Black Internationalism.* Cambridge, MA: Harvard University Press, 2003.
Edwards, Harry. *The Revolt of the Black Athlete.* New York: Macmillan, 1969.
Elliot, Jeffrey M., ed. *Conversations with Maya Angelou.* Jackson and London: University Press of Mississippi, 1989.

Enstice, Wayne, and Janis Stockhouse. *Jazzwomen: Conversations with Twenty-One Musicians*. Bloomington: Indiana University Press, 2004.

Esedebe, P. Olisanwuche. *Pan-Africanism: The Idea and Movement, 1776–1991*. 2nd edition. Washington, DC: Howard University Press, 1994.

Evanzz, Karl. *The Messenger: The Rise and Fall of Elijah Muhammad*. New York: Vintage Books, 2001.

Fanon, Frantz. *The Wretched of the Earth*. Translated by Constance Farrington. New York: Grove Press, 1963.

———. *Toward the African Revolution: Political Essays*. Translated by Haakon Chevalier. New York: Grove Press, 1967.

Fairclough, Adam. *Better Day Coming: Blacks and Equality, 1890–2000*. New York: Penguin, 2001.

Farred, Grant. *What's My Name?: Black Vernacular Intellectuals*. Minneapolis: University of Minnesota Press, 2003.

Ford, Tanisha C. *Liberated Threads: Black Women, Style, and the Global Politics of Soul*. Chapel Hill: University of North Carolina Press, 2015.

Forman, James. *The Making of Black Revolutionaries: A Personal Account*. New York: Macmillan, 1972.

———. *High Tide of Black Resistance*. Seattle, WA: Open Hand Publishing, 1994.

Franklin, John Hope, and August Meier, eds. *Black Leaders of the Twentieth Century*. Chicago: University of Illinois Press, 1982.

Gaines, Kevin K. *American Africans in Ghana: Black Expatriates and the Civil Rights Era*. Chapel Hill: University of North Carolina Press, 2006.

Gardell, Mattias. *In the Name of Elijah Muhammad: Louis Farrakhan and the Nation of Islam*. Durham, NC: Duke University Press, 2005.

Geary, Daniel. *Beyond Civil Rights: The Moynihan Report and Its Legacy*. Philadelphia: University of Pennsylvania Press, 2015.

Geiss, Imanuel. *The Pan-African Movement: A History of Pan-Africanism in America, Europe, and Africa*. Translated by Ann Keep. New York: Africana Publishing Co., 1974.

Geschwender, James A., ed. *The Black Revolt*. Englewood Cliffs, NJ: Prentice-Hall, 1971.

Gilroy, Paul. *The Black Atlantic: Modernity and Double Consciousness*. Cambridge, MA: Harvard University Press, 1993.

Gilyard, Keith. *John Oliver Killens: A Life of Black Literary Activism*. Athens: University of Georgia Press, 2010.

Gomez, Michael A. *Black Crescent: The Experience and Legacy of African Muslims in the Americas*. New York: Cambridge University Press, 2005.

Gomez, Michael A., ed. *Diasporic Africa: A Reader*. New York: New York University Press, 2006.

Gore, Dayo. *Radicalism at the Crossroads: African American Women Activists in the Cold War*. New York: New York University Press, 2011.

Gore, Dayo, Jeanne Theoharis, and Komozi Woodard, eds., *Want to Start a Revolution? Radical Women in the Black Freedom Struggle*. New York: New York University Press, 2009.

Gosse, Van. *Where the Boys Are: Cuba, Cold War America and the Making of a New Left*. New York: Verso, 1993.

Graham, Hugh Davis. *Civil Rights and the Presidency: Race and Gender in American Politics, 1960–1972*. New York: Oxford University Press, 1992.

Green, Reginald H., and Ann Seidman. *Unity or Poverty? The Economics of Pan-Africanism*. Baltimore, MD: Penguin, 1968.

Guy-Sheftall, Beverly, ed. *Words of Fire: An Anthology of African-American Feminist Thought*. New York: New Press, 1995.

Hansberry, Lorraine. *A Raisin in the Sun: The Unfilmed Original Screenplay*. Edited by Robert Nemiroff. New York: Plume, 1992.

———. *The Critical Last Plays*. Edited by Robert Nemiroff. New York: Plume, 1983.

Harris, Joseph, ed. *Global Dimensions of the African Diaspora*. Washington, DC: Howard University Press, 1982.

Harris, William J., ed. *The Leroi Jones/Amiri Baraka Reader*. New York: Thunder's Mouth Press, 1991.

Harris, Robert, Nyota Harris, and Grandassa Harris, eds. *Carlos Cooks and Black Nationalism from Garvey to Malcolm*. Dover, MA: Majority Press, 1991.

Harrison, Paul Carter, et al., eds. *Black Theatre: Ritual Performance in the African Diaspora*. Philadelphia: Temple University Press, 2002.

Haywood, Harry. *Black Bolshevik: Autobiography of an Afro-American Communist*. Chicago: Liberator Press, 1978.

Hill, Errol G., and James V. Hatch. *A History of African American Theatre*. Cambridge: Cambridge University Press, 2003.

Hilliard, David. *This Side of Glory: The Autobiography of David Hilliard and the Story of the Black Panther Party*. Boston: Little, Brown, 1993.

Hilliard, David, and Donald Wiese, eds. *The Huey P. Newton Reader*. New York: Seven Stories Press, 2002.

Hilliard, David, Keith Zimmerman, and Kent Zimmerman. *Huey: The Spirit of the Panther*. New York: Thunder's Mouth Press, 2006.

Hine, Darlene Clark, et al., *African Americans: A Concise History*. Vol. 1. Upper Saddle River, NJ: Prentice Hall, 2004. 125–26.

Ho, Fred, and Bill V. Mullen, eds. *Afro Asia: Revolutionary Political and Cultural Connections between African Americans and Asian Americans*. Durham, NC: Duke University Press, 2008.

Holmes, Linda Janet, and Cheryl A. Wall, eds. *Savoring the Salt: The Legacy of Toni Cade Bambara*. Philadelphia: Temple University Press, 2008.

Horne, Alistair. *A Savage War of Peace: Algeria, 1954–1962*. New York: Penguin Books, 1987.

Horne, Gerald. *The Fire This Time: The Watts Uprising and the 1960s*. Charlottesville: University Press of Virginia, 1995.

Howe, Irving. *The Radical Imagination: An Anthology from Dissent Magazine.* New York: New American Library, 1967.

Hunton, W. Alphaeus. *Decision in Africa: Sources of Current Conflict.* New York: International Publishers, 1957.

Isaacs, Harold R. *The New World of Negro Americans.* New York: Viking Press, 1963.

Iton, Richard. *In Search of the Black Fantastic: Politics and Popular Culture in the Post–Civil Rights Era.* Oxford: Oxford University Press, 2008.

Jackson, Esther Cooper, ed. *Freedomways Reader: Prophets in Their Own Country.* Boulder, CO: Westview Press, 2000.

Jackson, Lawrence P. *Indignant Generation: A Narrative History of African American Writers and Critics, 1934–1960.* Princeton, NJ: Princeton University Press, 2011.

Jamal, Hakim A. *From the Dead Level: Malcolm X and the Organization of Afro-American Unity.* Springfield, MA: Masjid At-Tawhid, 1971.

Jamal, Mumia-Abu. *We Want Freedom: A Life in the Black Panther Party.* Boston: South End Press, 2008.

James, Darius. *That's Blaxploitation: Roots of the Baadasssss 'Tude (Rated X by an All-White Jury).* New York: St. Martin's Griffin, 1995.

Jayawardena, Kumari. *Feminism and Nationalism in the Third World.* London: Zed Books, 1986.

Jeffries, Judson L. *Huey P. Newton: The Radical Theorist.* Jackson: University of Mississippi Press, 2002.

Jeffries, Judson L., ed. *Comrades: A Local History of the Black Panther Party.* Bloomington: Indiana University Press, 2007.

Johnson, Abby Arthur, and Ronald Mayberry Johnson. *Propaganda and Aesthetics: The Literary Politics of African-American Magazines in the Twentieth Century.* Amherst: University of Massachusetts Press, 1979.

Jones, Charles E., ed. *The Black Panther Party Reconsidered.* Baltimore, MD: Black Classic Press, 1998.

Jones, LeRoi (Amiri Baraka). *Home: Social Essays.* Hopewell, NJ: Ecco Press, 1998.

Joseph, Peniel E. *Waiting 'Til the Midnight Hour: A Narrative History of Black Power in America.* New York: Henry Holt, 2006.

Joseph, Peniel E., ed. *The Black Power Movement: Rethinking the Civil Rights–Black Power Era.* New York: Routledge, 2006.

Kelley, Robin D. G. *Freedom Dreams: The Black Radical Imagination.* Boston: Beacon Press, 2002.

———. *Thelonious Monk: The Life and Times of an American Original.* New York: Simon and Schuster, 2009.

Kessler, Lauren. *The Dissident Press: Alternative Journalism in American History.* Beverly Hills, CA: Sage Publications, 1984.

King, Martin Luther, Jr. *The Autobiography of Martin Luther King, Jr.* Edited by Clayborne Carson. New York: Warner Books, 1998.

King, Woodie and Earl Anthony, eds. *Black Poets and Prophets*. New York: New American Library, 1972.

Kofsky, Frank. *Black Nationalism and the Revolution in Music*. New York: Beacon, 1970.

Legum, Colin. *Pan-Africanism: A Short Political Guide*. New York: Praeger, 1965.

Lemelle, Sidney J., and Robin D. G. Kelley, eds. *Imagining Home: Class, Culture and Nationalism in the African Diaspora*. New York: Verso, 1994.

Lewis, David Levering, ed. *W. E .B. Du Bois, A Reader*. New York: Henry Holt & Company, 1995.

Lincoln, C. Eric. *The Black Muslims in America*. Boston: Beacon Press, 1961.

Lott, Eric. *Love and Theft: Blackface Minstrelsy and the American Working Class*. Oxford: Oxford University Press, 1995.

Lynd, Staughton. *Intellectual Origins of American Radicalism*. Cambridge, MA: Harvard University Press, 1982.

Lynn, Conrad. *There Is a Fountain: The Autobiography of Conrad Lynn*. Brooklyn: Lawrence Hill, 1993.

McCarthy, Timothy, and John McMillian. *The Radical Reader: A Documentary History of the American Radical Tradition*. New York: New Press, 2003.

McDuffie, Erik S. *Sojourning for Freedom: Black Women, American Communism, and the Making of Black Left Feminism*. Durham, NC: Duke University Press, 2011.

Magubane, Bernard M. *The Ties That Bind: African-American Consciousness of Africa*. Trenton, NJ: Africa World Press, 1994.

Marqusee, Mark. *Redemption Song: Muhammad Ali and the Spirit of the Sixties*. London and New York: Verso Books, 1999.

Mazrui, Ali A., ed. *UNESCO General History of Africa*. Vol. 8: *Africa since 1935*. Berkeley: University of California Press, 1999.

Meriwether, James H. *Proudly We Can Be Africans: Black Americans and Africa, 1935–1961*. Chapel Hill: University of North Carolina Press, 2002.

Mills, Nicolaus, ed. *Legacy of Dissent: 40 Years of Writing from Dissent Magazine*. New York: Simon and Schuster, 1994.

Mills, Nicolaus and Michael Walzer, eds., *50 Years of Dissent*. New Haven, CT: Yale University Press, 2004.

Milne, June. *Kwame Nkrumah: A Biography*. London: Panaf Books, 2000.

Murch, Donna. *Living for the City: Migration, Education, and the Rise of the Black Panther Party in Oakland, California*. Chapel Hill: University of North Carolina Press, 2010.

Mullen, Bill V., and James Smethurst, eds. *Left of the Color Line: Race, Radicalism, and Twentieth Century Literature of the United States*. Chapel Hill: University of North Carolina Press, 2003.

Nash, Jay Robert, and Stanley Ralph Ross. *The Motion Picture Guide, 1927–1983*. Vol. 1: A–B. Chicago: Cinebooks, 1985.

Neal, Larry, and Amiri Baraka, eds. *Black Fire*. Baltimore, MD: Black Classic Press, 1968.

Neal, Larry. *Visions of a Liberated Future: Black Arts Movement Writings*. Edited by Michael Schwartz. New York: Thunder Mouth's Press, 1989.

Nelson, Jack, Kenneth Carlson, and Thomas Linton, eds. *Radical Ideas and the Schools*. New York: Holt, Rinehart and Winston, 1972.

Nemiroff, Robert, ed. *A Raisin in the Sun: The Unofficial Screenplay*. New York: Plume, 1992.

———. *The Collected Last Plays*. New York: Plume, 1983.

Nkrumah, Kwame. *Africa Must Unite*. London: Heinemann, 1963.

———. *Forward Ever: The Life of Kwame Nkrumah*. London: Panaf Books, 1977.

Nujoma, Sam. *Where Others Wavered: The Autobiography of Sam Nujoma*. London: Panaf Books, 2001.

O'Reilly, Kenneth. *"Racial Matters:" The FBI's Secret File on Black America, 1960–1972*. New York: Free Press, 1989.

Ogbar, Jeffrey O. G. *Black Power: Radical Politics and African American Identity*. Baltimore, MD: Johns Hopkins University Press, 2004.

Ongiri, Amy Abugo. *Spectacular Blackness: The Cultural Politics of the Black Power Movement and the Search for a Black Aesthetic*. Charlottesville: University of Virginia, 2010.

Panaf Books, Editors of *Panaf Great Lives: Eduardo Mondlane*. London: Panaf Books, 1978.

Patterson, William L., ed. *We Charge Genocide: The Crime of the Government against the Negro People, A Petition to the United Nations*. New York: International Publishers, 1951.

Pearson, Hugh. *When Harlem Nearly Killed King: The 1958 Stabbing of Dr. Martin Luther King, Jr.* New York: Seven Stories, 2002.

Perkins, Margo. *Autobiography as Activism: Three Black Women of the Sixties*. Jackson: University Press of Mississippi, 2000.

Plummer, Brenda Gayle. *In Search of Power: African Americans in the Era of Decolonization, 1956–1974*. Cambridge: Cambridge University Press, 2013.

———. *Rising Wind: Black Americans and U.S. Foreign Affairs, 1935–1960*. Chapel Hill: University of North Carolina Press, 1996.

Plummer, Brenda Gayle, ed. *Window on Freedom: Race, Civil Rights, and Foreign Affairs, 1945–1988*. Chapel Hill: University of North Carolina Press, 2003.

Porter, Eric C. *What is this Thing Called Jazz? African American Musicians as Artists, Critics and Activists*. Berkeley: University of California Press, 2002.

Powell, Richard J. *Black Art and Culture in the 20th Century*. New York: Thames and Hudson, 1997.

Prashad, Vijay. *Everybody Was Kung Fu Fighting: Afro-Asian Connections and the Myth of Cultural Purity*. Boston: Beacon Press, 2001.

Quaison-Sackey, Alex. *Africa Unbound: Reflections of an African Statesman*. New York: Prager, 1963.

Rabaka, Reiland. *Africana Critical Theory: Reconstructing the Black Radical Tradition from W. E. B. Du Bois and C. L. R. James to Frantz Fanon and Amilcar Cabral*. Lanham, MD: Lexington Books, 2009.

Rainwater, Lee and William L. Yancey, eds. *The Moynihan Report and the Politics of Controversy*. Cambridge, MA: MIT Press, 1967.

Roberts, Dick. *Revolution in the Congo* (pamphlet). New York: Pathfinder Press, 1965.

Robinson, Cedric. *Black Marxism: The Making of the Black Radical Tradition*. Chapel Hill: University of North Carolina Press, 2000 (1983).

Robinson, Jackie. *Baseball Has Done It*. New York: Ig Publishing, 2005.

Roth, Betina. *Separate Roads to Feminism: Black, Chicana, and White Feminist Movements in America's Second Wave*. Cambridge: Cambridge University Press, 2004.

Said, Edward. *Representations of the Intellectual*. New York: Vintage, 1996.

Sales, William W., Jr. *From Civil Rights to Black Liberation: Malcolm X and the Organization of Afro-American Unity*. Boston: South End Press, 1994.

Saul, Scott. *Freedom Is, Freedom Ain't: Jazz and the Making of the Sixties*. Cambridge, MA: Harvard University Press, 2003.

Schrecker, Ellen. *Many Are the Crimes: McCarthyism in America*. Princeton, NJ: Princeton University Press, 1998.

Schulman, Bruce J. *Lyndon B. Johnson and American Liberalism: A Brief Biography with Documents*. 2nd edition. Boston: Bedford/St. Martins, 2007.

Scott, Jack. *The Athletic Revolution*. New York: Free Press, 1971.

Self, Robert O. *American Babylon: Race and the Struggle for Postwar Oakland*. Princeton, NJ: Princeton University Press, 2003.

Shapiro, Herbert. *White Violence and Black Response: From Reconstruction to Montgomery*. Amherst: University of Massachusetts Press, 1988.

Singh, Nikhil Pal. *Black Is a Country: Race and the Unfinished Struggle for Democracy*. Cambridge, MA: Harvard University Press, 2004.

Singham, A. W., and Shirley Hune. *Non-Alignment in an Age of Alignments*. Westport, CT: Zed Books, 1986.

Sitkoff, Harvard. *The Struggle for Black Equality, 1954–1992*. Rev. ed. New York: Hill & Wang, 1993.

Smethurst, James. *The Black Arts Movement: Literary Nationalism in the 1960s and 1970s*. Chapel Hill: University of North Carolina Press, 2005.

Springer, Kimberley. *Living for the Revolution: Black Feminist Organizations, 1968–1980*. Durham, NC, and London: Duke University Press, 2005.

Springer, Kimberley, ed. *Still Lifting, Still Climbing: African American Women's Contemporary Activism*. New York: New York University Press, 1999.

Spivak, Gayatri. *The Post-Colonial Critic: Interviews, Strategies, Dialogues*. Edited by Sara Harasym. New York: Routledge, 1990.

Staniland, Martin. *American Intellectuals and African Nationalists, 1955–1970*. New Haven, CT: Yale University Press, 1991.
Steinberg, Stephen. *Turning Back: The Retreat from Racial Justice in American Thought and Policy*. Boston: Beacon Press, 1995.
Stetson, Erlene, ed. *Black Sister: Poetry by Black American Women, 1746–1980*. Bloomington: Indiana University Press, 1981.
Theoharis, Jeanne, and Komozi Woodard, eds. *Freedom North: Black Freedom Struggles Outside the South, 1940–1980*. New York: Palgrave MacMillan, 2003.
———. *Groundwork: Local Black Freedom Movements in America*. New York: New York University Press, 2005.
Ture, Kwame and Charles V. Hamilton. *Black Power: The Politics of Liberation*. New York: Vintage, 1992.
Turner, W. Burghardt, and Joyce Moore Turner, eds. *Richard B. Moore: Caribbean Militant in Harlem, Collected Writings, 1920–1972*. Bloomington: Indiana University Press, 1992.
Tyson, Timothy. *Radio Free Dixie: Robert F. Williams and the Roots of Black Power*. Chapel Hill: University of North Carolina Press, 1999.
Urban, Wayne. *Black Scholar: Horace Mann Bond, 1904–1972*. Athens: University of Georgia Press, 1992.
Van De Burg, William L. *New Day in Babylon: The Black Power Movement and American Culture, 1965–1975*. Chicago: Chicago University Press, 1992.
Vogel, Todd, ed. *The Black Press: New Literary and Historical Essays*. New Brunswick, NJ: Rutgers University Press, 2001.
Von Eschen, Penny. *Race against Empire: Black Americans and Anticolonialism, 1937–1957*. Ithaca, NY: Cornell University Press, 1997.
wa Thiong'o, Ngugi. *Writers in Politics: A Re-Engagement with Issues of Literature and Society*. 1981. Reprint; Portsmouth, NH: Heineman, 1997.
Wagstaff, Thomas. *Black Power: The Radical Response to White America*. Beverly Hills, CA: Glencoe Press, 1969.
Wald, Alan. *Writing from the Left: New Essays on Radical Culture and Politics*. New York: Verso, 1994.
Ward, Stephen M., ed. *Pages from a Black Radical's Notebook: A James Boggs Reader*. Detroit, MI: Wayne State University Press, 2011.
Washington, James M., ed. *A Testament of Hope: The Essential Writings and Speeches of Martin Luther King, Jr.* New York: HarperCollins, 1991.
Watts, Jerry G. *Amiri Baraka: The Politics and Art of a Black Intellectual*. New York: New York University Press, 2001.
Watts, Jerry G., ed., *Harold Cruse's The Crisis of the Negro Intellectual Reconsidered*. New York: Routledge, 2004.
Weinstein, James. *The Long Detour: The History and Future of the American Left*. Cambridge, MA: Westview Press, 2003.
West, Cornel, ed., *The Radical King*. Boston: Beacon Press, 2015.

Whalen, Carmen Theresa, and Victor Vasquez-Hernandez, eds. *The Puerto Rican Diaspora: Historical Perspectives*. Philadelphia: Temple University Press, 2005.

Williams, Rhonda Y. *Concrete Demands: The Search for Black Power in the 20th Century*. New York: Routledge, 2015.

Wilmore, Gayraud S. *Black Religion and Black Radicalism: An Examination of the Black Experience in Religion*. Garden City, NY: Doubleday, 1973.

Wilson, Sandra Kathryn, ed. *In Search of Democracy: The NAACP Writings of James Weldon Johnson, Walter White and Roy Wilkins, 1920–1977*. New York: Oxford University Press, 1999.

Woodard, Komozi. *A Nation within a Nation: Amiri Baraka and Black Power Politics*. Chapel Hill: University of North Carolina Press, 1999.

Wright, Richard. *The Color Curtain: A Report on the Bandung Conference*. 1956. Reprint; Jackson, MS: Banner Books, 1994.

X, Malcolm. *The Autobiography of Malcolm X*. New York: Ballantine Books, 1964.

———. *By Any Means Necessary*. Edited by George Breitman. New York: Pathfinder, 1970.

———. *The Final Speeches: February 1965*. New York: Pathfinder, 1992.

Young, Cynthia A. *Soul Power: Culture, Radicalism and the Making of a U.S. Third World Left*. Durham, NC: Duke University Press, 2006.

Zinn, Howard. *SNCC: The New Abolitionists*. 1964. Reprint; Cambridge, MA: South End Press, 2002.

Zirin, Dave. *A People's History of Sports in the United States*. New York: New Press, 2008.

Articles, Book Chapters, and Dissertations

Ahmad, Muhammad (Max Stanford). "The Roots of the Pan-African Revolution." *Black Scholar*, May 1972, 48–55.

Allen, Ernest, Jr. "The New Negro: Explorations in Identity and Social Consciousness, 1910–1922." In *The Cultural Moment*, ed. Adele Heller and Lois Rudnick, 48–68. New Brunswick, NJ: Rutgers University Press, 1991.

———. "When Japan Was Champion of the Darker Nations: Satokata Takahashi and the Flowering of Black Messianic Nationalism." *Black Scholar* 24 (Winter 1994): 23–46.

———. "Waiting for Tojo: The Pro-Japan Vigils of Black Missourians, 1932–1943." *Gateway Heritage* 16 (Fall 1995): 38–55.

———. "Minister Louis Farrakhan and the Continuing Evolution of the Nation of Islam." In *The Farrakhan Factor: African American Writers on Leadership, Nationhood, and Minister Louis Farrakhan*, ed. Amy Alexander, 52–102. New York: Grove Press, 1998.

Anon. [Ernest Mkalimoto]. "Revolutionary Nationalism and the Class Struggle." Unpublished pamphlet of the League of Revolutionary Black Workers, 1970.

Asante, S. K. B., and David Chanaiwa. "Pan-Africanism and Regional Integration." In *UNESCO General History of Africa*. Vol. 8: *Africa since 1935*, ed. Ali A. Mazrui, 724–43. Berkeley: University of California Press, 1999.

Baker, James. "The American Society of African Culture." *Journal of Modern African Studies* 4, no. 3 (November 1966): 367–69.

Baraka, Amiri. "A Critical Reevaluation: A Raisin in the Sun's Enduring Passion." In *A Raisin in the Sun/The Sign in Sidney Brustein's Window*, 9–20. New York: Vintage, 1995.

Baskerville, John D. "Free Jazz; A Reflection of Black Power Ideology." *Journal of Black Studies* 24, no. 4 (June 1994): 484–97.

Beal, Frances. "Double Jeopardy: To Be Black and Female." In *Words of Fire: An Anthology of African-American Feminist Thought*, ed. Beverly Guy-Sheftall. New York: New Press, 1995.

Beveridge, Lowell Pierson, Jr. "The Theory and Practice of White Supremacy in South Africa, 1910–1913." Master's thesis, Columbia University, 1953.

Bradley, Stefan M. "Gym Crow Must Go! The 1968–1969 Student and Community Protests at Columbia in the City of New York." Ph.D. dissertation, University of Missouri, Columbia, 2003.

Brown, Marion. "The Negro in the Fine Arts." In *American Negro Reference Book*, ed. John P. Davis, 766–74. Englewood Cliffs, NJ: Prentice-Hall, 1967.

Campbell, Horace. "Pan-Africanism in the Twenty-First Century." In *Pan-Africanism: Politics, Economy and Social Change in the Twenty-First Century*, ed. Tajudeen Abdul-Raheem, 212–28. London: Pluto Press, 1996.

Canby, Vincent. "Bland Exteriors and Madness Within." *New York Times*. April 9, 1971, 23.

Cha-Jua, Sundiata, and Clarence Lang. "The Long Movement as Vampire: Temporal and Spatial Fallacies in Recent Black Freedom Studies." *Journal of African American History* 92, no. 2 (Spring 2007): 265–88.

Chick, C. A., Sr. "The American Negroes' Changing Attitude toward Africa." *Journal of Negro Education* 31 (Autumn 1962): 531–35.

Clark, Kenneth B. "HARYOU: AN Experiment." In *Harlem: A Community in Transition*, ed. John Henrik Clarke. New York: Citadel, 1964.

———. "HARYOU-ACT in Harlem: The Dream That Went Astray." In *Harlem USA*, ed. John Henrik Clarke. Brooklyn: A&B Publishers, 1971.

Clarke, John Henrik. "The New Afro-American Nationalism." *Freedomways* 1, no. 3 (Fall 1961): 285–95.

———. "The African Heritage Studies Association (AHSA): Some Notes on the Conflict with the African Studies Association (ASA) and the Fight to Reclaim African History." *Issue: A Journal of Opinion* 6, nos. 2/3 (Summer–Autumn 1976): 5–11.

———. "The Influence of Arthur A. Schomburg on My Concept of Africana Studies." *Phylon* 49, nos. 1 and 2 (Spring–Summer 1992): 4–9.

Clemons, Michael L., and Charles E. Jones. "Global Solidarity: The Black Panther Party in the International Arena." In *Liberation, Imagination and the Black Panther Party: A New Look at the Panthers and their Legacy*, ed. Kathleen Cleaver and George Katsiaficas, 20–39. New York: Routledge, 2001.

Crawford, Margo Natalie. "Black Light on the Wall of Respect: The Chicago Black Arts Movement." In *New Thoughts on the Black Arts Movement*, ed. Lisa G. Collins and Margo Natalie Crawford, 23–42. New Brunswick, NJ: Rutgers University Press, 2006.

Cruse, Harold. "Revolutionary Nationalism and the Afro-American [1962]." In *Rebellion or Revolution?*, 74–96. New York: Morrow, 1968.

Davis, Henry Vance. "Harold Wright Cruse: The Early Years and the Jewish Factor." *The Black Scholar* 35, no. 4 (Winter 2006): 17–31.

———. "Dixie Senator Attacks African Nations." *Chicago Daily Defender*, December 3, 1962.

Drake, St. Clair. "The International Implications of Race and Race Relations." *Journal of Negro Education* 20, no. 3 (Summer 1951): 261–78.

———. "Pan-Africanism: What Is It?" *Africa Today*, January 1959, 6–10.

———. "Negro Americans and the Africa Interest." In *The American Negro Reference Book*, ed. John P. Davis, 662–705. Englewood Cliffs, NJ: Prentice-Hall, 1966.

———. "Diaspora Studies and Pan-Africanism." In *Global Dimensions of the African Diaspora*, ed. Joseph E. Harris. Washington, DC: Howard University Press, 1983.

Duganne, Erina. "Transcending the Fixity of Race: The Kamoinge Workshop and the Question of a 'Black Aesthetic' in Photography." In *New Thoughts on the Black Arts Movement*, ed. Lisa G. Collins and Margo Natalie Crawford, 187–209. New Brunswick, NJ: Rutgers University Press, 2006.

Elaigwu, J. Isawa, and Ali A. Mazrui. "Nation-building and Changing Political Structures." In *UNESCO General History of Africa*. Vol. 8: *Africa since 1935*, ed. Ali A. Mazrui, 435–67. Berkeley: University of California Press, 1999).

Engel, Julien. "The African-American Institute." *African Studies Bulletin* 6, no. 3 (October 1963): 13–18.

Fenderson, Jonathan. "'Journey toward a Black Aesthetic': Hoyt Fuller, the Black Arts Movement and the Black Intellectual Community." Ph.D. dissertation, University of Massachusetts, W. E. B. Du Bois Department of Afro-American Studies, Amherst, 2011.

Foster, Badi G. "U.S, Foreign Policy toward Africa: An Afro-American Perspective." *Issue: A Journal of Opinion* 2, no. 2 (Summer 1972): 45–51.

Frazier, Robeson Taj. "Thunder in the East: China, Exiled Crusaders, and the Unevenness of Black Internationalism," *American Quarterly* 63, no. 4 (December 2011): 929–53.

Gibbs, David N. "Hammarsjkold, the United Nations, and the Congo Crisis, 1960–1, A Reinterpretation," *Journal of Modern African Studies*, 31, no. 1 (1993): 163–74.

Gibson, Richard. "Richard Wright's 'Island of Hallucination' and the 'Gibson Affair.'" *Modern Fiction Studies* 51, no. 4 (Winter 2005): 896–920.

Gilstrap, Max K. "Mr. Stevenson and Africa," *Christian Science Monitor*, July 7, 1955.

Goldman, Peter. "Malcolm X: Witness for the Prosecution." In *Black Leaders of the Twentieth Century*, ed. John Hope Franklin and August Meier, 305–30. Urbana and Chicago: University of Illinois Press, 1982.

Gordon, Edmund T., and Mark Anderson. "Conceptualizing the African Diaspora." In *Advances in Education in Diverse Communities: Research, Policy and Praxis*, Vol. 1, ed. Carol Camp-Yeakey, 229–39. Bingley, UK: Emerald Group Publishing, 2000.

Gosse, Van. "More Than Just a Politician: Notes on the Life and Times of Harold Cruse." In *Harold Cruse's The Crisis of the Negro Intellectual Reconsidered*, ed. Jerry G. Watts. New York: Routledge, 2004.

Granton, E. Fannie. "Africa's Famous Model: Mrs. Yahne Sangare. *Jet*, June 22, 1967, 40–42.

Harrison, Bonnie Claudia. "Diasporadas: Black Women and the Fine Art of Activism." *Meridians* 2, no. 2 (2002): 163–84.

Henderson, Errol Anthony. "Shadow of a Clue." In *Liberation, Imagination and the Black Panther Party*, ed. Kathleen Cleaver and George Katsiaficas, 197–207. New York: Routledge, 2001.

Henry, Charles, and Tunua Thrash, "U.S. Human Rights Petitions before the UN." *The Black Scholar* 26, nos. 3–4, (Fall–Winter 1996): 60–73.

Hentoff, Nat. "How Wonderful to Be a Black Woman." *New York Times*, January 14, 1968.

Hill, Adelaide Cromwell. "What Is Africa to Us?" In *The Black Power Revolt*, ed. Floyd Barbour, 127–35. Porter Sargeant: Boston, 1968.

Irele, F. Abiola. "What Is Africa to Me? Africa in the Black Diaspora Imagination." *Souls* 7, no. 3–4 (Summer–Fall 2005): 26–46.

Ismaili-Abu Bakr, Rashidah. "Slightly Autobiographical: The 1960s on the Lower East Side." *African American Review* 27, no. 4 (1993): 585–89.

Isaacs, Harold R. "The American Negro and Africa: Some Notes." *Phylon* 20 (Fall 1959): 219–33.

———. "Back to Africa." *New Yorker*, May 13, 1961.

Johnson, Thomas A. "Renaissance in Black Poetry Expresses Anger." *New York Times*, April 25, 1969, 49.

Jones, Meta DuEwa. "Politics, Process and (Jazz) Performance: Amiri Baraka's 'It's Nation Time.'" *African American Review* 37, nos. 2/3 (Summer–Autumn 2003): 245–52.

Jones, Theodore. "Negro Boy Killed; 300 Harass Police." *New York Times*, July 17, 1964, 1.

Joseph, Peniel. "Where Blackness Is Bright? Cuba, Africa and Black Liberation during the Age of Civil Rights." *New Formations* 45 (Winter 2001–2): 111–24.

Joyce, Joyce A. "Gil Scott-Heron: Larry Neal's Quintessential Artist." In *So Far, So Good* by Gil Scott-Heron, 73–83. Chicago: Third World Press, 1990.

Ki-Zerbo, Joseph, et al. "Nation-building and Changing Political Values." In *UNESCO General History of Africa*. Vol. 8: *Africa since 1935*, ed. Ali A. Mazrui, 468–98. Berkeley: University of California Press, 1999.

Kelley, Robin D. G. "New Monastery: Monk and the Jazz Avant-Garde." *Black Music Research Journal* 19, no. 2 (Autumn 1999): 135–68.

———. "Into the Fire: 1970 to the Present." In *To Make Our World Anew: A History of African Americans*, ed. Robin D. G. Kelley and Earl Lewis. Oxford: Oxford University Press, 2000.

Knight, Frederick. "Justifiable Homicide, Police Brutality, or Government Repression? The 1962 Police Shooting of Seven Members of the Nation of Islam." *Journal of Negro History* 79, no. 2 (Spring 1994): 182–96.

"La. Senator Makes Visit to Mali Republic." *Chicago Daily Defender*, October 27, 1962, 3.

Lewis, Harold O. "American Education and Civil Rights in an International Perspective." *Journal of Negro Education* 34, no. 3 (Summer 1965): 239–48.

Massolo, Arthur. "Stevenson Tells Negroes to 'Proceed Gradually' toward Desegregation." *Greensboro Daily News*, February 8, 1956.

———. "Negro Leaders Deny Harlem Mad at Adlai." *New York Post*, September 9, 1956.

M'Bokolo, Elikia. "Equatorial West Africa." In *UNESCO General History of Africa*. Vol. 8: *Africa since 1935*, ed. Ali A. Mazrui, 192–220. Berkeley: University of California Press, 1999.

Michaels, Walter Benn. "Race into Culture: A Critical Genealogy of Cultural Identity." *Critical Inquiry* 18, no. 4 (1992): 655–85.

Moore, Richard B. "Africa Conscious Harlem." In *Harlem: A Community in Transition*, ed. John Henrik Clarke, 77–96. 3rd edition. New York: Citadel Press, 1964.

Morgan, Gordon D. "Exploratory Study of Problems of Academic Adjustment of Nigerian Studies in America." *Journal of Negro Education* 32, no. 3 (Summer 1963): 208–17.

Neal, Lawrence P. "Black Power in the International Context." In *The Black Power Revolt*, ed. Floyd Barbour, 136–46. Porter Sargeant: Boston, 1968.

Nkrumah, Kwame. "Peace! The World from African Eyes: Address by Osagayefo Kwame Nkrumah, President of the Republic of Ghana, September 23, 1960." Chicago: Afro-American Heritage Association, 1960.

Patterson, Tiffany Ruby, and Robin D .G. Kelley. "Unfinished Migrations: Reflections on the African Diaspora and the Making of the Modern World." *African Studies Review* 43, no. 1 (April 2000): 11–45.

Plummer, Brenda Gayle. "The Afro-American Response to the Occupation of Haiti, 1915–1934." *Phylon* 43, no. 2 (2nd quarter 1982): 125–43.

Rabaka, Reiland. "Malcolm X and/as Critical Theory: Philosophy, Radical Politics, and the African American Search for Social Justice." *Journal of Black Studies* 33, no. 2 (November 2002): 145–65.

Reston, James. "Copper Sun, Scarlet Sea, What Is Africa to Me?" *New York Times*, March 12, 1961.

"Riot in Gallery Halts U.N. Debate." *New York Times*, Feb. 16, 1961, 1.

Rodriguez, Besenia. "'De la Esclavitud Yanqui a la Libertad Cubana': U.S. Black Radicals, the Cuban Revolution and the Formation of a Tricontinental Ideology." *Radical History Review* 92 (Spring 2005): 62–87.

Rowe, Cyprian Lamar. "Crisis in African Studies: The Birth of the African Heritage Studies Association." *Black Academy Review* 1, no. 3 (Fall 1970): 3–10.

Sanchez, Sonia. "Ruminations/Reflections." In *Black Women Writers, 1950–1980: A Critical Evaluation*, ed. Mari Evans. New York: Doubleday, 1984.

Schanberg, Sydney H. "Legislature Meets Today." *New York Times*, January 3, 1968, 1, 2.

Self, Robert O. "'Negro Leadership and Negro Money': African American Political Organizing in Oakland before the Panthers." In *Freedom North: Black Freedom Struggles outside the South, 1940–1980*, ed. Jeanne Theoharis and Komozi Woodard, 93–124. New York: Palgrave MacMillan, 2003.

Shepperson, George. "Notes on Negro American Influences on the Emergence of African Nationalism." *Journal of African History* 1 (1960): 299–312.

———. "Pan-Africanism and pan-Africanism: Some Historical Notes." *Phylon* 23 (Winter 1962): 346–58.

Sibley, John. "2 Harlem Demands Accepted by Mayor." *New York Times*, August 7, 1964, 1, 12.

Skrentny, John David. "The Effect of the Cold War on African American Civil Rights: America and the World Audience, 1945–1968." *Theory and Society* 27, no. 2 (April 1968): 237–85.

Smethurst, James. "Poetry and Sympathy: New York, the Left and the Rise of Black Arts." In *Left of the Color Line: Race, Radicalism, and Twentieth Century Literature of the United States*, ed. Bill V. Mullen and James Smethurst. Chapel Hill: University of North Carolina Press, 2003.

———. "Black Arts South: Rethinking New Orleans and the Black Arts Movement in the Wake of Hurricane Katrina." In *Radicalism in the South since Reconstruction*, ed. Chris Green, Rachel Rubin, and James Smethurst, 128–47. New York: Palgrave MacMillan, 2006.

Stevenson, Adlai. "The New Africa: A Guide and a Proposal," *Harper's Magazine*, May 1960.

Taylor, Ula Y. "The Historical Evolution of Black Feminist Theory and Praxis." *Journal of Black Studies* 29, no. 2 (December 1998): 234–53.

Teague, Robert L. "Negroes Say Conditions in U.S. Explain Nationalists' Militancy: Negroes Explain Extremist Drives." *New York Times*, March 2, 1961, 1.

Thomas, Lorenzo. "The Shadow World: New York's Umbra Workshop and Origins of the Black Arts Movement." *Callaloo* 4 (October 1978): 53–72.

Thomas, Tansey. "A Very Black Sister." *Third World News*. May 27, 1971, 5.

Tinson, Christopher M. "Voice of the Black Protest Movement: Notes on the *Liberator* Magazine and Black Radicalism in the Early 1960s." *The Black Scholar* 37, no. 4 (Winter 2008): 1–15.

"Uganda Bars Ellender; Rips Segregation Views." *Chicago Daily Defender.* December 4, 1962.

Wallerstein, Immanuel. "Africa in the Capitalist World." In *The Essential Wallerstein*, 39–68. New York: New Press, 2000.

Walker, Victor Leo, II. "Archetype and Masking in LeRoi Jones/Amiri Baraka's *Dutchman*." In *Black Theatre: Ritual Performance in the African Diaspora*, ed. Paul Carter Harrison et al., 236–43. Philadelphia: Temple University Press, 2002.

Wilkinson, Michelle Joan. "In the Tradition of Revolution: The Socio-Aesthetics of Black and Puerto Rican Arts Movements, 1962–1982." Ph.D. dissertation, Emory University, 2001.

Williams, Rhonda Y. "Black Women, Urban Politics and Engendering Black Power." In *The Black Power Movement: Rethinking the Civil Rights—Black Power Era*, edited by Peniel Joseph, 79–104. New York: Routledge, 2006.

Williams, Walter L. "Black Journalism's Opinions about Africa during the Late 19th Century." *Phylon* 34 (September 1973): 224–35.

Woodard, Komozi. "Amiri Baraka, the Congress of African People, and Black Power Politics from the 1961 United Nations Protest to the 1972 Gary Convention." In *The Black Power Movement: Rethinking the Civil Rights—Black Power Era*, ed. Peniel E. Joseph. New York: Routledge, 2006.

ya Salaam, Kalamu. "Black Theatre—the Way It Is: An Interview with Woodie King, Jr." *African American Review* 31, no. 4 (Winter 1997): 647–58.

Index

Note: Page numbers in *italics* refer to illustrations.

AACCC. *See* Afro-American Cultural Center Committee
AASF. *See* African American Students Foundation
Abdul, Etta Bernice Shreeve, 78
Abdul, Hamid, 78
Abdul, Raoul, 78
Achebe, Chinua, 41
ACOA. *See* American Committee on Africa
"Act Black," 138
Action for South Africa, 24, 27
Actors, black: discrimination against, 189–90, 193–94; on television, 198. *See also* Film; Theater; *specific actors*
Adderley, Cannonball, 88
Addison, Florence, 64, 92
Adefumi, Baba Oseijerman, 211
Advertisements, LCA, 22, 34
Advisory board of *Liberator:* Baldwin in, 124, 125, 127; Communist Party ties to, 135; Davis in, 49, 124, 127; establishment of, 49; members in 1962, 49; members in 1963, 124; members in 1965, 177; number of members of, 147; women members of, 77
Aesthetics, 12, 185–234; African culture and, 188–90; autonomous institutions for, calls for, 186, 188, 193, 199, 200–201, 224, 226; and beauty standards for black women, 85–87, 96–97; evolution of *Liberator*'s coverage of, 186; of *Liberator*, Neal's impact on, 12, 181; scope of *Liberator*'s coverage of, 187. *See also* Artists; *specific genres*
Afra-Arts gallery, 221
Africa: African American understanding of, 69–70; culture of, 188–90; decline in *Liberator* coverage of, 62, 70, 72–73, 255n78; explosion of coups in, 66–67; independence in (*See* African independence); Malcolm X's travels in, 167–69; matrilineal customs in, 109; Soviet vs. U.S. influence in, 14, 15; Stevenson's influence on U.S. relations with, 18–19; tribalism in, 60; U.S. foreign policy toward, 44–45, 59. *See also specific countries*
Africa, Year of, 14, 15, 39
Africa Blood and Guts (film), 72
"Africa Freedom Day," 28
Africa Seen by American Negro Scholars (AMSAC), 41
Africa Unbound (Quaison-Sackey), 255n83
African-American Institute, 40, 252n23
African American Research Institute, 29
African Americans. *See* Men, African American; Women, African American; *specific issues, organizations, and people*
African American Students Foundation (AASF), 28, 47

African Cultural Group of the U.S.A., 190
African diaspora: on African independence, 17; and Diasporadas, 94; shifts in attitudes of, 14
African Freedom Day Observance, 77
African independence, 13–73; as central focus of *Liberator*, 1–2, 11, 22, 243n3; and Cold War, 14, 15; end of era of, 66–67; number of *Liberator* articles on, 45; number of nations achieving, 15; as part of struggle for black liberation in U.S., 32; Stevenson on, 18–19; UN role in, 54; U.S. organizations supporting, 27–32, 39–40. *See also specific countries*
African National Congress (ANC), 27, 58, 61
African Nationalist Pioneer Movement (ANPM), 32, 39, 86
"African Night Festival," 189
African Pilot (periodical), 42
African Review (periodical), 194
"African Roots of War" (Du Bois), 66, 104
African Scholarship Program of American Universities, 252n23
"African Scorecard," 66
African students, in U.S.: ACOA's connection to, 28, 47; Beveridge family sponsorship of, 27, 251n18; in Kennedy Airlift, 28, 59; *Liberator*'s coverage of, 45, 46–48; scholarships for, 47–48, 252n23
African Studies Association, 40
Africobra, 221, 225
Afric-sploitation films, 72, 256n114
Afro-American, use of term, 157
Afro-American Association, 137–38, 143
Afro-American Cultural Center Committee (AACCC), 137, 196
Afro-American Heritage Week, 77–78
Afro-American Institute, 143–45
Afro-American Research Institute, 122, 143–44
"Afro-American Woman" (Lomax), 95–96
"Afro-American Youth and the Bandung World" (Touré), 132, 141–42
"Afternoon in Africa, An" event, 189
Aguta, Margaret, 64, 92
Ahmad, Muhammad (Max Stanford): Cruse's influence on, 135; at "Forum 66" conference, 211; impact on radicalism of *Liberator*, 177; on Malcolm X, 166, 174; at National Afroamerican Student Conference, 133; in RAM, 166, 177; "Revolutionary Nationalism and the Afroamerican Student," 176; on Watts's interracial marriage, 68, 129
Ain't No Ambulances for No Nigguhs Tonight (Crouch), 232
Ain't Supposed to Die a Natural Death (Van Peebles), 194
Algarín, Miguel, 231
Algeria, 23, 57–58
"Algerian Story, The" (Gibson), 248n25
Alhambra Theatre, 200
Ali, Muhammad: boxing career of, 214; Sankore's letter to, 164–65; against Vietnam War, 105, 216–17
All-African Peoples' Conference, 45, 48
All-African Students Association, 49
All-African Students Union of the Americas, 48
Allen, Ernie, "Revolutionary Nationalism and the Class Struggle," 245n28
Allen, Robert L., 9
Alliances. *See* Interracial alliances
Amen Corner, The (Baldwin), 212–13
American Committee on Africa (ACOA), 27–29; and African students, 28, 47; establishment of, 27–28; in ideological spectrum, 40; Isaacs in,

14; LCA in competition with, 27, 28–29; mission of, 28
American Jewish Committee, 128
American National Theatre and Academy Playhouse (ANTA), 200
American Negro Leadership Conference on Africa (ANLCA), 40, 54–56
American-Nigerian Chamber of Commerce, 41–42
American Society of African Culture (AMSAC), 39–43; annual meetings of, 14, 41; Beveridge (Pete) in, 24; CIA ties to, 24, 41, 43; in Cold War, 40; cultural exchanges of, 41; establishment of, 40; in ideological spectrum, 39, 40; LCA in competition with, 27, 28–29; objectives of, 40; publishing projects of, 41; writer's conference of, 208
American Writer and His Roots, The (AMSAC), 41
AMSAC. *See* American Society of African Culture
ANC. *See* African National Congress
Angelou, Maya: activism of, 27; in *The Blacks*, 194; as expatriate in Ghana, 151, 168, 194; on March on Washington, 151; marriage to Make, 35; as Monroe Defense Committee sponsor, 34
Angola, 48–49, 252n28
ANLCA. *See* American Negro Leadership Conference on Africa
ANPM. *See* African Nationalist Pioneer Movement
ANTA. *See* American National Theatre and Academy Playhouse
Anthony, Paul, 227
Anticapitalism: in black radicalism, 3; of LCA, 33
Anticolonialism: as central focus of *Liberator*, 1–2, 13; Fanon's influence on, 153; *Liberator*'s coverage of, 44–46; in South Africa, 61; spread of, 3. *See also* African independence
Anti-imperialism: and civil rights movement, 45; of LCA, 29, 41; in perspective of *Liberator*, 41; spread of, 3
Anti-Semitism: Ellis on, 125–31; *Liberator* accused of, 121; Moore on, 130
Antubam, Kofi, 41
Apartheid, in Namibia, 54. *See also* South African apartheid
Arab students, in U.S., 46, 47
Architecture, Watts's career in, 16, 23, 111–12
Army, U.S., Beveridge (Pete) in, 26
Art and Social Change (Bradley and Esche), 218, 276n95
Artists, black, 12, 185–234; autonomous institutions for, calls for, 186, 188, 193, 199, 200–201, 224, 226; and Black Nationalism, 199–200; Neal on new wave of, 185–86, 187; in New York, 140, 218–21; political involvement by, 99, 186, 222; white judgment of value of, 205, 223–24, 227; women, 77, 94; works of, in *Liberator*, 77, 94, 218–21. *See also* Black Arts Movement; *specific artists and genres*
Association for the Study of Negro Life and History (ASNLH), 24, 27, 32, 63, 152
Athletes, black, 213–17
Atomic bomb, 62
Attica Blues (Shepp), 225
Autobiography of Malcolm X, 154
Autobiography of Martin Luther King Jr., 146
Avant garde, in jazz, 222
Azikiwe, Nnamdi, 43–44, 52–53

Baffoe, T. D., 62
Bain, Myrna, 93
Baker, Ella, 27

Baker, Houston, 241
Baldwin, James, 124–31; in ACOA events, 28; in advisory board of *Liberator*, 124, 125, 127, 177; *The Amen Corner*, 212–13; *Blues for Mr. Charlie*, 200; on Congo Crisis protests, 19; on cover of *Liberator*, 124; criticism of perspective of, 200, 210, 264n12; departure from *Liberator*, 121, 127–31; fame of, 124; impact on radicalism of *Liberator*, 12, 124–31; internationalism of, 124; on Jewish-black relations, 128–31; in LCA forums, 35, 125; as Monroe Defense Committee sponsor, 34; Neal on role of, 205, 210; "Not 100 Years of Freedom," 124–25; "Sonny's Blues," 139; writing in *Liberator*, 24, 125
Ballad for Bimshire (musical), 198
Baltimore Afro-American (newspaper), 51, 56, 67
Bambara, Toni Cade, 115–18; *The Black Woman*, 12, 103, 114; career of, 116, 118; education of, 116; *Gorilla My Love*, 116; in last years of *Liberator*, 236; "The Manipulators," 116; on origins of revolution, 119; *The Salt Eaters*, 116; *The Sea Birds Are Still Alive*, 116; "Sweet Town," 116; *Tales and Stories for Black Folk*, 116; transnationalism of, 117
Bandung Conference (1955), 15, 182
Baptista, Joao, 48–49
Baraka, Amiri (Leroi Jones): in BARTS, 122, 185, 212; "Black Art," 131, 182, 228; *Black Fire*, 212; *Black Mass*, 202, 208; *Black Music*, 278n127; *Blues People*, 147, 197, 204, 207; Cruse's influence on, 132; *Dutchman*, 202, 207; in editorial board of *Liberator*, 176–77; *Experimental Death Unit #1*, 212; impact on aesthetics of *Liberator*, 12; jazz criticism by, 221–22, 226; on March on Washington, 149–51; as Monroe Defense Committee sponsor, 34; Neal's articles on, 181–82, 202, 203–4, 207; on Neal's influence, 204; on *Raisin* (Hansberry), 90; *The Slave*, 203; *The Toilet*, 203, 212; and Touré, 140, 202; and Young Lords, 230
Bardonille, Priscilla, 86
Barth, Cecil Elombe, 86
Barth, Ronald, 86
BARTS. *See* Black Arts Repertory and Theater School
Baseball, 214–15, 216
Baseball Has Done It (Robinson), 216
Bashir, Mustapha, 140
Basketball, 213–14
Batsio, Kojo, 64
Battle-Kalibala, Evelyn. *See* Kalibala, Evelyn
Beal, Fran, 244n10; "Double Jeopardy," 9, 74, 96
Bearden, Romare, 221
Beauty standards, 85–87, 96–97
Belgium, 247n21. *See also* Congo Crisis
Belgrave, Cynthia, 91
Bell, Derrick, 184
Bell, Frederick, 97
Ben Bella, Ahmed, 57–58
Beveridge, Hortense "Tee" Sie, 24–27, 26; activism of, 24–27, 74–75; African students sponsored by, 27, 251n18; film career of, 25, 27; lack of articles in *Liberator*, 75; marriage of, 25–26; travels of, 25
Beveridge, Lowell "Pete," 24–27, 26; activism of, 24; on actors facing discrimination, 189; on African diplomats, 190; on African leaders, deaths of, 48–49; on African students, 48; African students sponsored by, 27, 251n18; in ASNLH, 63, 152; career of, 24; in Communist Party, 24, 46, 135; on Congo Crisis,

20, 46; departure from LCA, 24; in editorial board of *Liberator*, 24, 49, 121; education of, 46, 63; in establishment of LCA, 22; in executive board of *Liberator*, 197; financial support of *Liberator* by, 34; on Ford, 192; as frequent contributor to *Liberator*, 24; as ghost-writer for Watts, 267n81, 271n161; on growth of LCA and *Liberator*, 49, 123; on Hansberry, 78, 90–91; Hunton as mentor to, 50; impact on *Liberator*, 121; introduction to Watts, 16; on Malcolm X, 162; on Mandela, 53; on March on Washington, 145; marriage of, 25–26; roles in LCA, 23–24; roles in *Liberator*, 24, 121; "Two Faces of America," 59, 254n69; "Why AMSAC Festival Was a Flop," 42; Wilson recruited by, 152

Bigart, Homer, 127

"Big Brother" (Watts), 238–39

Bin-Hassan, Umar, 229–30, 232; *Suspenders*, 230

Birmingham, 16th Street Baptist Church bombing in, 89, 147

"Birth Control" (Watts), 112–13

Birth control, 103, 112–13

Black, C., 130

Black Americans. *See* Men, African American; Women, African American; *specific issues, organizations, and people*

"Black Art" (Baraka), 131, 182, 228

"Black Art and Fanon's Third Phase" (Fuller), 183

Black Arts Movement: Baraka's role in, 202; Detroit as locus of, 211, 275n70; emergence of, 86–87, 191–93, 204–5; "Forum 66" conference in, 211; and Harlem Renaissance, links between, 191; in ideological diversity of *Liberator*, 4; jazz in, 222; journals in, 6–7; literature in, 208; Neal's influence on, 181, 204–5; poetry in, 208, 212; regionalization in, 209–10; theater in, 192–94, 208; Touré in, 192; as translocal, 7; and Umbra Poets Workshop, 192; visual art in, 218–21; women's role in, 7. *See also specific artists and genres*

Black Arts Movement, The (Smethurst), 6–7

Black Arts Repertory and Theater School (BARTS), 122, 185, 204–5, 212

Black Boogaloo (Neal), 212

Black Bourgeoisie (Frazier), 176

Black Challenge, The (periodical), 40

Black consciousness: African culture in, 188–89; of athletes, 216; Baraka's approach to, 182

Black Fire (Neal and Baraka), 212

Black Ice (Patterson), 212

Black internationalism. *See* Internationalism

Black left, women pioneers of, 76–84

Black liberation: African independence as part of struggle for, 32; black consciousness in, 188–89; black journals on, 6–7; in ideological diversity of *Liberator*, 4, 132; *Liberator*'s coverage of struggle for, 20; Malcolm X in struggle for, 164–66, 174, 179, 182; white support for, 24, 127; women's role in, 7–8, 74–75, 77

Black Lives Matter, 241–42

Black Mass (Baraka), 202, 208

Black men. *See* Men

Black Music (Baraka), 278n127

"Black Music Predicament, The" (Qamar), 227–28

Black Muslims in America, The (Lincoln), 154, 155

"Black Muslims in Crisis" (Russell), 159–60

"Black Nationalism and the Arts" (Ford), 199–200

Black Nationalism: in art, 199–200; and beauty standards for women, 85–86; and Communist Party, 7; in community feminism, 244n10; in Congo Crisis protests, 17–18, 19–20, 30–31; Cruse on roots of, 134, 160, 199; and Harlem Riots, 170–72; in ideological spectrum of black radicalism, 4; and interracial marriage, 92; Malcolm X on definition of, 165, 166; after Malcolm X's assassination, 173; in Nation of Islam, 11; in origins of *Liberator*, 3; vs. radicalism, 11

Black Nationalism: A Search for an Identity in America (Essien-Udom), 154

Black Panther Party, 125, 142, 213

Black Power: Boggs on, 178, 182–83; in ideological diversity of *Liberator*, 4; *Liberator*'s anticipation of rise of, 1, 5; mainstream press on, 182; Watts's criticism of leaders of, 237–38; women's role in, 7

Black Power Movement, The (Joseph), 8

Black Power: The Politics of Liberation (Ture and Hamilton), 9

"Black Power: A Scientific Concept Whose Time Has Come" (Boggs), 178

"Black Power/White Backlash" (CBS News Special), 111

Black press. *See* Press

Black radicalism, 12, 120–84; Baldwin's influence on, 124–31; Black Nationalism in, 11; of Cruse, 131–36; cultural producers in, 123; Fanon's influence on, 153; ideological spectrum of, 4, 39, 132; as internationalist, 3; and Jewish-black relations, 125–31; *Liberator* in defining of, 5, 184; of Malcolm X (*See* X, Malcolm); and March on Washington, 145–51; New York as hub of, 32; origins of, 2; reemergence and rise of, in 1960s, 2–3; among students, 138; of Touré, 132–35, 139–42; tradition of, 9–11, 39; writing as form of activism in, 6

"Black Revolution in Music" (Neal), 224–25

Black Scholar (journal), 6

Black Sun (film), 88, 259n40

Black Tramp, The (White), 212

Black Woman, The: An Anthology (Bambara), 12, 103, 114, 116

"Black Woman to Black Man" (Stokes), 107–8

Black women. *See* Women

"Black Writer's Role, The" (Neal), 181, 205–8, 210

Blacks, The (Genet), 192, 194–95

Blancs, Les (Hansberry), 194

"Blues" (Sanchez), 99

Blues for Mr. Charlie (Baldwin), 200

Blues People (Baraka), 147, 197, 204, 207

Boggs, Grace Lee, 12, 83, 211

Boggs, James: on black population in urban areas, 112; on Black Power, 178, 182–83; "Black Power: A Scientific Concept Whose Time Has Come," 178; connections to East Coast, 211; on integration, 178; in last years of *Liberator*, 235

Boggs, Vernon, 70

Bogle, Donald, 199

Bogues, Anthony, 10–11

Bond, Horace Mann, 41

Bond, Jean Carey, 113–14

Book reviews, in *Liberator*, 12. *See also specific books*

Bookstores, black, 139

Booth, William H., 28

Bourgeois nationalism, 245n28

Bourgeois reformism, 133

Bowen, Robert, 222

Bowling, Frank, 221

Boxing, 214
Boyd, Herb, 128
Bradley, Will, *Art and Social Change*, 218, 276n95
Branton, Wiley, 64
Brasz, Marc, 222, 228
Brecht, Bertolt, *The Exception and the Rule*, 218
Breitman, George, 166
Briggs, Cyril, 197
Britain: in African coups, 66; Africans in, 65; in South African apartheid, 61, 62; Southern Rhodesia under, 65
Broadway theater, 189, 192, 193
Brooklyn Reform Democratic Club, 24
"Brother" (Scott-Heron), 236
Brown, James, 185
Brown, John, 80
Brown, Marion, 228, 278n136
Brown, Oscar, Jr., 87
Brummit, Houston, 193
Bryant, Hazel, 91
Bryant, Mary Ann, 85
Buckley, William F., 46
Buggs, Clara, 86
Bulger, Lucille, 81, 89
Bullins, Ed, 201
Bunche, Ralph, 19, 20, 78, 257n10
Burgos, Adrian, Jr., 214–15
Burrows, Vinie, 93
Burundi, 62
Businesses, black, call for expansion of, 137–38
Butler, Barbara, 106–7, 262n109
"Buy Black," 138

CAA. *See* Council on African Affairs
Cabral, Amilcar, 28
Cade, Toni. *See* Bambara, Toni Cade
Caine, Michael, 201
California: distribution of *Liberator* in, 33; *Liberator*'s coverage of, 137–38; Nation of Islam in, 155–56

"California Revolt, The" (Warden), 137–38
Callender, Herbert, 162, 269n126
Cambridge, Edmund, 193, 198
Cambridge, Godfrey, 198
Cameroon, 48
CANA. *See* Committee for the Advancement of the Negro in Architecture
Capitalism: anti-, 3, 33; racial, 9, 29, 33, 44
Carlson, Kenneth, *Radical Ideas and the Schools*, 10
Carmichael, Stokely (Kwame Ture), 9, 111; *Black Power*, 9
Carroll, Vinnette, 91
Cartoons, in *Liberator*, 170, 240
Carty, Leo, 151, 170, 176, 219
Catlett, Elizabeth, 94
CAWAH. *See* Cultural Association for Women of African Heritage
CBS, "Black Power/White Backlash" News Special on, 111
CENP. *See* Committee for the Employment of Negro Performers
"Centennial Celebration of the Birth of Tuskegee" (Stevens), 225
Central African Students' Union of America, Inc., 47
Central Intelligence Agency (CIA): in African coups, 66; AMSAC ties to, 24, 41, 43; in Ghana, 168
Chicago, in Black Arts Movement, 275n70
Chicago Defender (newspaper), 59
Childress, Alice, 27
China! (film), 217
Chinnery, Lois, 97
Chisholm, Shirley, 24
Chrichlow, Ernest, 27
Christianity: feminist critique of, 100–101; Malcolm X's critique of, 178
CIA. *See* Central Intelligence Agency

Circulation and distribution, of *Liberator*: in Detroit, 33, 211; expansion of, 138–39; in first years, 33–34, 45, 123–24

Citizen Care Committee, 81

Civil Rights Act of 1964, 145, 151

Civil rights movement: achievements of, 2; and anti-imperial movement, 45; criticism of leaders of, 111, 148, 171; Freedom Rides in, 36, 50; gradualism in, 3, 19, 35, 145; impact of March on Washington on, 145–46; Jewish support for, 127; LCA on, 35–36; limitations of, 2–3; Malcolm X on, 164; in rise of black radicalism, 2–3

Clark, Edward, 221

Clark, Kenneth, 107

Clark, Mamie Phipps, 107

Clarke, Austin, *The Meeting Point*, 116

Clarke, John Henrik: on African independence, 31; on African influences in Harlem, 60; in *The American Writer and His Roots*, 41; and Davis's letter on Jewish-black relations, 129; in editorial board of *Liberator*, 24; and Ghanaian coup, 65–66; in Harlem Writer's Guild, 191; on ideological spectrum of radicalism, 39, 40; as Monroe Defense Committee sponsor, 34; and National Afroamerican Student Conference, 133; on Nation of Islam, 154–55; "The New Afro-American Nationalism," 13, 36, 140, 187; on Powell, 159, 269n116; and *Purlie Victorious* (Davis), 198; Russell's (Charlie) introduction to, 139

Clay, Cassius. *See* Ali, Muhammad

Cleage, Albert, 142–43; on cover of *Liberator*, 126; in Freedom Now Party, 269n124; LCA's praise for, 36; "Struggle for Survival," 160

Clean-city campaigns, 89

Cleveland (Ohio), Afro-American Institute in, 143–45

Clothing, African-derived styles of, 86, 259n35

CNA. *See* Committee for the Negro in the Arts

Coffee Concerts, 78

Cohen, Hettie, 207

"Cold Reception for AMSAC in Nigeria, A" (*Liberator*), 42

Cold War: and African independence, 14, 15; AMSAC in, 40; Council on African Affairs during, 29

Coleman, Gladys, 81

Coleman, Ornette, 222, 223, 224, 228

Collins, Addie Mae, 89, 147

Colonialism, economic, 127. *See also* Anticolonialism

Colony, domestic/internal: African Americans as, 3; Harlem as, 172

Color Curtain, The (Wright), 182

Coltrane, John, 225, 227, 228

Columbia University, 107

Combahee River Collective, 119

Committee for the Advancement of the Negro in Architecture (CANA), 16

Committee for the Employment of Negro Performers (CENP), 189–90, 193–94

Committee for the Negro in the Arts (CNA), 16, 25

Committee on Race and Class in World Affairs (CORAC), 41

Common Sense Clinic, 83

Communist Party: Beveridge (Pete) in, 24, 46, 135; Beveridge (Tee) in, 25; and Black Nationalism, 7; Cruse in, 135

Community feminism, 4, 100, 244n10

Community League on 159th Street, 81

Concerned Black Women, 96

Congo, tribalism in, 60

Congo Crisis, 17–22; Black Nationalist protests on, 17–18, 19–20, 30–31; LCA's response to, 14, 17–22, 30, 53;

Liberator's coverage of, 14, 20, 45–46, 53, 247n21. *See also* Lumumba, Patrice
Congress of Racial Equality (CORE): and Afro-American Institute, 144; Boggs (Vernon) on, 70; jazz at, 228; in Lee's trip to Harlem, 68; radicalization of, 122; on residential segregation, 84; women's role in, 84
Connor, James, 235
Conscription, in Vietnam War, 104–5
Contraception. *See* Birth control
Cook, Mercer, 41
Cooks, Carlos, 32, 39–40, 86
Cool World, The (Miller), 194
CORAC. *See* Committee on Race and Class in World Affairs
CORE. *See* Congress of Racial Equality
Cortez, Jayne, 222
Cosby, John, Jr., 105
Council on African Affairs (CAA): and Action for South Africa, 27; AMSAC formation as response to, 40; Beveridges in, 25–26, 50; dissolution of, 29
Coups: explosion of, in 1965–66, 66–67; in Ghana (1966), 64, 65–67
Cover, of *Liberator*: art by women on, 77; Baldwin on, 124; Cleage on, *126*; Davis and Dee on, 80, 128, 189; Hansberry on, *79, 90*; Malcolm X on, 160, *175*; Nelmes on, 86; Powell on, *150*; Richardson on, 81, *82*
Crawford, Vicki L., 76
Cricket (periodical), 226
Crisis of the Negro Intellectual, The (Cruse), 78, 122, 132, 134–35, 136
"Criticism Is Not Anti-Semitism" (Moore), 130, 197
Crouch, Stanley, *Ain't No Ambulances for No Nigguhs Tonight*, 232
Cruse, Harold, 131–36; and Afro-American Institute, 144; *The Crisis of the Negro Intellectual*, 78, 122, 132, 134–35, 136; criticism of *Liberator* by, 122, 132, 134; cultural revolution called for by, 132–34; departure from *Liberator*, 135–36; "The Economics of Black Nationalism," 134, 169–70; Gibson's feud with, 22; on Harlem as domestic colony, 172; on ideological diversity of *Liberator*, 132; impact on radicalism of *Liberator*, 12, 120–22, 135; on interracial alliances, 131–32, 134; on Jewish-black relations, 135; "Marxism and the Negro," 134; *Rebellion or Revolution?*, 120, 122, 134, 244n8; "Rebellion or Revolution?," 133–34, 147, 196–97; "The Roots of Black Nationalism," 134, 160, 199; "Third Party," 134; Touré influenced by, 132, 135, 142
"Crux of Black Non-Violence, The" (Schomburg), 83
"Cry Freedom" (Touré), 140, 192, 209
Cry in the Night (Greenwood), 196
Cry of My People, The (Shepp), 225
Cuba, 23
Cudjoe, Selwyn, 70–72
Cultural Association for Women of African Heritage (CAWAH), 32, 39
Cultural events: of LCA, 188, 189, 190; rise of *Liberator*'s coverage of, 188–89
Cultural genealogy, 206
Cultural heritage, in identity of black radicals, 3
Cultural nationalism, 3, 178–79
Cultural producers, black radicals as, 123
Cultural revolution, Cruse's call for, 132–34
Culture: African, *Liberator*'s coverage of, 188–90; black folk, 224
Cumbo, Kattie, 89–90, 102, 177, 259n47

Danska, Herbert, 229
Dark to Dark (Russell), 139

Dark, Alvin, 214
Davis, John A., 41
Davis, Ossie, 127–30; as advisor to LCA, 81; in advisory board of *Liberator*, 49, 124, 127, 177; in *Ballad for Bimshire*, 198; and CENP, 190; on cover of *Liberator*, 80, 128, 189; departure from *Liberator*, 121, 127–30; on Genet's plays, 195; on Jewish-black relations, 128–29; in Lee's trip to Harlem, 68; *Liberator*'s honoring of, 81, 128; on Malcolm X, 180; as Monroe Defense Committee sponsor, 34; in Negro History Week, 88, 189; *Purlie Victorious*, 128, 189, 198–99
DeCarava, Roy, 27, 173, 218–20; *The Sound I Saw*, 220; *The Sweet Flypaper of Life*, 220
Dee, Ruby: and CENP, 190; on cover of *Liberator*, 80, 128, 189; in Lee's trip to Harlem, 68; *Liberator*'s honoring of, 81, 128; as Monroe Defense Committee sponsor, 34; in Negro History Week, 88, 189; in *The Nurses*, 198; in *Purlie Victorious*, 198
Defender of the Angels (Kimbrough), 117
Demonstrations. *See* Protests
Dent, Tom, 140
Derby, Doris, 201
Desegregation. *See* Integration
Detroit: distribution of *Liberator* in, 33, 211; "Forum 66" conference in, 211; as locus of Black Arts Movement, 211, 275n70; Northern Negro Grassroots Leadership Conference in, 83, 160
"Development of Leroi Jones" (Neal), 181, 207
Diaspora. *See* African diaspora
Diasporadas, 94
Dissent (magazine), 179, 271n177
Dissident press, 8, 10
Distribution, of *Liberator*. *See* Circulation and distribution

Dixon, Ivan, 217
Doe, Christie, 27
Domestic Personal Service Workers, 96
Donaldson, Jeff, 231
Donaldson, Lou, 258n34
"Double Jeopardy" (Beal), 9, 74, 96
Douglas, Emory, 276n95
Douglass, Frederick, 157, 158
Down Beat (magazine), 221, 223–24, 226, 277n107, 278n126
Draft, in Vietnam War, 104–5
Drake, St. Clair: in *Africa Seen by American Negro Scholars*, 41; at ANLCA, 55; on black organizations, 40; on Ghanaian independence, 51; "Negro Americans, the African Interest, and Power Structures in Africa and America," 55, 254n51
Drug abuse, 80
Du Bois, Shirley Graham, 65, 76, 168, 194
Du Bois, W. E. B.: "African Roots of War," 66, 104; in Council on African Affairs, 29; death of, 151, 196; *Encyclopedia Africana* project of, 52; Garvey's conflict with, 142; and Hunton, 50, 252n31; LCA on, 36; on "rising tide of color," 13; *The World and Africa*, 44
Duganne, Erina, 219
Dust Tracks on Road (Hurston), 212
Dutchman (Baraka), 202, 207

East Side, West Side (television show), 198
Ebony (magazine), 96–97, 212
Economic colonialism, 127
Economic imperialism, 47
Economic justice, 2
Economic nationalism, 85
Economic segregation, 35–36
Economic self-sufficiency, 3

"Economics of Black Nationalism, The" (Cruse), 134, 169–70
Editorial board of *Liberator*: Ford in, 176, 195, 201; Gibson in, 67, 69; members in 1961, 24; members in 1962, 49; members in 1965, 176–77; Riley in, 176, 214
Education: Beveridge's (Pete) interest in, 46; as function of *Liberator*, 63; integration in, 101–2, 137; radicalism in theories of, 9–10. *See also* Students
Edwards, Brent Hayes, 5
Edwards, Harry, 215
Ellender, Allen J., 59
Ellington, Duke, 205
Ellis, Eddie: on black-Jewish relations, 125–31; in Black Panther Party, 125, 213; "Is Revolutionary Theatre in Tune with the People?," 213; in meeting with *Ebony*, 97; theater criticism by, 213
Ellison, Ralph: Baldwin compared to, 124; *Invisible Man*, 140, 153, 203, 206; Neal on role of, 181, 205–6; *Shadow and Act*, 203
Emancipation Proclamation, 80, 124; Centennial of, 157, 158
Emasculation, 108, 113–14
Encyclopedia Africana (Du Bois and Hunton), 52
Endfield, Cy, 201
Engel, Julien, 252n23
Epton, Bill, 61, 146
Erby, Nelson, 125
Esannason, Harold, 219
Esche, Charles, *Art and Social Change*, 218, 276n95
Essien-Udom, E. U., *Black Nationalism: A Search for an Identity in America*, 154
Ethel Barrymore Theatre, 212
Evers, Medgar, 146
Exception and the Rule, The (Brecht), 218

Exiles, intellectuals as, 38–39
"Exiles No More" (Tillman), 160
Expatriates, African American, in Ghana, 151–52, 168
Experimental Death Unit #1 (Baraka), 212

Fair Play for Cuba Committee (FPCC), 22, 23, 34, 138
Family life: in Africa, 109; matriarchal, 109, 110, 114; Moynihan Report on, 110
Fanon, Frantz, 135, 153; *The Wretched of the Earth*, 153, 183
"Farewell to Liberals" (Miller), 243n6
Farmer, James, 36, 64, 145
Farred, Grant, 122–23
Faubus, Orval, 68
Fax, Elton, 41
Federal Bureau of Investigation (FBI), 25, 26
Feelings, Muriel, *Zamani Goes to Market*, 219
Feelings, Tom, 105, 176, 197, 219, 235; *Zamani Goes to Market*, 219
Feminism: black left, 76–84; community, 4, 100, 244n10; organizational phase of black, 262n103; second wave, 74, 106
Figueiredo, Elisio, 49, 252n28
Films: Afric-sploitation, 72, 256n114; reviews of, in *Liberator*, 12, 116, 201, 217. *See also specific films*
Finances: of LCA, 34; of *Liberator*, 34, 45, 123, 236, 237
Finkenstaedt, James, 33, 134, 158, 197
Finkenstaedt, Rose: arrival at *Liberator*, 33; on black voters, 80; on black women activists, 81; on distribution of *Liberator*, 33; on drug abuse, 80; on Nation of Islam, 81, 158; "Never on Christmas," 158; as staff writer for *Liberator*, 77; "Which Road to Freedom?," 143

Fire Music (Shepp), 225
Fitch, Bob, 66
Five Spot (jazz club), 221–22, 223
Fletcher, Robert, 61
FLN. *See* National Liberation Front
Flood, Curt, 216
Folk culture, black, 224
Food, African, 190
For Love of Ivy (film), 88
Ford, Clebert, 192–202; acting career of, 192, 194–95, 201; advocacy for black theater by, 186, 193–95, 198, 200–202; on autonomous artistic institutions, need for, 186, 193, 199, 200–201; "Black Nationalism and the Arts," 199–200; in CENP, 189–90, 193–94; departure from *Liberator*, 201; in editorial board of *Liberator*, 176, 195, 201; in executive board of *Liberator*, 197; film reviews by, 201; on Gregory, 195, 196; at March on Washington, 146; "The Responsibility of Black Artists," 195; on television shows, 198; theater criticism by, 192, 194–95, 198, 200; on Umbra Poets Workshop, 192; writing career of, 192
Ford Foundation, 42
Fordham University, Watts at, 238, 239–40
Foreign policy, U.S., toward Africa, 44–45, 59
Forman, James, 68, 151
"Forum 66" conference, 211
Foster, Wendell, 28
Four Lives in the Be-Bop Business (Spellman), 228
FPCC. *See* Fair Play for Cuba Committee
Fraser, Len, Jr., 133
Frazier, E. Franklin, 41; *Black Bourgeoisie*, 176
"Frederick Douglass and Emancipation" (Moore), 158

Freedom (newsletter), 26, 50, 90
Freedom Now Party, 269n124
Freedom Rides, 36, 50
Freedomways (journal): on *The Blacks* (Genet), 195; Clarke's role in, 24; Davis's letter on Jewish-black relations in, 129; duration of, 236; Howard's articles in, 57; ideology of, vs. *Liberator*, 143; influence on *Liberator*, 77; and National Afroamerican Student Conference, 133; support for *Liberator* from, 49
Freeman, Al, Jr., 200, 230
Freeman, Donald, 133, 144–45
Free Southern Theatre, 200–201
FRELIMO. *See* Mozambique Liberation Front
Fuller, C. H., Jr., "Black Art and Fanon's Third Phase," 183
Fuller, Meta Vaux Warrick, 94
Fundi (film), 27

Gaines, Kevin, 168
Galamison, Milton, 191
Gandhi, Mahatma, 10
Garment workers, 80, 130
Garnett, Henry Highland, 173
Garrison, Jimmy, 223, 224
Garvey, Amy Jacques, 244n10
Garvey, Marcus, 86, 141, 142, 144
Garveyism, 32, 141
Gaston, Rosetta, 152
Gayle, Addison, 236
Gbedey, Regine, 64, 92
Gender: in Black Arts Movement, 7; hierarchy of, 96, 108–9. *See also* Men; Women
Genealogy, cultural, 206
Genet, Jean, *The Blacks*, 192, 194–95
Ghana: African American expatriates in, 151–52, 168; Angelou in, 151, 168, 194; coup of 1966 in, 64, 65–67; Du Bois's death in, 151; independence for

(*See* Ghanaian independence); Malcolm X's travels in, 168–69; and March on Washington, 151–52; Organization of Afro-American Unity in, 168–69; in UN, 63–64, 255n83
Ghana Evening News (newspaper), 51
Ghanaian Broadcasting Corporation, 194
Ghanaian independence, 14–15; fifth anniversary of, 43–44; Howard on, 57; independence of other African nations linked to, 15, 50; Kennedy on, 59; LCA on, 14, 17; *Liberator*'s coverage of, 14, 43–44, 50–52; and pan-African unity, 15, 43–44
Ghanaian Times (newspaper), 62, 151, 194
Gibson, Katy, 92
Gibson, Ray, 228
Gibson, Richard, 22–23; activism of, 22–23, 34; on African American understanding of Africa, 69–70; on Algerian revolution, 57–58; "The Algerian Story," 248n25; on Black Nationalist protest at UN, 18; on East African independence, 67; in editorial board of *Liberator*, 67, 69; in establishment of LCA, 22; as executive secretary of LCA, 23–24; as frequent contributor to *Liberator*, 24; on Ghanaian coup, 65–66; home of, 18, 32; on Israel, 69; in last years of *Liberator*, 235; on Make (Vusumzi), 35; as Monroe Defense Committee sponsor, 34; on Moynihan, 111; on Quaison-Sackey, 64; questions about credibility of, 67–68, 248n25; in *Révolution Africaine*, 22, 56, 58, 67; "Richard Gibson Reports" by, 22, 72; role at *Liberator*, 22, 65, 235, 248n25; travels of, 22, 23, 58, 64–65; Watts's friendship with, 22, 23, 68
Gibson, Sarah, 58

Gilligan, Thomas, 170, 171
Gizenga, Antoine, 53
Glasgow, Adele, 78
Golden, Maurice, 33
Goldman, Phaon, 174
Goldwater, Barry, 68
Gomez, Michael, 154
Goncalves, Carlos, 78, 125
Gone Are the Days (film), 199
Gonzales, Juan, 230
Gore, Dayo, 76, 249n45
Gorilla My Love (Bambara), 116
Gospel music, 224
Gosse, Van, 255n78
Gradualism, civil rights, 3, 19, 35, 145
Graffiti artists, 221
Grandassa Models of Harlem, 86, 258n34
Graves, Milford, 224–25
Gray, Jesse, 162
Grayson, William, 97
Great Britain. *See* Britain
Great Society, 95
Greene, Felix, 217
Greenwood, Frank, 137, 196; *Cry in the Night*, 196
Greenwood, Vera, 196
Gregory, Dick, 195, 196, 229
Grey, Jesse, 34
Grimes, Henry, 228
Guardian, The (newspaper), 52
Guns at Batasi (film), 217
Guy, Rosa, 27, 30–31
Guzman, Yoruba, 230
Gyando, Eddy, 27, 251n18

Hairstyles, black, 85–86
Hambrick, Edith, 108
Hamilton, Bobb, 211
Hamilton, Charles, *Black Power*, 9
Hammarskjöld, Dag, 17–18, 19, 247n21
Hampton, Fred, 142

Hansberry, Lorraine: activism of, 27, 78; in Afro-American Heritage Week, 78; *Les Blancs*, 194; career of, 90–91; Coffee Concerts sponsored by, 78; on Congo Crisis protests, 19–20; on cover of *Liberator, 79,* 90; death of, 90; and Kennedy Airlift, 28; *Liberator*'s tribute to, 90–91; marriage of, 92; Negro History Week speech by, 78, 125; *A Raisin in the Sun*, 90, 91; *The Sign in Sidney Brustein's Window*, 91, 203; support for *Liberator* by, 78

Hansberry, William Leo, 41

Happy Ending (Ward), 202

Harlem: African influences in, 60–61; basketball in, 213–14; black women activists in, 81, 89; as domestic colony, 172; Jewish-black relations in, 125, 128; Lee's visit to, 68; Mboya's visit to, 70–72; Nation of Islam in, 154; police brutality in, 89; Riots of 1964 in, 170–72; visual arts in, 218–21

Harlem Anti-Colonial Committee, 61

Harlem Defense Council (HDC), 170–71

Harlem Parents Committee, 68

Harlem People's Parliament, 68, 211

Harlem Renaissance, 191

Harlem Writer's Guild (HWG): duration of, 236; on Lumumba's assassination, 19; and On Guard for Freedom, 30; Russell (Carlos) in, 191; Russell (Charlie) in, 139, 191, 197

Harlem Youth Unlimited (HARYOU), 125, 171

Harper's Magazine, 18–19

Harrison, Bonnie Claudia, 94

HARYOU. *See* Harlem Youth Unlimited

"Has Jazz Lost Its Roots?" (Russell), 223

Hatch, James, 91

Hate That Hate Produced, The (documentary), 159

HDC. *See* Harlem Defense Council

Henderson, David, "Keep On Pushin'," 209

Hentoff, Nat, 223, 226

Hernton, Calvin, 140; "Jitterbuggin' in the Streets," 209

Hetherington, H. A., 52

Hicks, Calvin, 18, 19, 32, 34, 250n59

Hill, Adelaide Cromwell, 41

Hill, Errol, 91

Hobson, Charles, 224

Holocaust, 127, 130

Holt, Len: in advisory board of *Liberator*, 49; on civil rights movement in South, 258n28; in editorial board of *Liberator*, 176; on Freedom Rides, 50; on Harlem Riots, 171–72; on Malcolm X, 182

Homegirls (Smith), 116

Homosexuality, of Rustin, 180

Honeybaby, Honeybaby (film), 27

Hooks, Robert, 202, 229

Hoover, J. Edgar, 147

"Hot Irons and Black Nationalism" (Mason), 85

Houser, George, 28

Housing discrimination, 84

Howard, Charles P.: on African coups, 66–67; on African leaders, deaths of, 57; career of, 56–57; at "Forum 66" conference, 211; News Syndicate of, 57, 66–67; as UN correspondent, 56–57, 62; on Verwoerd's assassination, 68

Howard University, 72

Hughes, Langston: and Abdul (Raoul), 78; on African influences in Harlem, 60; Coffee Concerts sponsored by, 78; in Harlem Writer's Guild, 191; "Junior Addict," 191, 192; and Neal, 205; "The Negro Artist and the Racial Mountain," 1, 2, 195; "The Negro Speaks of Rivers," 78; *The Prodigal Son*, 218; support for

Liberator by, 130, 265n25; *The Sweet Flypaper of Life*, 220; *Tambourines to Glory*, 198
Hughes, Virginia, 93
Human rights, Malcolm X on, 164, 172
Humphrey, Dona, 97
Hunton, Dorothy, 50, 51, 76
Hunton, W. Alpheaus: in Council on African Affairs, 29; and Du Bois, 50, 252n31; *Encyclopedia Africana* project of, 52; on Ghanaian independence, 51; praise for LCA from, 50
Hurston, Zora Neale: *Dust Tracks on Road*, 212; *Jonah's Gourd Vine*, 212
Hurwitz, Leo, 27
HWG. *See* Harlem Writer's Guild

IATSE. *See* International Alliance of Theatrical Stage Employees
Identity, of black radicals, 3
Ideological diversity, in *Liberator*, 4, 132
"I Have a Dream" (King), 146
ILGWU. *See* International Ladies Garment Workers Union
Imperialism: economic, 47; in Vietnam War, 103–4. *See also* Anti-imperialism
Indignant Generation, The (Jackson), 6
Institute for International Education, 46
Integration: of baseball, 216; black women in debate over, 89–90, 101–2; and interracial marriage, 92; Neal on, 177–79; school, 101–2, 137; vs. separatism, debate over, 5; skepticism in *Liberator* about, 35–36; in theater, 194; Touré on, 142; Watts on, 35–36, 55
Intellectuals: African, 11, 40; as exiles, 38–39; vernacular, 123
Internal colony, African Americans as, 3
International Alliance of Theatrical Stage Employees (IATSE), 25
Internationalism, black: Africa as central to, 243n3; of Baldwin, 124; in black radicalism, 3; of LCA, 31; in *Liberator*, 5–6; of Malcolm X, 164, 166; of Touré, 140–42
International Ladies Garment Workers Union (ILGWU), 80, 130
Interracial alliances: Black Panther Party on, 142; Cruse on, 131–32, 134; in LCA, 17, 33; Rustin on, 179; Watts on, 157–58
Interracial dating and marriage: by Beveridges, 25–26; by Hansberry, 92; Jewish, 127; *Liberator*'s coverage of, 92, 107; by Watts, 68, 92, 127, 129
In the Castle of My Skin (Lamming), 208
Invisible Man (Ellison), 140, 153, 203, 206
Isaacs, Harold R., 14; *The New World of Negro Americans*, 60, 254n73
"Is *Ebony* Killing Black Women" (Rodgers), 96–97
Ismaili Abu Bakr, Rashidah, 140; "Scenes of Home," 105
Israel, 47, 69
Israeli Socialist Organization, 69
"Is Revolutionary Theatre in Tune with the People?" (Ellis), 213
Iton, Richard, 187

Jackson, Donald, 64
Jackson, Esther Cooper, 76–77
Jackson, Lawrence, 38, 39; *The Indignant Generation*, 6
Jacobson, Helen, 78
Japan: atomic bomb used in, 62; Lincoln and Roach on tour in, 87–88; Winter Olympics in, 215
Jazz, 221–28; free, 222, 223, 224; in Japan, 87–88; Malcolm X's speeches compared to, 204; and politics, 222; rise in mainstream attention to, 221–22; spirituality of, 224–25, 226–27; Thomas (Bedwick) inspired by, 220; and visual art, 220, 225; white audience of, 222, 223–24, 227

Jazz criticism, in *Liberator*, 187, 222–28; by Brasz, 222, 228; by Neal, 222, 224–26; by Qamar, 222, 227–28; by Russell (Charlie), 198, 222, 224; by Spellman, 222, 228
Jazz poetry, 228–32
Jerome, Jocelyn, 61
Jett, Ruth, 27
Jewish-black relations: Baldwin on, 128–31; in civil rights movement, 127; Cruse on, 135; Davis on, 128–29; Ellis's series on, 125–31; Neal on, 210–11. *See also* Anti-Semitism
"Jitterbuggin' in the Streets" (Hernton), 209
Joans, Ted, 222
Johnson, Audrey, 78
Johnson, Edwina, 93
Johnson, John H., 96
Johnson, Lyndon, 64, 93, 95
Johnson, M. P., 107
Johnson, Roy, 200
Jonah's Gourd Vine (Hurston), 212
Jones, Bill, 61
Jones, Elayne V., 27
Jones, Leroi. *See* Baraka, Amiri
Joseph, Peniel, 138, 155; *The Black Power Movement*, 8
Joyce, Joyce A., 232
"Junior Addict" (Hughes), 191, 192

Kahn, Eddie, 88
Kahn, Tom, 179
Kain, Gylan, 229–30, 232
Kajumbula, Nancy, 64, 92
Kalibala, Ernest, 24, 59
Kalibala, Evelyn: activism of, 27; in editorial board of *Liberator*, 49; in executive board of *Liberator*, 197; in last years of *Liberator*, 235; as secretary at *Liberator*, 177; as social director of LCA, 24, 77

Kamoinge Gallery and Workshop, 219–20
Karenga, Maulana, 138
Kaunda, Kenneth, 28
"Keep On Pushin'" (Henderson), 209
Keita, Modibo, 63
Kelley, Robin D. G., 3, 186, 222
Kennedy, John F.: on ACOA, 28; Africa policy of, 59; assassination of, 151, 160, 221; black leaders recruited by, 64; on March on Washington, 148; Watts's criticism of, 147
Kennedy, Robert, 147
Kennedy Airlift, 28, 59
Kenya, 67, 70–72
Kerina, Jane, 27
Kerina, Mbrumba, 27, 28
Kessler, Lauren, 8
Keutcha, Julienne, 64, 92
Killens, John O., 30, 35, 135, 191, 211
Kilson, Martin, 41
Kimbrough, Jess, *Defender of the Angels*, 117
King, Charles T. O., II, 263n116
King, Martin Luther, Jr.: and ACOA, 28; autobiography of, 146; cartoons of, in *Liberator*, 170; criticism of, in *Liberator*, 5, 36, 80, 98, 111, 145, 147–48; "I Have a Dream," 146; Malcolm X on, 165–66; in March on Washington, 145–49; Poor People's March led by, 106; radicalism of, 10; U.S. government interests in Africa represented by, 64; on Vietnam War, 103, 262n92
King, Woodie, 201, 202, 229–30, 274n39
Kochiyama, Yuri, 68
Kofsky, Frank, 226
Kooper, Markus, 27
Korean War, 26
Kotto, Yaphet, 217
Kozonguizi, Jariretundu, 27, 59

Kulchur (periodical), 226
Kwanguvu, Umoja, 131

Labor Youth League, 25
Lacy, Leslie, 168
LaGrone, Oliver, 211
Lamb, Lucretia, 81
Lamming, George, *In the Castle of My Skin*, 208
Last Poets, The, 229–32
Lateef, Yusef, 88
Lawrence, Jacob, 27, 41, 221
Lawson, James, 32
LCA. *See* Liberation Committee for Africa
Leaks, Sylvester, 61, 198
Lee, Carl, 198
Lee, Don (Haki Madhubuti), 232; "A Poem for Black Women," 106
Lee, Franz J. T., 68
Left: New, 4, 37, 121; Old, 4, 33, 135; women pioneers of, 76–84
"Legacy of Malcolm X, The" (Spellman), 176
"Lenox Avenue Sunday" (Neal), 209
"Leroi Jones Will Get Us All in Trouble" (Russell), 199
Lev, Ray, 27
Lewis, Edmonia, 94
Lewis, Ida, 78
Liberalism: failure of, 3, 243n6; Neal's critique of, 210–11
Liberation Committee for Africa (LCA), 11, 14–37; aims of, 16–17, 20; anticapitalism of, 33; on civil rights movement, 35–36; in competition with other organizations, 27–29; complexity of challenges facing, 29; on Congo Crisis, 14, 17–22, 30, 53; cultural events of, 188, 189, 190; establishment of, 16, 20, 22, 29, 122; executive committee of, 23–24, 190; on Ghanaian independence, 14, 17;

"Nationalism, Colonialism, and the United States" forum by, 35; origins of *Liberator* in, 4, 11, 20; pan-Africanism of, 31; white allies in, 17, 33; women's influence on, 76–77. *See also specific members*
Liberator: advisory board of (*See* Advisory board); central focus of, 1–2, 11, 20; circulation of (*See* Circulation); cover of (*See* Cover); decline of, 233, 235–36; as "dissident" press, 8, 10; editorial board of (*See* Editorial board); executive board of, 147, 197; finances of, 34, 45, 123, 236, 237; gaps in scholarship on, 1, 8; ideological diversity in, 4, 132; influence of, 3–4; legacy of, 12, 240–42; logo of, 219; masthead of, 13, 20, 91, 93, 224; origins of, 3–4, 11; production of, 33, 77, 121, 235. *See also specific articles, topics, and writers*
Liberator volume 1 (1961): March (first issue), 20, 48; June, 48; July, 154–55; September, 45, 251n15; December, 45–46, 47; lack of volume number for, 251n15
Liberator volume 2 (1962): January, 189; February, 42; March, 42; May, 49–50, 155; June, 156–57
Liberator volume 3 (1963): January, 53–55, 79–80; February, 55–56, 80, 158, 189; March, 81, 158, 190; April, 57–58, 192; May, 85, 139, 159, 192, 194; June, 59–60, 254n69; July, 85–86, 130; August, 130, 145; September, 146, 196; October, 132, 141, 146–51, 196–97; November, 81–83, 82, 134; December, 83, 126, 128, 143
Liberator volume 4 (1964): January, 87; March, 134; April, 134, 160–62; May, 62, 134, 162; June, 134, 202; July, 134, 141, 150, 167, 169–70, 200; August,

Liberator volume 3 (1963) (cont.) 134, 223; September, 171–72; October, 202; November, 132; December, 79, 90–91, 202, 203

Liberator volume 5 (1965): January, 63–64, 172, 176, 202, 224; February, 132, 141–42; March, 173–74, 220; April, 174, 175, 212, 220; May, 91–92, 153, 176, 212; June, 176; September, 224–25; December, 65, 110–11

Liberator volume 6 (1966): January, 125–27, 131, 181–82, 207; February, 125, 127, 133, 182, 207; March, 96–97; April, 125, 127; May, 98–100, 103; June, 208, 227–28; July, 131, 210–11; August, 228; November, 219

Liberator volume 7 (1967): January, 182; February, 103–5; April, 182; May, 105, 131, 182; July, 183; November, 106

Liberator volume 8 (1968): March, 236–37; April, 106; June, 107; July, 262n100; August, 116; September, 262n109; November, 116; December, 107–8, 116

Liberator volume 9 (1969): May, 112–14; July, 72

Liberator volume 10 (1970): January, 235; February, 230, 237; July, 117; November, 231; December, 238–39

Liberator volume 11 (1971), March (final issue), 12, 240

Liebowitz, Sheldon, 125

Lincoln, Abbey, 87–89; activism of, 27, 88–89; *Black Sun* music by, 88, 259n40; career of, 87–88; in Congo Crisis protests, 18; home of, 18, 32; marriage of, 87, 88; as Monroe Defense Committee sponsor, 34; in Negro History Week, 189; in *Nothing But a Man*, 217; poetry in *Liberator* by, 87; on tour in Japan, 87–88; *We Insist! Freedom Now Suite*, 32, 87, 88, 189

Lincoln, C. Eric, *The Black Muslims in America*, 154, 155

Linton, Thomas, *Radical Ideas and the Schools*, 10

Liston, Sonny, 190

Literature, black: in Black Arts Movement, 208; Neal's approach to history of, 205–8; reviews of, in *Liberator*, 12, 116, 153. *See also* Poetry; Writers

Living for the Revolution (Springer), 7–8

Lockhart, Calvin, 27

Logan, Giuseppi, 224–25

Logan, Rayford, 41

Logo, of *Liberator*, 219

Lomax, Betty Frank, 99; "Afro-American Woman," 95–96

Lomax, Louis, 159

Long, Amelia, 98–99

Los Angeles, Nation of Islam in, 155–56, 196

Loving, Al, 221

Lucas, W. Francis, 264n12

Luciano, Felipe, 229–32

Lumet, Sidney, 217

Lumumba, Patrice, assassination of, 17–22; and Hammarskjöld's death, 247n21; LCA's response to, 14, 17–22, 30, 53; *Liberator*'s coverage of, 14, 20, 53, 247n21; and Malcolm X, 174; in Negro History Week, 88; vs. Olympio's assassination, 57; protests after, 17–18, 19–20, 30–31

Lundberg, Ferdinand, *The Rich and the Super-Rich*, 263n109

Lynn, Conrad, 61

MacWilliams, Pairlie, 81

Madhubuti, Haki. *See* Lee, Don

Mahoney, Bill, 171–72, 235

Mailer, Norman, 223, 226

Make, Vusumzi, 27, 35

Makiwane, Tennysen, 61

Malcolm X, 153–70, *161*; and Ali, 216–17; assassination of, 68, 122, 173–77; autobiography of, 154; and Bandung Conference, 182; on Black Nationalism, 165, 166; on cover of *Liberator*, 160, *175*; in "Cry Freedom" (Touré), 140; on Harlem as domestic colony, 172; impact on radicalism of *Liberator*, 12, 91, 122; on imperialism of U.S., 103; internationalism of, 164, 166; and Kennedy Airlift, 28; on Kennedy's assassination, 160; on King, 165–66; LCA's praise for, 36; legacy of, 176, 182; *Liberator*'s coverage of, 154–67; on March on Washington, 146; as model of black masculinity, 96, 100, 101, 180, 217; in Nation of Islam, 154–58; Nation of Islam left by, 122, 160–62; Nkrumah's meeting with, 65; at Northern Negro Grassroots Leadership Conference, 83, 160; in OAAU, 122, 166, 168–69, 173; on police violence, 155–56; political evolution of, 122, 158, 160–63, 166, 169; Russell's (Carlos) interview with, *161*, 163–67, 191; Rustin's criticism of, 179–80; on self-defense, 160–61; Shepp's *Fire Music* dedicated to, 225; travels in Africa, 167–69; on Vietnam War, 105

"Malcolm X: International Statesman" (Touré), 132–33

Male supremacy, 96

Mali, 63

Mallory, Mae, 18, 36, 61

Malone, James, 235

Mandela, Nelson, 53, 56

"Manipulators, The" (Bambara), 116

March on Washington (1963), 145–51; attendance at, 145–46; as "Farce on Washington," 111, 146; Ghanaian expatriates on, 151–52; King on impact of, 146; *Liberator*'s coverage of, 111, 145–51, 196; Rustin's role in, 179

Marriage. *See* Interracial dating and marriage

Marshall, Paule, 34

Martin, Milton, 219, 220

"Marxism and the Negro" (Cruse), 134

Masculinity, black: Ali as model of, 217; and emasculation, 108, 113–14; idealized notions of, 180–81; Lomax's critique of, 95–96; Malcolm X as model of, 96, 100, 101, 180, 217; Moore's critique of, 100–101

Mason, Eleanor, "Hot Irons and Black Nationalism," 85

Masthead, of *Liberator*, 13, 20, 91, 93, 224

Mathews, Ronnie, 88

Matriarchal families, 109, 110, 114

Matrilineal customs, 109

Mayfield, Ana, 34

Mayfield, Curtis, 242

Mayfield, Julian: in *The American Writer and His Roots*, 41; as expatriate in Ghana, 151–52, 168; in *Ghana Evening News*, 51; on Ghanaian independence, 51; on Hansberry, 90; on March on Washington, 151–52; as Monroe Defense Committee sponsor, 34; reprinted articles in *Liberator* by, 51; "Uncle Tom Goes to Africa," 151–52, 268n91

Maynard, Valerie, 83, 94, 218

Mboya, Tom, 28, 70–72

McKissick, Floyd, 68

McLean, Jackie, 228

McLucas, Leroy, 146, 219

McNair, Denise, 89, 147

MDC. *See* Monroe Defense Committee

Meade, Matthew, 140

Media. *See* Press

Meeting Point, The (Clarke), 116

Melone, Thomas, 41

Men, African American: black women's writing on relationships with, 107–9; emasculation of, 108, 113–14; in gender hierarchy, 96, 108–9; in interracial relationships, 92, 107; male supremacy among, 96; universal plight of, 59. *See also* Masculinity

Meredith, Burgess, 200

Meriwether, James, 14

Merrick, David, 198

Merritt College, 138

Mexico, Olympics in, 215

Michaux, Louis H., 49, 68, 124

Midwest, as locus of Black Arts Movement, 211, 275n70

Miller, Loren, "Farewell to Liberals," 243n6

Miller, Warren, *The Cool World*, 194

Miss National Standard of Beauty Contests, 86

Mitchell, Loften, 193

MMI. *See* Muslim Mosque, Inc.

Mobley, Ora, 61

Mocumbi, Pascoal, 28

Moncur, Grachan, III, 225, 228

"Monde Des Noires, Le" (exhibition), 219

Mondlane, Eduardo, 28, 54–55

Monk, Thelonious, 88, 221–22, 224

Monkey on a String (Viertal), 116

Monroe Defense Committee (MDC), 34, 144

Moon, Marjorie, 91

Moore, Audley (Queen Mother), 76–77

Moore, Louise: on domestic workers, 91; on double jeopardy of black women, 96; feminism of, 100–101; on masculinity, 100–101; "When Will the Real Black Man Stand Up?," 98, 99

Moore, Richard B.: in advisory board of *Liberator*, 49, 124, 130, 156–57, 177; on African influences in Harlem, 60; in Communist Party, 135; "Criticism Is Not Anti-Semitism," 130, 197; "Frederick Douglass and Emancipation," 158; in Harlem Anti-Colonial Committee, 61; on Nation of Islam, 156–57; open letter to editor by, 156–58

Moore, Willard, 49

Moral Mondays, 242

Morton, Hugh X., 158

Moses, Gilbert, 201

Mothers Defense Committee, 89

Moumie, Felix Roland, 48

Mount Vernon/New Rochelle Women's Group, 101–3

Moynihan, Daniel P., 110–14

Moynihan Report, 108, 110–14

Mozambique Liberation Front (FRELIMO), 28

Mpolo, Maurice, 19

Muhammad, Elijah, 154–60

Mulzac, Hugh, 49, 124

Muralists, 218, 221

Murch, Donna, 138

Murphy, George B., Jr., 49, 124, 135

Murphy, Michael J., 162, 171

Murray, Sunny, 228

Music: African, 190; gospel, 224. *See also* Jazz

Musical theater, 193, 198

Muslim Brotherhood, 39

Muslim Mosque, Inc. (MMI), 166

NAACP. *See* National Association for the Advancement of Colored People

NALC. *See* Negro American Labor Council

Namibia, 27, 53–54

Nasser, Gamal Abdel, 50

Nation, The (magazine), 17, 243n6

National Afroamerican Student Conference, 133, 141

National Association for the Advancement of Colored People (NAACP), 5, 39, 152

National Black Theatre, 202
Nationalism, in black radicalism: bourgeois, 245n28; cultural, 3, 178–79; economic, 85; vs. internationalism, 3; revolutionary, 3, 100, 177, 244n8, 246n28; spread of, 39–40; Touré on, 141, 142; varying degrees of, 39. *See also* Black Nationalism
"Nationalism, Colonialism, and the United States" (1961 forum), 35
National Liberation Army (Angola), 48–49
National Liberation Front (FLN, Algeria), 23, 58
Nation of Islam (NOI), 154–61; Black Nationalism in, 11; cultural and political influence of, 154; doctrine of, 154; on frugality, 138; growth of, 154; *Liberator*'s coverage of, 81, 154–60; Malcolm X's separation from, 122, 160–62; police violence against, 155–57, 196; recruitment by, 165; separatist philosophy of, 5; Touré on influence of, 141
NATO. *See* North Atlantic Treaty Organization
"Natural Hair, Yes—Hot Irons, No" (Nelmes), 85–86
Neal, Evelyn, 115
Neal, Larry, 176–81, 202–18; as arts and culture editor of *Liberator*, 177, 183, 187, 202–3, 206; on autonomous artistic institutions, need for, 186, 224, 226; Bambara compared to, 117; on Baraka, 181–82, 202, 203–4; *Black Boogaloo*, 212; *Black Fire*, 212; "Black Revolution in Music," 224–25; "The Black Writer's Role," 181, 205–8, 210; career of, 211–12; Cruse's influence on, 132; cultural nationalism of, 178–79; departure from *Liberator*, 68, 211–12, 213, 226; "Development of Leroi Jones," 181–82, 207; in editorial board of *Liberator*, 176–77; education of, 202; on Ellison, 181, 203, 205–6; final article in *Liberator*, 211; first article in *Liberator*, 202; at "Forum 66" conference, 211; on Hansberry, 90, 91, 203; impact on aesthetics of *Liberator*, 12, 181, 187; impact on radicalism of *Liberator*, 177; on integration, 177–79; jazz criticism by, 222, 224–26; on Jewish-black relations, 210–11; "Lenox Avenue Sunday," 209; liberalism critiqued by, 210–11; on literature in Black Arts Movement, 208; on Malcolm X's assassination, 174, 177, 204; on Malcolm X's legacy, 182, 185, 204; on Malcolm X's program, 179–80; on Malcolm X's speeches, 204; marriage of, 211; on masculinity, 180–81; on new wave of black artists, 185–86, 187; "On Malcolm X," 185–86; on politics and art, link between, 222; in RAM, 177, 178; on Rustin, 177–80; on visual artists, 221; on women's issues, 90
Negative radicalism, 10
"Negritude" (Russell), 191
Negro, use of term, 86, 157
Negro American Labor Council (NALC), 171
"Negro Americans, the African Interest, and Power Structures in Africa and America" (Drake), 55, 254n51
"Negro Artist and the Racial Mountain, The" (Hughes), 1, 2, 195
Negro Digest (magazine), 226, 268n91
Negro Ensemble Company, 202
Negro Family, The (Moynihan). *See* Moynihan Report
Negro History Week, 78, 88, 125, 189
"Negro Is Obsolete, The" (Watts), 12, 110–11

Negro Newspaper Publishers, 51
"Negro Speaks of Rivers, The" (Hughes), 78
"Negro Writers and His Roots" conference (1959), 22–23
Nelmes, Rose, "Natural Hair, Yes—Hot Irons, No," 85–86
Nelson, David, 229–31
Nelson, Jack, *Radical Ideas and the Schools*, 10
Neocolonialism: drug abuse as indication of, 80; in Israeli aggression, 69; rise of, 53; warnings about dangers of, 50
"Never on Christmas" (Finkenstaedt), 158
"New Afro-American Nationalism, The" (Clarke), 13, 36, 140, 187
"New Afro-American Writer, The" (Touré), 132, 140–41, 147, 196–97, 207
New Federal Theatre, 201
New Group, The, 198
New Left, 4, 37, 121
New Rochelle Women's Group, 101–3, 119
Newton, Huey P., 138
New World of Negro Americans, The (Isaacs), 60, 254n73
New York City: arts scene in, 140, 218–21; Black Nationalist groups in, 17–18, 31–32; distribution of *Liberator* in, 33–34; as hub of black radicalism, 32; *Liberator* based in, 4, 32; "Negro Writers and His Roots" conference in, 22–23. *See also* Harlem
New York Times (newspaper): ads for *Liberator* in, 34; on *The Amen Corner* (Baldwin), 212–13; on Baldwin and Davis's departure from *Liberator*, 127, 129; on black police officers, 171; on Callender's arrest, 269n126; on Congo Crisis protests in U.S., 17, 19–20; on incorporation of LCA, 122; *Liberator*'s criticism of Congo Crisis coverage of, 46; on Nation of Islam, 155; on *Right On!* (film), 229–30; on Rockefeller's Urban Development Corporation, 106
NGOs. *See* Nongovernmental organizations
Nicholas, Denise, 211
Nichols, Denise, 99
Nichols, Herbie, 228
Nigeria: *Liberator*'s coverage of, 41–43, 52–53; Malcolm X's travels in, 167–68; and pan-African unity, 43–44
Nigerian Information Service (NIS), 52
Night Song (Williams), 229
Nikkatsu Studios, 88
NIS. *See* Nigerian Information Service
Nkrumah, Kwame, 50–52; and African student organizations, 48; assassination attempts against, 52; Howard on, 57; LCA on, 36, 43; Malcolm X's meeting with, 168; overthrow of, 64, 65–67; on pan-African unity, 15, 42, 43–44; and Quaison-Sackey, 63, 255n83; on "United States of Africa," 42; U.S. expatriates invited by, 168
NOI. *See* Nation of Islam
Nokwe, Duma, 61
Nongovernmental organizations (NGOs), 31, 40–42
Nonviolence: black radicals' critique of, 3, 83, 167; and Christianity, 101; LCA's opposition to, 35, 36; *Liberator*'s coverage of, 83, 170
North Atlantic Treaty Organization (NATO), 35
Northern Negro Grassroots Leadership Conference (1963), 83, 160
Northern Rhodesia, 17, 45
"Not 100 Years of Freedom" (Baldwin), 124–25
Nothing But a Man (film), 88, 217

Novels. *See* Literature
Nuclear weapons, 50, 51, 62
Nujoma, Sam, 54
Nurses, The (television show), 198
Nyobe, Um, 48

OAAU. *See* Organization of Afro-American Unity
OAU. *See* Organization of African Unity
OBAC. *See* Organization of Black American Culture
Obama, Barack, 143, 241
Obote, Milton, 58–59
Ofuatey-Kodjoe, W., 59–60
Ogbar, Jeffrey, 154
Okito, Joseph, 19
Olatunji, Michael, 189
Old Left, 4, 33, 135
Olympic games, 215
Olympio, Silvanus, 57
O'Neal, Frederick, 198
O'Neal, John, 201
On Guard for Freedom, 18, 19, 30, 32, 39, 250n59
"On Malcolm X" (Neal), 185–86
Operation Crossroads Africa, 40
Oppenheimer, Mary, 66
Organization of African Unity (OAU), 63, 70, 168
Organization of Afro-American Unity (OAAU): after assassination of Malcolm X, 173; establishment of, 122, 166, 168; Ghanaian branch of, 168–69; Neal on significance of, 179
Organization of Black American Culture (OBAC), 221
Original Last Poets, 229
Ortiz, Juan, 230
Overstreet, Joe, 218, 219, 221
Overton, Joseph, 171
Oyewole, Abiodun, 229, 232

Padmore, George, 168
Pan-African Congress (South Africa), 35, 37
Pan-Africanism: in African student organizations, 48; Ghana vs. Nigeria on, 43–44; in ideological diversity of *Liberator*, 4; in ideological spectrum of black radicalism, 4; LCA position on, 31, 43; *Liberator*'s defense of, 59–60; Nkrumah on, 15, 42, 43–44
Pan-Africanism Reconsidered (AMSAC), 41
Pan-African Students' Union of the Americas, 48
Paperback Theatre, 230
Parker, Charlie, 223
Parker, William H., 155
Patterson, Charles, *Black Ice*, 212
Patterson, Louise, 78
Patton, Gwendolyn, 103–5
Pawnbroker, The (film), 217
Peace Corps, 40
Peace movement, critique of, 80
Peery, Pat, 113–14
Periodicals, black: "dissident," 8; as precursors to Black Studies departments, 241; scholarship on role of, 6–7. *See also specific publications*
Peters, Brock, 217
Photography, *Liberator*'s coverage of, 219–20
"Pilgrimage, The" (Wilson), 147, 148–49
Pindell, Howardena, 221
Piñero, Miguel, 231
Pittsburgh Courier (newspaper), 46
Planned Parenthood, 102
Plummer, Brenda Gayle, 40
"Poem at Thirty" (Sanchez), 99
"Poem for Black Women, A" (Lee), 106
"Poem for My Father, A" (Sanchez), 114–15
Poetry: in Black Arts Movement, 208, 212; epic, 209; jazz, 228–32

Poetry, in *Liberator*: by Baraka, 131, 182; from Black Arts Movement, 212; by Hughes, 191, 192; by Ismaili Abu Bakr, 105; by Lee (Don), 106; by Princeton, 106; by Russell (Carlos), 191; by Sanchez, 98, 99, 106, 114–15; by Touré, 140, 192, 209

Poitier, Juanita, 98, 99

Poitier, Sidney, 27, 88, 98

Police officers: black, 117, 171; Jewish, 125–27; at March on Washington, 148–49

Police state, U.S. as, 62

Police violence: in Harlem Riots, 170–71; against Nation of Islam, 155–57, 196; in rise of black radicalism, 2–3; at Talladega College, 49–50; women activists on, 89

Political autonomy, 3, 109

Political parties, call for all-black, 196–97, 233

Politicians, black, 142–43

Politics, and art, link between, 99, 186, 222

POMUSICART, 220, 223

Pontiflet, Theodore, 222

Poor People's March, 106

Porter, Wyndam, 219, 220

Positive radicalism, 10

Poverty, war on, 93

Powell, Adam Clayton, Jr.: on cover of *Liberator*, 150; LCA's praise for, 36; *Liberator*'s coverage of, 142, 159; and Malcolm X, 158, 159; political career of, 158

Powell, James, 170

Presidential elections, U.S., 19, 202

Press, black: "dissident," 8, 10; on Ellender's trip to Africa, 59; scholarship on role of, 6–7; Worthy on responsibilities of, 51–52. *See also specific publications*

Press, mainstream: ads for LCA in, 22, 34; on Black Power, 182; challenged by LCA, 46, 51–52; on *Liberator*, 13. *See also specific publications*

Price, Richard, 235

Primus, Pearl, 41

Princeton, Irma, 106

Printing, of *Liberator*, 33

Prodigal Son, The (Hughes), 218

Production, of *Liberator*, 33, 77, 121, 235

Progressive Labor Party, 170

Project Uplift Gallery, 94

Protests and demonstrations: anti-apartheid, 61–62; on Congo Crisis, 17–18, 19–20, 30–31

Provisional Committee for a Free Africa, 39

Puerto Ricans, 230–31, 279n144

Pullen, Don, 225

Purlie Victorious (Davis), 128, 189, 198–99

Qamar, Nadi: "The Black Music Predicament," 227–28; jazz criticism by, 222, 227–28

Quaison-Sackey, Alex: *Africa Unbound*, 255n83; as UN representative, 63–64, 255n83

Racial capitalism, 9, 29, 33, 44

Racial integration. *See* Integration

Racial segregation. *See* Segregation

Racial violence: in Freedom Rides, 36; in rise of black radicalism, 2–3. *See also* Police violence

Racism, U.S.: vs. African tribalism, 60; in baseball, 214–15; in Moynihan Report, 108; in Vietnam War, 104

Radical Ideas and the Schools (Nelson, Carlson, and Linton), 10

Radicalism: definition of, 10; negative vs. positive, 10. *See also specific types*

Rahman, Abdul, 219, 220

Rahman, Rose, 220
Rainbow Coalition, 142
Raisin in the Sun, A (Hansberry), 90, 91
RAM. *See* Revolutionary Action Movement
Randall, Dudley, 211
Randolph, A. Philip, 111
Randolph, Jimmy, 198
Reading groups, 139
Rebellion or Revolution? (Cruse book), 120, 122, 134, 244n8
"Rebellion or Revolution?" (Cruse articles), 133–34, 147, 196–97
Redding, Saunders, 41
Reed, Ishmael, 140
Reese, Albert X., 158
Religion: feminist critique of, 100–101; and nonviolence, 83
Representations of the Intellectual (Said), 38–39
Reproductive rights, 102–3
Resha, Robert, 61
Residential segregation, 84
"Responsibility of Black Artists, The" (Ford), 195
Révolution Africaine (journal), 22, 56, 58, 67, 248n25
Revolutionary Action Movement (RAM): and Afro-American Institute, 144; Ahmad in, 166, 177; departure of members from *Liberator*, 68; emergence of, 122; impact on radicalism of *Liberator*, 174, 177; Malcolm X in, 166; on Malcolm X's assassination, 68, 174, 177; Neal in, 177, 178; in radicalization of other organizations, 177; on revolutionary nationalism, 177, 244n8
Revolutionary nationalism, 3, 100, 177, 244n8, 246n28
"Revolutionary Nationalism and the Afro-American" (Cruse), 244n8

"Revolutionary Nationalism and the Afroamerican Student" (Ahmad), 176
"Revolutionary Nationalism and the Class Struggle" (Allen), 245n28
Revolutionary socialism, 166
Rich and the Super-Rich, The (Lundberg), 263n109
Richards, Beah (Beulah Richardson): in Afro-American Heritage Week, 78; in *The Amen Corner*, 212–13; in *Purlie Victorious*, 198; on SNCC, 84, 258n28
Richardson, Gloria, 36, 81–83, *82*, 143
Right On! (film), 229–30
Right On! (Last Poets), 229–31
Riley, Clayton, 212–18; on *The Amen Corner* (Baldwin), 212–13; arrival at *Liberator*, 213; on athletes, 213–17; Bambara compared to, 117; on black women's activism, 89; on civil rights leadership, 171; Cruse's influence on, 135; in editorial board of *Liberator*, 176, 214; film reviews by, 217; in last years of *Liberator*, 235; on poetry in Black Arts Movement, 212; on *Right On!*, 229, 230
Ringgold, Faith, 231
Roach, Max: on Afro-American Institute, 144; article in *Liberator* by, 87; *Black Sun* music by, 88, 259n40; in Congo Crisis protests, 18; home of, 18, 32; marriage of, 87, 88; as Monroe Defense Committee sponsor, 34; in Negro History Week, 189; on tour in Japan, 87–88; *We Insist! Freedom Now Suite*, 32, 87, 88, 189
Robertson, Carole, 89, 147
Robeson, Eslanda, 79
Robeson, Paul, 29, 50, 79, 90
Robinson, Jackie, 28, 78, 105, 257n10; *Baseball Has Done It*, 216
Robinson, Johnny, 147
Robinson, Patricia, 101–3
Rockefeller, Nelson, 106, 272n11

Rodgers, Evelyn, 99, 211; "Is *Ebony* Killing Black Women," 96–97
Roemer, Michael, 217
"Role of the Afro-American Artist, The" conference, 204
"Roots of Black Nationalism, The" (Cruse), 134, 160, 199
Rosenberg, Ethel, 26
Rosenberg, Julius, 26
Roth, Benita, 7–8, 76, 102, 108
Rouse, Jacqueline Anne, 76
Rubadiri, David, 41
Russell, Bertrand, 196
Russell, Bill, 33, 190, 215, 216
Russell, Carlos E., *161*; Afro-Panamanian heritage of, 153, 190, 191; on athletes, 213, 215; on "Black Muslims in Crisis," 159–60; career of, 191; on eclecticism of *Liberator*, 132; in editorial board of *Liberator*, 176; education of, 191; on Ellender's trip to Africa, 59, 254n69; in executive board of LCA, 190; in executive board of *Liberator*, 197; on Lumumba assassination, 57; Malcolm X interviewed by, *161*, 163–67, 191; on Malcolm X's assassination, 174; at March on Washington, 146; "Negritude," 191; on nonviolence, 167; notable cultural and political interviews by, 190–91; poetry of, 191
Russell, Charlie L.: Baldwin's influence on, 139; "Black Muslims in Crisis," 159–60; on *Blues People* (Baraka), 197; career of, 139, 197–98; *Dark to Dark*, 139; Davis interviewed by, 128, 198–99; in distribution of *Liberator*, 33; on *Dutchman* (Baraka), 202; in editorial board of *Liberator*, 176; education of, 139; in Harlem Writer's Guild, 139, 191, 197; "Has Jazz Lost Its Roots?," 223; on Hughes, 265n25;

jazz criticism by, 198, 222, 224; "Leroi Jones Will Get Us All in Trouble," 199; at March on Washington, 146
Rustin, Bayard: and ACOA, 28; homosexuality of, 180; on Malcolm X, 179–80; in March on Washington, 179; as Monroe Defense Committee sponsor, 34; Neal's criticism of, 177–80; Watts's criticism of, 111
Rwangasore, Louis, 77

Said, Edward W., 242; *Representations of the Intellectual*, 38–39
Salaam, Uthman A., 49
Salazar, António de Oliveira, 55, 253n49
Salt Eaters, The (Bambara), 116
Sanchez, Juan, 231
Sanchez, Sonia, 98–99; "Blues," 99; on interracial dating, 107; "Poem at Thirty," 99; "A Poem for My Father," 114–15; "To All Brothers," 106; "to blk/record/buyers," 262n100; and Watts, 115
Sanders, Edith, 72
Sands, Diana, 27, 200
San Francisco, distribution of *Liberator* in, 33
San Francisco State University, 138
Sangare, Louis, 109
Sangare, Yahne, 69, 72, 109–10, 263n116
Sankore, Shelby, 164–65
Saul, Scott, 228
Savage, Augusta, 94
"Scenes of Home" (Ismaili Abu Bakr), 105
Scholarships, for African students, 47–48, 252n23
Schomburg, Edith, 93; "The Crux of Black Non-Violence," 83
School integration, 101–2

Schuyler, George, 46
Scott-Heron, Gil, "Brother," 236
Sea Birds Are Still Alive, The (Bambara), 116
Sealy, Lloyd George, 171
Segregation: economic, 35–36; residential, 84; Supreme Court on, 36
Self-defense: Malcolm X on, 160–61; position of LCA on, 36; position of *Liberator* on, 5; Stewart on, 83; Watts on, 112, 148
Self-determination, 3
Self-sufficiency, economic, 3
Servicemen's Defense Committee, 26
Sexuality: black female, 116; of Rustin, 180
Shadow and Act (Ellison), 203
Shange, Ntozake, 91
Sharpeville Massacre, 56
Shepard, George, 28
Shepp, Archie, 225–26; *Attica Blues*, 225; *The Cry of My People*, 225; *Fire Music*, 225
Shervington, Florence, 49, 77
Shomrin Society, 125–27
Sie, Rachel Hall, 25
Sie, Thorgues Tor, Sr., 25
Sign in Sidney Brustein's Window, The (Hansberry), 91, 203
Silvera, Frank, 212, 213
Sisulu, Walter, 56
Sitkoff, Harvard, 146, 154
Six-Day War, 69
Skidmore, Owings and Merrill, 16
Slave, The (Baraka), 203
Smethurst, James, 211; *The Black Arts Movement*, 6–7
Smith, Barbara, *Homegirls*, 116
Smith, Frank, 131
SNCC. *See* Student Nonviolent Coordinating Committee
Snellings, Rolland. *See* Touré, Askia
Social events, of LCA, 24, 77–78

Socialism: *Liberator*'s approach to, 33; Malcolm X on, 164, 166; revolutionary, 166
"Sonny's Blues" (Baldwin), 139
Soulbook (periodical), 67–68
Soul Circle, 144
Sound I Saw, The (DeCarava), 220
South Africa: African National Congress of, 27, 58, 61; Israel compared to, 69; Pan-African Congress of, 35, 37; Sharpeville Massacre in, 56
South African apartheid: assassination of architect of, 68; *Liberator*'s coverage of, 35, 56, 58, 61, 68; Make in struggle against, 35; Mandela in struggle against, 53, 56; UN on, 61–62; U.S. role in, 61, 62
South African Freedom News, 58
Southern Christian Leadership Conference, 101
Southern Rhodesia (Zimbabwe), 65
South West Africa (Namibia), 27, 53–54
South West Africa National Union (SWANU), 27, 53–54, 59
South West Africa People's Organization (SWAPO), 54
Soviet Union, influence in Africa, 14, 15. *See also* Cold War
Sowande, Fela, 190
Sparks, Selma: in advisory board of *Liberator*, 49, 77, 124; on garment workers, 79–80, 130; in Harlem Anti-Colonial Committee, 61; travels in Ghana, 51; on Women's Strike for Peace, 83
Spellman, A. B.: *Four Lives in the Be-Bop Business*, 228; jazz criticism by, 222, 228; "The Legacy of Malcolm X," 176
Spencer, Christine, 198
"Sphere of influence" theory, 66

Spirituality: of music, 224–25, 226–27; Neal's desire for renewal of, 178–79
"Spiritual Voices of Black America" (exhibition), 228
Spivak, Gayatri, 226
Sports, 213–17
Spotlight on Africa (periodical), 50
Springer, Kimberly, *Living for the Revolution,* 7–8
Stanford, Max. *See* Ahmad, Muhammad
Star of the Morning (musical), 193
Steinberg, Stephen, 112
Stevens, Nelson, 225, 278n125; "Centennial Celebration of the Birth of Tuskegee," 225
Stevenson, Adlai, 15, 17–19, 30, 62
Stewart, Merle, 83
St. Jacques, Raymond, 217
Stokes, Gail A., "Black Woman to Black Man," 107–8
Stokes, Joan, 49
Stokes, Ronald, 50, 155–57, 196
Stone, Chuck, 28
Street Speaker, The (periodical), 40
Strickland, Calvin, 223
"Struggle for Survival" (Cleage), 160
Student Nonviolent Coordinating Committee (SNCC), 68, 84, 122
Students: African American, radicalization of, 138; Arab, 46, 47. *See also* African students
Studio Museum, 221
Styron, William, 264n12
Sun Ra, 228
"Sunrise" (Touré), 209
Supreme Court, U.S., 36
Suspenders (Bin-Hassan), 230
Sutherland, Bill, 28
SWANU. *See* South West Africa National Union
SWAPO. *See* South West Africa People's Organization

Sweet Flypaper of Life, The (DeCarava and Hughes), 220
Sweet Love, Bitter (film), 229
"Sweet Town" (Bambara), 116
Sykes, Ossie, 57, 64, 170, 174, 176

Tales and Stories for Black Folk (Bambara), 116
Talladega College, 50
Tambo, Oliver, 27, 28, 58
Tambourines to Glory (Hughes), 198
Tanzania, 67
Taubman, Howard, 212–13
Taylor, Cecil, 223, 228
Taylor, Ula Y., 100, 244n10
Teenage pregnancy, 102
Teer, Barbara Ann, 201, 202
Tekle, Afewerk, 41
Tell, Diallo, 78
Thant, U, 62, 64
Theater, 192–202; in Black Arts Movement, 192–94, 208; Black Nationalism in, 199; Broadway, 189, 192, 193; Ford's advocacy for black, 186, 193–95, 198, 200–202. *See also specific plays and writers*
Theater criticism, in *Liberator*: by Ellis, 213; by Ford, 192, 194–95, 198, 200; by Riley, 212–13, 218
Theoharis, Jeanne, 76, 249n45
"Third Party" (Cruse), 134
Third World News (newspaper), 117–18
Third World Women's Alliance, 119
Thomas, Bedwick, 219, 220
Thomas, Evelyn, 81
Thomas, Mildred, 89
Thompson, Rosa, 78
Tillman, James, "Exiles No More," 160
Time magazine, 221
"To All Brothers" (Sanchez), 106
Toame, Khalil, 69
"to blk/record/buyers" (Sanchez), 262n100

Togo, 57
Toilet, The (Baraka), 203, 212
Torn, Rip, 200
Touré, Askia, 132–35, 139–42; "Afro-American Youth and the Bandung World," 132, 141–42; and Baraka, 140, 202; Cruse's influence on, 132, 135, 142; "Cry Freedom," 140, 192, 209; departure from *Liberator*, 68; on epic poetry, 209; on Harlem as domestic colony, 172; impact on aesthetics of *Liberator*, 12; impact on radicalism of *Liberator*, 177; internationalism of, 140–42; on Malcolm X, 132–33, 140, 174, 182; "Malcolm X: International Statesman," 132–33; on mentors, 135; name change by, 139; on National Afroamerican Student Conference, 133, 141; on Neal, 202–3; "The New Afro-American Writer," 132, 140–41, 147, 196–97, 207; "Sunrise," 209; "Toward Repudiating Western Values," 132; in Umbra Poets Workshop, 192; "Unchain the Lion," 141; on western values in art, 94
Touring Artists Group, 196
"Toward Repudiating Western Values" (Touré), 132
Tribalism, vs. racism, 60
"Truth Posters," 108
Tshombe, Moïse, 46
Tubman, Harriet, 80, 101
Ture, Kwame. *See* Carmichael, Stokely
Turner, Lorenzo, 41
20th Century Creators, 220
"Two Faces of America" *(Liberator)*, 59, 254n69

UANM. *See* Universal African Nationalist Movement
Uganda, 58–59, 67
Umbra Poets Workshop, 192
Umkonto we Sizwe, 56

"Unchain the Lion" (Touré), Askia, 141
"Uncle Tom Goes to Africa" (Mayfield), 151–52, 268n91
UNIA. *See* Universal Negro Improvement Association
Union of Populations of Cameroon (UPC), 48
United African Nationalist Movement, 32
United Council of Harlem Organizations (Unity Council), 171
United Nations (UN): African American representation at, 16; in African cultural events, 190; in African independence, 54, 62; African women representatives at, 64, 91–92; Angola in, 252n28; antiapartheid protests at, 61–62; Congo Crisis protests at, 17–18, 19–20, 30; Ghana in, 63–64, 255n83; Gibson's work with, 23; Harlem Anti-Colonial Committee rally at, 61; Howard as correspondent at, 56–57, 62; *Liberator*'s coverage of, 62, 63–64; on Namibia, 54; press gallery of, 57, 62; Stevenson as U.S. ambassador to, 17–19, 30; U.S. influence in, 54; Watts's access to, 62, 63
"United States of Africa," 42
Universal African Legion, Inc., 32
Universal African Nationalist Movement (UANM), 39
Universal Art Studio, 220
Universal Negro Improvement Association (UNIA), 86
University of California, Berkeley, 137, 138
University of California, Santa Barbara, 117–18
UPC. *See* Union of Populations of Cameroon
Urban areas: rebellions in, 106–7, 111–12; renewal in, 106–7

Urban Development Corporation, 106
Uris, Percy, 107

Van Cortland, Beverly, 93
Van Peebles, Melvin, *Ain't Supposed to Die a Natural Death*, 194
Veii, Gerson, 53
Verges, Jacques, 62, 248n25
Vernacular intellectual tradition, 123
Verwoerd, Hendrik, 55, 68, 253n49
Viera, Raphael, 230
Viertal, Joseph, *Monkey on a String*, 116
Vietnam War: Ali's opposition to, 105, 216–17; and Great Society, 95; women writers on, 103–5
Violence. *See* Nonviolence; Police violence; Racial violence
Visual artists, 218–21; and jazz, 220, 225; in New York, 140, 218–21; works of, in *Liberator*, 77, 94, 218–21. *See also specific artists*
Voice of Africa, 51, 52
Von Eschen, Penny, 29
Voters, black, 80

Wade, Virgil, 147
Wagner, Robert, 159, 171, 269n126
Wali, Obi, 133
Walker, Ann, 77
Walker, David, 173
Walker, Earl, 84
Walker, Mildred Pitts, 84
Wallace, George, 68, 147
Wallace, Mike, 13, 111, 159
Wallerstein, Immanuel, 70–72
Ward, Douglas Turner, *Happy Ending*, 202
Ward, Steven, 244n10
Warden, Donald, "The California Revolt," 137–38
Warren Wilson College, 47–48
Washington, D.C. *See* March on Washington

Washington, Leon H., Jr., 196
Wattley, Pernella, 61
Watts, Daniel H., *21, 238*; on African independence, 16, 29, 47; on African students, 47–48; on ANLCA, 54–56; architectural career of, 16, 23, 111–12; Beveridge (Pete) as ghost-writer for, 267n81, 271n161; Beveridge's (Pete) introduction to, 16; "Big Brother," 238–39; "Birth Control," 112–13; on Black Nationalist demonstration at UN, 17–18; Caribbean roots of, 153; as chairman of LCA, 23–24; compartmentalization by, 249n35; on Congo Crisis, 19, 20, 30, 46; on *Ebony*, 97; in editorial board of *Liberator*, 24, 49; education of, 111; in establishment of LCA, 22; in executive board of *Liberator*, 197; financial support of *Liberator* by, 34; as frequent contributor to *Liberator*, 24; Gibson's friendship with, 22, 23, 68; on growth of LCA and *Liberator*, 49, 123–24; home of, 32; on integration, 35–36, 55; on interracial alliances, 157–58; on Israel, 69; and Jewish-black relations, 125, 128–31; in last years of *Liberator*, 235–40; in legacy of *Liberator*, 12; on Malcolm X, 160–62, 169, 173–74, 182; on March on Washington, 145–48; marriage of, 68, 92, 127, 129; as Monroe Defense Committee sponsor, 34; on Moore's letter to editor, 157–58; on Moynihan Report, 110–12; and Neal, 202–3, 205; "The Negro Is Obsolete," 12, 110–11; in *The New World of Negro Americans* (Isaacs), 60, 254n73; at Northern Negro Leadership Conference, 83; on nuclear weapons, 62; in On Guard for Freedom, 250n59; photography by, 219; as polarizing figure, 233; in production of *Liberator*, 33, 121;

pseudonyms of, 130; on Richardson, 81–83; roles in *Liberator*, 24; on self-defense, 112, 148; teaching career of, 239–40; in UN press gallery, 62, 63; women writers cultivated by, 109, 115
Watts, Marilyn Lieberman, 32, 33, 111, 249n35
We Insist! Freedom Now Suite (album), 32, 87, 88, 189
Weiss, Cora, 28
Weiss, Peter, 28
Welburn, Ron, 231–32
Welensky, Roy, 55, 253n49
Welfare, 203
Wesley, Cynthia, 89, 147
West, Jennifer, 202
West Coast, *Liberator*'s coverage of, 137–38
Weston, Randy, 41
Wheeldin, Lynn, 136
"When Will the Real Black Man Stand Up?" (Moore), 98, 99
"Which Road to Freedom?" (Finkenstaedt), 143
White, Helene, 86
White, Nat, *The Black Tramp*, 212
Whites: as allies of LCA, 17, 33; on jazz, 222, 223–24, 227; judgment of black artists by, 205, 223–24, 227; support for black liberation among, 24, 127
White supremacy: vs. male supremacy, 96; in South Africa, 56, 58
"Why AMSAC Festival Was a Flop" (Beveridge), 42
Wilkes, Quinton, 238
Wilkins, Roy, 64, 145
Wilkinson, Michelle, 185, 231
William Morrow publishers, 33
Williams, Bert, 193
Williams, Clarence, III, 230
Williams, Jim, 195
Williams, John A., *Night Song*, 229

Williams, Rhonda Y., 7–8
Williams, Robert F.: and Harlem Anti-Colonial Committee, 61; on Harlem as domestic colony, 172; and National Afroamerican Student Conference, 133; on nonviolence, 83, 167; praise in *Liberator* for, 36; support committees for, 34, 138; UN protests inspired by, 18
Wilson, Charlie E., 152–53; on arguments at *Liberator*, 172; on black leadership crisis, 171; career of, 152–53; Caribbean roots of, 153; Cruse's influence on, 135; departure from *Liberator*, 177; in editorial board of *Liberator*, 176; education of, 152; in executive board of *Liberator*, 197; Fanon's influence on, 153; and Jewish-black relations, 121; on Malcolm X, 176; on March on Washington, 146, 148–49, 196; "The Pilgrimage," 147, 148–49; on RAM, 177; travels in Africa, 152; on women's issues, 90
Wilson, Nancy, 105
Windom, Alice, 151, 168
Wingate, Livingston, 171
Women, African: film depictions of, 201; photos of, in *Liberator*, 91–92; political independence sought by, 109; at UN, 64, 91–92
Women, African American, 11–12, 74–119; in Afro-American Heritage Week, 77–78; beauty standards for, 85–87, 96–97; birth control use by, 103, 112–13; in Black Arts Movement, 7; in integration debate, 89–90, 101–2; LCA influenced by, 76–77; *Liberator*'s coverage of activism by, 81; as "long-distance runners" in activism, 27, 249n45; on male supremacy, 96; matriarchal families of, 109, 110, 114; and Moynihan

Women, African American (cont.)
Report, 108, 110; as pioneers of black left, 76–84; on police brutality, 89; review of scholarship on, 7–8; sexuality of, 116; subjects of *Liberator* articles by, 75–76; on Vietnam War, 103–5; at writers' conference by *Liberator*, 93. *See also specific women*

Women's rights. *See* Feminism

Women's Strike for Peace, 83

Woodard, Komozi, 76, 249n45

Woods, Barbara, 76

Woods, Jacqueline D., 94–95

Woodson, Carter G., 32

World and Africa, The (Du Bois), 44

World War II: atomic bomb in, 62; Holocaust in, 127, 130

"World without the Bomb, The" conference, 51, 80

Worthy, William: on Afro-American Institute, 144; on all-black political party, 196–97; in antiapartheid protests, 61–62; in Harlem Anti-Colonial Committee, 61; on mainstream press, 51–52; in "Nationalism, Colonialism, and the United States" forum, 35; passport revoked, 53, 61; praise in *Liberator* for, 36; reprinted articles in *Liberator* by, 51; travels of, 139

Wretched of the Earth, The (Fanon), 153, 183

Wright, Richard, 124, 182, 205–6; *The Color Curtain*, 182

Wright, Sarah, 32, 140

Writers, black, 191–92; AMSAC-sponsored conference for, 208; critique of western values of, 183, 202; expansion of opportunities for, 235–36; *Liberator*-sponsored conference for, 92–93; mentorship among, 191; militant, 141; Neal on audience of, 208; Neal on role of, 181, 205–8, 210; white writers' judgment of, 223–24; writing as form of activism for, 6

ya Salaam, Kalamu, 229

Year of Africa, 14, 15, 39

Yergan, Max, 46

Yorty, Samuel, 155, 156

Young, Cynthia, 5

Young, Whitney, 36, 64

Young Lords, 229–31, 233–34

Zamani Goes to Market (Feelings and Feelings), 219

Zambia, 72

Zimbabwe, 65

Zionism, 47, 69

Zirin, Dave, 215

Zuber, Paul, 49

Zulu (film), 201